# JACK ⁘ RIPPER
## AT LAST?

### THE MYSTERIOUS MURDERS OF
## GEORGE CHAPMAN

The Hastings Press
hastings.press@gmail.com
www.hastingspress.co.uk


Casebound edition published 2013 ISBN 978-1904-109-273
Paperback edition published 2014 ISBN 978-1904-109-228
Ebook edition published 2014 ISBN 978-1-904-109-297
Printed in Poland by Booksfactory.co.uk

Cover photograph: George Chapman © Metropolitan Police
Book interior and jacket design by the author


By the same author:
*Women of Victorian Sussex: Their Lives, Occupations and Dealings with the Law*
*Notable Sussex Women: 580 Biographical Sketches*
*Railwaywomen: Exploitation, Betrayal and Triumph in the Workplace*

# CONTENTS

In Memoriam

**Mary Spink**
**Bessie Taylor**
**Maud Marsh**

# ACKNOWLEDGEMENTS

I am grateful to Mark Ripper for sharing thousands of images of crucial primary source documents, and for his generosity in critiquing the text. Many thanks to Kate Haigh for rooting out a plethora of typos; to Stephen Thomas for the book *Trial of George Chapman*; to Adrian Hancock for the hand-drawn maps; to David Green for the index; to Debra Arif for many press cuttings and lookups; to Val Brown for researching Willie Spink's war record; to Jon Menges for the *S.S. Wieland* passenger list and other documents; to How Brown and Chris Scott for making the O'Donnell Manuscript accessible; to Stewart P. Evans for the petition for mercy, cuttings from *Shurey's Illustrated* and the *Weekly News* and the images of Abberline and Pinchin Street; to Neal Shelden for his article 'Severin Kłosowski and his Victims'; to Steven Russell for scans from *The True Face of Jack the Ripper*; to How Brown for cuttings from US newspapers; to Rob Clack for the plan of Tewkesbury Buildings; to Gareth Williams for his research on feldshers, and to Keith Skinner for suggesting the title *Jack the Ripper at Last?* Lastly, thanks to the members of casebook.org and jtrforums.com, especially Gareth Williams, Norma Buddle, Erin Sigler, 'Errata', Chris George and Wolf Vanderlinden, for their Chapman-related postings.

# A NOTE TO READERS

George Chapman was the pseudonym of Seweryn Kłosowski, pronounced 'Severin Kwo-sov-ski'. Rather than resorting to the awkward and ugly construction 'Kłosowski/ Chapman', I generally refer to him as 'Kłosowski' when writing of his life prior to the autumn of 1895 (when he changed his name) and thence 'Chapman'.

Biographical notes about most of the people mentioned in the narrative, and further information about the Crown public house in Southwark, can be found in Appendices II and III.

I have made all reasonable efforts to contact copyright holders for permission to use photographs and other illustrative material, and apologise for any omissions or errors in the form of credits given. Corrections will be made for future printings.

Helena Wojtczak
Sussex, 2014

# INTRODUCTION

Interest in George Chapman has for the past few decades focussed entirely on assessing and debating whether or not he was Jack the Ripper — or the Whitechapel Murderer — the uncatchable, knife-wielding maniac who stalked the streets of east London in the late 1880s. But a century ago Chapman also had two soubriquets — the Southwark Poisoner and the Borough Poisoner — and was infamous across the English-speaking world. Dubbed 'the foulest criminal of the early twentieth century',[1] he was placed 'among the most loathsome murderers in criminal history'.[2] According to the British Parliamentary Papers, 'the annals of crime perhaps do not contain a more remarkable story of cold-blooded murder'.[3] Chapman attracted and deserved such damning comments because he had perpetrated three mysterious, seemingly pointless, apparently motiveless and yet exceptionally cruel murders, about which he maintained a stubborn silence all the way to the gallows, provoking the *Daily Mail* to remark:

> Never in the history of crime has such a case been before the public; there is an element of mystery about the whole affair; the prisoner himself, Sphinx-like...presents a psychological problem which affords much study.[4]

His refusal to either present a defence or admit his guilt was puzzling. In this respect, although he was caught, tried and hanged, his case was never satisfactorily solved.

Nowadays the murders which George Chapman committed receive attention almost exclusively as evidence to support or contradict the 'Chapman–Ripper theory'. It is only because he is a Ripper suspect that numerous versions of his life story appear in books, newspapers and magazines, in public talks and on websites. However, much of what is written is gossip and rumour which, when analysed, is unsupported. Unsubstantiated speculation is habitually presented as fact, misunderstandings are perpetuated, errors are repeated and myths retold, not only on amateurs' websites but also within printed books written by respected authors and issued by major publishers. A surprising number make mistakes with significant dates and names, or muddle the sequence of events. Chapman's childhood and youth, his profession, his sexual and marital life, and his poisoning murders are routinely misrepresented. I have yet to read an account of his life, no matter how brief — and no matter how eminent the writer — that is correct in every detail.

Owing to the ubiquity of misinformation about Chapman within secondary sources, I have relied mostly on the primary ones: foreign-language documents, official records, court witnesses and contemporaneous newspapers; but even they have shortcomings and must always be regarded with a sceptical eye.

---

1 Furniss, H. (ed) *Famous Crimes Past and Present*, Vol. IX, No. 109, c. 1908, Caxton House.
2 Marjoribanks, E. (1932) *Carson the Advocate*, Macmillan. Reprinted 2005, Kessinger, p304.
3 Return showing the Working of the Regulations for carrying out the Prosecution of Offences Act 1879 & 1884. British Parliamentary Papers, Vol. 56, HMSO, 1902. Pub as the *Blue Book*, 1903, p12–16.
4 *Daily Mail*, 16th March 1903.

# THE PRIMARY SOURCES

### DOCUMENTS IN RUSSIAN

Kłosowski spent the first two decades of his life in a part of Poland that was occupied by the Russia Empire, and so his personal documents — found by police in 1902 — were in Russian. They consisted of his birth record and testimonials relating to his schooling, apprenticeship and early employment. Their current whereabouts is unknown, but an English translation was published in 1930 in H.L. Adam's book *Trial of George Chapman* and is reproduced here in Appendix I. Some words were mistranslated, leading later researchers to misconstrue certain facts, as I shall soon explain.

### OFFICIAL RECORDS

A former casebook.org member called 'Adamkle' contacted various agencies in Poland in 2009, including the National Archives, the Regional Court and Prosecutor's Office, and both Warsaw hospitals associated with Kłosowski, but none had any records pertaining to him, because most Polish official records and archives were destroyed during the Second World War. The Metropolitan Police file on Chapman detailing his investigation in 1902/1903 has not survived. (British) National Archives file HO 144/680/101992 comprises correspondence and official papers relating to Chapman's trial and execution, including his petition, exhumation orders, Mr Justice Grantham's notes, and his death certificate. File HO 144/581/A63521 contains documents from Chapman's private prosecution of Hilda Oxenford and Alfred Clarke, one of which bears a copy of his signature.

Other useful official sources include censuses, birth, marriage and death records and ships' passenger lists. The reliability of these depends on their having been correctly recorded at the time and subsequently accurately transcribed. They frequently bear spelling and other mistakes. Ships' passenger lists were hastily scribbled and are difficult to decipher; transcriptions carried out during digitalisation are riddled with errata; even the censuses cannot be trusted, because they relied not only upon correct transcription but also upon householders' honesty. A biography of Chapman appears in the British Parliamentary Papers, published as the *Blue Book* in June 1903.[5] Although it is detailed, some statements have been shown to be wildly inaccurate, making it an unreliable source.

### WITNESS TESTIMONY

A summation of Chapman's trial at the Central Criminal Court can be viewed at oldbaileyonline.org, whilst notes of the relevant proceedings at Southwark coroner's court and Southwark police court are held at the National Archives (CRIM 1/84 and HO 144/680/101992). All three also appear in *Trial of George Chapman*. The transcriptions are in all cases abbreviated, a court clerk's précis of what was said. Their accuracy

---

5 The BPP consists of the working papers of Parliament, including *Hansard* (the daily record of proceedings), other papers produced by parliament and its committees, and papers presented to parliament by outside bodies. It was not widely read by the general public.

depends on him having correctly heard the words spoken and recording them faithfully by hand and, later, on the diligence of a copy-typist. Unsurprisingly, they are full of mistakes and misspellings, which have been repeated by authors and other researchers who have used the transcripts as their source.

The witnesses who gave evidence during Chapman's murder trial were speaking up to fifteen years after the events they described, and in some cases about a man they knew only casually. Their statements are subject to the vagaries of human memory and depend on honesty and impartiality.

## NEWSPAPERS

Press articles proved to be valuable sources. As well as publishing testimony that was omitted as irrelevant by court clerks in their official transcripts of hearings in the police court and Chapman's Old Bailey trial, newspapers added life and colour to their own court reports by describing witnesses' physical attributes and attire, and by remarking on Chapman's demeanour and facial expressions as he listened to their testimony. Reporters also passed comment on the general scene in the courtrooms, the overspill crowds clamouring for admittance, and moments when the words or gestures of witnesses or counsel provoked a response from the public gallery. As a delightful bonus, some publications provided pen-sketches or woodcuts of the witnesses, the victims, the legal teams and the accused.

## THE CRIME MUSEUM

Scotland Yard's famous archive, previously called the Black Museum, currently holds nothing related to Chapman except police mugshots of him and sketches of witnesses and others present at his trial. In the 1930s, E.T. Woodhall reported seeing Chapman's death mask, but it was probably that of Frederick Bailey Deeming.[6] Since then, claims have been made that various artefacts belonging to Chapman were held there, including a case of razors, chemistry textbooks, a hangman's diary and a 'magic bottle'.[7] In 1993 Gordon Honeycombe featured Chapman's poison crimes in a book bearing the title *More Murders of the Black Museum,* but omitted to state which items related to Chapman were supposedly held there.

Keith Skinner, a volunteer at the Crime Museum, said recently that the museum's old catalogue covers the period 1870 to 1914, after which new accessions were not recorded for a period of sixty-five years until, in the early 1980s, the curator began a new one. There is no reference to George Chapman (or Seweryn Kłosowski) in either catalogue, which suggests that, if items relating to him were ever held, they must have been placed there after June 1914 and removed by the early 80s.[8]

6 Aliffe, A. 'Guardian of the Great: A brief biography of E.T. Woodhall', *Ripperologist* No. 11, June 1997. Woodhall was the author of *Jack the Ripper or When London Walked in Terror* (1937).
7 (Magic bottle) *Corpus Christi Caller-Times,* 8th December 1957.
8 Email correspondence with the author, June 2012.

*Image: a court reporter's sketch of George Chapman, from The Echo.*

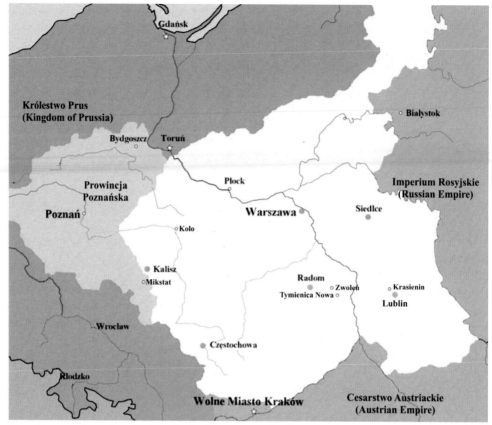

*The white area shows the Kingdom of Poland (Congress Poland) as it was between 1815 and 1915. Kłosowski was born in Nagórna, half a mile east of Koło, and later lived in Krasienin, Zwoleń, Warsaw and Tymienica Nowa. His wife came from Mikstat, in the province of Posen (now Poznań), then in Prussia.*

*The hamlet of Nagórna in the 1930s. Now absorbed into Koło, Nagórna exists only as a street name.*

# THE LIFE OF SEWERYN KŁOSOWSKI

Seweryn Kłosowski came into the world on the morning of 14th December 1865. All that is known about his family is the religion, names and ages of his parents. They were Roman Catholic; his father Antoni was a thirty-year-old carpenter;[9] his mother Emilia was twenty-nine and had the maiden name Ulatowska. Some renditions of his life history state that 'Antoniovich' was his middle name, but according to his birth certificate he did not have one. 'Antoniovich' was a patronymic given according to Russian custom; it simply means that his father's name was Antoni. Seweryn's birthplace was the hamlet of Nagórna, a suburb of Koło, a small town between Poznań and Warsaw. There is no record of how long his family lived there but, before Seweryn was eight, they moved 160 miles east to Krasienin, some nine miles north-west of Lublin. This was also a hamlet; even today the population is under 300.

In the 1860s, Poland had not been an independent nation state for seven decades. Its land had been appropriated and parcelled out between Russia, Prussia and Austria. Since 1815, both Koło and Krasienin had been part of the Kingdom of Poland (also called Congress Poland[10]), a puppet state of the Russian Empire.

In October 1873, shortly before his eighth birthday, Seweryn was enrolled in Krasienin village school. He left six years and eight months later with nothing more than a certificate of good conduct. This was probably all that was available to children of his humble background; elementary schools in rural Polish backwaters would have offered a very basic education — mainly the 'Three Rs' — and no formal academic qualifications. Seweryn would have been bilingual. Ethnic Polish children spoke their mother tongue at home and their schooling was carried out in the language of the occupying state. They also acquired a knowledge of Yiddish that varied from person to person according to how much interaction they had with Poland's large Jewish community.

On 1st December 1880, two weeks short of his fifteenth birthday, Seweryn began an apprenticeship in a medical clinic in the village of Zwoleń, about thirty miles from Krasienin. Statistics for the 1880s are unavailable, but in the 1860s Zwoleń was home to nearly 3,000 people, generally farmers or artisans, residing in just 325 houses, most of which were timber-built. The population was increasing: by 1907 it exceeded 7,000.[11] About half the residents were Jewish, including thirty-five-year-old Moshko Rappaport, to whom the fourteen-year-old Seweryn was apprenticed.[12]

---

9 Kłosowski's marriage certificate (1889) gave his father's profession as 'hairdresser'.
10 So named because it was created during the Congress of Vienna.
11 www.sztetl.org.pl (accessed 16th May 2013).
12 His children and grandchildren lived in Zwoleń until the Second World War, when eighty per cent of Zwoleń was destroyed and its entire Jewish population (with very few exceptions) perished.

The most misleading of the myths associated with Kłosowski is that he was trained and qualified to perform invasive surgery, a misconception which impacts strongly on his candidacy as Jack the Ripper. Although it is repeatedly asserted that Kłosowski was apprenticed to a 'senior surgeon', this is not the case. The mistake arose from the incorrect translation of his Russian documents into English. Moshko Rappaport was not a *chirurg* (the Polish for surgeon) but a *starszy felczer*. *Starszy* means 'senior' and *felczer* means 'feldsher', a profession common in Eastern Europe but which has no equivalent in Britain.

The word 'feldsher' derives from the German *feldscherer*, meaning 'field-shearer' — a military barber. In the seventeenth century, the Prussian Army suffered a shortage of field surgeons, and so its feldshers were trained to double up as wound dressers. Peter the Great of Russia borrowed the idea, introducing them into his own army around 1700. With extra training they evolved into medical orderlies who could assist army surgeons in various ways. When they retired, many feldshers settled in rural areas where, although illiterate and poorly trained, they were consulted by the peasantry because doctors were so rare and expensive. As the population grew they were increasingly relied upon, despite being — on the whole — 'ignorant, unsavoury, and usually alcoholic'.[13] Eventually the problem was solved: any man who wished to practise as a civilian feldsher in Russia had first to undergo formal training by apprenticeship followed by attending a feldsher school.

Once qualified, about two-thirds became nurse-practitioners in clinics in small towns or villages, and the remainder worked as doctors' or surgeons' assistants in hospitals, as nurses in educational or industrial workplaces, as medical orderlies in the army or as government sanitary inspectors.

Clinic-based feldshers gave first aid, delivered babies, pulled teeth, reset fractures, lanced boils, and treated haemorrhoids, abscesses, burns, sprains and other common ailments. Even in the 1880s they still performed medieval procedures such as bloodletting (by cupping and leeching)[14] and purging.[15] Hospital-based feldshers carried out the technical and practical tasks of nursing. They changed dressings, assisted during surgery, applied poultices and leeches, administered enemas and stepped in to perform anything judged as indecent for female nurses.[16] They were not trained, expected or permitted to cut open a torso or interfere with internal organs.

---

13 Ramer, Samuel C. (1976). 'Who Was the Russian Feldsher?' *Bulletin of the History of Medicine*, 50:213–225. Ramer, Samuel C. (1996). 'Professionalism and Politics: The Russian Feldsher Movement, 1891–1918', in Balzer, H. (ed) (1996) *Russia's Missing Middle Class: the Professions in Russian History*, Sharpe.
14 Bloodletting dates back to antiquity. An imbalance of the four main bodily humours (blood, phlegm, black bile and yellow bile) was treated by bloodletting, purging and vomiting. Virtually every known medical condition was once treated by these methods. In cupping, the heated rim of a cup is applied to the skin, forming an air-tight seal. As the air inside the cup cools it contracts, forming a partial vacuum; the cup sucks the skin, pulling in soft tissue, and drawing blood to that area. With leeching, a live leech is attached by its sucker onto the patient's skin. It bites into the flesh, and sucks in as much blood as it can hold within its body.
15 To evacuate the bowels as a cathartic measure.
16 All feldshers were male until 1871, when female students were accepted. After a few decades, most feldshers were female.

*The Rynek (market square) at Zwoleń. This photo was taken during the First World War, but the scene would not have changed since Kłosowski lived there in the 1870s and 1880s. In 1939, Rappaport's son was a feldsher with a clinic at Rynek 20. This was perhaps also the location of his father's clinic, where Kłosowski was an apprentice. From author's collection.*

*Central Warsaw (from an English-language street plan of 1922) showing (circled, left) Muranowska Street, which was just south of Kovel (now Warszawa Gdańska) station and close to the Russian military citadel. Circled, right, is Praga Hospital, where Kłosowski worked and studied.*

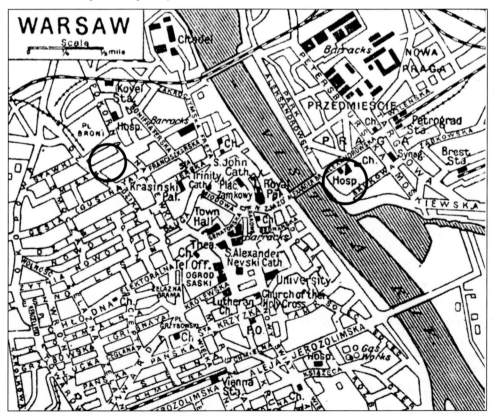

The myth that Kłosowski was a 'surgeon' originated from Joseph Petrykowski.[17] Engaged by the Metropolitan Police in 1902 to translate Kłosowski's documents into English, he rendered the Russian word фельдшер (feldsher) as 'surgeon'. Russian-born Natalia McGovern, a Home Office interpreter currently employed by the Metropolitan Police, recently confirmed that Petrykowski had made a mistake.[18] One can describe a feldsher as a medical orderly, hospital auxiliary, paramedic, doctor's assistant or male nurse, but they were most assuredly not surgeons in today's meaning of the word. As Kłosowski's documents are missing, we are denied the opportunity to re-examine the original foreign text and undertake another translation.

However, shortly after Petrykowski's translation was made, a Russian Pole called Wolff Levisohn, who had worked as a feldsher for seven years, gave a sworn deposition at Southwark police court that a feldsher was 'an assistant to a doctor, what you call here a practical nurse, who put on bandages and that sort of thing, when the doctor tells him'.[19] Levisohn's words are conveniently overlooked (or blatantly ignored) by those who propose Kłosowski as Jack the Ripper, because his description fails to support the claim that feldshers were surgeons.

Since it is now clear that Petrykowski mistranslated *felczer* as 'surgeon', it therefore follows that all related words he rendered into English — such as 'surgery' and 'surgical' — also do not refer to invasive procedures. The following three paragraphs must be read with that in mind because they derive from Petrykowski's translation. The issue is further complicated by the ambiguity of the word 'surgeon' (and its derivatives) in English. Nowadays we reserve 'surgeon' to refer exclusively to someone who invasively cuts into bodies, but the terms doctor, physician and surgeon have in the past been used interchangeably. Even today the workplace of British GPs, dentists, chiropodists and even opticians is called a 'surgery', though no (invasive) surgery is performed there.

In late 1882 Senior Feldsher Moshko Rappaport placed his sixteen-year-old apprentice Seweryn Kłosowski on the registry of pupils of the Surgical Society of Radom (the nearest large town to Zwoleń). A copy of his birth certificate was obtained, and the local magistrate issued a reference to attest that he was 'a well-behaved man, and was never found guilty of any crime whatever'. Presumably these two documents, along with a fee of one rouble, were a requirement of registration.

On 1st June 1885, when Kłosowski was nineteen, his four-and-a-half-year apprenticeship was complete. Rappaport issued a testimonial declaring that his protégé had discharged all his duties accurately and was diligent, of exemplary conduct, and had 'studied with zeal the science of surgery'. Dr Olstetski, who signed a similar certificate, revealed what the medical profession in 1880s Poland meant by the 'science of surgery': 'Cupping by means of glasses, leeches, and other assistance'. This constitutes further confirmation that Kłosowski was not a surgeon: it is not feasible that, when preparing testimonials to help a young man to obtain employment in the medical field, his mentors would trumpet his competency in medieval bloodletting techniques and yet omit to state — even as an afterthought — that he was also fully trained and qualified to perform invasive surgery.

---

17 Mistranscribed in the primary sources as 'Betrikowski' or 'Petrickowski'.
18 Personal interview with the author, April 2012.
19 *Northampton Mercury*, 9th January 1903.

Armed with his references and certificates, Kłosowski sought employment as a feldsher. In the summer of 1885 he moved seventy miles north to the city of Warsaw, where he worked as an assistant to surgeon Mr Olszański of Praga Hospital, from 20th August to 1st February. He also attended a course in 'practical surgery' run by a Mr Krynicki, between 1st October and 1st January 1886. (This course probably presented the latest techniques for removing warts, furuncles, verrucas, etc.) On 20th January[20] he became an assistant to surgeon Mr Moszkowski at an unrecorded location in Warsaw, and was still in his service in November 1886. Both surgeons issued glowing references: Olszański said his assistant 'fulfilled the whole of his duties with zeal', and Moszkowski stated that he 'performed his surgical functions with a full knowledge of the subject'.

Three weeks before Kłosowski's twenty-first birthday, he was issued with an internal passport. It describes him as 'height, medium; hair, of a dark shade; eyes, blue; nose and mouth, medium; chin and face, longish; birthmarks, none.' Valid for one year from 24th November 1886, it had to be surrendered when expired (which it was not: it was still in his possession in 1902). Such passports were in use throughout the Russian Empire between 1800 and 1914. Since there were no physical borders or passport control points, in practice they were identity cards, issued to people who wished to travel between their usual home and another town, or to reside somewhere temporarily. As Kłosowski had already lived in Warsaw for over a year, perhaps students and minors did not need one and the acquisition of a passport was made necessary by either the termination of his studies or his turning twenty-one. On the other hand, it may have been issued in preparation for military service.

From 1st January 1874, men living in Russia (and the countries subsumed into the Russian Empire) were subject to conscription to military service from the age of twenty-one. Men who had received secondary and higher education had to serve between six months and four years. Students, men without brothers, and the sole breadwinners of families were exempt (this amounted to fifty per cent of potential draftees).[21] Petrykowski remarked in his 1902 translation that the passport was given to Kłosowski 'on his recruiting in 1886'. His comment is mysterious because nothing related to military service was found among Kłosowski's documents.

A law passed in Poland in 1842 had authorised the creation of feldsher clinics, each one run by a *starszy felczer*, who took in apprentices for a certain duration, at the end of which the lads could enrol in a two-year course at the Imperial University of Warsaw Feldshers' School and themselves become fully-qualified feldshers. Kłosowski's documents seem to indicate that he purposely collected all the necessary paperwork required to enter the school.

In November 1886 Kłosowski was living in Tymienica Nowa, a rural hamlet seven miles from Zwoleń and about halfway between Radom and Lublin. He may have been working in a feldsher clinic, or perhaps his parents had moved the family

---

20 There is a twelve-day overlap with his job with Olszański; however, Kłosowski stated that the jobs were consecutive. See Appendix I for his statement and the text of the surgeons' and tutor's references.
21 Years later 'Chapman' claimed to have no brothers. He also claimed he was not Polish, so perhaps no credence can be placed on that statement.

home there.[22] Weeks later he had returned to Warsaw, where, from his lodgings at 16 Muranovskaja Street, a Jewish district on the west side of the Vistula River,[23] he addressed a letter of petition to 'His Excellency, the Dean of the Medical Faculty of the Imperial University of Warsaw'. Petrykowski's translation reads: 'I have the honour to request your Excellency to grant me permission to undergo the examination for the purpose of receiving the degree of Junior Surgeon. I enclose herewith the required documents.' The letter would have been in Russian[24] and 'junior surgeon' was in all probability a mistranslation of 'junior feldsher'.

Kłosowski needed to pass the exam in order to enrol on the feldsher course. Had he done so, his pride in earning such a prestigious certificate would surely have led him to stow it carefully among the bundle of papers he brought to London, but no such document was found. Nor does any record exist to show whether he enrolled on the two-year course, let alone completed it.

His most recently dated Russian document was a receipt for four roubles to confirm payment of his monthly hospital fee. It was issued by the Warsaw Society of Assistant Surgeons (probably a mistranslation of 'Surgeons' Assistants') on 28th February 1887 and reminded him that his next payment was due on '3 March'. (This is an error: a fee paid monthly would be due on 31st March.) After this we lose track of him for eighteen months until a witness places him in London in August 1888.

Several writers have asserted that between February 1887 and August 1888 Kłosowski travelled around Poland as a barber-surgeon; others claim that he married and fathered one, two or three children. According to H.L. Adam, he left his position at Praga Hospital 'suddenly' in November 1886 and 'journeyed to Warsaw'. In fact, Praga is a district of central Warsaw. There, wrote Adam, he enlisted in the Imperial Russian Army in December 1886, but his military service 'was of short duration', because 'about eighteen months afterwards he sailed for England'.[25] This would date his arrival in London as June 1888, however, if he joined the army in December 1886, why was he still paying hospital tuition fees in February 1887? If he was a military feldsher based at Warsaw barracks, he might have attended feldsher classes at the hospital. Alternatively, maybe he failed his exam, could no longer claim exemption as a student and, rather than be forcibly conscripted into the army of the country that had obliterated his own, fled to London. Perhaps he was recruited into the Imperial Russian Navy and deserted whilst on shore leave. If so, perhaps he concealed his desertion by destroying any documents related to his conscription or military service. It is even possible that he completed the two-year feldsher course, remaining in Warsaw until late 1888.

---

22 Currently, an Antoni Kłosowski owns a metalworks in Stalowa Wola, about seventy miles from Tymienica Nowa and about fifty from Krasienin. He might be related to Seweryn.

23 In Polish it was Ulica Muranowska (Muranów Street). Muranów was called the 'Jewish Capital of Europe'. During the Second World War the area became part of the Warsaw Ghetto, was completely razed to the ground and has since been completely rebuilt. Nothing remains of Muranowska Street but its name, which has been assigned to a street which is not on the old street's footprint.

24 When the Russians took over Warsaw University in 1871, they banned the Polish language, installed Russian lecturers, and gave the remaining Polish staff two years to become fluent in Russian, on pain of dismissal. Consequently, all Polish students had to know Russian to university level in order to study there. The university was evacuated to Russia in 1915, and the Polish university was restored.

25 Adam, H.L. (1930) *Trial of George Chapman,* William Hodge, p2.

Kłosowski's passport provides a clue to the date he left Poland. It was valid for a year and had to be given up before a replacement could be issued. That he failed to surrender it and get a new one suggests that by the expiry date, 23rd November 1887, he had left the country.

## EMIGRATION

Theories about Kłosowski performing military service are mere speculation. In reality, nobody knows why he abandoned his career, family, friends, homeland and culture. No clue reveals his initial destination when leaving Poland. He could have travelled straight to London or spent time in another country. One uncorroborated account, mentioned in an Australian newspaper, claimed that he lived for a while at Scheveningen in the Netherlands.[26] As there are no ships' records, nobody can say if he travelled alone, or with a friend or family member. Whatever his reasons for leaving, and wherever he went, Kłosowski risked a blind leap into an uncertain future. He carried with him a copy of his birth certificate, documentation relating to his schooling and feldsher training, a passport valid only within the Kingdom of Poland, and a book in Polish entitled *Five Hundred Prescriptions for Diseases and Complaints*,[27] which was signed 'S. Kłosowski' and dated '1885' on the first and last pages.

At that time, hordes of people were leaving Eastern Europe, heading mainly for the UK and USA. Tsar Alexander II was assassinated in 1881 and, because his death was attributed to a Jewish conspiracy, thousands of Russian and Polish Jews were murdered in a wave of pogroms (anti-Semitic riots), causing hundreds of thousands to flee. The UK's Jewish population grew sixfold in three decades, from 46,000 in 1882 to 300,000 by 1914. There was also a mass emigration of ethnic Poles from their homeland, prompted by an aversion to forced conscription into the armies of the occupying states, their oppressive policies against everything Polish (such as Catholicism, language and customs) combined with enforced Germanisation or Russification, and a series of failed uprisings against the occupying forces.

If Kłosowski travelled directly from Poland to England he probably left from Hamburg in the German Empire, on a vessel in which steerage passengers were herded together like cattle and slept on straw. He may have sailed to Hull, though the more obvious choice would have been London, where ships disembarked at St Katharine Docks, just east of the Tower of London. Until 1894, immigrants' first sight of the great city was Irongate Stairs, a flight of stone steps that rose out of the Thames directly beneath where Tower Bridge is today.[28] In 1901 George R. Sims wondered,

> What must these people feel as they get their first glimpse of London? All they can see is a blurred and blotted line of wharves and grim buildings, and when at last they land it is in a dark archway crowded with loafers and touts all busily trying to confuse them, to seize their luggage, almost fighting to get possession of it.[29]

---

26 *The Register* (Adelaide). 28th July 1921.
27 If that title is correct, in Polish it would have been *Pięćset Recept na Choroby i Dolegliwosci*.
28 When Tower Bridge was built in 1894, Irongate Wharf was moved slightly west.
29 'Sweated London', in Sims, G.R. (1901) *Living London*, Cassell.

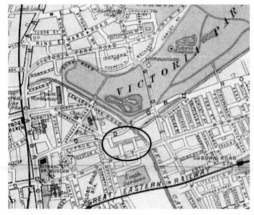

*Cranbrook Street about 1900. It was halfway between Cambridge Heath and Coborn Road railway stations.*

To protect their fellow religionists from local villains, the Jewish community in London had 'agents that meet every boat, and, addressing them in their own language, help them get their scanty belongings from the docks and advise and direct them to lodgings and homes and shelters'.[30] Perhaps they also helped Kłosowski to find accommodation.

Some researchers believe that Kłosowski's first home in London was a room in a house in a cul-de-sac abutting Regent's Canal, just south of Old Ford Lock. This was in Bow, a cheap, shabby, working-class area just over two miles from the docks. His initial and surname, along with the address '54 Cranbrook Street', were later found inscribed within his Polish book of medical remedies (which suggests an intention to stay longer than a few nights or weeks). Bow was inhabited mainly by indigenous Londoners, and perhaps he struggled to communicate, which may have prompted his move to an area populated by Eastern Europeans.[31]

According to the *Daily Telegraph*, Kłosowski 'came to England penniless, like most other undesirable aliens'.[32] Although the writer offered nothing to support this alleged impoverishment, it is true that Kłosowski was one of hundreds of thousands of immigrants from Eastern Europe who ended up living in overcrowded conditions in the slums of the East End whilst competing with the indigenous population, as well as an influx of Irish people, for low-paid work. 'Aliens', as they were called, often met with prejudice, suspicion and resentment, not only from the ignorant but also from the educated, literate and influential who inform public opinion, such as judges, teachers, social commentators, politicians and the press.

The date of Kłosowski's arrival in London has yet to be established, despite researchers' attempts to locate him within ships' manifests or to extrapolate the date from the testimony of those who knew him in those days. He could have arrived as early as March 1887 or as late as October 1888. According to one source, on Bank Holiday Monday 6th August 1888 Ethel Radin 'gave a party to a small number of Poles, whom [Kłosowski], who was new to the country and lonely, was anxious to meet.'[33] Mrs Radin was speaking in 1930, when she was in her sixties, and was casting her

---

30 'Sweated London', in Sims, G.R. (1901) *Living London*, Cassell.
31 He may have lived in Cranbrook Street at a later date, but it must have been before 1895, the year he ceased to use the name Kłosowski.
32 Quoted in the *Southland Times* (NZ), 25th March 1903.
33 *Thomson's Weekly News*, 21st June 1930.

mind back forty years, but the date may have stuck in her memory because, just hours after the party, a woman called Martha Tabram was brutally murdered a couple of miles away, and the shocking news hit the headlines the next day.

## WORKING LIFE

In London, Seweryn Kłosowski did not follow the profession for which he had trained since the age of fourteen. He may have abandoned his vocation whilst still in Poland, either because he failed his junior feldsher exam, or because he was dissuaded from practising since discovering feldshers' lowly status and poor reputation within the Polish/Russian healthcare system. Perhaps Moshko Rappaport failed to mention that many of his colleagues felt so undervalued that they had organised themselves into a professional body to campaign for greater recognition and respect. Impassioned letters to their journal revealed that they felt 'exploited, abused and unjustly maligned',[34] most especially by doctors, whose poor opinion of them was — most unfairly — based on the incompetence of their unqualified forebears. Maybe this is what prompted Kłosowski to give up the profession which he had worked so hard to qualify for and begin a completely new life in London, the city of seemingly infinite possibilities.

He may have believed that the certificates and testimonials that proved his apprenticeship to a feldsher and subsequent employment placed him above the common mob of Eastern European émigrés. Given the heavy reliance upon — and ubiquity of — feldshers throughout the Russian Empire, he would have no reason to suspect that they did not exist everywhere, nor that, in England, the nursing profession was open only to women.[35]

Unless he had studied privately by acquiring textbooks, or had engaged a tutor before leaving Poland, Kłosowski would have known no English. He needed to find an occupation in which he could get by until he became fluent. An East End barber's assistant need not speak English: nearly all his clients were from Poland and the rest spoke Russian or Yiddish. What is more, the job made use of his skills, because in those days barbers carried out minor cosmetic procedures such as removing unsightly growths (warts, moles, etc) and also used chemical substances to treat dandruff and various minor skin conditions. According to Harry Furniss, Kłosowski

> found a flourishing Polish club in Clerkenwell, where he met a number of his compatriots, who soon helped him to get work...He was advised to set up as a hairdresser and by the aid of his Polish acquaintances he soon obtained a billet as assistant to a barber, with whom he remained for a short time till he had acquired enough English to set up on his own account.[36]

About 1887 or 1888,[37] Kłosowski worked for hairdresser Abraham Radin in Limehouse. The area was home to large numbers of Eastern Europeans and Radin

34 Professionalism and Politics: The Russian Feldsher Movement 1891-1918, in Balzer, H (1996) *Russia's missing middle class: the professions in Russian History*, Sharpe, New York, p121.
35 In 1880s England there were untrained nurses (older women whose skills derived from raising their own children) and, from 1860, hospital-trained, certificated nurses. Their training was based on the programme created by Florence Nightingale, which did not admit male students.
36 Furniss, H. (ed) *Famous Crimes Past and Present*, Vol. IX, No. 109, c. 1908, Caxton House.
37 In early 1903, Mrs Radin stated that Kłosowski worked for her husband 'about fifteen years ago.'

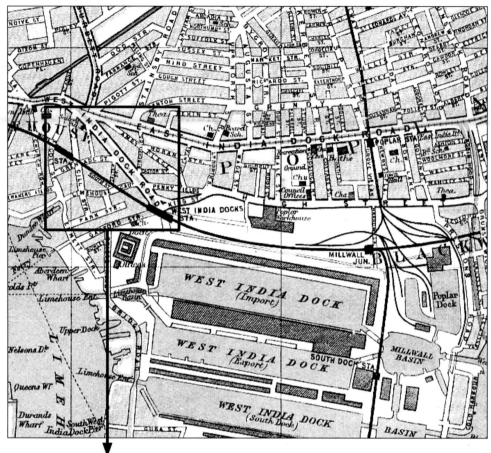

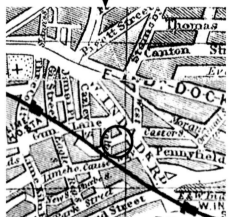

Limehouse and Poplar on a map of 1908.

West India Dock Road (on a map of 1888). No. 70 was on the west side, on the corner of Robert Street (the short, unlabelled road between Gun Lane and Limehouse Causeway). The railway stations are Limehouse (left) and West India Docks.

and his wife Ethel were Lithuanian Jews. The couple — who at twenty-two were the same age as Kłosowski — had a baby named Solomon, whom Kłosowski helped nurse through an illness by the use of poultices. According to Mrs Radin, Kłosowski 'had a wife with him', but who this mystery woman was has not yet come to light. Mrs Radin disclosed that her husband had the Limehouse shop for eighteen months. We do not know when they arrived or when they left. However, we know that Solomon was born at 70 West India Dock Road on 26th May 1887, and that Kłosowski worked for them for five months. This means they must have arrived between November 1885 and May 1887 and they must have left between June 1887 and December 1888.

During his apprenticeship Kłosowski may have learned barbering techniques. He probably started by shaving Radin's customers (with a cut-throat razor) whilst being brought up to speed in hair-cutting. The work of an East End barber was neither artistic nor glamorous, but basic and cheap. As Gareth Williams has so eloquently pointed out:

> This isn't Vidal Sassoon or Trevor Sorbie territory...it's pudden-basin for the kids, it's trimming Shmuel Ashkenazi's hair, it's chasing the lice out of Karol Jankowski's beard, and lancing Melnick's boils. All for 2d or 3d a go.[38]

## STEPNEY

When Kłosowski had been with them for about five months, the Radin family moved home and business to 7 Aldgate High Street. Kłosowski took over their Limehouse premises for a short time before opening his own barbershop in Stepney. He must have moved (or had firm plans to do so) no later than December 1888, for he is listed at 126 Cable Street (as 'Severyn Glosovski, hair dresser') in the 1889 Post Office Directory, and December was the deadline for submissions for inclusion.

Cable Street is near the River Thames and gained its name from the mile-long ropes that were twisted into cables for ships' sails and other maritime uses. It was a rough area with a long-held (and well-deserved) reputation for harbouring thieves, brothels and opium dens. A low, brick-built, arched viaduct ran parallel to the street, carrying the London & Blackwall Railway between Shadwell and Leman Street stations, and onwards to Fenchurch Street. Facing this viaduct, between the junctions with Betts Street and Prince's Square, stood No. 126, part of a tall, flat-fronted, brick-faced terrace with shops on the ground floor and living accommodation above. English and Eastern Europeans lived and traded cheek-by-jowl: flanking Kłosowski's salon were Emma Skelsey's coffee house and a bakery owned by Cecilia Nordheim, a widow from Prussia. Among his other industrious neighbours were tripe-dressers and tobacconists, fishmongers and furniture brokers, drapers and dressmakers.

Kłosowski lived above his shop and, as there were nine rooms over two floors, doubtless many others shared the premises. There is no record for the time he lived there, but a year after he moved out the 1891 census listed eighteen residents, all of them working-class Jews from Russian Poland. Because of the influx of aliens, and rent increases of twenty-five per cent over the previous two decades, such overcrowding

---

38 Sam Flynn (Gareth Williams), jtrforums.com, 13th May 2007.

*126 Cable Street (with open windows) in 1943. Source of image unknown.*

*Cable Street on a map of 1897. 126 was located on the south side, just beneath the letter 'B' in CABLE. The road opposite the letter 'B' is Grove Street. The Pinchin Street Torso was found in Arch 16, under the railway line, near the 'P' in Pinchin Street.*

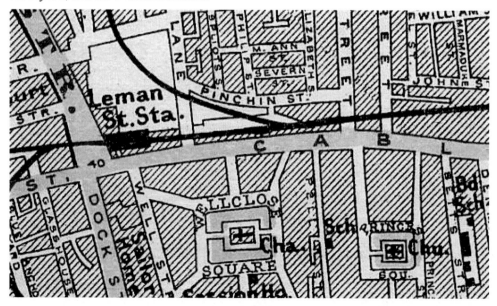

Press sketches related to the two Whitechapel murders which some researchers associate with Kłosowski. In both cases the association is purely geographical: he lived near to locations in which the bodies were discovered.

Above: the murder of Martha Tabram in George Yard, off Whitechapel High Street, on 7<sup>th</sup> August 1888, from the Illustrated Police News. Below: the discovery of a torso in a railway arch in Stepney in September 1889. The artist is in Pinchin Street, looking south at Arch 16, where East End gawpers are being held back by a cordon of police. From the Pictorial News.

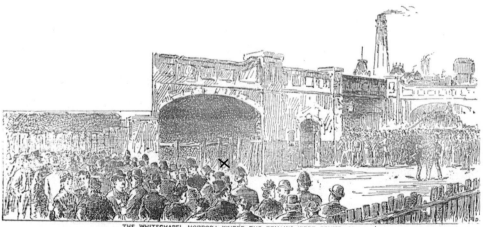

was typical in the East End: over half of its 900,000 inhabitants occupied flats with fewer than five rooms, with an average occupancy of two persons per room.

Whilst Kłosowski was living at 126 Cable Street, a gruesome discovery was made nearby. During a routine beat on 10th September 1889, PC William Pennett found the decomposing, headless corpse of a woman, without legs but with both arms, in the westernmost arch of the railway viaduct alongside Pinchin Street,[39] just a couple of minutes' walk from Kłosowski's home and shop.

## LUCY BADERSKA

The Baderski family hailed from Mikstat, a small but historic Polish village in the county of Ostrzeszów, within the province of Wielkopolska. At the time it was called Mixstadt in the county of Schildberg in the Province of Posen (Poznań) and all inhabitants were forced to learn, speak and read German for official purposes. The area had fallen under Prussian rule after the Second Partition of Poland in 1793 and was part of the Duchy of Warsaw from 1807 until 1815, when it was returned to Prussia. In 1871 the residents of Mikstat numbered 1,437 (comprising 1,249 Catholics, thirty-six Protestants and 152 Jews). Over the following decades, the natural increase in population was almost matched by emigration: by 1905 it had grown to just 1,462.

The father of the Baderski family, Józef, was a farmer. Nothing is known of his wife, but perhaps her name was Stanisława, given the prevalence of that name (and its male equivalent) among her children and grandchildren. We do not know how many offspring they produced but, over the course of a decade, four daughters and one or two sons emigrated piecemeal to London. The girls were Maria, born in 1868; Łucja, 1871; Stanisława, 1873; and Józefina, 1876. Their elder brother, Stanisław, was born in 1864. (I believe there was a second brother, called Władysław.) The first to arrive in London was Maria (Mary), who may have travelled with her brother Stanisław, or Frank Polaczek, or both. Frank, a hairdresser, was also born in Mikstat and when Mary married him in London on 15th May 1887 Stanisław was a witness. Łucja (Lucy) arrived in London about 1889 and her younger sister Stanisława, a tailoress, was to follow in 1890, the year Stanisław married a fellow Polish émigrée. Józefina was the last to come over, arriving by 1898, the year she married Polish cabinetmaker Stanisław Kamiński.

During 1889 Kłosowski spent Sunday evenings enjoying the company of his compatriots at the Polish Club in St John's Square, Clerkenwell, a shabby area in which the Salvation Army had recently opened a doss house. He made the acquaintance of Lucy Baderska, recently arrived from Poland and sharing lodgings at Green Street, Bethnal Green, with Stanisław, Mary and Frank. At just eighteen, Lucy was five years younger than Kłosowski, but they seem to have taken a shine to one another, for they began courting and he gave her a photo of himself, which she posted to her father in Mikstat. Presumably he passed muster with her folks back home as well as in London, for they were married on Tuesday 29th October by Father Joseph Verres at the German Roman Catholic church of St Boniface in Union Street (now Adler Street), immediately behind Whitechapel

---

39 The viaduct carried a spur line to Commercial Road Goods Depot. Though the line has long since closed, the viaduct and arches remain and are the subject of a campaign to preserve them.

parish church.[40] The couple's ages were recorded as twenty-four and nineteen, in line with Polish custom, which counts age as the one reached at the next birthday. The address of both bride and groom was 126 Cable Street, but Lucy is not likely to have moved in unchaperoned until after the wedding. The couple had been acquainted for only four or five weeks, and the reason for the hasty marriage is unknown. Although Roman Catholicism imposed strict rules against fornication, Kłosowski was later to demonstrate just how easily he could persuade women to abandon their moral code, and so maybe Lucy was pregnant with a child she subsequently miscarried. On the other hand, she may have disliked living with her siblings or impatient to escape from their overcrowded lodgings. Many years later, Stanisław revealed that he had been unhappy at the pair marrying so soon.

There are two clues to the existence of a second brother. A Władysław Baderski was a witness to the marriage (as was Maria, whose surname was misspelled 'Polachek') and Stanisław stated that, although he missed the church ceremony, he went to the reception at Cable Street 'with his brother'. (They arrived too late: the wedding feast had ended.)[41]

In January 1890 Kłosowski again appeared — as 'Severyn Closovski' — in the local trade directory. According to Stanisław, in about April the couple moved to Commercial Street and later to nearby Greenfield Street, where Lucy's younger sister Stanisława found them living when she arrived from Poland in about August that year. By that time, Kłosowski was working in a barbershop in the cellar of the White Hart public house at 89 Whitechapel High Street. At some point he took over as proprietor of the shop, and remained there until mid-1891.

Lucy gave birth to a son, Władysław, at the White Hart on 6th September 1890. Researchers have cited the address on the child's birth certificate as proof that the couple lived in the cellar, but they may have rented a room above the pub. Judging by recent photographs, there was no habitable accommodation in the cellar and no census from 1841 to 1911 lists any barber living there. In common with half of East End children at that time, Władysław did not survive babyhood: he died at home on 3rd March 1891, of cardiac asthenia following a bout of pneumonia.

At this time, the Kłosowskis were living at Tewkesbury Buildings, a terrace of fourteen small, overcrowded houses in a courtyard reached via a narrow alleyway between 99 and 100 Whitechapel High Street, just a few doors to the west of the White Hart and close to the junction with Leman Street, or via John Bull yard, which led to Commercial Street.[42] The national census, taken a month later, shows the couple sharing No. 2 with six others: a young couple with a toddler, an older couple,

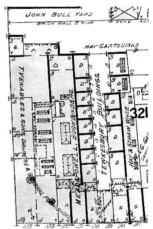

*Tewkesbury Buildings.*

---

40 The deutschsprachige katholische Gemeinde St Bonifacius. Mary Baderska had also married there. The registration district was Mile End Old Town.
41 Baderski mentioned this in court in 1903. I can find no marriage or death records for Władysław.
42 A row of eight cramped, flat-fronted, three-storey homes facing six slightly larger ones. Twelve had no gardens (their frontages were only 15ft apart and their rear walls abutted industrial buildings).

and a lodger. Eight people may seem a lot, but next door at No. 1, sixteen were somehow shoe-horned in. Apart from the Kłosowskis, everyone at No. 2 was Jewish. The young couple were Jacob Limberg, a costermonger, and his wife Jane, a former umbrella maker. They were born in Spitalfields, but their fathers were cigar makers from Amsterdam. The older pair were a seventy-year-old shopkeeper with the unlikely name of Barnet Barnet and his wife, Betsy, fourteen years his junior. Each family had only one room, and the Kłosowskis shared theirs with a lodger — an eighteen-year-old Pole named Max Starke. He was a hairdresser's assistant, so perhaps he also worked under the White Hart.[43]

Only one other man with the surname Kłosowski appears in London records at that time. Curiously, he was also a hairdresser. In 1891 he lived and worked at 195 Blackfriars Road, close to where Seweryn would one day lease a public house. Born in 1861, Oscar Kłosowski was the perfect age to have been Seweryn's elder brother, but — alas — he came from Germany.[44]

## A TRIP TO AMERICA

In the spring or summer of 1891, the Kłosowskis sailed to the United States. According to Lucy's sister Stanisława, they left at around Whitsuntide, which was in mid-May, but extensive searches of ships' passenger lists and Ellis Island immigration records for that month drew a blank. The closest match found is a record of a twenty-seven-year-old barber called 'Severin Klosowsky' travelling with his twenty-year-old wife on the Red Star Line's S.S. Friesland, occupying cabin 2B and arriving in New York on 28th July.[45] The man's name is correct phonetically and his profession spot-on, as was his wife's age. However, he was two years older than Kłosowski and his wife's scribbled name looks like 'Any'. Moreover, the Friesland sailed from Antwerp in Belgium with no stopping point in England and the Klosowskys were listed as German citizens, travelling from Germany. If the Klosowskys were in fact the Kłosowskis, perhaps they visited Lucy's family in Poland and then stopped off in Germany en route to Antwerp docks, and the ship's clerk misheard or misunderstood them and wrongly recorded them as German nationals.

The Friesland was one of the safest vessels afloat. Having been built just two years earlier, it had every modern convenience, including electric lighting throughout. Maybe the couple caught a glimpse of the magnificent staterooms and saloons on their way down to the 'comfortable quarters for 800 immigrants', which consisted of steerage rooms that were 'well lighted and well ventilated'.[46]

No document or witness statement reveals what the Kłosowskis did, nor where they lived, after they arrived in New York. Lucy's siblings Stanisław and Stanisława stated merely that the couple went to the USA and returned separately. Only two clues point to their whereabouts. In 1903 Kłosowski wrote a short autobiography in which he reeled off the names of many streets and districts of New York, which points

---

43 Max married Russian-born Tilly Gluckstein and become proprietor of his own salon in Houndsditch.
44 There are no death or marriage records associated with him, nor any offspring, suggesting that after 1901 he either changed his surname or left the country.
45 Researcher Roger Palmer is responsible for finding this record. The Klosowskys shared the cabin with a twenty-year-old Englishman called Thomas H. Edward.
46 www.norwayheritage.com (accessed 16th May 2013).

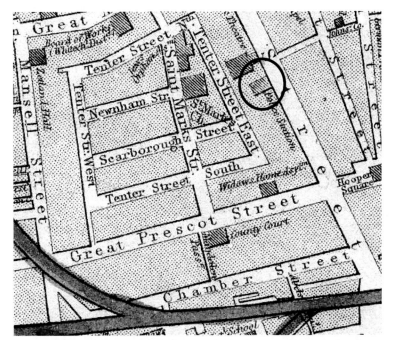

*Scarborough Street on a map of 1868. The police station circled was Leman Street, part of H Division (Whitechapel), which investigated the Whitechapel murders. The dark, forked line is the London & Blackwall Railway, between Fenchurch Street station to the west and Leman Street station to the east.*

to an intimate knowledge of the city gained from personal experience. The other clue is an anecdote about Kłosowski threatening to kill Lucy in Jersey City. (This will be discussed in Part Six.) All we know for certain about their time in the USA is that, within a few weeks of their arrival, Lucy again became pregnant.

### A RETURN TO LONDON

Aged twenty, and about five months into her second pregnancy, Lucy travelled back to England on the Inman Line's *S.S. City of Berlin*, which left New York on 11th January 1892. Built in Scotland in 1875, in its first year it broke the records for the fastest transatlantic crossing in both directions and could carry 202 first class and 1,500 steerage passengers. On arrival at Liverpool about 20th January, Lucy made her way to London, where she moved into a rented room with her sister Stanisława, then eighteen. This lodging was in Scarborough Street, a residential backstreet between Mansell Street and Leman Street, a few minutes' walk from Whitechapel High Street, in an area known as Goodman's Fields. No. 26 was an eight-roomed house which, nine months earlier, in the spring of 1891, had been shared by two families, both headed by Polish-born Jewish tailors: Aaron Logette, his wife Jane and their two baby sons, and Charles Cooper, his wife Sarah and their two infant daughters.[47] One couple may still have been living there the following January and let the room to Lucy and her sister.

47 The Logettes had lived there for at least eighteen months, for Benjamin was born there in October 1889.It is interesting that Polish-born Charles Cooper had adopted an English name; perhaps this influenced Kłosowski's later name-change.

Numerous authors have professed to know why Lucy returned from the US without Kłosowski. According to the British Parliamentary Papers (BPP)[48] she left because of his violence and womanising (having obtained her fare from her father in Poland). Sugden claims that she was 'terrified' of him and Buddle declares that she 'fled back to England in terror', and yet there is no evidence that Kłosowski was unfaithful to Lucy, nor that she was scared of him. Her departure could have been a mutually agreed decision to avoid her making a long sea voyage in late pregnancy.

Perhaps Kłosowski stayed on awhile because he could earn more in the USA and wanted to maximise their nest-egg, especially with a baby on the way. Years later he claimed to have worked as a barber and a steward on board transatlantic ships; perhaps that accounts for his whereabouts from January to May 1892. Ten years later, a slip of paper discovered among Kłosowski's documents bore the words: 'Came from America in 1893, independent.' Did he misremember the year or return to America in 1893? The note continued: 'Deposits £100, when from America I had £1,000.' This appears to suggest that he brought £1,000 home from the States. As that is the equivalent of £100,000 today, he certainly did not earn it as a barber.[49] We know that, eight years later. he performed illegal abortions, so it is possible that he made that vast sum in a similar manner in the US.

Baby Cecilia was born at 26 Scarborough Street on 12th May 1892 and, according to Stanisława, Kłosowski turned up two weeks later accompanied by his brother-in-law.[50] If Lucy had cabled him when the child was born, that would have given him about two weeks to disengage from whatever he was doing and travel to her. If they knew approximately when the baby was due, the date he would sail to London may even have been decided months before, but he miscalculated. If Lucy had fled from him, Kłosowski may have guessed the baby's due date and returned of his own accord, even though he was unwelcome, and then either bullied, manipulated or charmed Lucy into a reconciliation.

A clue to the state of their marriage lies in Stanisława's actions. She moved out of the rented room in order to give the couple privacy. Would she have done so if her sister lived 'in terror' of Kłosowski? Or was she somehow ousted by him? Stanisława, even when appearing as a witness for the prosecution at Kłosowski's trial for murder in 1903, did not hint at any contretemps between husband and wife. On the other hand, Stanisława said that she never saw Kłosowski again, although he and Lucy were together for at least another year and she lived within walking distance. This suggests an estrangement or argument.

Three months after she left them at Scarborough Street, Stanisława (still a teenager) married thirty-one-year-old Varsovian Wilhelm Rauch and set up home at 292 Burdett Road, Poplar, where Stanisława, who anglicised her name to 'Stella', bore twelve children. According to Lucy's great-grandson, the Rauches 'did not mix much with Lucy and her family'.[51]

48 Return showing the Working of the Regulations for carrying out the Prosecution of Offences Act 1879 & 1884. British Parliamentary Papers, Vol. 56, HMSO, 1902. Pub as the Blue Book, 1903, p12–16.
49 £1 then is worth roughly £100 today; a shilling, about £5; a penny, about 40p.
50 The brother-in-law was not named. At the time, he had only one: Frank Polaczek. However, it makes more sense that it was Stanisława's future husband, who was courting her at that time.
51 David J. Brown, in O'Donnell, K., Parlour, A. and Parlour, S. (1997) Jack the Ripper Whitechapel murders, Ten Bells Publishing.

On 20th June 1892 Kłosowski presented himself at the office of the registrar of births, deaths and marriages and reported the birth of his daughter. From then until the autumn of 1893 the couple's movements went unrecorded. He could have returned to the USA (as suggested by his aforementioned memo), worked on board ships, or been a barber in London. Only two things are certain about their movements. Firstly, they lived at some point at an unknown address in the City Road area. In 1891 Lucy's sister Mary, her husband Frank Polaczek and their three children occupied three rooms above Frank's hairdressing shop at 209 City Road.[52] Maybe the Kłosowskis lodged with them, or in rented rooms close to them, and perhaps Frank gave Kłosowski a job as a barber. Secondly, between June 1892 and the autumn of 1893, Lucy left Kłosowski.

The couple's estrangement marked the end of a turbulent three years in Lucy's life. In that short time she had left her homeland and her parents, sailed to England, experienced a whirlwind courtship, a hasty marriage, pregnancy, childbirth and the death of her first baby. She had moved home at least eight times, emigrated to the US, returned alone and pregnant, given birth in her husband's absence and, ultimately, left him and became a single mother. She was still only twenty-one.

H.L. Adam cited Kłosowski's 'insistent and open immorality' as the cause of the couple's estrangement, although he offered no proof of this. He added that Kłosowski made no attempt to get custody of the *two children*, an error that throws doubt on his knowledge of Kłosowski's life.[53] Because of the poor social, legal and financial position of women at that time, no wife left her husband on a mere whim. Victorian society condemned marital separation as self-indulgent, socially embarrassing and deeply shameful. Furthermore, no woman would choose to be a single parent — especially a poor East End immigrant woman without means or profession — unless her marital situation was utterly unendurable. Lucy must have had a compelling reason to walk out on her husband and breadwinner and to deprive Cecilia of her father.

### SARAH ANN CHAPMAN

Sometime in 1893 Kłosowski became assistant to hairdresser and umbrella maker John Haddon at 3 Market Buildings, West Green Road (later renumbered 5 West Green Road), Tottenham. It must have been a busy and successful establishment: Haddon employed a couple of assistants and an errand boy. That autumn Kłosowski met a dressmaker named Sarah Ann Chapman, known as 'Annie'. Her origins and age have not yet been established, but she appears to have been about twenty. Before long she had moved in with him in a flat above Haddon's as his 'housekeeper' (a Victorian euphemism for mistress at a time when cohabitation was universally condemned as living 'in sin'). The writer of the BPP article claimed that Annie had 'practically no alternative', but did not explain why he thought her options so limited. He suggested that Kłosowski had promised to marry Annie in order to persuade her to allow sexual activities then, having had his wicked way, refused to honour the promise. In fact he was not free to marry, and divorcing Lucy would have taken years and involved

---

52 By 1895 they had moved to 205 and by 1899 they were at 179.
53 The mistake that there were two children was repeated in Wilson, C. and Pitman, P. (1962) *Encyclopedia of Murder*, Putnam and also in Rumbelow, D. (2004) *The Complete Jack the Ripper*, Penguin.

considerable expense. Among the working classes, estranged spouses simply lived apart and, if either cohabited with someone else, the woman adopted the man's surname for the sake of outward respectability.

One day in the autumn of 1894 Kłosowski met Lucy by chance in the street. A discussion ensued, and she consented to return to him:

> He removed her furniture to his premises where, to her surprise, she found that he was already living with a woman. A quarrel ensued, but the parties settled their differences somehow and all lived in the house together, [Kłosowski] apparently dividing his favours between the two women. After a time, disputes arose and Miss Chapman left the house.[54]

Some writers have assumed that Kłosowski persuaded the women to indulge in three-in-a-bed frolics. This is an absurd suggestion, given the moral code of the era. Under oath several years later, Annie said that Kłosowski brought Lucy home and introduced her as his wife, they shared the house for six weeks until December 1894, then she (Annie) left. Kłosowski had possibly convinced Lucy that Annie was genuinely his housekeeper and persuaded Annie to play along. Perhaps Lucy became suspicious and insisted the 'other woman' leave, or maybe Annie felt her number one place in his heart and his household had been usurped and left of her own accord. All we know for certain is that, when Annie moved out, she was about a month pregnant.

After Annie's departure, Lucy again left her husband, this time permanently. It is impossible to determine when they split up: it could have been the same day Annie left or at any point over the following year.

Sometime in 1894, Kłosowski took over the lease of a shop at 656 Tottenham High Road from John Haddon. Within a year he had moved again. Further south on the same road, businessman Henry Pincott owned a tobacconist shop at 520 and also the adjoining building, 518, which he let through a friend, legal clerk William Lemain Bray. Kłosowski took the lease on 518 on 7th January 1895, paying his weekly rent to Mr Bray. He set up home upstairs and opened a barbershop on the ground floor under the grand name 'The Criterion Toilet'.[55]

Despite having lost his son and daughter, when Annie called on Kłosowski to inform him that she was expecting a baby, he gave her the brush-off. He even declined her plea for a reference to help her find paid work. Their final meeting occurred in February or March 1895, when he cycled to her home in Albert Road, Tottenham. No record exists of what was said, but clearly they did not reach a mutually acceptable agreement, because Annie subsequently consulted William Bray (in his capacity as clerk to solicitor Frederick Braund) several times to ask for legal advice. She had the right to obtain an affiliation order enabling a magistrate to compel Kłosowski to contribute financially towards the child's upbringing; however, giving evidence in 1903, Bray did not reveal if he had informed Annie of her legal rights; nor did she mention whether she had pursued that route.

---

54 Return showing the Working of the Regulations for carrying out the Prosecution of Offences Act 1879 & 1884. British Parliamentary Papers, Vol. 56, HMSO, 1902. Pub as the *Blue Book*, 1903, p12–16.
55 The building currently above the shops at 518 and 520 appears to be Victorian.

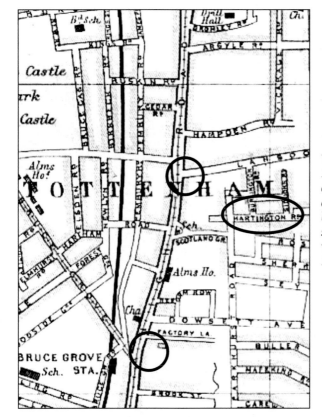

*Tottenham High Road on a map of 1908. Kłosowski's barbershops are circled. The top one is 656 (on the corner of Lansdowne Rd); the one below is 518, opposite Bruce Grove station. Also marked is Hartington Rd, where Annie Chapman was living in 1903.*

About the middle of 1895, Kłosowski became an employee once again, this time in a barbershop at 7 Church Lane, a razor's throw from the Great Eastern Railway's Leytonstone station.[56] He told the owner, a thirty-year-old, German-born man called William Wengel, that he could not provide employers' references because he was self-employed and his shop had failed. However, he may have given up the shop to evade Annie Chapman's expected or threatened affiliation suit.

Kłosowski worked at Wengel's for about seven months, during which time he was a 'quiet, industrious man earning about 30s a week,[57] and behaving in a proper way'.[58] His English colleagues struggled with his surname. Eventually they nicknamed him 'Shaloski' because, as Alfred Wicken later explained, it was 'a matter of picking up his name as we could'.

Giving up his own shop rendered Kłosowski homeless, so he asked John Ward, a customer with a nearby tailoring business at 3 Church Lane, whose wife Caroline let rooms, if he could lodge with them. In the autumn of 1895 Kłosowski moved into the Wards' home in Forest Road, Leytonstone, a short walk from his workplace.

Annie Chapman gave birth on 8th August 1895 in Edmonton Workhouse, Bridport Road, about a mile north of Kłosowski's former shop in Tottenham. She named her son William Kłosowski Chapman.

---

56 Leytonstone station is now part of the London Underground system.
57 Unskilled men earned 20 to 25 shillings a week; a skilled man (e.g. mason, compositor, watchmaker) would earn about £3 a week.
58 *Southwark & Bermondsey Recorder*, 3rd January 1903.

*Church Lane, looking east from the railway station, across the junction with Kirkdale Road, c. 1914. Evans & Davies (first awning) was at No. 25. Wengel's hairdresser (No. 7) is on the same side but further along, opposite St John-the-Baptist church, which can be seen in the centre of the photograph.*

*Leytonstone (from a 1908 map) showing Church Lane and Forest Road, a short walk away.*

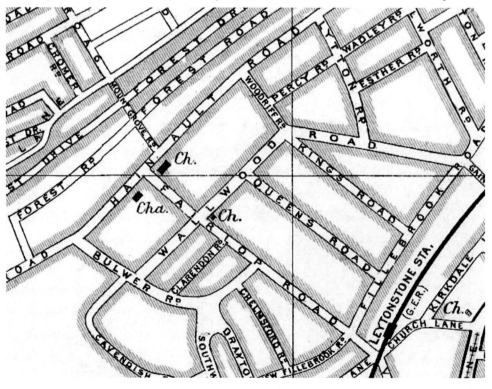

# THE CRIMES OF GEORGE CHAPMAN

## MARY SPINK

Mary's parents, William Renton and Annie Smith, may have first met in the early 1850s, when he was a young hosiery salesman at 56 Briggate, in Leeds city centre, and she lived above her family's pork butcher's shop at No. 70. They married on 13ᵗʰ January 1858 and Mary Isabella Renton was born on 14ᵗʰ August, at Lowtown, near Pudsey, between Bradford and Leeds. William was by then a linen draper, but changed profession to that of pork butcher by the time their second daughter, Clara, was born in 1861.

Annie Smith's younger sister Sarah married William Renton's younger brother Alfred and the couple had three sons: Joseph in 1861, Edgar in 1864 and John in 1865. When John was five weeks old Alfred died, aged just twenty-seven. The widowed Sarah took her three boys to Briggate to live with their grandmother, Mary Farrar Smith, widow of Joseph.

Joseph Smith had died in 1863, leaving a handsome estate of nearly £4,000, worth about £400,000 today. The sum of £570 was earmarked for his granddaughter Mary Renton, in the form of a trust fund that she could access at age twenty-one. Doubtless similar bequests were made to Clara, Sarah and other kin. When Joseph died, his widow took over the business. Listed as a pork butcher in the census, Mary Smith owned and managed the shop and employed professionally trained men. Her son-in-law William Renton was working for her when he and Annie had their third child, George, in 1866. He died as a baby, then Annie succumbed to TB in 1868 and, just eight months later, William also died. Their daughters Mary and Clara, as orphans aged ten and seven, went to live with their grandmother, their aunt Sarah and their three boy cousins above the Briggate shop. The 1871 census shows all seven in residence, along with a cook and a general servant.

Sarah Renton remarried in 1872. Her new husband Henry Midgley, just twenty-two, acquired a ready-made family consisting of Sarah's three boys, aged eleven, eight and seven, and her nieces Mary and Clara, then fourteen and eleven. Within three years the couple had added two more children.⁵⁹

On census day in 1881 Mary was visiting a relative, William Crampton, at Raglan Street, Leeds, whilst Clara was lodging nearby and working for a confectioner. The Midgleys had settled in Headingley, where Henry worked as a butcher and Sarah's sons, now teenagers, were learning trades (dyer, plumber's mate and pawnbroker's

---

59 Annie, born 1873 and William, born 1875. A third child, Edward, was born and died in 1881.

assistant). About 1882, the Midgley family moved to London and set up home at Sydney Villas, Mornington Road, Leytonstone. Mary accompanied them, but Clara stayed behind and married a butcher called John Farrer in March 1883. Henry Midgley opened a pork butcher's shop in Leytonstone, in which he employed Mary as cashier. It is possible that the move to London and the purchase of the shop was funded by Sarah's inheritance from her father.

In March 1883 Sarah gave birth to her seventh child. Just one month later, she died.[60] Sarah had been the lynchpin of the family and her death fractured the link between the Rentons and the Midgleys and led to the breakup of the household. In June, Henry christened the baby Sarah, after her late mother, but by then no longer had a shop; he was living in Clapton and working as a foreman. Just five months later, he married Emma Parker and in April 1885 they emigrated to California, taking Henry's three children, then aged twelve, ten and two. His three stepsons, Joseph, Edgar and John Renton, by then grown up and self-supporting, remained in east London.

Within three months of her aunt Sarah's death, Mary Renton, then twenty-four, became pregnant by a railway porter five years her senior. He enjoyed the splendidly Dickensian name of Shadrach Spink and had grown up — the fifth of nine children — at Banningham windmill in Norfolk, where his father was the miller and farmed fifty-two acres. Shadrach and Mary married on 16th December 1883 at St Paul's church, Bow Common, Burdett Road, Stepney, whilst residing at 2 King John Street, near Stepney Green. The baby, Shadrach Sayer Spink, was born on 26th April 1884 at 6 Forest Road, Leytonstone.

According to Joseph Renton, his cousin Mary's marriage to Spink was unhappy: he told a court in 1902 that Spink was 'not a sober man' and Mary was 'also intemperate'. Mary's former landlord John Ward told a different story: when he knew her (seven years after she separated from Shadrach) she indulged in drink only once a month, on the day she received her income from her trust fund. Whatever the truth, after only five years of marriage, and seven months into her second pregnancy, Spink abandoned Mary, taking their four-year-old boy to live on his grandfather's farm in Norfolk. Mary never saw either of them again.

Perhaps one of the Renton brothers stayed on at Sydney Villas after Henry Midgley moved out, because Mary's second child, William Alfred Spink, was born there on 8th December 1888. When the census was taken in April 1891 she was living in rented accommodation at 1 Mornington Road,[61] and was better off than many single mothers, since she enjoyed the exclusive use of three rooms, and in a superior area. Over £500 remained in her trust fund, from which she drew just under £2 a month. If she continued to live that frugally, her inheritance would last at least two decades.

Mary does not appear to have been on close terms with her cousins, though they lived nearby. Joseph and John Renton had married siblings Mary and Louisa Sampson in 1885 and 1887 respectively. John died in 1889. Edgar — who remained unmarried — may have suffered poor health, because he lived with Joseph and his family until his death in 1898, at the age of just thirty-four. Mary saw her sister Clara for the final time about 1893, the year Clara gave birth to her fourth child.[62] Whilst

60 Sarah Renton left £102 in her will, worth about £10,000 today.
61 This may have been the same house as Sydney Villas, but numbered instead of named.
62 In 1903 Clara revealed that she had not seen Mary 'for ten years'.

Clara's large brood may have made travelling difficult, that Mary did not take Willie to visit his aunt and cousins in Leeds hints at a family rift.

By 1895 Mary and Willie were lodging with John and Caroline Ward at Forest Road, Leytonstone — the same street in which her elder son, Shadrach, had been born seven years previously.[63] In the autumn a handsome young barber took a room in the same house. At twenty-nine, he was seven years her junior and his name was George Chapman.

Seweryn Kłosowski's change of identity coincided with the time that Annie Chapman's child was due, so perhaps its purpose was to help him to dodge an affiliation order from Annie which, if successful, would have obliged him to pay towards the maintenance of the child. We do not know why he chose that particular name, but it takes a wry sense of humour to take the surname of a person from whom one wishes to hide. Discarding his real name also helped him to evade any financial claim from his estranged wife.

Landlady Caroline Ward, a fifty-year-old mother of five, whose youngest was then nine, could tolerate having a deserted wife under the roof of her respectable lodging house, but was scandalised when she caught Chapman kissing Mrs Spink on the stairs. She expressed her disapproval to her husband, who conveyed it to Chapman, warning him: 'We cannot allow that sort of thing to go on.' The romancer's response was to assure Ward that his actions were not improper because he had asked Mrs Spink to marry him. Although the Wards knew Shadrach Spink (he had been a porter at their local station) they did not question Mary's bigamous intentions. Perhaps she told them the lie she later told others: that her husband had been killed whilst working on the railway. Shadrach's absence made her explanation seem feasible (he had returned to Norfolk). What story she invented to explain her elder son's simultaneous disappearance is anybody's guess.

On Sunday 27th October 1895, the courting couple went out together for the day. When they returned at 11pm Chapman declared to the Wards: 'Allow me to present you to my wife.' The next day he opened his diary and recorded an entry in his poor written English: 'to Mabele Spins married'. 'Mabele' was perhaps his pet name for her, a conflation of 'Mary' and 'Isabella' (her family always called her 'Isabella'). According to some sources, Mary believed that a fake religious ceremony conjured up by Chapman was genuine. However, that would mean she was happy to commit bigamy, which, being illegal, was surely worse than living 'in sin', which was viewed as merely immoral. Brian Marriner has claimed that Chapman faked the marriage because he was 'pressured by the persistent badgering of her relatives'.[64] But Mary rarely saw her family, so their interference seems highly unlikely.

Seven years later John Ward recalled that George Chapman 'told so many tales we never knew when to believe him. He was the biggest liar I have ever met.' Chapman, said Ward, always carried a loaded revolver in a black leather bag, and grumbled about the difficulty he was experiencing in accessing Mary's inheritance. Henry Dacre, the trustee of her fund, even travelled down from Otley in Yorkshire to discuss matters with 'Mr and Mrs Chapman', but what passed between them has not come to light.

---

63 The Wards had not yet moved to Forest Road when Shadrach was born.
64 Marriner, B. (1993) *Murder with Venom*, True Crime Library, p27.

Early in 1896, as Chapman was making plans to move to the Sussex seaside with Mary and his newly acquired stepson William, his own son of the same name died in poverty. He was not quite six months old. Nobody knows whether Chapman was aware of his son's death, nor if he cared a jot about the child that he and Annie had created, nor if her fate had even once crossed his mind since he abandoned her in early pregnancy. Equally, we do not know if he felt any concern for the welfare of his estranged wife, or his daughter Cecilia, then approaching her fourth birthday.

## HASTINGS

In March 1896, Chapman gave both his employer and his landlord a week's notice and packed his belongings in preparation for his new life in Hastings with Mary and Willie. The change of town may have been prompted by the desire to make a fresh start somewhere that their pasts were not likely to be exposed and where nobody knew his real name. After all, in the East End Chapman ran the risk of bumping into his ex-wife, her siblings, their spouses and Annie Chapman; he may also have worried that Shadrach Spink might reappear.

According to some sources, the first hairdressing shop the couple leased in Hastings was in a location that was unsuitable because the neighbourhood was too poor.[65] The mistake probably occurred through lack of local knowledge or insufficient funds. Once they had got their bearings they deduced that their shop would be most likely to prosper in the bustling shopping thoroughfare of George Street.

Mary's trust fund was to bankroll the business. The problem with accessing her money that prompted Chapman's gripe to John Ward could explain why, instead of contacting her trustee direct, they chose to incur legal costs by engaging a solicitor. In May 1896 Mary — using the name 'Mrs Chapman' — asked Hastings solicitor Frederick G. Langham[66] to obtain a portion of the remainder of her inheritance from the trustee. Of her £500 she requested £195. On receipt of the money Langham deducted his (substantial) fee of £3.3s and sent Mary a cheque for the balance of £191.17s to 'Mrs Chapman'. This was deposited in an account in that name at the local branch of Lloyds Bank at 17 Wellington Place. The shop lease was purchased on 11th June 1896 for £195, the equivalent of nearly £20,000 today.

The Hastings shop was not, as H.L. Adam stated, an 'old-established hairdressing business'. In fact the premises did not exist until 1894 and had never been a hairdresser's or barber's shop. It was part of the former Albion Hotel, built in 1831 in a grand style to attract affluent guests. Although its frontage, on Marine Parade, faced the English Channel, business declined and some guest-rooms were converted into flats (Royal Albion Mansions). By 1894 the public rooms on the ground floor had been divided: the front became the Royal Albion public house and hotel; the rear was partitioned into a short row of lock-up shops, each let to a small business. Chapman leased the one at the western end of the row — its formal address was No. 1, 33 George Street — and set up as a barber, umbrella repairer and stick merchant.

George Street is a long and narrow road which runs parallel to — and eventually joins — the seafront. In the 1890s it was crowded with shoppers from early

---

65 Adam, H.L. (1930) *Trial of George Chapman*, William Hodge, p6.
66 Of Langham, Son and Douglas, 44a Robertson Street.

morning until late evening because of its plethora of small shops, street-stalls, pubs and eating places. Chapman's barbershop was opposite the entrance to the West Hill Lift, which had opened in 1891 and was a hugely popular attraction, drawing thousands of visitors.

The Chapmans' shop had no living accommodation, so they lived in lodging houses in which furnished rooms and apartments were let, mostly to members of the artisan class, who shared the communal kitchen, scullery and WC. From March 1896 they lived in Hill Street, then in February 1897 they moved to Cobourg Place, two minutes' walk away. Both houses were among the more superior and spacious in Hastings Old Town, much of which comprised overcrowded slums. 10 Hill Street was (and still is) a four-storey, eighteenth-century house, fronted by a narrow pavement, and hung from the top floor to the first with attractive terracotta tiles. When the census was taken in 1891 it was home to sixteen people in five separate households. 1 Cobourg Place was a larger and more modern house which, in 1891, was being shared between just five people living in two households, each comprising four rooms.

Hastings offered a wide range of amusements and leisure activities, and there were clubs and societies to suit most tastes, including Chapman's known hobbies of photography and cycling. Maybe he and Mary joined the many organised two-wheeled excursions to rural locations. As Chapman later became a publican they doubtless enjoyed visiting some of the numerous local hostelries — maybe this is where the desire to run a pub originated. The town's theatres and concert halls drew noted performers from around the globe. As he was evidently a fan of the piano, perhaps Chapman attended the recital given by his Polish compatriot, the internationally famous virtuoso Ignacy Paderewski, at the Kursaal in nearby Bexhill in June 1897.[67]

George Street contained plenty of shops to interest the Chapman family, including a toy dealer (which maybe supplied a present for Willie's eighth birthday), a photographic shop and numerous retailers of clothes, shoes and foodstuffs. No. 8 was a well-established sports shop owned by Archibald and John Stoakes. The brothers were gunmakers and agents for bicycle manufacturers and, as Chapman was a cyclist with an interest in firearms, it seems likely that he was drawn to their premises. They were also purveyors of nautical menswear, so perhaps this was where he acquired the double-breasted naval-style blazer and the peaked sailing cap with which he was later associated.

Few of Chapman's countrymen lived in Hastings, but there were over 150 Germans, one of whom owned a hairdressing salon just eight doors away. Theodore Oscar Henze and Chapman were of similar age and both had English partners. Clara Henze hailed from Bishop's Stortford, where, coincidentally, Chapman would later take a lease on a pub (perhaps she gave her home town a glowing recommendation). Theodore's expertise was, clearly, far superior to Chapman's. His advert in the local directory read: *T.O. Henze, Hairdresser & Perfumer, Wig & Ornamental Hair Manufacturer, 28, George St, Hastings. Ladies' Combings made up to any Design at Moderate Prices. Ladies and Gentlemen waited on at their own Residences.* According to one press report, Chapman was not to be outdone: he circulated handbills under the title *Professor Chapman*

---

67 Paderewski was to become prime minister of Poland in 1919, shortly after it regained independence.

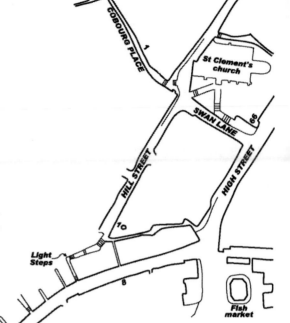

A plan of George Street, Hastings, c. 1896. Chapman's shop is labelled 'A'. Also shown are Light Steps, 10 Hill St. 1 Cobourg Place, and the chemist's shop at 66 High St.

Below: left: a photo of Chapman's barbershop from a March 1903 edition of the Southwark & Bermondsey Recorder. Haircuts were threepence and the shop sold fireworks. The report did not say if the photo was taken in Chapman's day or in 1903 (six years after he left).

Below: the same view today. Photo by the author.

*The Royal Albion today, with the entrance to the West Hill Lift visible to its left.*

*The shops behind the former Royal Albion Hotel, showing it former entrance (in the right-hand corner of the photo). Chapman's shop unit is in the centre of the photo, to the left of the woman in white. Both photos from author's collection.*

and Co, and claimed to have *large experience in America, Paris, and various places on the Continent, also in skin diseases and the Hair Restoration Hospital, &c.*[68]

One of Chapman's regular clients was William Davison, an American pharmacist who visited two or three times a week to be shaved. The pair found much common ground. Chapman expressed great interest in pharmaceutical matters and purchased a couple of old medical books from Davison, who found him 'an intellectual man to talk to on medical subjects.'[69] As Davison had lived in the East End throughout the 1860s and 70s, perhaps they aired their pet theories about who was responsible for the series of horrific murders that occurred in Whitechapel some years after Davison had moved away but soon after Chapman arrived. When topics related to medicine and the East End were thoroughly exhausted, they had another common theme to explore: Davison was a native of New York, and Chapman had spent a year in the US and possessed a detailed knowledge of New York geography, presumably from living there.

### HASTINGS TALES

In late October 1902 press reporters travelled to various places in which Chapman had resided. Among those who visited Hastings were correspondents for *Lloyd's Weekly* and *Shurey's Illustrated*. Their intention was to collect anecdotes from locals who had known Chapman and Mary five years previously. In those days ordinary people found it thrilling to see their words in print and this may have led some to exaggerate and even invent tall tales to satisfy an eager reporter. One can well imagine a garrulous old salt realising that the more yarns he could spin for the gullible young hack, the more beers or whiskies would be lined up on the counter to lubricate his voice box and loosen his tongue. The collected anecdotes were used to cobble together a story of Chapman's life in Hastings.

According to locals, Mary wore her fair hair 'as short as a man's' and helped Chapman in his business:

> In those days lady barbers had not been heard of — at any rate, on the south coast. Mrs Chapman was the pioneer. Dressed in a smart apron, and with sleeves rolled up over her plump arms, she set to and acted as lady latherer — and the customers began to come in a good deal more numerously. She even tried her hand at shaving, but never took it up seriously.[70]

> Then a piano was hired, and put in the front of the shop, where all could see — and hear. Upon the advent of customers Mrs. Chapman would first lather them energetically, wipe her hands, and then sit down at the piano and play popular airs while her husband worked the razor. These 'Musical Shaves' became quite a feature of the neighbourhood, and the result was that the once quiet hairdressing salon did very decent business.[71]

---

68 *Manchester Courier*, 31st October 1902.
69 Davison's evidence at the Old Bailey, where his name is misspelled 'Davidson'.
70 *Lloyd's Weekly*, 2nd November 1902.
71 *Shurey's Illustrated*, 8th November 1902.

Locals also revealed that Chapman had purchased a sailing boat called *Mosquito*. According to *Lloyd's*, he donned a nautical suit and P & O cap and boasted that he would one day cross to Boulogne. In reality he only sailed up and down the coast.

H.L. Adam is cited as an authority on Chapman, yet he drew heavily upon these second-hand anecdotes in his 1930 book *Trial of George Chapman*. He also changed some tales and embellished others. (For example, whereas *Lloyd's* stated that Chapman was 'generally regarded as an adventurous sort of person', he changed this to, 'He was generally regarded as a hazardous person.') Perhaps Adam's choice of word was more accurate. According to one story, the *Mosquito* capsized and its occupants were jettisoned into the sea and were rescued by fishermen. H.L. Adam's retelling of the mishap also included some speculative comments:

> In the light of subsequent events one would like to know how this accident happened. It would be interesting, too, to know if both, or only one, of the occupants of the boat could swim; particularly as the two were not then living very happily together, on account, it was thought, of the lady's habitual drunkenness.[72]

When R.M. Gordon reworked that paragraph in 2008 he decided to answer Adam's questions by adding details he could not possibly have known: firstly that Chapman 'could swim and, if reports are correct, swim quite well', and also that 'The fishermen thought them both on the point of drawing [sic] when they were pulled from the sea, but Chapman was a good actor so his condition may have been overstated, by himself of course.'[73] According to Adam and Gordon, only Mary and Chapman were in the boat, but the *Illustrated Police News* sketch of the incident depicted a third person on board: the small face of a young boy can be seen, indicating that the artist thought Willie had accompanied them on the hair-raising adventure.

Both *Shurey's Illustrated* and *Lloyd's Weekly* reported that young Willie Spink had a miserable time in Hastings and claimed that, when Mary and Chapman went home to their comfortable lodgings, he was left to spend the night 'either in the shop or in the cellar underneath it'.[74] A quarter-of-a-century later this unsubstantiated tale was embellished by H.L. Adam who, for reasons unknown, described the cellar as 'foul', despite having no knowledge of its condition.[75] In his own retelling, in 2000, R.M. Gordon added rodents and maternal inadequacy to give the story additional melodrama:

> Chapman showed his contempt for her son by having him sleep in a cellar below his barbershop, in the company of rats and filth. The alcoholic Mrs Spink was not a very protective mother.[76]

The 'rats and filth' apparently failed to deter Mary from using the cellar herself as a place to enjoy a drink in secret. According to *Shurey's* (the story is absent from *Lloyd's*), whilst Chapman attended to customers she would sneak into the cellar and pass up jugs 'through the glass ventilator to be filled with beer at the public-house across the

72 Adam, H.L. (1930) *Trial of George Chapman*, William Hodge, p7.
73 Gordon, R.M. (2008) *The Poison Murders of Jack the Ripper*, McFarland, p62.
74 *Shurey's Illustrated*, 8th November 1902.
75 Adam, H.L. (1930) *Trial of George Chapman*, William Hodge, p6.
76 Gordon, R.M. (2000) *Alias Jack the Ripper: Beyond the Usual Whitechapel Suspects*, McFarland, p252.

*A sketch of Chapman's barbershop in 1902, from the Illustrated Police News.*

*A photograph of the premises, now Albion Books, taken recently by the author from a similar angle.*

road.'[77] The ventilator and the pub (the Albion Shades) existed, but as access to the cellar was via a trapdoor in the shop Mary could not have gone down there without Chapman's knowledge.

A photograph exists of Chapman and his family on board *Mosquito*, but there is no corroborative evidence that he capsized it, nor that Mary lathered customers or played a piano in the shop, nor that Willie slept in the cellar. These anecdotes were not mentioned by any of the six Hastings-based witnesses who spoke under oath at Chapman's trial; they all derived from unnamed reporters who supposedly obtained them from anonymous, untraceable local gossips. Despite this, these tales have become so firmly attached to Chapman's story that their veracity is never questioned.

*Shurey's* also told its readers that 'the earliest record' of Chapman 'begins with his life on the sea, where he filled various roles, mainly as a ships' steward, and sometimes as ships' barber'.[78] If we swallow uncritically the story of the musical shaves, why not believe that he worked on board ships?

## PHILANDERING AND VIOLENCE

Chapman had many good reasons to count his blessings. He and his mistress ran a 'feel-good' service business in a busy part of an historic and lively seaside town, enjoyed an abundance of fresh air and fresh fish, had no money troubles, lived in above-average lodgings and had a young boy to amuse and educate. The 'musical shaves' anecdote — if true — reveals a fun aspect to their working lives, and their hobbies of sailing and cycling provided pleasant and healthy diversions. He had (maybe) narrowly cheated death in the English Channel. And yet Chapman still felt entitled to more.

His eye settled upon Alice Penfold, six years his junior and employed as a domestic servant to a Mrs Field. One Sunday evening whilst she was out for a walk Chapman chatted her up. Though married to one woman and cohabiting with another, he claimed to be a bachelor and the manager of William Slade's pianoforte and music warehouse.[79] He called on Miss Penfold and took her out on a few dates. On one occasion she mentioned having a cold and he thoughtfully sent some medicinal powders to her at Mrs Field's house, together with a note signed 'George Smith'. Miss Penfold evidently did not trust him, because she threw the packets of medication onto the fire. During their final meeting she accompanied him to nearby St Leonards-on-Sea to view a public house which was for sale. However, she did not wish to continue their acquaintance. 'I did not want the man,' she explained, 'but he kept following me about.'[80]

It was in Hastings that Chapman began to treat Mary badly. One writer claimed that he manipulated and controlled her by acting moodily:

> Instead of feeling desperately in love with her, he grew cold, used to speak of her harshly, and, after a period of 'sulks' would again grow very affectionate, and 'make it up'.[81]

77 *Shurey's Illustrated*, 8th November 1902.
78 *Ibid*.
79 In 1903 Mr Slade was so appalled at having his good name linked with that of Chapman that he wrote to his local paper to refute having ever employed him.
80 Miss Penfold's evidence at the Old Bailey in 1903.
81 Furniss, H. (ed) *Famous Crimes Past and Present*, Vol. IX, No. 109, c.1908. Caxton House.

*Mary Spink and George Chapman, from Famous Crimes*

*'Musical shaves', from the Illustrated Police News.*

Hill Street, Hastings, 1898.

1 Cobourg Place, Hastings.

10 Hill Street, Hastings (tall, dark-tiled house).

66 High Street, Hastings.

*Top left: photo by John H.B. Fletcher, reproduced in Elleray, D. Robert,*
*Hastings, A Pictorial History, Phillimore, 1979. Other photos by the author.*

*Hastings fishermen battling to save the Chapmans. Sketch created from the artist's imagination, based on a magazine article created from anecdotal material. From the Illustrated Police News.*

*Right to left: George Chapman, Mary Spink, Willie and an unknown friend on board the Mosquito. From the Southwark & Bermondsey Recorder.*

Years later it emerged that Chapman was also physically violent to Mary. Neighbours heard her crying out in the middle of the night and saw bruises on her face and marks around her throat. Annie Helsdown, a fellow lodger at 10 Hill Street, revealed that the couple frequently quarrelled and, once or twice, when her face was very red, Mary admitted that Chapman had slapped her.[82] Author Gordon Honeycombe surmised that Chapman was provoked to violence by Mary's drinking,[83] but others suspect it was an attempt to make her leave him and that, when his plan failed, he tried to get rid of her in another manner. David Wilson has suggested that capsizing *Mosquito* 'may have been a first, botched attempt' by Chapman 'to rid himself of a "wife" who was no longer wanted or needed'.[84]

## POISON

Tartar emetic is a yellowish-white powder containing antimony, a colourless, odourless substance that has been utilised for medicinal purposes for more than 3,000 years. The Ancient Egyptians used antimony to treat skin complaints, ulcers and burns, and in the Middle Ages it was a common cure for a hangover (it emptied the stomach by causing vomiting). It was the subject of controversy for a few hundred years, but by the seventeenth century again found favour within the medical profession. A recipe for tartar emetic first appeared in 1631 and it began to be used by eminent physicians to cure all manner of ailments. For a century and a half from 1747 it was among the ingredients of James's Powder, a popular remedy for fever. By the late nineteenth century its popularity had declined (partly because it had been used to commit murder) but it was still available from any local chemist, although by law the purchaser had to sign an official poisons' register and explain its intended use.

Tartar emetic was measured using an ancient system of apothecaries' weights, which divided a pound into twelve ounces, an ounce into eight drachms, a drachm into three scruples and a scruple into twenty grains. It had to be administered in minute quantities, for an overdose could kill the patient. Different individuals had varying sensitivity to tartar emetic but, as a rule of thumb, a one-off dose of up to a quarter of a grain was effective as medicine. One grain would be toxic but, luckily, it would act as its own antidote by causing the swallower to vomit, expelling the poison before it took effect. Large single doses of between three and six grains were dangerous, as vomiting would not clear the gastric system entirely, and life was consequently put in jeopardy. Doses of over six grains were often fatal, especially if expulsion was delayed, while ten grains would usually guarantee death.

Only an exceptionally cruel and wicked person would repeatedly administer sub-lethal doses of tartar emetic by stealth, because it caused excruciating stomach pains and constant vomiting, straining and purging, which led to a 'prolonged and painful struggle for life' as the victims 'reeled beneath repeated blows of the poison' until they died of dehydration, malnutrition, starvation and heart failure.[85]

---

82 Mrs Helsdown's deposition to Southwark police court.
83 Honeycombe, G. (1993) *More Murders of the Black Museum*, Hutchinson, p150.
84 Wilson, D.A. (2011) *History of British Serial Killing*. Amazon Kindle, no page numbers.
85 Emsley, J. (2006) *The Elements of Murder: A History of Poison*, OUP, p220. Whilst I trust Emsley as a source of information on poisons, his writings on George Chapman are inaccurate.

In February 1897 the couple moved to 1 Cobourg Place, where they lodged for seven months. Chapman must have obtained a supply of tartar emetic before they moved, because they were still living at Hill Street when Mary suffered her first attacks of severe stomach pain accompanied by the violent expulsion of green vomit. These occurred at intervals of about a week, but it seems that no doctor was consulted.

During the Chapmans' first month at Cobourg Place the house's owner Frank Greenaway, and his wife Harriet, also lived there. Chapman told Harriet that he was a Russian Pole who had been to America, and Mary told her that he kept a loaded revolver in the house, showing her its bag. Mary 'seemed dazed always', Harriet later recalled, adding that she attributed it to Mary's alcoholism: 'I put it down to the drink.'[86] The Greenaways lent the Chapmans their complete set of Cassell's *Family Physician: A Manual of Domestic Medicine, By Physicians and Surgeons of the Principal London Hospitals*. Harriet made repeated attempts to reclaim the set; she even sent her servant Edith Simmonds on a retrieval mission to Chapman's shop, but it was never recovered.

Chapman evidently did not have sufficient supplies of tartar emetic to continue dosing Mary. A few weeks after moving to Cobourg Place, on 2nd April 1897, whilst shaving pharmacist Mr Davison, he enquired if he might buy some. Receiving a favourable reply he visited Davison's establishment at 66 High Street where, amongst other items, he bought an ounce of the stuff for tuppence. Davison supplied it in a wide-mouthed bottle, to which he glued a red label bearing the handwritten words: *Poison. Tartar emetic; dose, one-sixth to one-quarter of a grain. To be used with caution,* appending his name and address. To comply with the law, Davison entered the sale in his official register of poisons. Chapman signed it, adding the words 'to take' as his reason for purchase. As one ounce was equivalent to just over 437 grains, and ten grains a fatal dose, he had purchased enough to kill more than forty people.

In the summer of 1897 'Mr and Mrs' Chapman began making plans to move back to London. Mary decided (or was persuaded) to withdraw the entire balance of her trust fund, which contained just under £300. But instead of consulting Mr Langham again, she chose a different solicitor, William Glenister.[87] He wrote to the trustee Mr Dacre and, after a good deal of pressure, received from him two cheques: one for £250 made out to 'Mrs Chapman', which he posted to Mary; the other for just over £48 which, on Mary's instructions, Glenister placed temporarily in his own account. He deducted his fee and retained the balance, awaiting her further instructions. Mary deposited the £250 cheque into her account at Lloyds Bank in Hastings. A week later she withdrew it in cash and handed it over to Chapman, who placed it in a new account in his sole name.

Having purchased the lease of the George Street shop in June 1896, Chapman sold it just fifteen months later, in September 1897.[88] It was purchased by thirty-seven-year-old Edwin Robinson, manager of a furniture shop at No. 44, directly opposite, who continued to operate it as a hairdresser's.

---

86 *Lloyd's Weekly*, 18th January 1903.
87 Of Davenport, Jones & Glenister, 8 Bank Buildings, Hastings.
88 According to H.L. Adam, Chapman owned the Hastings shop for only six months, an error he probably gleaned from *Lloyd's* or *Shurey's*.

Author John Emsley claimed that the couple left Hastings because Chapman was 'tiring of living by the sea'.[89] This seems unlikely. To paraphrase Dr Johnson, to be tired of 1890s Hastings one would have to be tired of life. The fact is, we do not know what prompted the move, nor why a man with an alcoholic partner chose to become the tenant of a beerhouse. Perhaps he was influenced by his old boss, William Wengel, a hairdresser who also ran a pub, or maybe he latched on to the idea after discovering that licensees enjoyed a high income.

In September 1897 Chapman began his new career as a licensed victualler. After viewing potential premises in St Leonards, he'd had a change of heart and decided instead to return to London, where he paid £56.16s for a short lease on a beerhouse (a pub that could sell only beer and cider, not spirits or wine). Under the 1869 Wine and Beerhouse Act, Chapman was required to apply to a magistrate and to submit personal references from people who could vouch for his good character over a number of years. Nobody in his life fulfilled these requirements, so he must have obtained false references. Unfortunately the record of his referees no longer exists. As Mary was above him socially and had respectable relations, it was perhaps someone she knew. Once a person secured a licence for one premises, he need not provide references when applying for subsequent licences, so Chapman was set for life.

Chapman took Mary Spink back to London to be landlady of his beerhouse. He then wrote to Alice Penfold three times inviting her to visit. How he would have squared her presence with Mary we shall never discover, for Miss Penfold declined his invitations and failed to respond to his letters — in fact, she destroyed them.

On 28th September Chapman opened an account at the London, City & Midland Bank at 93 Great Eastern Street, about 300 metres from his beerhouse. He deposited £230 (of which £150 comprised the actual notes withdrawn by Mary from Lloyds in Hastings) and a further £21.10s soon after. Mary requested the remainder of her trust money from Mr Glenister (her solicitor in Hastings) and on 30th September received his cheque for just over £33, which she deposited in Chapman's account. At this point, every penny of Mary's nest-egg had been transferred to Chapman, a total of nearly £500, the equivalent of about £50,000 today.

The Prince of Wales stood at 20 Bartholomew Square, on the corner of Lizard Street. The square was located just off Old Street, in the parish of St Luke, Finsbury, and its freehold was owned by St Bartholomew's Hospital, hence its name. The beerhouse was a modest establishment located in a down-at-heel, working-class backstreet surrounded by terraced houses and shops with accommodation above, in which people lived in overcrowded conditions. Retail shops were interspersed with artisans' workrooms and some light industry devoted to the manufacture of boots, cabinets and surgical instruments. Most of the locals were born within a mile or two of the square and counted among their number a feather curler, a fur sewer, an umbrella coverer, a bookbinder's gold-blocker, a plate glass beveller and a watch dial painter. Although fully employed they were not well-off. Booth's researcher George Duckworth undertook an investigatory walk around Bartholomew Square with

89 Emsley, J. (2006) *The Elements of Murder: A History of Poison*, OUP, p244.

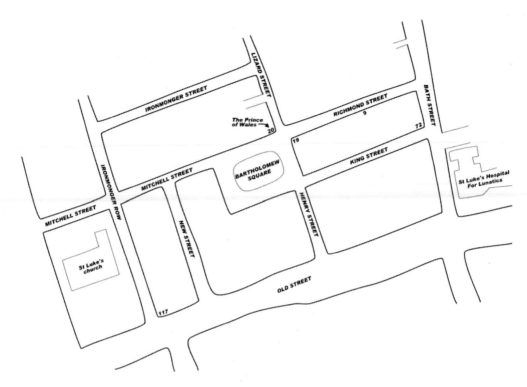

A plan of Bartholomew Square as it was in 1897, showing the location of the Prince of Wales at No. 20, No. 19, 9 Richmond Street, 72 Bath Street, 117 Old Street, St Luke's Church and the hospital for lunatics.

The square in 1963, taken from the corner of King Street, looking across the playground to the Mitchell Street exit. The site of the Prince of Wales beerhouse is just out of shot on the far right. The modern commercial buildings on the right suggest wartime bombing and rebuilding. The original buildings were probably uniformly like those on the left. Photo from Chris Mitchell.

Sergeant Richard Machell in June 1898. He noted that the area used to be a 'rough spot' but, as houses were 'being done up', it was improving. He designated the area 'Poor, 18s to 21s a week for a moderate family', although some of the neighbouring streets, Duckworth noted, housed 'a large proportion of thieves and housebreakers'. He also mentioned that, instead of the usual gardens, there was an asphalt-covered playground in the centre.[90] Willie Spink almost certainly played there.

According to one pressman, the Prince of Wales 'was not one with a big trade, and Chapman did little to attract customers'.[91] There were several other beer retailers and pubs within a few metres and so the trade was divided between them; however, a whist club met at the beerhouse once a week (its members organised concerts and outings), and business was sufficiently brisk for Chapman to engage a young couple.

Potman Richard Pagett was just approaching twenty; general-servant-cum-barmaid Susan Robinson was seventeen and pregnant (the couple were to marry in 1900). They heard Chapman grumble repeatedly about Mary's excessive fondness for alcohol. Sometimes when she entered the bar parlour[92] he would admonish her, within customers' earshot: 'Get out of it. You cannot get drunk here!' He kept medical books behind the counter and would peruse them during quiet times. When Mary became curious about them he told her he was 'studying how to stop you drinking'.[93]

Eventually Chapman confined Mary to one upstairs room and, when people asked for her, explained that she was suffering from delirium tremens (uncontrollable shaking caused by a sudden withdrawal from alcohol). He assumed total control of his prisoner, appointing himself sole supplier of everything she consumed. Susan was even reprimanded for taking Mary a non-alcoholic drink: 'You have no business up in that room!'[94]

Chapman was again administering tartar emetic to Mary, but was none too keen on having to deal with the copious, slimy green matter that the poison caused her to expel violently from both ends; nor could he attend her twenty-four hours a day. In the first week of December he asked a neighbour, Martha Doubleday, to sit by Mary's bed at night, take her to the toilet when she was able to stagger there, and deal with the chamber pots and soiled bed-linen when she couldn't. Mrs Doubleday was forty-five and no stranger to illness and death: she had been widowed twice and four of her eight children had died. She seems to have been fond of Mary, describing her as a 'nice, little-built person, with a fresh colour'.

As Mary's mysterious malady continued, Mrs Doubleday insisted that she needed a doctor. Susan agreed, and when Chapman displayed reluctance she threatened to shame him by calling in the workhouse doctor, who was paid from parish funds. This would tarnish Chapman's social standing by making him appear unable to afford the 2s 6d consultation fee.[95] Under mounting pressure he engaged the nearest GP, Dr Rogers, whose surgery was at 117 Old Street, on the corner of Ironmonger Row.

---

90 Booth, C. (1902) *Life and Labour of the People in London,* Macmillan. See booth.lse.ac.uk
91 *Manchester Courier,* 1st November 1902.
92 The front parlour of a house, which contained the bar from which alcoholic beverages were served.
93 *Daily Mail,* 1st January 1903.
94 Susan Pagett's testimony at the Old Bailey.
95 The equivalent to about £12.50 today.

John Frederick Rogers, a sixty-one-year-old Welshman, had qualified thirty-seven years previously and been in general practice ever since. After examining Mary he discussed her illness with Chapman in the bar parlour. Mrs Doubleday eavesdropped as Rogers warned that Mary was wasting away through malnutrition. He prescribed the appropriate medicines and recommended that Mrs Waymark, an unqualified but experienced sick-nurse, take over the night shift from Mrs Doubleday. Elizabeth Jane Waymark was forty-three and her life story matched Mrs Doubleday's. Widowed in her thirties, five of her eight children had died before the age of two.

As soon as Mrs Waymark met Mary, her experience told her that she was past help. She did everything in her power to make her patient comfortable, including giving her a much-needed bed bath and dressing her in a new chemise and nightgown that were a gift from Mrs Doubleday. She may have thought it unusual that Chapman insisted on being in sole charge of Mary's medication and nourishment; however, he was clearly such a loving husband that he just wanted to make certain that nothing was given to Mary that might exacerbate her illness. By then she was able to consume only beef tea, milk, or brandy-and-soda, all of which he prepared personally and in private — and all of which made her vomit. Mrs Waymark thought it rather odd, though, that when she fed Mary some Liebig's Meat Extract, she kept it down.

Jane Mumford, their neighbour at No. 19, began to attend Mary during the day. She wasn't a nurse but a mantle-maker by trade, and visited solely from kindness. Mrs Mumford asked Chapman about the books behind the counter. He explained that he was using them as a guide to giving Mary 'stuff to make her the better of the drink', adding that, when she recovered, he would 'tell her what he had been giving'.[96] He described the publications as 'doctors' books' collected during his previous career as a medic on board ships. Is this a clue that he had been a feldsher in the Russian Navy?

Several members of staff witnessed behaviour that they found strange or alarming. Mrs Doubleday watched Chapman enter Mary's bedroom and 'lean over' her. Once or twice he ordered Doubleday to wait outside, from where she once overheard Mary exclaim, 'Pray God, go away from me!' Upon learning from Mary that Chapman had put 'a red powder' into her medicine, Susan challenged him. He told her to take no notice, as Mary was 'delairious' [sic], but Susan warned him, 'Delairious or not, I quickly moved in and I can quickly move out.' Her fiancé later made a direct, blatant accusation: 'Mr Chapman,' he asserted, 'if you have no respect for your wife and want to kill her, I have respect for mine, and you won't kill her.'[97] The couple's next action sealed Mary's fate. They did not go to the police. They did not share their concerns with Dr Rogers, or even with Doubleday, Waymark or Mumford. They simply moved out. Had they acted differently, Mary's life may have been spared, along with those of his subsequent victims.

On Christmas morning, after severe vomiting and flooding,[98] Mary lost consciousness. Martha Doubleday and Elizabeth Waymark were in attendance, and young Willie waited anxiously in an adjacent room. Mrs Waymark sent for Chapman three times before he came upstairs. Mary put her emaciated arms out to him and

---

96 Mrs Mumford's witness testimony to the Old Bailey in 1903.
97 Evidence to Southwark police court, 21st January 1903.
98 A term commonly used in that era to mean uterine bleeding in excess of normal menses.

pleaded, 'Do kiss me', but he declined. At 1pm Mrs Waymark shouted down the stairwell: 'Chapman, come up, your wife's a-dying!' He was attending to something and did not respond immediately. Eventually he appeared, leaned over Mary and said, 'Polly, Polly, speak!' Realising she was dead he walked out of the room and began to weep. One o'clock was the Christmas Day opening time, but Mrs Doubleday remarked, 'You are not going to open the house after this!' Chapman's simple, unashamed reply was, 'Yes, I shall.' According to one source he added:

> 'There's a man hammering to get in now.' And down he went into the bar, and in a few minutes was busy laughing and joking with his customers on that bright Christmas morning as if he was as happy as the rest of the world. To one or two, it is true, he did remark that he had 'a bit of trouble' and when asked what was the matter, casually replied, 'Oh, the missus pegged it this morning'.[99]

Mary Spink was, by all accounts, plump, but when Mrs Waymark prepared her body for burial it was 'a mere skeleton'. Moreover, Mrs Doubleday exclaimed, 'it was in a shocking condition' and 'very much bruised.'[100] Dr Rogers issued a certificate stating that Mary had died of phthisis, which meant any disease that caused wasting of the body. He followed her to the grave just a few months later and so was never called to account for his misdiagnosis.

Undertaker Henry Pierce of 32 Featherstone Street, off City Road, was summoned to the premises that evening. Chapman ordered a coffin to be delivered that night but Pierce declared it impossible. He returned at noon the next day and, after obtaining all the particulars from the grieving widower, prepared a nameplate for 'Mary Isabella Chapman'. On 30th December Chapman, having stripped Mary of her fortune, had her buried in an unmarked, common, pauper's grave in a remote, north-west corner of St Patrick's Roman Catholic Cemetery, Leytonstone. (Nine years earlier, the pitiful remains of another Mary — Ripper victim Mary Jane Kelly — had been buried in the same cemetery.) Mary Spink's cheap elm coffin was interred in a hole eighteen feet deep and, within weeks, seven more were laid on top. Her cousin Joseph lived barely 500 metres from the cemetery, but Chapman did not contact him; consequently none of her family attended her funeral or could influence its arrangements.

Mary was killed just three months after leaving Hastings. This is significant because the move from seaside to city gave both parties the opportunity to reflect on the partnership and end it if either was unhappy. After all, they were not tied by marriage, nor had they produced a child, despite cohabiting for two years. Each chose to continue the relationship, but Mary may have felt constrained in her decision. By the time they left Hastings she had surrendered most of her inheritance to Chapman. The little she retained was sufficient to support herself and her son for only a year or two, after which she would be penniless. Leaving Chapman would render her destitute, forcing her to either go cap-in-hand to her relations or join the thousands of other women seeking unskilled, low-paid jobs. She may even have ended up in the dreaded workhouse.

---

99 Furniss, H. (ed) *Famous Crimes Past and Present*, Vol. IX, No. 109, c. 1908, Caxton House.
100 From their witness statements to the Old Bailey in 1903.

Willie Spink had turned nine a fortnight before his mother died. Raised fatherless, he had always relied upon her for everything. In his short life he had already endured much upheaval and loss, multiple house-moves, several changes of school, and — if certain accounts are to be believed — neglect, incarceration in a rat-infested cellar, and nearly being drowned. Lastly, he had witnessed his mother's distressing illness and tragic death. More than ever he needed stability, reassurance and security. Mary's death forced Willie into dependence upon his stepfather. Although Chapman had lived with the boy for two years, he evidently felt no love, attachment or even pity for the child whose mother he had killed in cold blood. He had no conscience about the loss he had inflicted and did not feel any obligation to compensate the boy by raising him. In fact he considered Willie a nuisance and wanted rid of him. But instead of contacting Mary's cousins Joseph and Edgar Renton, or her sister Clara Farrer, Chapman visited William Wengel to ask his advice about offloading the boy onto Dr Barnardo's, a charity for homeless orphans.

On 30th January 1898, five weeks after Mary's death, Chapman called at one of Dr Barnardo's homes and pretended that Willie was an orphan. An officer later visited the Prince of Wales beerhouse to enquire about Mary Spink's family. Chapman mentioned Joseph Renton but provided a false address for him. Somehow the officer managed to locate Renton and paid him a visit. Barnardo's then refused to take Willie, for they did not accept children who had living relatives.

It remains a mystery why Joseph Renton, once he learned of Mary's death from the Barnardo's officer, did not offer Willie a home. At that time Renton was married with three children aged three to eight, and his cousin — Mary's sister Clara — had four children aged between six and twelve. These were small families for that era, and yet the Rentons preferred Willie to go to an orphanage than to take him in. Nobody seems to have known Shadrach Spink's whereabouts.

Rejected by Barnardo's and unwanted by his blood relations, Willie remained by default at the Prince of Wales, and when Chapman's new girlfriend moved in around Easter, he was still there.

## BESSIE TAYLOR

Bessie was born into a cattle-farming family on 15th June 1861 at New Brook Farm, Lodge Lane, Dutton, about five miles from Northwich, Cheshire. Her name was officially registered as 'Bessey' but she was christened 'Bessie' at St Matthew's church, Stretton, near Lymm, on 14th July. The middle child of seven, she had one younger and three elder brothers, and two younger sisters, all born, as was typical in Victorian times, a year or two apart. Bessie grew up in a picturesque location on the east bank of the Trent and Mersey Canal. Her mother, Betsey, had been raised on her family's farm in Stretton, leaving home aged twenty-seven to marry twenty-one-year-old Thomas Parsonage Taylor. They built up a ninety-six acre farmstead and Thomas won awards for his prize heifers at agricultural shows. When Bessie was nine, the Taylors were living at Massey Brook Farm, Lymm; a decade later they had moved twenty miles south to Holly Bank Farm in Heatley Lane, Broomhall.

From April 1881 (when she appears in the census) until 1898 (when she met Chapman) there is no record of Bessie's life. This press report might help fill the gap:

*Bessie's birthplace, New Brook farmhouse, today.*

[Bessie] is described as a bright, intelligent, and attractive little maiden... She appeared to have been blessed with a lively vivacious temperament, and as early womanhood approached it would seem that the dull and monotonous life of the countryside made her restless and anxious to go out into the world. Eventually with the consent of her parents she accepted a situation as companion-housekeeper to a lady at Acton, near Nantwich. There she remained for some time, and by her industry, tact, and pleasant behaviour won the approval of her employer. She left this situation with the highest credentials to go to London as an assistant housekeeper at...a London city hotel, where she subsequently met Chapman. The latter paid her considerable attention, with the result that the then Miss Taylor became enamoured, and announced her intention of marrying him despite her parents' objections.[101]

Other sources say that, when she met Chapman, Bessie was not a hotel housekeeper in the city but a restaurant manager in the south London suburb of Peckham, where she shared lodgings with her friend Elizabeth Painter, with whom she had previously been in domestic service in nearby Streatham. According to H.L. Adam and others, Bessie applied for a job at the Prince of Wales, but it seems unfeasible that a woman who had reached the status of manager or housekeeper would seek employment as a lowly barmaid in a backstreet beerhouse. It is more likely that she met Chapman socially, fell for his moustachioed charm, and was persuaded to become his mistress, which at least bestowed upon her the status of landlady. Either way, having told her work colleagues that she was leaving 'to get married', about Easter 1898 Bessie moved into the Prince of Wales.

101 *Manchester Courier*, 31st October 1902 and 1st January 1903.

The BPP described Bessie as 'a person of agreeable manners...a careful, saving woman' who was 'possessed of some money and an excellent wardrobe and some good jewellery.'[102] J.R. Nash called her 'a naïve farmer's daughter',[103] hardly a fair description, considering she had supported herself for ten years as a single, independent career woman in the world's largest city. She had a number of things in common with Mary Spink. At thirty-six she was several years older than Chapman; she played the piano, was in robust health, enjoyed cycling, and was naturally plump. And, just like her predecessor, she either agreed to live 'in sin', or else started as Chapman's employee and later 'fell a victim to his lust'.[104] H.L. Adam was surprised by what he described as her 'surrender to the lustful publican' and asked, 'Why did she yield to Chapman, who was socially far below her, illiterate, and of repulsive appearance?'[105]

After living together for just a few weeks, one Sunday morning in July Bessie conspired with Chapman to feign a wedding. Adam suggested that they may have pretended to marry at St George's Roman Catholic Cathedral in Southwark. According to one newspaper, 'It is understood that her parents expostulated with her against marrying a man of whom she apparently knew little...but the girl was wilful and the connubial knot was tied.'[106] Some sources assert that Bessie's father despatched £50 (worth £5,000 today) as a wedding gift, but the BPP claimed that Chapman persuaded Bessie to ask her father for a loan of £50. Whichever way the money was obtained, a cheque arrived from Cheshire on 18th July 1898. According to Adam, it was 'intercepted and annexed' by Chapman, whilst the BPP claimed that he forged her signature in order to redirect it to himself and, indeed, Bessie's brother William was later shown the signature and confirmed that it was not hers. Records show that the cheque was credited to Chapman's account at the London, City & Midland Bank. He later deposited a further £305, in cash. The provenance of the larger sum is uncertain, it was probably a combination of money he took from Mary and earnings from the pub. It is not known whether it incorporated any of Bessie's nest-egg.

According to the *Manchester Courier*, 'Of [Bessie's] married life very little is known. She does not appear to have corresponded at any length with her parents or relatives, and certainly never made any complaints.'[107] Other sources stated that, soon after the wedding, Bessie took a trip to Cheshire to visit her folks and, whilst there, praised her spouse in the highest terms. After their return visit her parents expressed how delighted they were with Chapman — Mrs Taylor even went so far as

102 Return showing the Working of the Regulations for carrying out the Prosecution of Offences Act 1879 & 1884. British Parliamentary Papers, Vol. 56, HMSO, 1902. Pub as the *Blue Book*, 1903, p12–16.
103 Nash, J.R. (1990) *Encyclopaedia of World Crime*, Crime Books, p682.
104 So said Mr Justice Grantham at Chapman's trial.
105 Adam, H.L. (1930) *Trial of George Chapman*, William Hodge, p39–40.
106 *Manchester Courier*, 31st October 1902.
107 *Ibid.*

*Image: Bessie Taylor, from Famous Crimes.*

*Bessie Taylor and George Chapman, from Trial of George Chapman.*

to announce that she 'never saw a better husband.' Mr Taylor's dairy farming business occasionally took him to Jersey, and Chapman was always ready and willing to meet him at St Pancras or Euston and render him every assistance in crossing London to Waterloo station en route to Southampton Docks. Other members of the Taylor family were welcomed most cordially by Chapman when they visited. For recreation, the Chapmans cycled — sometimes with the Police Cycling Club — and on Sunday mornings occasionally rode to Peckham to visit Bessie's brother William, his wife Emma and Bessie's teenage nephews Tommy and Harry. William Taylor noted that Chapman treated his sister 'kindly and properly.'

Chapman's staff and customers concurred with the Taylors' positive view of the 'marriage'. A neighbour thought that the couple 'seemed to be fond of one another' and Bessie's friend Elizabeth Painter admitted that Chapman was 'pretty fair' with her and that they 'got on all right.' He did 'carry on' at Bessie from time to time, she revealed, but otherwise they were on very good terms. Miss Painter recalled that Chapman kissed her once or twice, but only whilst Bessie was present, and he never made inappropriate 'overtures' to her.

A few weeks after the 'wedding', Chapman decided to buy the lease of a public house in Hertfordshire. On 10th August 1898 he sold the lease of the Prince of Wales for £80 (almost £30 more than he paid for it) and moved thirty miles to the Grapes in Bishop's Stortford. The timber-and-plaster building dated back to the late 1600s and was called the Cherry Tree until the 1870s.[108] It was located on what is now South Street, on the corner of Apton Road. This was a busy shopping area, which suggests that the pub probably enjoyed good takings. At that time Chapman's balance at his London bank stood at just under £370. On 23rd August 1898 he withdrew the entire sum and closed the account.

Frederick Thomas Sanderson, a county court bailiff who stabled his horse nearby and made a habit of drinking at the Grapes every day, became very friendly with the new licensee, a family man with a pleasant wife and a nine-year-old son. Chapman regaled Fred with anecdotes about his erstwhile career as a steward on board transatlantic ships — the same yarns he had told in Hastings. Fred found Bessie to be in excellent health, other than suffering 'pains in her teeth'. Towards the end of the year Bessie's close friend Elizabeth Painter came for a fortnight's stay, partly to help in the bar whilst Bessie went into hospital for an operation to treat what Elizabeth called the 'lumps on her face, caused by her teeth'. Chapman asked Fred where he might purchase a will form, explaining — perhaps rather tactlessly — that he wanted Bessie to complete one because her health was so bad.

After Bessie came home, more than one person saw Chapman being brusque and rude to her, 'carrying on' at her, getting angry when the takings didn't quite add up, even throwing things at her. On one occasion he even frightened her with a revolver. Miss Painter explained that Bessie 'Didn't answer him back, but cried very much.'[109]

---

108 It was demolished in 1934 and replaced by a new Ind Coope pub also called the Grapes. That was demolished in 1967 and modern high street shops and a dentist now occupy the site.
109 *Southwark & Bermondsey Recorder,* 31st January 1903.

After just six months at the Grapes, a decision was made to return to London. Chapman and Bessie had lived together for almost a year, and if he found her an encumbrance, giving up the pub afforded him the perfect opportunity to offload her. Equally, unless Chapman was controlling her in some way, Bessie was free to leave. Each chose to continue the partnership, and took lodgings at 8 Haberdasher Street, Hoxton, about 400 metres east of Bartholomew Square and within walking distance of Elizabeth Painter's family home in Dufferin Street.[110]

In the fifteen months since Mary's death, Chapman had been stepfather to Willie Spink; Bessie had filled the role of stepmother and Miss Painter was his honorary auntie. But when Chapman began negotiating for the lease of a pub on the south side of the River Thames, he had no intention of taking the ten-year-old with him. On 20th March 1899, he decided to dump him in the nearest workhouse. He told Ernest Sibley, relieving officer for the parish of Shoreditch St Leonard's, that Willie's father had deserted his mother, who had since died, but this time he did not mention Joseph Renton. He gave as referees Miss E. Painter and his 'housekeeper' Miss B. Taylor. The officer duly admitted Willie to Shoreditch Workhouse, which at 204 Hoxton Street was barely half a mile away. A few weeks later, on 9th May, Willie was moved to the workhouse's dedicated children's home, opened a decade previously in the more lugubrious surroundings of rural Essex. For the remainder of his short life he never again saw Chapman, Bessie, Miss Painter, or his Renton relations, and he would never meet his father, his elder brother, or his kin in the Spink side.

Chapman had withdrawn £370 in cash when he closed his London bank account and moved to Bishop's Stortford. Judging by other transactions, landlords generally broke even on the buying and selling of pub leases, but in this case Chapman probably made a profit because, according to the Manchester Courier, he had upgraded the premises by fitting up the house 'with electric bells and other mechanical contrivances', work 'for which he is said to have a great bent'. The paper added that 'these proofs of his skill can still be seen'. He also built a shooting gallery, where he gave 'exhibitions of fancy shooting, and was regarded as a magnificent shot.'[111]

On 23rd March 1899 Chapman purchased the lease of the Monument public house from the old-established Meux's Brewery in Nine Elms Lane, Lambeth.[112] The price was £367.10s, of which £235 was paid by him in cash, whilst the brewery lent him the balance.[113] The Monument stood at 135 Union Street, a long, ancient road in Southwark. Its western end begins at Blackfriars Road, where the great Rowland Hill once preached in Surrey Chapel. A turning nearby leads to Nelson Square, where at No. 26 Percy Bysshe Shelley had attempted a ménage à trois in 1814. Moving eastwards, next to St Saviour's Charity School, on the corner of Red Cross Street, is Cross Bones, an ancient burial ground containing the remains of the women of the Bankside stews.[114] The eastern end of the street adjoins Borough High Street, close to London Bridge railway station.

---

110 In 1884, 1891 and 1901 her parents were recorded at 20, Block M, Dufferin Street.
111 Manchester Courier, 8th November 1902.
112 The Bridge House Estates Committee held the freehold.
113 Deposition of John Todhunter Earle, of Meux's Brewery, at Southwark police court.
114 The burial ground has recently received considerable publicity. www.crossbones.org.uk

The area had been residential until the nineteenth century, when it became 'gradually merged and finally submerged in an atmosphere of manufacturing.'[115] By 1899 it was dominated by the world-famous Hayward's Union Iron Works, whose foundry extended all the way down Princess Street and along Orange Street. Black smoke belched from its chimneys, infusing the air with a fragrance of molten iron that blended with the powerful aromas emanating from Pott's Vinegar Works and Barclay and Perkin's Brewery. The cacophony of hammering from the foundry mingled with the whistling and puffing of the steam engines and the clattering of carriage wheels passing across the rails of the South-Eastern & Chatham Railway that ran the length of Union Street on a low, brick-arched viaduct opposite the Monument's front door.

The locals were poor but they were not unemployed. Apart from the foundry workers, among the men were market porters, waterside labourers and bookbinders. The women included sack, bag and accoutrement makers, dust pickers, rabbit-skin pullers and laundresses. These industrious residents lived between and above multifarious shops which supplied all their daily needs for food, tobacco and newspapers and ensured that they would never go thirsty, for there were numerous coffee houses and no fewer than *ten* pubs in Union Street itself, supplemented by a dozen more located in the roads and alleys leading from it.[116] By a curious coincidence, the proprietor of the Red Lion in Union Street was also called George Chapman, and his wife's name was Annie.

The tightly-packed terraces of cramped shops and overcrowded homes built in the 1830s and 40s were interspersed not only with noisy, pungent industries, but also with large edifices housing charities and missions. These existed in all of London's poor districts and were created and run by middle class do-gooders or religious missionaries. Opposite the Monument stood Shaftesbury Hall and two social clubs run by All Hallow's church. Next-door-but-one to the Monument, seven Anglican nuns, members of the Clewer Sisters of Mercy, ran All Hallow's Mission and a day nursery for the infants of working mothers. All Hallow's parish church, just around the corner in Pepper Street, was 'grandly proportioned' and 'looked exactly like a Roman Catholic place of worship.'[117] Its rituals were also High Church. Bessie was a member of the congregation, but whether Chapman joined her is not known.

Bessie seems to have found contentment and friendship amongst the humble folk of Union Street. According to H.L. Adam she was 'much liked, being very genial with the customers and charitable to the poor.'[118] She was certainly more popular than Chapman, who reputedly upset the locals with his political views. The second Anglo-Boer War was in full swing, and he sided with the Boers against the British (perhaps because, being from Russian-occupied Poland, he sympathised with the plight of a country colonised by another). When he read that the British had sustained losses, he celebrated by 'firing a revolver repeatedly from the upper windows.'[119]

---

115 *Years of Reflection 1783–1953: The Story of Haywards in the Borough,* Haywards, 1955.
116 Those in Union Street were the Sun, the Three Jolly Gardeners, the Hand and Flower, the Cooper's Arms, the Marquis of Granby, the White Horse, the Catherine Wheel, the Rose and Crown (extant), the Red Lion (rebuilt and now called the Charles Dickens) and the Monument.
117 All Hallow's was almost entirely destroyed by a bomb during WWII. Booth, C. (1902) *Life and Labour of the People in London,* Series 3, Chapter 1, Macmillan. See also booth.lse.ac.uk
118 Adam, H.L. (1930) *Trial of George Chapman,* William Hodge, p10.
119 *The Echo,* 29th October 1902.

Towards the end of 1900, when the couple had been together for two-and-a-half years, Bessie began to suffer from chronic dyspepsia. She confided in a neighbour, Martha Stevens, who lived at No. 176. Mrs Stevens was fifty-three and, since separating from her husband sixteen years previously, had worked as a sick nurse whilst raising four children. After they flew the nest she adopted two little ones, who by this time were aged twelve and six. Mrs Stevens advised Bessie to go to hospital, and when she refused took her several times to see James Stoker, a local doctor she had known for a few years, at his surgery at 221 New Kent Road.

Bessie's health improved, then she had a relapse with identical symptoms. In mid-December Chapman called on Stoker to ask him for a suitable medicine to cure Bessie of her mysterious stomach ailment, which he was, of course, deliberately creating with his stockpile of tartar emetic. In a repeat of his behaviour during Mary's similar 'mystery' illness, Chapman prepared Bessie's meals himself, alone in the kitchen, away from prying eyes. And, just like Mary, she was always severely sick after eating his concoctions. Nobody in Chapman's life knew of Mary's fate, which allowed him to grow more daring: he began to ask others to carry the poisoned food upstairs and feed it to her on his behalf.

Everyone could see how kindly Chapman treated Bessie. Nurse Stevens, who had by then been hired to care for her professionally, stayed for about a fortnight. She confirmed that Chapman obtained everything she asked for on behalf of the patient. 'Nothing was spared, and he did everything...to make her happy and cured.' Similarly, Miss Painter remarked that, 'from his manner and behaviour he was desirous of doing the best he could'. He made sure that Bessie had 'all she wished in the way of food', and yet it was all wasted, for none was retained. Bessie began losing weight alarmingly, until, in her brother's words, his healthily-stout sister looked 'shrunken, thin, like a little old woman.'[120]

Shortly before Christmas Bessie's tummy trouble grew so severe that Nurse Stevens was asked to continue caring for her on a long-term basis. The repeated, uncontrollable bouts of vomiting and diarrhoea that was a peculiar green colour left Bessie so weak that before long she became bedridden. Miss Painter called in every evening after work; Dr Stoker visited daily — sometimes twice a day — for six weeks. He later recalled that Chapman was concerned, attentive, and 'in the room every time I visited her.'

James Morris Stoker was of a different generation to Mary Spink's physician, the late John Rogers, who had set up in practice before Stoker was born. The Irishman was thirty-five and had qualified just seven years previously.[121] Although his training was fresh and his knowledge up to date, he was as unable as Dr Rogers had been to discover the source of the patient's constant vomiting and purging, the burning sensation in her throat, or her excruciating stomach pains.

When Dr Stoker asked Chapman for permission to get a second opinion from Septimus Sunderland, an eminent specialist in women's complaints, 'he at once agreed'. Chapman asked Dr Sunderland what he thought was wrong and received the vague reply: 'uterine trouble.' Stoker, having established that Chapman was more

---

120 *Southwark & Bermondsey Recorder*, 17th and 31st January 1903.
121 Strangely, R.M. Gordon refers to him as 'the old doctor.'

than willing to have a third opinion, consulted a local GP, Dr Elliman, who diagnosed 'hysteria.'[122] According to Stoker, Chapman 'accepted that opinion, as he had accepted Dr Sunderland's.' A fourth doctor, Patrick Cotter, diagnosed cancer of the stomach or intestine, and so Stoker sent a portion of Bessie's vomit to the Clinical Research Association to be tested for signs of cancer. The results were negative.

Each time Stoker had suggested inviting another doctor to give his opinion, Chapman had readily acquiesced, and even invited the various medics to hold joint consultations in his club-room.[123] When he received bills from all four, Dr Stoker commented, Chapman 'did not grumble' about paying them. He seems to have been almost relishing their pontifications, as though they were all engaging in an entertaining and intriguing parlour game which he, of course, was controlling.

Bessie spent her final Christmas bed-bound and gravely ill. Nurse Stevens, who was already looking after her all day, began to stay overnight as well until, about mid-January 1901, Bessie's mother arrived from Cheshire. For two weeks the women shared the workload. Mrs Taylor prepared Bessie's food and sat by her bedside all night (whilst Chapman slept soundly in the parlour); Nurse Stevens administered the medicines and was in attendance during the day. The ladies' constant presence prevented Chapman from administering tartar emetic and Bessie's condition at long last improved. Everyone, including Chapman, expressed immense pleasure, and when Dr Stoker called one Sunday he was relieved to find his patient out of bed, dressed and merrily playing the piano in the club room. Stoker ended his daily visits, Nurse Stevens was discharged, and Mrs Taylor returned to Cheshire.

Within twenty-four hours of being left alone with Chapman, Bessie experienced another relapse and was worse than ever before. Her loving husband immediately re-engaged Nurse Stevens. Soon her condition became so severe that she could be fed only by rectal enemata, using a soft-rubber ball syringe with a long nozzle. This duty fell to Nurse Stevens, who again moved into the pub, this time for about six weeks. Miss Painter remarked that Bessie's eyes were 'glassy' and she 'seemed frightened', whilst Chapman 'appeared to be very kind and attentive' and, as his beloved grew worse, 'seemed very anxious'. Sometimes he would sit and weep copiously, pressing his handkerchief to his face. Then he would pull himself together, dry his eyes, and prepare for his loved one another meal or drink laced with tartar emetic.

Bessie received visits from the clergymen of All Hallow's church and its Clewer Sisters of Mercy. Her parents made the journey from Cheshire to sit anxiously at her bedside. When Miss Painter visited she would ask Chapman how Bessie was faring. Sometimes he would tease her by replying, 'Your friend is dead', and she would dash upstairs in great distress, only to find her alive.

At last Bessie rallied and 'seemed a bit brighter', but then, at about 1.30am on Wednesday 13th February 1901, Nurse Stevens called Chapman up to the top floor bedroom. However, as was the case with Mary Spink, he delayed and, by the time he attended, Bessie had died. Dr Stoker was summoned. He issued a certificate citing the cause of death as 'intestinal obstruction, vomiting and exhaustion.' After her visit on

---

122 A term applied by male physicians to women whose ailments they could not cure or whose behaviour they labelled as 'too' emotional. Modern medicine long ago rejected it as a genuine disorder.
123 A separate room in a pub that was hired by clubs and societies for meetings or parties.

7th February Miss Painter did not (or could not) visit for a week. When she arrived on Thursday 14th she found Chapman with Nurse Stevens in the bar parlour, where he was serving customers. When she asked about Bessie's health, Chapman told her that she was 'much about the same'. In fact, he had attended the registrar's office earlier that day — Valentine's Day — to register Bessie's death. It fell to Nurse Stevens to impart the bad news.

There was a female undertaker close to the Monument (Mrs Sarah Fentum), but Chapman engaged a grander one: Alfred Smith, of 122 Southwark Bridge Road. On 15th February, having removed, prepared and coffined Bessie's body, Mr Smith's manager conveyed it at 7am in a raven-black, horse-drawn hearse to St Pancras railway station, where it was loaded into a luggage van. In a nearby compartment sat Chapman, Bessie's mother and her son William.[124] On arrival at Lymm station, the coffin was unloaded and taken by hearse to St Mary's church, followed by Chapman and the Taylor family in a sombre mourning carriage. Bessie was interred in a family grave that would, within eighteen months, receive the remains of both her parents. The *In Memoriam* cards bore the popular verse: 'Farewell, my friends, fond and dear/ Weep not for me a single tear/For all that was or could be done/You plainly see my time was come.'

Bessie's brother William met all the funeral expenses because Chapman told him he had insufficient funds. This was a lie: he earned a handsome income from the pub and possessed capital of at least £300 (the equivalent to about £30,000 today). At the funeral, William later remarked, Chapman 'behaved in every way that I should expect a man to who had just lost his wife.' This was contradicted by the sexton, who was 'struck by Chapman's somewhat indifferent manner.'[125] Nurse Stevens believed that his grief was genuine, and continued to visit for another week or so to provide emotional and practical support, even helping out by pulling pints until a barmaid was engaged.

Despite still being married to Lucy, and masquerading as Bessie's husband for almost three years — and even burying her as 'Bessie Chapman' — when the national census was taken on 31st March 1901, Chapman pretended to be a bachelor. He also claimed to have been born in the USA.

## MAUD MARSH

For six months after Bessie's demise, Chapman supposedly employed a succession of barmaids, about whom nothing is known. The 1901 census lists a resident potman, eighteen-year-old Henry F. Hope, who may have had some connection to Bessie, as he was born in Cheshire. On Tuesday 20th August 1901, Chapman was perusing the publicans' daily newspaper, the *Morning Advertiser*, when he spotted this advertisement:

> Wanted, by a young lady, age 19, a SITUATION to learn the bar and assist in house. Address to M.M., Outwood, Sydenham Road, Croydon.[126]

---

124 Records are unclear about when, or whether Bessie's parents were in London when she died.
125 *Manchester Courier*, 31st October 1902.
126 Thanks to Neal Shelden, who found Maud's advertisement.

M.M. was actually eighteen, and Outwood was not her home but a house in which her mother was employed as residential housekeeper. Chapman was among nine licensees who responded. He sent a reply by postcard, saying to come at once, 'fare paid engaged or not'. It is a testament to the frequency of the postal service in those days that M.M. and her mother received the card within hours and were therefore able to take the train to London Bridge at 6pm the same day.

They introduced themselves as Miss Maud and Mrs Robert Marsh. Maud had experience of both domestic and bar work, having previously been employed in the curious role of nursemaid-cum-barmaid at the Duke of York, 50 Canterbury Road, near her family home in Longfellow Road, West Croydon.[127] For the past ten months she had been a domestic housemaid, and offered her employer as referee. Although she had once been prone to attacks of 'hysteria', Maud was an energetic, strong, healthy girl. Chapman offered her seven shillings (the equivalent to about £28 today) plus board and lodging, for a six-day week, the pub being closed on Sundays. Mother and daughter were pleased to hear that a charlady visited daily to perform the laundry and the rough chores, so Maud would be spared the heaviest domestic tasks.

Eliza Marsh, concerned for her daughter's moral welfare, hoped the ring on Chapman's finger signified the presence of a wife. To her disappointment, he explained that he was a widower. It wasn't considered decent for a young woman to live alone with a man — not even if he was her employer — but Chapman put Mrs Marsh's mind at rest: a respectable family shared the living accommodation above the pub. Reassured by this, and also by Chapman's charming manners and his social standing as a public house licensee, Mrs Marsh felt able to trust him not to take advantage of a naïve and vulnerable teenage girl young enough to be his daughter.

Chapman asked Maud to start work two days later — a Thursday — provided her character reference was satisfactory. Mrs Marsh gave her blessing, and each toasted Maud's successful interview with a refreshing glass of bitter. The next morning Chapman wrote two letters: one to Maud's previous employer, the other to Maud herself, deferring her starting date until the following Monday, 26th August.

On that Monday, Maud engaged her local carter, Mr Paterson, to convey her personal belongings to the Monument, and at about 7pm she went up by train. On arrival she discovered that the 'family upstairs' had moved out that morning and that no charlady was employed. Despite these disappointing surprises she stayed, and in her daily letters home reported that she liked her new place. Maud was 'attractive, vivacious, and well liked by the customers',[128] one of whom described her as 'a nice, high-spirited girl.'[129] When her father visited, Chapman told him that she 'shapes up very well in the business.'[130]

127 The former Duke of York is now flats.
128 *Daily Express*, 28th October 1902.
129 *Daily Express*, 29th October 1902.
130 *Coventry Evening Telegraph*, 11th November 1902.

*Image: Maud Marsh, from the Illustrated Police News.*

Within a week Chapman had given Maud a gold watch and chain and some rings. Mrs Marsh immediately became anxious: everyone knew that when a man gave a pretty girl jewellery it could mean only one thing. On Sunday 1st September she despatched her husband to investigate. He found Maud perfectly content. Shortly afterwards, however, Chapman proposed to Maud and then expected sexual favours on the strength of their betrothal. This was a common practice amongst working class couples who had been courting for a long time but, as this was not true in her case, Maud was unsure whether to permit such intimacy. On Wednesday 11th September she wrote to her mother:

> Just a line to say, on the q.t., Mr Chapman has gone out, so I now write this to you to say that George says if I don't let him have what he wants he will give me £35 and send me home. What shall I do? He does worry me so, but still I am engaged, and so it does not matter much, and if he does not marry me I can have a breach of promise case.

Maud meant that it would not matter if she surrendered her virginity to him and risked pregnancy, because he had promised to marry her. The £35 constituted two years' barmaid's wages, and Chapman may have offered to pay it directly to her rather than face a writ for breach of promise. This was a court action available to women against men who made a proposal of marriage and later retracted it. It existed to deter men from using false proposals to persuade women to engage in premarital sex and subsequently abandoning them, leaving them 'ruined', according to the morality of the day. Clearly, Maud was unaware that a woman under the age of twenty-one could not bring such an action.

Maud's mother replied to her letter promptly, telling her to come home at once; however, Maud reassured her that everything was now fine.

[Thursday] September 12th, 1901

> Dear Mother, your letter to hand this morning. I am very pleased to say there is nothing between us so far but only friendship, and I was silly enough to write that letter to you yesterday and hardly knew what I was doing. I had not been very well, and he tried to do the best for me, and I thought he was going to take advantage of me. Dear Mother, there is no need to worry about me, as I am all right here, and was sorry I wrote the letter to you, as I see different of him this morning. I had to show the letter from you to Mr Chapman, and was surprised at my own folly. After receiving such a nice letter from you last night, Mr Chapman said he will come down on Sunday if he does not have a different understanding between us. I am quite comfortable, and I am getting on all right. We must take things from a different light from this, but will tell you more when I come to see you. Hoping to hear from you before Sunday. I must close with love and best respects from Mr Chapman and myself — I remain, your loving daughter, Maud.

Mrs Marsh later admitted that she 'could not say if the second letter had been written solely by her daughter and on her own initiative'. Maud's comment *I had to show the letter from you* reveals that Chapman was already invading her privacy, and her sudden volte-face suggests that he was also manipulating her thoughts and actions.

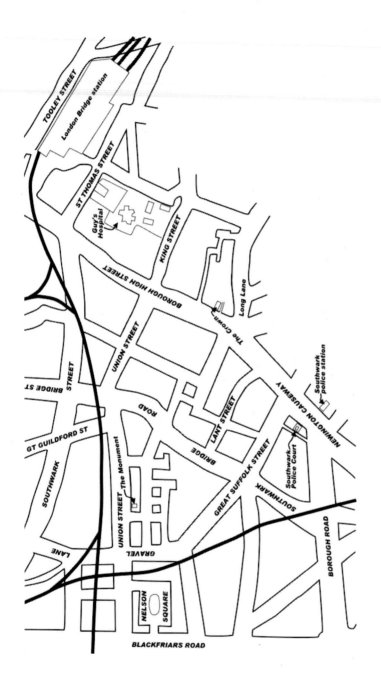

*Map of Southwark in 1900, showing the Monument, the Crown, the police court and police station, Guy's Hospital, and the railway lines and station. The police station, at 323 Borough High St (formerly, 50 Blackman St) was known colloquially as Stone's End, from the Stones' End tavern that previously occupied the site. At the rear were barracks housing police officers, their wives and children. The court was at 298 Borough High St (formerly, 58 Blackman St). Now demolished, David Bomberg House stands on the site.*

*Maud Marsh and George Chapman, from Trial of George Chapman. Sketches of the couple, copied by a newspaper artist from photographs they took of one another. From Shurey's Illustrated.*

Just two weeks after his first visit, Mr Marsh called on his daughter again, and was alarmed to hear that she had received an invitation to become *Mrs* Chapman. Marsh warned her not to do anything rash; it was too soon, and she barely knew the man.

Maud, blissfully ignorant of the fact that the bicycle her generous fiancé gave her had previously been ridden by two women he had murdered, cycled with him to Croydon on Sunday 15th September. Chapman told Mrs Marsh he wished to marry her daughter and she promised to discuss it that afternoon with her husband, then an in-patient at Croydon Hospital. On the following two Sunday mornings, Maud and Chapman cycled to visit Mr Marsh in hospital (where Chapman met Maud's twenty-year-old sister Alice for the first time), then they dropped in on Mrs Marsh, who was at Outwood with her other two children — Alfred, aged sixteen and Daisy, fifteen.[131] On 29th September Chapman asked Mrs Marsh and Alfred (who were housekeeping at 8 Litton Road) to witness his will. Post-dated 13th December 1901, it named Maud as executor and sole beneficiary. Impressed by Chapman's display of sincerity and responsibility, both Mr and Mrs Marsh consented in principle to his marrying Maud at some point in the future; however, each parent separately advised her not to get married without informing them in advance. When Chapman and Maud left they took Daisy with them to stay at the Monument for a month. The Marshes almost certainly sent her to act as both chaperone and spy. Both girls wrote many letters home, and one included an invitation from Maud asking her mother to visit on 13th October.

One day Maud and Chapman went shopping and returned with a fine wedding costume. Then, on the morning of Sunday 13th October, leaving Daisy and her friend Pollie Bowling[132] with instructions to mind the house, they drove away soon after 10am, reputedly in a carriage drawn by a pair of grey horses, to get married in 'a Roman Catholic chapel in Bishopsgate Street.' This was sheer nonsense. Chapman was still married to Lucy and, even if he had obtained a divorce, the Roman Catholic church did not allow divorcees to marry. According to one writer, Maud and Chapman merely paid a visit to a neighbour's public house (presumably, one that was open on Sundays).[133]

When Mrs Marsh arrived at the pub at 3pm, accompanied by a teenager called Jenny Field, she was chagrined to find confetti plentifully strewn about and Maud wearing a shiny, thick new wedding ring. Remonstrating with Maud, she was informed that the wedding plans had been kept secret because Chapman did not want a big fuss. Mrs Marsh asked to see the marriage certificate but Maud explained that, regretfully, her new husband had already locked it safely away with his other important papers. Although Mr Marsh was subsequently to ask on four separate occasions if he might view the document, Maud repeatedly dodged the issue.

After a late luncheon, the party of six went out on the underground railways so that Mrs Marsh could take her first trip on the Twopenny Tube. Borough station, just a few minutes away, was on the City & South London Railway (London's first

---

131 Daisy Harriett Helen Marsh. Different reports call her Daisy, Helen, Nellie or Harriet.
132 Probably Mary Ann Bowling, b1885, who appears in the 1901 census as a firework-factory hand, living at Church Road, Mitcham, with her widowed mother Eliza.
133 Furniss, H. (ed) *Famous Crimes Past and Present*, Vol. IX, No. 109, c. 1908, Caxton House.

electric line, now the Northern Line) which went to Bank, the interchange with the Central London Railway. The Central had opened just fifteen months previously and was instantly dubbed the 'Twopenny Tube' on account of its flat fare of two pence. Their afternoon of 'train-spotting' was followed by an evening at the Monument where, according to some sources, 'a band was engaged and festivities kept up to a late hour.'[134]

A week after the fake wedding, Daisy Marsh saw Chapman sending some boxes of clothing belonging to himself and Maud to her parents' house, and some other parcels to London Bridge station. About this time (according to Jack While), Philip Sharp, a chairmaker living round the corner at 26 Pepper Street, witnessed 'a load of costly furniture' being carried into the Monument.[135]

On 24th October Chapman absented himself from the pub, leaving Maud a note that read: 'Close up the house at the usual time, take what you can from the urns, etc., empty the tills, tell Jim Bloomfield if anyone asks for the guv'nor that he has gone into the country for a few days.'[136] (Bloomfield, a market porter, was their next-door neighbour at No. 137.) Maud and Daisy left the pub at 10.15pm to walk to London Bridge station, but Maud turned back, telling Daisy that she had forgotten to bring the ticket for something deposited at the station's cloak room. Reunited a few minutes later, they took the train to Croydon and made their way to the Marsh family home at 48 Stanley Road. In the early hours, Chapman sneaked back into his pub and set a fire in the cellar. He then joined Maud at Croydon, where they slept overnight. Maud told her family that she had been told to say, 'if any questions were asked', that the purpose of their visit was to see her father before he was readmitted to hospital the next day.

Jack While, a former fire reporter, wrote an article in the *Sunday Express* in 1931. 'The Most Exciting Fire I Ever Attended' recounted the story of 'Polish Jew' George Chapman's mysterious blaze:

> At 1.30am, on October 25, smoke was seen coming from the tavern. Two passers-by, having summoned the fire brigade [from Southwark Bridge Road] approached the building. The doors were open, but there was no one to be seen. When the fire was extinguished brigade officials and detectives examined the premises. They found that the tills were empty, that the place was practically destitute of furniture, and that there was nobody there. Suspicion was aroused.[137]

Daisy Marsh rose that morning to find Chapman in her family kitchen, nonchalantly eating breakfast, after which he and Maud caught a train to London Bridge and visited the Monument. After feigning shock at the devastation caused by a mysterious fire that had occurred during their overnight absence, and inspecting and assessing the damage, they returned to Croydon to collect their belongings. Alice was home, and they told her that the upper storeys were undamaged, so they would still be able to live there even though the pub could not trade.

---

134 *The Echo*, 29th October 1902.
135 'The Memories of a Fire Reporter: The Most Exciting Fire I ever Attended', *Sunday Express*, n.d., 1931.
136 *Ibid.*
137 *Ibid.*

*The Metropolitan Fire Brigade going out 'on a shout'. From Free London, 1901.*

Chapman read While's report of the fire in the *Daily Chronicle*. Its final sentence infuriated him: 'Last night the police were making enquiries for the landlord, a Mr George Chapman, who had disappeared.' He stormed off to the newspaper's offices and threatened an action for libel. Later, While visited the Monument and assured Chapman that there was no malice in his report. Chapman became belligerent and repeatedly demanded While's name and address (so that a writ could be issued). While lost his temper and, after a shouting match, Chapman left the bar. While worried that he might return armed with a revolver,[138] and went out into the street. As he chatted to a salvage man Chapman appeared, circled him and glared at him menacingly from head to foot, but did not attack him.

The *Morning Advertiser* also reported the fire, and again Chapman was outraged by the insinuation within its final remarks: 'No trace could be found of the landlord. The police are pursuing investigations.'[139] Chapman served a writ for libel, determined to extract substantial damages, but it was swiftly withdrawn after he was confronted with 'certain evidence' by the police and the Salvage Corps.[140] This doubtless included the highly incriminating note that he had written to Maud, which she had carelessly discarded in the bar parlour, where it was later found by the police.

138 Presumably locals had told While about the gun when he viewed the burnt remains of the pub.
139 *Morning Advertiser*, 25th October 1902, quoted in *Lloyd's Weekly*, 2nd November 1902.
140 The London Salvage Corps was a private service created by insurance companies to salvage and protect premises and goods involved in fires. Its No. 3 station was opposite the headquarters of the Metropolitan Fire Brigade Station in Southwark Bridge Road. It was disbanded in 1982.

Superintendent Blyth carried out an investigation for the insurance company. He discovered that Chapman had insured the contents of the Monument for the massive — and unwarranted — sum of £400, whilst the brewery had a policy on the building for £1,700. Blyth concluded that the fire 'had started amid a quantity of straw and rubbish close to a rum cask, and was probably caused by a candle being inserted in the rubbish and allowed to burn down'.[141] This method provided the opportunity for Chapman to create an alibi by placing himself in Croydon by the time the fire took full hold. The insurance company paid only a portion of Chapman's claim (some sources suggest it paid nothing) and cancelled his policy. He 'came within an ace of being arrested for arson', Jack While remarked, and pointed out that, had Chapman gone to prison, Maud's life would have been saved. 'Fate, however, willed otherwise', he concluded.

Despite failing to obtain the insurance payout, Chapman had plenty of cash in hand. He approached public house brokers J. and S. Motion and asked them to find him another pub.[142] On 11th November 1901 he paid just over £258 to the New Phoenix Brewery in Peckham Road, Camberwell, for the lease of the Crown public house, a few minutes' walk from the Monument. He and Maud began to manage the pub just before Christmas, but continued sleeping at the Monument until its lease expired on 5th January 1902, when they moved into the Crown. After managing the pub for a few weeks, its licence was transferred to him on 19th February 1902, two days after Maud's nineteenth birthday. Chapman paid the New Phoenix Brewery £60 for fittings and £160 for utensils. His annual rent was set at £75 and the bill for the supply of beer would be £40 a month.

Meux's Brewery paid Chapman £100 for what remained of the fittings at the Monument, but it never reopened. Its windows were boarded up and a 'site for sale' notice exhibited. It made one last, ghostly appearance in a street directory in 1902, after which neither the pub (No. 135) nor its neighbours at 131 and 133 appear in any directory. Newspapers reported in July 1903 that the building — which had 'attained an unenviable notoriety' — was to be demolished by London County Council.[143]

The Crown, Chapman's most prominent pub to date, stood at 213 Borough High Street, an ancient road linking the City, via London Bridge, to Surrey and the south. It was located at the junction of six busy roads, surrounded by popular shops, just along from the main post office, a few paces from the landmark of St George-the-Martyr parish church, around the corner from Borough station on the City & South London Railway and Borough Road station on the City Branch of the London, Chatham & Dover Railway. It was one of a long terrace of shops that ended at the entrance to the carriage-drive of London Bridge station.

Although the Crown was only sixty years old, there was a plethora of historic hostelries nearby, prompting Dr William Rendle to publish The Inns of Old Southwark in 1888. The most celebrated and ancient was the Tabard, built about 1306 and immortalised by Geoffrey Chaucer as the place his pilgrims assembled before setting off for Canterbury. Other local pubs had links with Shakespeare and Ben Johnson.

---

141 'The Memories of a Fire Reporter: The Most Exciting Fire I ever Attended', Sunday Express, n.d. 1931.
142 Brothers James Shepherd Motion and Sidney Herbert Motion were also auctioneers and licensed property valuers. Their offices were at 42 Bloomsbury Square, in central London.
143 Northampton Mercury, 24th July 1903. Wykeham House, a dismal block of flats, now covers the site.

John Harvard, for whom Harvard University is named, was born and raised in the Borough in the early 1600s and inherited the Queen's Head, 105 Borough High Street, from his mother.[144]

Southwark also has strong associations with Charles Dickens. In 1824, at the age of twelve, he lodged with his sister in Lant Street, off Borough High Street, whilst most of their family was incarcerated for three months in Marshalsea debtors' prison, at that time situated just metres to the north-east of the site of the Crown. Lant Street is mentioned in *The Pickwick Papers*, and Dickens was in later life a customer of the George, a galleried coaching inn rebuilt in 1676 (which still trades as a pub and is owned by the National Trust). The entrance to the Crown was panelled with painted tiles representing scenes from Dickens's novel *Little Dorrit*. Dorrit was a debtor's daughter, born and raised within the confines of the Marshalsea, who was baptised and married in St George-the-Martyr church. In January 1902 Little Dorrit's Playground was opened, just north of Marshalsea Road, providing another reminder of the area's literary connections.[145]

Adjacent to the Crown stood William Barker's, the largest mourning warehouse in London. Thanks to the Victorian cult of mourning, it had expanded from one shop in 1853 to occupy a parade of six by 1901 and drew hundreds of shoppers every day, supplying the Crown with a steady stream of customers wishing to drown their sorrows. Guy's Hospital was a short walk away. It, too, contributed to the Crown's coffers, for medical students frequented its billiard room. Chapman's new pub was also close to Newington Sessions, a police station, a magistrates' court and a coroner's court, all of which drew public, press and members of the legal profession to the area. Surrounded by thriving businesses, legal and medical establishments and sites of historic interest, and served by railways, omnibuses and trams used by thousands of people every hour, the Crown could not fail to bring its landlord a very large income. The locals, however, were not prosperous. Although in 1899 Booth's investigator designated Borough High Street itself as 'middle class', he noted that in the courts that led off the High Street,

> There is in this part a great concentration of evil living and low conditions of life...It contains a number of courts and small streets which for vice, poverty, and crowding, are unrivalled in London, and as an aggregate area of low life form perhaps the most serious blot to be found on the whole of our map. The down-at-heel, overcrowded dwellings were inhabited by a very poor and sometimes bad class of people.[146]

This was an area populated by the indigenous British: about two-thirds had been born within a couple of miles and most of the rest were English. 'They are the dregs of this, not the scum of any other population', added Booth's investigator and, indeed, the foreign residents could be counted on the fingers of one hand.

Many people living on the breadline eschewed church-going at a time when it was flourishing among the better-off. The rector of St George-the-Martyr described the religious condition of his parish as 'depressing, almost hopelessly so'. He regretted

---

144 The Queen's Head closed in 1886.
145 The area features in *Oliver Twist, Little Dorrit, David Copperfield* and *Barnaby Rudge*.
146 Booth, C. (1902) *Life and Labour of the People in London*, Macmillan. See also booth.lse.ac.uk

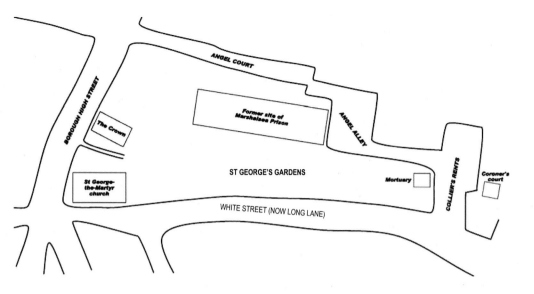

A map showing the location of the Crown, the former Marshalsea Prison, St George-the-Martyr church, and the mortuary and coroner's court. Angel Court led to 205 Borough High Street. Collier's Rents was filled with overcrowded, slum tenement buildings. The coroner's court was located in a former chapel of ease, built in 1776 and converted into a mission hall in 1883. The mortuary backed onto the east side of a small public garden created on St George's burial ground, which was bounded to the north by an old wall belonging to Marshalsea Prison, and on the west by the backyards of the buildings on Borough High St, including the Crown. After being bombed during the Second World War, Collier's Rents was widened, re-aligned and renamed Tennis Street. The site now contains the 1950s Tabard Garden Estate and a modern coroner's court stands opposite the site of the original; alongside is a Victorian building which may have been the mortuary.

Below: Chapman's next-door neighbour was a mourning warehouse.

that the church had 'lost its hold over the great bulk of the people' and feared that thousands were 'living lives of practical heathenism'.[147]

The Crown was a tall, narrow, three-storey building. The front doors led straight from the pavement into the saloon bar, from which a wide, curtained doorway led through to a billiard room at the rear of the building. The accommodation above comprised a living room, kitchen, scullery and toilet on the first floor and three bedrooms on the top floor.

After 'Mr and Mrs Chapman' moved in, Maud ceased to write letters home, but her parents were informed of her progress and wellbeing by their other children, each of whom visited often, usually on a Sunday when the pub was closed. Despite the large age gap the newlyweds were perfectly content and 'always playing and larking'. Chapman was a generous husband and a hospitable host. Although Maud's father rarely visited, he was satisfied that his daughter had married well.

Beneath his charming exterior Chapman was far from an ideal husband. He showed signs of being unreasonably possessive when Maud interacted with other men, and yet expected her to serve at the bar. One customer remarked that Chapman became 'very jealous if he saw her talking to anybody for more than a minute or two.'[148] Maud's married sister Louisa Morris began to gain the impression that Maud was sometimes afraid of him. Once, during a tram ride to Streatham, she had begun to weep. 'Look how late it is!' she exclaimed anxiously, adding, 'You don't know what my husband is.' Louisa guessed: 'What, has he been hitting you?' Maud replied, 'Yes, more than once. He held my hair and banged my head.' 'Didn't you pay him back?' Louisa enquired. 'Yes,' Maud assured her, 'I kicked him.'

The same month as they moved to the Crown, Chapman made Maud pregnant. One day in Maud's bedroom Louisa noticed a curious ball syringe with a white nozzle and asked Maud what it was for.

> She said: George used it. I asked 'On you?' she replied, 'Yes.' I asked 'What for?' She said she was a fortnight over her time and that George had used injections on her with this syringe. I picked up a bottle on the mantel... There were some frozen crystals in it. I took the cork out and it smelt of carbolic. She said: 'Put it down, he's coming.' My sister told me George had done it and it brought on flooding and then he used it again to stop the flooding...I told her one day afterwards that I did not think it was right...She told me 2 or 3 different times...that Chapman had given her some stuff to take. I asked what for. She said, 'George does not want any children yet but after we get enough [money] to live private I could have as many as I like then'.[149]

Chapman's actions were illegal: under the 1861 Offences Against the Person Act, performing an abortion carried a maximum sentence of life imprisonment.

As well as physical trauma, Chapman's actions caused Maud emotional pain, for she was not only eager but also impatient to become a mother. Louisa testified that Maud was 'grieved' at Chapman's refusal to have children, and stated that she

---

147 Booth, C. (1902) *Life and Labour of the People in London*, Macmillan. See also booth.lse.ac.uk
148 *Daily Express*, 29th October 1902.
149 Louisa Morris's evidence at the Old Bailey.

would 'get very distressed'.[150] Even Chapman admitted that, each time Louisa brought her baby Clara to visit, 'After she had gone Maud would sit and cry for a long time.'[151] During 1902 Louisa became pregnant with her second child, news that must have been hard for Maud to bear.

## THE SHARES SCAM

In the spring of 1902 Chapman and Maud committed perjury at both Southwark police court and Newington Sessions when Chapman prosecuted Alfred Clarke and a woman going by the name of 'Hilda Oxenford' for false pretences. The case would lead Chapman to meet a policeman called George Godley. In 1888 Godley had been a sergeant in Whitechapel Division, where he was part of the team hunting Jack the Ripper. By 1902 he was forty-five, in his twenty-fifth year with the Metropolitan Police, and a detective inspector in Southwark Division.

Alfred Clarke was a smartly dressed, sharp-brained thirty-two-year-old who spent his life perpetrating frauds involving shares and cheques. Recently discharged from Liverpool's Walton Prison, he was keen to get back into the game. In 1900 he had lodged in Liverpool with merchant's widow Matilda Gillmor and conducted an affair with her married daughter.[152] Mrs Gillmor owned 35,000 shares in the Caledonian Gold Mining Company. She entrusted him with two of the certificates in order to ascertain their value and sell them on her behalf. Clarke discovered that the mining company had been dissolved on 12th March that year, rendering the shares worthless. He conveyed this news to Mrs Gillmor, but did not return the certificates because he knew their potential to defraud. Later he stole from her twenty-four more certificates and some diamond rings worth nearly £100, and absconded to London, where he found lodgings at 14 Bonham Road, Brixton.

Almost nothing is known about Hilda, his female accomplice. I suspect it is now impossible to discover her true identity. In the 1901 census for 45 Fairmount Road, Brixton, she claimed to be a twenty-four-year-old Liverpudlian married to a forty-two-year-old travelling salesman called Walter Oxenford. Walter was indeed married, but not to Hilda; his real wife, Ada, was alive and well, having taken her daughter to live on the Isle of Man. A son, then fifteen, lived with Walter.[153] Without a marriage record, we cannot ascertain Hilda's maiden name. A search revealed that over a hundred girls called Hilda were born in the Liverpool area between 1886 and 1888. Not only could she be any one of them, but also her forename, age and birthplace may be fictitious.

Clarke asked Hilda to masquerade as the Matilda Gillmor named on the shares certificates, in order to extract loans from people by offering the certificates as security. They tried to borrow £1 from Charles Beckwith Barton of the Flower of the

150 Adam, H.L. (1930) *Trial of George Chapman*, William Hodge, p87.
151 Sergeant Kemp's testimony to the Old Bailey.
152 Matilda's name is sometimes misspelled as Gillmore or Gilmour. Her address on the certificates was 23 Hertford Street, Liscard. In the 1901 census she was forty-five and living 'on her own means' in Churchill Street, Toxteth, having been widowed in 1896. Her twenty-one-year-old married daughter May (then estranged from her husband) and May's baby Vera lived with her. May had an affair with Clarke and was eventually named as co-respondent in his divorce in 1907.
153 In the 1911 census Ada Oxenford appears as married for twenty-seven years. The only marriage record found for Walter is related to his wedding to Mary Annie Raper in 1903.

The Crown today. The original building has been demolished and rebuilt, but the decorative façade has been painstakingly reinstated. The ground floor frontage has been radically altered: in Chapman's day there were two narrow, arched doorways either side of a central window. Photo: Christian Jaud.

A map of 1897 showing the position of Southwark police station opposite the police court, either side of the 'B' in 'Borough (High Street), which leads off top right.

Also shown are Newington Sessions house and, alongside it, the recreation ground that was once the site of Horsemonger Lane Gaol.

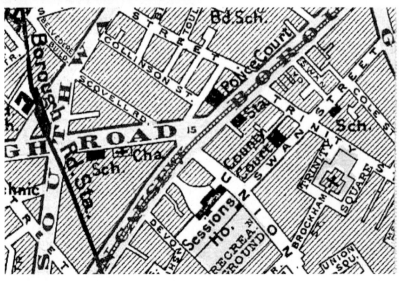

Forest public house at 123 Blackfriars Road, but he declined. Hilda was a customer of the Crown, but Chapman did not know her name. Posing as Mrs Gillmor she engaged him in conversation, winning his trust and respect by casually giving him certain personal information: her husband owned a tobacconist's shop at 292 Wandsworth Road and she owned a property at 55 Brixton Hill. She said that she was an account collector for two large companies of cigar-makers in Manchester and Liverpool. In order to submit her accounts on time, she needed to borrow some cash until some tardy London customers paid her.

According to Hilda, Chapman lent her a total of £9. She borrowed £2 on 9th March, which she repaid. It had been secured with a share certificate, which Chapman returned. She borrowed a further £4 on 14th March, and £3 on 15th, giving him further certificates. There was £7 outstanding. Hilda claimed that Clarke had asked her to obtain the loans on behalf of Matilda Gillmor, who was his mother-in-law. He waited outside the pub each time Hilda borrowed money from Chapman, and she handed over the cash to him. She did not disclose the nature of her relationship with Clarke, why she took part in the transactions, nor whether she was paid a fee.

According to Chapman, on 9th March 1902 he lent 'Mrs Gillmor' £400, to be repaid by 20th. She left as security two certificates in her name for 1,500 shares worth 5s each and showed him that she held further certificates for 5,000 shares. On 15th March she borrowed another £300, leaving another share certificate and promising to repay the money on 28th. On 16th she called yet again, asking him to advance her £1 on a cheque, so she could pay her taxi fare home. He declined, asking when she was going to repay the £700. She told him she would settle up the following day, but failed to show.

Both parties agreed that, on 19th March, Clarke had called at the Crown to settle Hilda's debts. But because Clarke was unaware of the sum owed and declined to give his name, Chapman refused to tell him anything or to accept any money, so Clarke agreed to return later, accompanied by 'Mrs Gillmor'. When they failed to show, Chapman went to the Caledonian Gold Mining Company's offices, which according to 'Mrs Gillmor' were at 22 Queen Victoria Street, Blackfriars. Finding no trace of the company he went to the stock exchange, where he discovered that the shares were worthless. A visit to 55 Brixton Hill proved fruitless: no Mrs Gillmor lived there.

Clarke was probably attempting to perpetrate a con similar to a long firm fraud (a type of sting for which he was later jailed). The plan was to build Chapman's trust by creating a pattern of borrowing and repaying, increasing the amounts each time, and always leaving as security share certificates whose value greatly exceeded the sum owed. Once Chapman had complete confidence that monies lent would always be repaid, Hilda would borrow one final, huge amount and hand it to Clarke, who would then abscond. Clarke ensured that the only name ever revealed to Chapman was that of the blameless widow Mrs Gillmor, who lived hundreds of miles away and had, in any case, long since left the address written on the certificates. Clarke usually perpetrated his frauds in concert with another man but this time he needed a female accomplice to match the female name on the certificates. It is still not known whether Hilda was privy to Clarke's ultimate sting. Perhaps he was simply using her to borrow the monies and intended to flee without her once the final, large amount was extracted, and leave her to take the rap.

But Chapman wasn't as naïve as Clarke had hoped. He smelled a rat and decided to teach Hilda a lesson for treating him as a fool. Inflating a hundredfold the amount she had borrowed he consulted a solicitor, who referred him to Angus Scott Lewis, assistant Director of Public Prosecutions, who passed the matter to Southwark police for investigation. On 4th April Inspector Godley instructed Detective Sergeant William Smith to make enquiries. A little over a week later, after reading Smith's report, Lewis thought Chapman's story unfeasible — who in his right mind would hand over such an enormous sum of money to a stranger? (£700 is the equivalent to £70,000 today.) He refused to prosecute. Upon hearing this, Chapman decided to take out a private prosecution at his own expense.

On 16th April George Chapman applied to magistrate Cecil Chapman for a warrant for the arrest of 'Matilda Gillmor' and, under that name, Hilda was arrested at her home six days later. Declaring herself to be Mrs Oxenford, she vehemently denied the accusation. Sergeant Smith took her to Southwark police station to be identified by George Chapman, charged her with obtaining £700 by false pretences, then escorted her across the road to the magistrates' court, where she appeared every week for five weeks to be repeatedly remanded. Robert Marsh managed the Crown on several occasions to allow Chapman and Maud to attend court.

At the first hearing, on 22nd April, Cecil Chapman was on the bench, Henry Sydney prosecuted and E.H.A. Newman defended. When she heard Chapman swear on the Holy Bible that she had borrowed not £7 but £700, Hilda Oxenford must have been astounded. To add verisimilitude to his story, Chapman provided exact details: he had handed over £400 in notes and gold on 9th March and a further £300 on 15th and had kept a record of the serial numbers of the banknotes. The police copied down the numbers.

At the second hearing, on 29th April, Maud Marsh, posing as 'Mrs Chapman', confirmed her husband's version of events, swearing on oath that she had witnessed the conversation on 9th March and seen 'the guv'nor' — as she always called him — hand over the money to 'Mrs Gillmor', who signed a receipt in a book. The following week, Stanley Mackinder gave evidence. He had co-owned the tobacconist at 292 Wandsworth Road with Augustus Martin for five years and, although he was acquainted with the lady in the dock, had attended public houses with her and given her his card, she was certainly not his wife. Evidence was also brought to show that she had lied about owning 55 Brixton Hill, which was occupied by Temple Chevalier Martin, chief clerk at Lambeth police court, and his sons, one of whom was a barrister and another a Home Office official. 'Mrs Gillmor' had been proved a downright liar.

Images: above right, Cecil Chapman, from Trial of George Chapman; above: Henry Sydney, from the Illustrated Police News.

On 13th May Mr Sydney applied for a warrant to be issued for Clarke's arrest. As soon as Clarke heard about it, which was two weeks later, he surrendered himself to

Southwark police. By the time the court reconvened on 28th May, the police were referring to the accused as Hilda Oxenford (instead of Matilda Gillmor) and had charged Clarke with conspiring with her. The fraudsters were bailed to appear at Newington Sessions the following month.

The sessions house was built in the 1790s along with the adjacent Horsemonger Lane Gaol, the site of 135 public executions. After the gaol closed, its gallows — which had been erected on the flat roof of the gatehouse so gawpers could get a clear and unobstructed view of the hangings — were transferred to Wandsworth Prison.[154]

Chapman's private prosecution was heard by Richard Loveland Loveland KC, deputy chairman of the North and South London Sessions. Arthur Hutton was the prosecuting counsel. Barrister Henry Goodwin Rooth appeared for Hilda Oxenford. Clarke retained E.H.A. Newman as his solicitor but did not engage a barrister, preferring to conduct his own defence in court which, according to reports, he did most ably and eloquently. Bail was granted for Hilda but was declined for Clarke in view of his criminal record, which included a conviction for stealing silk (1897) and three for false pretences (Oct 1900, Nov 1900, Feb 1901). Clearly, his prison sentences (six months, eight months, twelve months and six months, each time with hard labour) had failed to either reform or deter him. Clarke's solicitor appealed to Mr Justice Wright, who allowed him bail on his own recognisances of £100 plus £100 surety from Mr Lees, clerk to Mr Newman.

The witnesses repeated the testimony they had given at the magistrates' court. In cases such as this, the plaintiff was required to provide evidence to show that he withdrew the disputed sum of money from his bank account. When asked why he was unable to provide such proof, Chapman said he had given up using banks in 1898. The defence refused to believe that anyone would keep £700 just lying about casually in a drawer, and reminded him that there was a penalty for perjury. Chapman stuck to his story. As his takings were about £40 a week (about forty times the income of most of his customers), the disputed sum could be accumulated in a matter of months. Mr Hutton, for the prosecution, pointed out that Chapman would hardly have gone to all the trouble of bringing a private prosecution, which entailed considerable expense in engaging a solicitor and barrister, if the amount owed had been a mere £7, as Oxenford and Clarke alleged. After the real Mrs Gillmor — who had been subpoenaed — gave her evidence, Clarke accused her of lying. He had cohabited with her daughter and then abandoned her (owing to her immorality, he said) and therefore the mother's evidence amounted to nothing more than 'malicious perjury' in retaliation. He also accused Chapman of perjury and his solicitor twice applied for a warrant of perjury against the publican, but was advised to await the result of the trial.

In fact, both sides were committing perjury. Hilda claimed she was acquainted with Clarke for just a few days at the time she agreed to borrow money on his behalf, but Sergeant Smith brought proof to show that they had known one another for (at least) some months. (He also stated that Clarke had been 'going about getting women under his influence'.) Walter Oxenford testified that he and Hilda had been

154 The gaol was demolished in 1881 and the site turned into a public park. The sessions house was rebuilt in 1921 and is still in use. Horsemonger Lane was called Union Road in Chapman's day and is now Harper Road.

married for fourteen years,[155] but there is no record of their marriage and Ada, the woman he had married in 1884, was still alive. Maud Marsh claimed to be Chapman's wife (although, when asked, she declined to say when they had married; perhaps she thought that if she gave a specific year, parish records could be checked). Although a press reporter remarked that Chapman's accent 'denotes German extraction',[156] the Pole claimed he was a South American who had been to Australia and the Cape before landing up in 1893 in England, where he had set up in business as a hairdresser in Hastings, after which he had leased a series of public houses in Dover and London.[157]

With no independent witnesses and no physical evidence, the case hinged on which couple the jury believed. On one side were Mr and Mrs George Chapman, a highly respectable married couple running a successful and prosperous local business. Smartly dressed and well groomed, they paid their bills and taxes and had never been in any trouble with the law. Chapman in particular was a veritable pillar of the community. That he had been landlord of a succession of licensed premises proved he was of good social and financial standing, especially as it was necessary to provide solid character references to obtain a publican's licence.

On the other side was Clarke, an incorrigible conman and jailbird with a criminal record as long as your arm. Then there was Hilda, apparently a shameless adulteress, masquerading under a false identity stolen from an innocent widow. She had readily consorted with a notorious fraudster and eagerly involved herself in his wicked deception. Her tall tales of owning a house, being married to a tobacconist and working for a cigar-maker all proved beyond doubt that she was a habitual liar. It is no wonder that the one honest thing she said — that she had borrowed only £7 from Chapman — was not believed.

As Clarke's criminal past and Hilda's multiple lies were unveiled, the Chapmans appeared to grow progressively more reputable in contrast. Predictably, the jurymen had no difficulty in returning a guilty verdict. Clarke was sentenced to three years' imprisonment and two years' police supervision for conspiracy and obtaining money by false pretences. Hilda was saved by institutionalised sexism: she was assumed to have been acting entirely under her male accomplice's evil influence and was, therefore, acquitted.[158]

It is deeply ironic that the jury believed the Chapmans, who were both using false names and had recently committed arson and perpetrated an insurance fraud. Chapman had lied on oath about his nationality, his past and his marital status and would, just months later, commit his third cold-blooded and motiveless murder.

### SUMMER AT THE CROWN

In June 1902 Bessie Taylor's father was killed in a trap accident. Somebody must have told Chapman, because he cycled to William Taylor's home in Peckham to offer his condolences. Thomas Parsonage Taylor had died just sixteen months after his daughter, and his heartbroken widow passed away peacefully two months later. Their coffins were buried above Bessie's in the family grave in Lymm churchyard.

---

155 In the 1901 census, Hilda claimed to be twenty-four years of age.
156 *Daily Mail*, 28th October 1902.
157 The documentary evidence shows that he moved directly from Hastings to London.
158 *Southwark & Bermondsey Recorder*, 28th June 1902; *The Times*, 23rd and 30th April, 7th and 28th May 1902.

Queen Victoria had died two weeks before Bessie and the coronation pageant of her son and successor, Edward VII, was set for 26th June. Business owners along the route placed adverts in the local papers offering viewing seats in their upper front rooms. Chapman did not state his fee, but others nearby were charging between 20s and 25s per person. He claimed to have space for seventy people which, even at 20s a head, was set to net him the colossal sum of £70 (worth £7,000 today) for just a few hours of inconvenience. The increase in sales of drinks would add a substantial amount of additional profit, especially if the spectators started to gather early in the morning and their revels continued until late at night. However, the new king was struck down with appendicitis, the coronation deferred until August and the procession rescheduled for late October.

One Saturday in mid-June Chapman asked Florence Rayner, a regular lunchtime customer, to manage the bar on the following Monday. Florence was a twenty-three-year-old dressmaker with experience of the pub trade. Pleased with the way she ran the business, he offered her a permanent position at five shillings a week plus bed and board. Chapman instigated a curious arrangement whereby Maud would work behind the bar alone whilst he took his main meal with Florence, then Maud would eat her dinner whilst Florence sat with her. During their shared repasts, Chapman flirted with Florence and kissed her — sometimes 'constantly' — but she did not object: 'I could not help myself', she later explained. After about a fortnight he asked, 'Be my sweetheart, will you?' and pleaded with her several times to elope to America with him. He'd even devised a plan to send her out first, then sell the pub and join her. Months later the police found a letter from auctioneers Biggs & Co, dated 8th September 1902, informing Chapman that they had not yet found a buyer for the Crown. This suggests it had been on the market for at least a few weeks.

One day whilst they were flirting, Florence reminded Chapman that he had a wife. He retorted: 'If I gave her *that*' — snapping his fingers — 'she would be no more Mrs Chapman.' Florence interpreted his gesture to mean that he would give her a 'pinch' of some substance, but perhaps he meant he could order Maud to pack her bags and leave. Florence Rayner once found Maud weeping because Chapman had forbidden her to visit her sister, and she heard him threaten Maud, warning: 'If you go out today you will stop out.' (Strangely, Florence later testified that she 'never saw them quarrel' and that Chapman was 'always kind' to Maud.)

According to the BPP, 'disagreements arose' between Maud and Chapman in connection with a trip to America which he proposed to take without her. What is more, the writer claimed that Maud raised with Chapman the subjects of the arson and the prosecution of Clarke and Oxenford, and hinted that she was 'in a position to disclose awkward things if he left her behind'. In early July, Maud was ill for one day with unexplained vomiting, diarrhoea and flooding. She was nursed by the Marshes' family friend Mrs Eliza Bowling, mother of Pollie.

Florence moved out on a Tuesday in mid-July. Accounts of why she left are contradictory. The BPP stated that Chapman threw her out for refusing to have sex with him; other sources claim that Maud fired her out of jealousy. Chapman told Florence's brother that he'd sacked her for being drunk. Florence said Maud gave her notice for being insufficiently physically robust to perform the full range of public house duties, and then, whilst she was working out her notice, Chapman walked uninvited into her bedroom during her rest break one afternoon, prompting her to immediately pack her bags and leave.

The day after she left, Florence visited Chapman in order to obtain a work reference. She seemed tipsy, so he took her by the throat and threw her out. A policeman who happened to be passing arrested her and locked her in a cell overnight. The next morning a magistrate fined her 2s 6d for being drunk and disorderly.

Soon afterwards, Maud engaged Miss Louisa Cole as cook, general servant and ad-hoc barmaid.

## CLARKE'S APPEAL

In June Alfred Clarke had been taken to Wandsworth Prison, where he immediately told the governor, Major Knox, that his conviction was a miscarriage of justice and so he wished to petition the Home Secretary. But he was not given sufficient paper upon which to make his statement in full, so he delayed sending the petition until he was transferred to Chelmsford Prison where, incredibly, he met with exactly the same obstruction and was forced to condense his story in order to fit it onto the small amount of paper provided. It was, therefore, August by the time his petition was dispatched. He claimed that his conviction was illegal, a judicial error, because the flimsy evidence against him amounted to his holding some share certificates and being acquainted with Hilda Oxenford. He had not borrowed any money from Chapman and had not been present when the loans from the publican to Mrs Oxenford took place. How, then, could he possibly be guilty of obtaining money by false pretences? It was Oxenford alone who had used the worthless shares to obtain money and, he argued, she had done so without his knowledge or consent. There was, in fact, nothing whatever to link him to the crimes, other than the word of Hilda Oxenford — a proven liar! Furthermore, in a conspiracy case, *both* parties must be found guilty, or neither. A lone person cannot be guilty of conspiracy. If Hilda was innocent of any crime, it was absurd to convict him of conspiring with her. After a month's wait, Clarke learned that his appeal had been rejected. He was permitted to petition again, on fresh grounds of points of law, but that met the same fate.

## MAUD'S ILLNESS

On Friday 25th July Maud's sister Alice received a postcard bearing the words 'Come by the workmen's train. George is ill.'[159] On her arrival early the next morning Alice found Chapman in perfect health and serving customers in the lounge bar. Perplexed, she asked where Maud was and he replied, 'In bed, dying fast.' Alice sprinted upstairs to find Maud sitting up in bed, a cup of senna tea in one hand, whilst in the other she held a sugar lump, presumably to make the tea palatable (according to *Materia Medica* it had a 'nauseous and disgusting flavour'). Maud confided in Alice: 'George has made this, but I cannot take it, because it makes me sick'.[160] This suggests he put tartar emetic in the senna tea for its purgative qualities. Senna was a common cure for constipation and was also used in folk medicine to cause the uterus to contract in order to induce labour; perhaps Chapman believed it could also precipitate a miscarriage.

---

159 Workmen's trains were the first ones to run each morning; they were cheaper than rush-hour trains.
160 *Southwark & Bermondsey Recorder,* 22nd November 1902.

Having confided in Louisa, Maud now divulged to Alice that Chapman had used a syringe inside her. She did not need to say why; Alice already knew from Louisa that its purpose was to prevent Maud having a child. Maud explained that she had been in bed for three days, during which time had been 'unable to use her bowels'. Alice insisted her sister be medically examined, Maud acceded, but was so weak that it took her an hour to dress, even with Alice's help. Chapman gave them his blessing and 2s 6d, the consulting fee for a doctor, but warned them not to go to Guy's Hospital, because he did not want 'the fellows to mess her about'. However, the doctor was not at home so Alice decided to take Maud to Guy's. The sisters were obliged to pass by the Crown, so they crossed the street and, with the road full of horse-drawn carriages, bicycles, omnibuses and trams, and both pavements teeming with pedestrians, there was almost no chance of Chapman spotting them.

At Guy's, Maud was examined by half-a-dozen doctors and medical students, one of whom, Alice recalled, 'pressed a sponge dipped in carbolic against her back passage'. She was given castor oil to take immediately, and white powder with which to syringe herself rectally at home. As time was getting on, Maud sent Alice back to the Crown to help Chapman run the bar, whilst she stayed on at Guy's, where she eventually fainted. Hearing that Maud had gone to the hospital, Chapman became angry: 'That is all she wanted to go for, for these fellows to mess her about!' Later, Maud returned alone to find Chapman cross with her for being gone for so long.

The following morning, Sunday 27th July, Maud disclosed to Alice that Chapman had again given her 'stuff' to drink against her will. When asked why she consumed it, Maud exclaimed, 'Because he stands by me while I drink it, so I have to!' Hours later she became ill again and the next day was admitted to Guy's, where she stayed until 20th August in No. 17 bed, Queen Victoria Ward. She had a fever, her heart raced at 110 beats a minute, her bowels were obstructed and she vomited sporadically. For the first fortnight her temperature was between 102 and 104 degrees, then it suddenly dropped to normal. Maud could not be properly examined because she found being touched excruciatingly painful; she also refused examination of 'certain parts'. She was ostensibly under the care of obstetrician James Henry Targett, but he never once examined her — or even spoke to her — leaving that chore to his students and juniors, none of whom detected that she had been poisoned. Targett diagnosed inflammation of the peritoneum, then changed his mind and opted for consumption of the bowel, for which he prescribed opiates. The possibility of her being poisoned did not enter his mind.

When Mrs Marsh visited, Maud told her she had 'constipation so bad and that her inside had come down and was inflamed...owing to the straining'. Mrs Marsh did not drop in at the Crown, because she and Chapman had fallen out about something. Louisa saw Maud frequently, and when she discovered that Chapman had not visited for a couple of days, despite living so close by, she took his place at the bar to allow him to cycle to Guy's with a parcel of clean clothes for Maud. He told Louisa that the hospitalisation was Maud's own fault because she should have taken the medicine he gave her, adding, 'When she comes out of this she will do as I tell her.'[161] When she

161 Return showing the Working of the Regulations for carrying out the Prosecution of Offences Act 1879 & 1884. British Parliamentary Papers, Vol. 56, 1902. Published as the Blue Book, 1903, p12–16.

*Eliza and Robert Marsh, from Famous Crimes.*

remarked on how strange it was that the doctors could not find a cause for Maud's illness, he replied: 'I could give her a bit like *that*' (pressing a thumb to a fingertip) 'and fifty doctors would not find it out.' When she asked what he meant he walked away, muttering 'Never mind.'

Maud passed some of her time reading and writing letters to her family. Once, Alice wrote to her and was perplexed at receiving no response. She later discovered (via Louisa) that Chapman had forbidden Maud to reply. Two of Maud's letters to Chapman were later read out in court. Her pencilled words read:

> My dear husband — just a line to let you know I am no better. I had no sleep last night; was in pain all night long and have not been much better to-day. I will try, dear George, to get better so as to come home and help you. My own darling husband, I think this is all, so, with love, I remain your ever true and loving wife, Maud.

> My dearest George — a line as promised. I had a good night's sleep last night and feel very much better this morning. The doctor said when he saw me I had not got a very good prospect, which meant I was not going on so well as he would like me to do, I think, all this time. So, with fond love, I remain, yours for ever, Maud. My temperature is still going higher.[162]

Despite having treated Florence dismissively when she had called upon him for a work reference, Chapman relented a few days later, and on the strength of it she had landed a job at the Foresters' Arms, Peckham.[163] According to Florence, when Maud had been in Guy's for three weeks, Chapman turned up at her new workplace and said, 'If you had not been such a fool you would have been at the Crown now.' Whether he meant as his barmaid or his mistress is unclear.

In hospital, away from Chapman's ministrations, Maud made a full recovery. She told Louisa that Chapman 'strongly objected' to her being examined by doctors and, when she wrote telling him that she was now sufficiently pain-free to undergo an intimate examination, he had immediately taken her home by cab.

---

162 *Southwark & Bermondsey Recorder,* 15th November 1902.
163 The Old Bailey court transcript wrongly states it was the Foresters at Twickenham. The Foresters' Arms was at 182 Peckham High St, close to Florence's parents' home in Cerise Street.

One day Chapman, Maud, her mother and Louisa were taking tea together when Maud asked, 'What do you think, Lou? George says I shall not live to see twenty-eight.' Louisa replied, 'Pooh, how does he know?' Chapman insisted: 'More you won't,' to which Maud retorted: 'Remember, I have been ill once, and this' — she pointed to herself — 'is a long liver.' Chapman smirked: 'We shall see.' Despite Chapman's comments, and even when she suffered a relapse soon after returning home, Maud still did not suspect him. Mrs Marsh later recalled:

> During the whole of my daughter's last illness she never suggested any cause for it. She never said one word to lead one to suppose that she doubted her husband for a moment, or that he had been unfaithful to her with other women. She appeared perfectly happy and contented to the last, apart from her illness.[164]

One day in the first week of October, Maud suffered a bout of diarrhoea, but recovered the next day and walked with her sister Louisa to the Monument to see if anything was being done with the derelict, burned-out building. Later they browsed the market stalls at New Cut, where Maud consumed seed-cake, tomatoes and lemonade, without ill effects. Back at the Crown, they enjoyed bread and butter with celery for afternoon tea. Louisa left when Chapman summoned Maud downstairs to work in the bar by blowing his whistle (his method of communicating between floors). A few days later Louisa received a letter from Maud reporting that she was again ill in bed with the same symptoms.

On Friday 10th October Chapman walked the half-mile to Dr Stoker's surgery in the New Kent Road and told him that his current girlfriend had developed the same mysterious illness that had killed his ex. Stoker called on Maud at 10.30pm and from then barely missed a day until she died. Consulting the same doctor twice was far more risky than engaging one who knew nothing of Bessie's demise, but by this time Chapman seemed to enjoy taking risks. He told Stoker that the doctors at Guy's had changed their opinion two or three times about the cause of Maud's illness. Perhaps he was covertly boasting about his ability to fool the medical profession.

Louisa and Edward Morris also visited on the evening of Friday 10th October and, at Maud's request, Louisa returned the next day and stayed the rest of the weekend. She gave Maud Bovril and toast on the Saturday, and roast pork, potatoes and greens on the Sunday. To her delight, Maud ate it all and kept it down. Later, Louisa left Maud alone with Chapman for about an hour, and that night Maud became very ill, so bad that at times she did not even recognise her. Maud asked repeatedly for brandy and soda, which Chapman prepared, and he also brought her ginger beer and, later, some champagne. Each time she consumed anything supplied by him she suffered a burning sensation in her throat, dreadful stomach pains, and was repeatedly, violently sick.

Dr Stoker prescribed all the correct remedies, including catechu, ipecacuanha, morphia, and a mixture of bismuth, opium and chalk. Maud would rally, and then become ill again. By Wednesday 15th Stoker had prohibited all feeding by mouth and ordered her to be nourished rectally with beef tea suppositories; he also introduced morphia by the same means. For this procedure he recommended that Maud again become an in-patient; however, when she began to sob at the thought of being

164 Mrs Marsh's deposition at the police court.

confined to hospital a second time, he agreed that a trained nurse could be engaged to carry out the procedure at home.

Chapman later shared several concerned but friendly conversations with Stoker about Maud's condition, during which neither his words nor his demeanour betrayed that he was deliberately inflicting the illness he sought to cure. On the contrary, Stoker later testified that Chapman 'appeared to be kind and solicitous to his wife, she appeared to be fond of him; I had never the slightest idea of anything being wrong'. He also pointed out that Chapman had raised no objection whatever to his examining Maud's vomit or excreta, of which he found copious amounts in a pail in the bedroom. Years later Dr Stoker remembered Chapman as 'a most plausible man — the very last man in the world you would suspect of being the author of such heartless crimes'. He continued:

> I can see him now, broken with distress at the illness of his wife, urging me to spare no trouble or expense to get well again the woman he outwardly professed to love so dearly, yet all the time was secretly, slowly, and fiendishly poisoning.[165]

On 16th October Chapman asked a regular customer, a garrulous charwoman named Jessie Toon, to come in daily to look after Maud. She had previously been hired to clean the billiard room, and Maud rather liked her cheery, chatty personality. Chapman told Jessie that Maud was 'very bad indeed' and issued her with a whistle to call him upstairs if necessary. 'I won't have another doctor', he added. 'If the hospital doctors can't find out what is wrong with her, who can?'[166] Chapman would not allow Jessie to prepare Maud's food or drink, and to obtain drinking water she was required to wait at the foot of the stairs whilst he filled a jug out of her line of sight.

Dr Stoker thought Jessie 'intelligent, capable and sober', and asked her to feed Maud with the rectal injector. She refused and so, although it was considered a shockingly indecent act for a non-medical man to carry out on a woman — even his own wife — Chapman assumed the task himself. He used the same ball syringe, made of green rubber and with a white nozzle, that he had used to flush out the contents of Maud's womb. As per Dr Stoker's orders, he filled the ball with various 'meals', concocted from beef tea, raw egg, milk and brandy. Jessie, who was often present during the procedure, said that Maud objected because they caused her horrendous pain and made her limbs go rigid. Because Maud refused to take Dr Stoker's medicines, Chapman added them to the syringe, along with his usual pinch of tartar emetic, so that everything she drank, ate or received *per rectum* was swiftly and violently expelled — to be cleaned up by the unfortunate Mrs Toon. Afterwards Chapman always washed the syringe himself, then placed it in water in a half-pint tumbler on the kitchen windowsill. Eventually Jessie offered to administer the injections, to avoid Chapman having to absent himself from the bar, but Maud told her: 'He is a very funny man, Jessie, but he has done it so far, so let him go on.'[167]

---

165 'Murderer Unmasked by a Doctor.' *Daily Express*, 8th December 1930. The article also revealed that James Stoker still possessed a small bottle that had figured prominently in the trial.
166 Return showing the Working of the Regulations for carrying out the Prosecution of Offences Act 1879 & 1884. British Parliamentary Papers, Vol. 56, HMSO, 1902. Pub as the *Blue Book*, 1903, p12–16.
167 *Southwark & Bermondsey Recorder*, 22nd November 1902.

In his autobiography Charlie Chaplin — born in nearby Walworth in 1889 — claimed to have met Chapman about this time. Chaplin purported to be endowed with a sixth sense, and cited an incident in which he, as a boy of thirteen, entered the Crown and asked for a glass of water:

> A bluff, amiable gentleman with a dark moustache served me. For some reason I could not drink the water. I pretended to but as soon as the man turned to talk to a customer I put the glass down and left. Two weeks later, George Chapman, proprietor of the Crown public house in the London Bridge Road, [sic] was charged with murdering five wives [sic] by poisoning them with strychnine [sic]. His latest victim was dying in a room above the saloon the day he gave me the glass of water.[168]

According to Mrs Marsh, during Maud's final three days Chapman 'appeared to show her every possible attention'. Jessie remarked that husband and wife 'appeared to be on very good terms. He got everything she asked for; he constantly came to her while she was ill, and seemed anxious about her.' This was echoed by Miss Cole, the live-in servant: 'He always treated her kindly...and they were on affectionate terms.'[169]

At 7pm on Saturday 18th October, Robert Marsh arrived at the Crown to find his daughter confined to bed with 'internal pains and other distressing symptoms'.[170] He thought it odd that, whenever she asked for water, Chapman would leave the room and return with a discoloured liquid that caused her to throw up. (Clearly, Chapman had become so audacious that he was poisoning Maud while her father watched.) Adulteration with tartar emetic would not cause the discolouration of the water, so perhaps Chapman was giving her something else unwholesome. About this time Mr Marsh began to feel a little uneasy, to the point of wondering whether his daughter was 'not having fair play'. And yet he could not convince himself that such a thing could be possible. The obstacle was that Chapman and Maud were so happy together and it was obvious to anyone that they truly adored one another. Moreover, it was plain to see that Chapman was doing everything he possibly could to find a cure, and he was also helpful and co-operative, always answering the family's questions with frankness and honesty.

On Sunday 19th October, Jessie was Maud's only visitor. She watched Chapman gently pull down his patient's lower eyelids and examine her eyes, and then use a stethoscope to check the function of her heart. At noon the next day Mrs Marsh and Louisa arrived together. Maud was so ill she could barely speak, prompting Louisa to sound out Chapman about getting another doctor, since Stoker was baffled. His response was that Stoker was the best, and 'if the best can't find out, fifty can't find out'. Mrs Marsh repeated the suggestion later, but Chapman was emphatic: 'No, it is no good'. To assuage Maud's raging thirst, caused by chronic dehydration, Jessie gave her lumps of ice to suck, then brandy and soda, which she could not keep down. In

---

168 Chaplin, C. (2003) *My Autobiography*, Penguin, p344. Chaplin also had a 'psychic' experience in connection with Edgar Edwards. He claimed that Edwards was an old gent of sixty-five who had acquired five grocery stores by bludgeoning their owners to death. In fact he was forty-four when hanged for the murder of one couple and their baby.
169 Their court testimony.
170 *South London Press*, 16th November 1902.

the presence of Jessie Toon, Chapman dipped a beef suppository into Vaseline and inserted it into Maud. Soon afterwards she expelled that and vomited again, and everything that emerged was — in the words of Mrs Toon —'green as grass'. Maud was in such agony with abdominal and rectal pain that her mother placed hot towels over her body in a feeble attempt to give some relief.

Dr Stoker arrived later and admitted: 'I am at my wits' end to know what to do'. Mrs Marsh asked if he minded her fetching their family GP, Dr Grapel. Far from objecting, he was eager to obtain assistance with this case, which he found both puzzling and personally distressing. When Alice arrived, Mrs Marsh sent her immediately back home to Croydon to ask her father to fetch Grapel.

As Alice and Louisa prepared to leave at about 7.30pm, Maud declared, 'Goodbye, you won't see me again.' Mrs Marsh spent an anxious night sitting in an armchair by her daughter's side, whilst Chapman slept soundly, fully dressed, on the other bed. In the morning Maud attributed her illness to the rabbit Miss Cole had served for dinner, despite the obvious fact that everyone else who ate it suffered no ill effects.

At 9am on Tuesday 21st October, Mr Marsh called upon Dr Francis Grapel, a bright, keen, recently qualified thirty-two-year-old. Marsh told him he was dissatisfied with Stoker and was starting to suspect that Chapman might be up to no good. He invited Dr Grapel to travel up to Southwark and give his opinion. Marsh then returned immediately to his daughter's bedside.

Shortly afterwards, Dr Stoker shared with Mrs Marsh his fear that Maud would never get out of bed again. If Maud died, Mrs Marsh replied, she would pay for a private post-mortem. Jessie Toon conveyed this remark to Chapman, who retorted: 'She wants to have her cut about and show me up, the old cat' (Victorian slang for someone who kept another under surveillance). He continued: 'Be careful Jessie what you say to her, and take particular notice of what she says to you, and in the course of conversation just ask her if there is anything wrong or any foul play'.

When Dr Grapel arrived unannounced at about 3pm, Chapman declared that they already had a doctor, and mumbled something unintelligible about 'fifty others' as he turned to serve a customer. He sent Miss Cole to fetch Dr Stoker whilst Dr Grapel waited in the bar, discussing Maud's illness with Mrs Marsh. When Stoker arrived the two young medics examined Maud in the presence of Jessie Toon and Mrs Marsh. They found her semi-comatose and with a coated tongue. Her breathing was shallow and yet her pulse was racing. Dr Grapel was particularly struck by Maud's skin tone, which he later described as 'a colour that would make you turn; a dirty jaundice'. He also noted that she 'writhed in pain when touched'.[171] Stoker suggested that Maud had ingested an irritant poison, possibly ptomaine. Later he told Jessie (knowing she would relay it to Chapman) that if Maud died he intended to conduct a post-mortem.[172]

Dr Grapel began to ponder the notion of arsenical poisoning. He raised the subject with Mrs Marsh, who mentioned the rabbit Miss Cole had bought from the street market in the New Cut. He replied, 'You don't find arsenic in rabbits.' On

---

171 *The Echo*, 25th November 1902.
172 Return showing the Working of the Regulations for carrying out the Prosecution of Offences Act 1879 & 1884. British Parliamentary Papers, Vol. 56, HMSO, 1902. Pub as the *Blue Book*, 1903, p12–16.

the train home to Croydon, Grapel wondered how else arsenic might have entered Maud's stomach. Of course it crossed his mind that the poisoning could have been deliberate, but he felt unable to voice his suspicions to Dr Stoker because, as he explained later, 'a diagnosis of repeated doses of arsenic is tantamount to accusing someone of murder'.

In the bar that evening, Chapman griped to Mr Marsh about Dr Grapel's visit. Though he had been happy for several doctors to examine Bessie, this time he resented the interference of even one other.

After sitting with his daughter for three hours, Robert Marsh discerned an improvement in her condition. Before leaving he remarked, 'I think my daughter will pull through now, George.' He was taken aback at Chapman's reply: 'She will never get up no more.' This seems to have been the moment when suspicion began to take a firmer hold within Robert Marsh's mind, prompting him to enquire if Chapman had seen anyone else with a similar illness. 'Yes', he replied. Marsh probed further: 'Was your other wife like it?' Chapman admitted that she had been 'Just about the same way'. But Marsh still suppressed his suspicions. It was impossible to remove Maud from Chapman's care without making a direct, monstrous — and indeed slanderous — accusation of attempted murder, something that Marsh felt unable to do.

That night Jessie Toon went home in the early hours, whilst Mrs Marsh settled down to spend a second consecutive night on a green plush chair beside Maud's bed. After setting a bottle of brandy and a soda syphon within Mrs Marsh's reach, Chapman again went to sleep on the other bed. About 4am Mrs Marsh gave her daughter a tablespoon of the brandy, which she vomited. Mrs Marsh had consumed no food for many hours, only tea and draught stout. She felt emotionally drained and in dire need of a pick-me-up. About 5am she took a little of the brandy herself, mixed with some cold water from a jug that Chapman had placed in a large pan of ice just outside the bedroom door. Two hours later she suffered a bout of severe diarrhoea and vomiting, necessitating six trips downstairs to the toilet, situated on the first floor. Clearly, Chapman had slipped tartar emetic into the brandy or the water or both, and had by then become so reckless that he took no precautions to prevent anyone else from drinking it.

On the morning of 22nd October, a little after 7am, Chapman rose, examined Maud, helped her to turn over to make herself more comfortable and then went downstairs to open the pub as usual. Mrs Marsh asked the servant to fetch Jessie Toon, who arrived at 8am to hear that Mrs Marsh had also been ill. (Chapman attributed it to her sitting up for two nights.) He spent the day manning the bar and now and again climbing the stairs to check up on his wife and her carers. Jessie offered Maud some brandy, but she raised her hand and exclaimed, 'No, no, no!' She drank some water that Chapman had supplied and immediately had a fit. Her arms turned the colour of port wine and her hands and lips went black, then she evacuated a large quantity of green diarrhoea onto the bed, which Jessie and Mrs Marsh mopped up with cloths and towels. Mrs Marsh told the servant to put them in the rubbish bin (she ignored this and put them in with the household laundry).

Jessie later claimed that she tasted a little of Maud's brandy. It brought tears to her eyes and burned her lips and tongue, so she had bolted downstairs to the kitchen to wash out her mouth and hastily gobble down a wedge of bread and butter to take away the nasty taste.

Meanwhile, in Croydon, Mr Marsh called at Dr Grapel's at 10am. The doctor said that, in his opinion, Maud had somehow been poisoned with arsenic but, being a robust girl, would recover once the sickness had passed.

Just after noon, with her mother and Chapman in attendance, Maud suddenly tried to throw off her bed-coverings, saying, 'Take them all off, I am going.' Chapman asked, 'Where?' She replied, 'Goodbye, George', and died. Chapman gently closed her eyes, sat with her awhile, then stepped out onto the landing, where he broke down in floods of tears. Mrs Marsh described him as 'dreadfully upset'. The pair later had a discussion, during which he agreed to let her take Maud's belongings home but asked her to come back and stay with him at the Crown until after the funeral.

Dr Stoker received a note by hand from Chapman informing him of Maud's death. He went to the Crown immediately and was astounded to discover it open for business. 'There was nothing to indicate there had been a death there', he remarked. Upstairs, standing around Maud's bed, he found Mrs Marsh, Jessie Toon and the grief-stricken widower, who was in the process of wiping tears from his eyes, which were noticeably red and sore. Chapman's voice cracked as he muttered forlornly, 'She died at 12 o'clock.'

Taking Chapman into another room, Stoker informed him that he was unable to issue a death certificate. According to Jessie, Chapman 'seemed dumbfounded' at this news. Stoker added that he would conduct a post-mortem 'just to satisfy myself', because he could not yet determine the exact cause of death. Chapman did not raise any objection, but said, 'I do not see the use of it.' Stoker asked him to suggest what killed Maud. He replied, 'Exhaustion.' Stoker asked what caused the exhaustion. Chapman said, 'Diarrhoea and vomiting.' But when asked what caused the diarrhoea and vomiting, he fell silent. Years later Stoker said: 'He must have known...that the game was up, yet all he said was, "Very well, do everything you think proper".'[173]

About 4pm Mr Marsh received a telegram from his wife informing him that Maud had died. He went straight to Dr Grapel, who was astonished because in his opinion she had been on the mend. Grapel suspected that another dose of poison had been administered. Remembering that Dr Stoker intended to conduct a post-mortem, he immediately sent a telegram advising him to test for arsenic, following it later with a letter detailing his reasons.

Dr Stoker, knowing that Maud was not married, acted correctly when he secured her mother's permission to perform a post-mortem. There was a legal requirement for him to also obtain the coroner's authority, but this he failed to do. Instead, he walked to the Old Vestry Hall at 81 Borough Road, where he met the clerk of the medical department of Southwark Borough Council, from whom he obtained verbal permission to remove the body to the mortuary and conduct the post-mortem.

That evening Chapman cycled to 122 Southwark Bridge Road, the premises of Alfred Smith, the undertaker. 'I have got some trouble,' he told Smith, 'I've lost my missus.' He reminded Smith that he had conducted his previous wife's funeral, but Smith had no recollection of it. Chapman also informed him of the planned post-

---

173 *Daily Express*, 8th December 1930.

mortem, and Smith explained that he was not permitted to remove the body without permission from the coroner's officer.

At 11.50pm Dr Stoker contacted Frank Gilbert, the keeper of St George's mortuary at Collier's Rents (which was separated from the pub only by St George's Gardens, a public open space) and asked him to convey a corpse from the Crown to the mortuary. About midnight, Gilbert visited Chapman, who asked him to fetch Alfred Smith and remove Maud's body immediately. Gilbert protested that it was far too late at night, but at Chapman's insistence he called upon Smith, who informed Gilbert that his staff had gone home, and suggested he knock up Mr Tull, the shop manager, at his home at 11 Warwick Street, Blackfriars. Tull refused to move the body that night, but promised to attend the Crown at 5am (the pub was due to open at 5.30am). Gilbert then walked back to the pub and angered Chapman by informing him that the body could not be removed for another five hours.

When Tull and Gilbert arrived at 5.30am on Thursday 23rd, Chapman's first remark was: 'You are late!' It was 6am by the time they removed Maud's corpse. As they placed it on the mortuary slab Chapman walked in unannounced and said he wanted Maud buried as quickly as possible. Then he returned to his pub, opening up about an hour later than usual.

That evening Frank Gilbert was having a drink in the Crown when Chapman asked him if Alice Marsh and her aunt might view the body. About 8.30pm all four walked the short distance to the mortuary and, as they approached the door, Chapman linked his arm through Alice's. After viewing the body he told Gilbert: 'I want it made a quiet job. As you know I don't want her buried from the Crown, where there is public business'. He asked if her funeral could be commenced from the mortuary.

At 10.40pm Dr Stoker began his post-mortem with two fellow Irishmen — Dr Patrick Cotter and Dr Theodore Poirotte (a physician-accoucheur) — and Dr Herbert French, who would one day be physician to George V and the royal household. According to George R. Sims:

> In the dark hours of the evening, when all was quiet and the gates of the public garden locked, the doctors had completed their task. As they stood together talking the mortuary keeper's quick ears caught the sound of a footstep on the gravel path outside. He instantly opened the door and saw the figure of a man disappear in the direction of the back wall of the Crown public-house. Mr Chapman, the landlord, had crept in the darkness to the door of the mortuary in the hope of overhearing the conclusion at which the doctors might arrive after the examination of the body of the dead barmaid.[174]

The doctors could discover nothing abnormal that could have caused Maud's death, which further increased Stoker's suspicions. He carefully placed Maud's stomach and its contents, a piece of liver and a portion of rectum, in two glass jars and ended the post-mortem at 11.55pm. The next morning Stoker took the jars to the Clinical Research Association, situated nearby at 1 Southwark Street, on the corner of Borough High Street. Heeding the telegram received from Dr Grapel, he asked public analyst Richard Bodmer to test for irritant poisons — especially arsenic. Dr Bodmer

---

174 *Lloyd's Weekly*, 8th December 1907.

*'The door in the wall where Chapman waited while the post mortem was being held.' From Lloyd's Weekly.*

found 'an appreciable amount' and the association's secretary, C.H. Wells, sent a written report to this effect to Dr Stoker, who received it at 6.30pm. This prompted him to consult Dr Cotter again and to contact the authorities. Only later did Bodmer perform further tests, which revealed the presence of more antimony than arsenic.

About midnight, Stoker informed the police of Bodmer's findings, and also posted a letter to the City and Southwark Coroner, Dr Frederick Joseph Waldo. By informing both the police and the coroner, he initiated two separate investigations into Maud's death. At Southwark police station, which at 323 Borough High Street was just a short walk from the Crown, Detective Inspector Godley read Stoker's report, and at 4.19am despatched a telegram to the coroner.

Meanwhile at the Crown, Mrs Marsh and Miss Cole helped Chapman behind the bar. Jessie Toon called on Thursday 23rd to see Maud's body but found she was too late. Chapman quizzed her about the hue of Maud's faecal matter on the day of her death, curious to know if it was black. 'No,' Jessie replied, 'it was green, like the vomit.' Later that afternoon, Alice Marsh visited and took tea with her mother and Chapman. Although Maud had barely been one day dead, Chapman remarked tactlessly, 'There is a chance for you as barmaid now. Will you come, Al?' She replied, rather more tactfully, that London did not suit her.

The next day Jessie called for her wages. Chapman asked how much he owed for five days' work and she replied, '15s won't hurt you'. This was quite high for the menial tasks she had performed, and yet Chapman voluntarily topped it up to 20s, and asked if she would do the laundry the following week. When she remarked that the heavily soiled towels and cloths should have been washed out already, he revealed that he had destroyed them. She requested a glass of rum (on the house) but he refused: 'I won't give you any rum, as you talk so if you have rum.' Jessie said, 'Well, if people ask me about Mrs Chapman...' Chapman interjected, 'You need not say anything.'

At about 9am on Saturday 25th October Mr Gilbert visited Chapman, who asked him again if the funeral, which he had booked for Monday 27th, could start from the mortuary, as he did not want 'any fuss' outside the pub. However, the coroner had instructed Gilbert not to allow the body to be moved and so he informed Chapman that the funeral had been cancelled.

Saturday 25th October was the date that every resident of Southwark had eagerly anticipated: the delayed royal pageant and procession was finally going to happen. Just after 2.30pm, His Majesty King Edward VII and his wife Queen Alexandra, together with a plethora of other royals, assorted aristocrats and hundreds of military personnel resplendent in full regalia, were going to pass Chapman's front door. Not only was this a once-in-a-lifetime event, he also expected to make a tidy profit from letting seats and standing room in his upper front rooms to those wanting a bird's-eye view of the spectacle, and from the exponential increase in sales of drinks to hordes of thirsty spectators hell-bent on celebrating in style. *The Times* remarked that the scene was 'never likely to be forgotten...by those who witnessed it', and that the event was an especially significant one in the lives of south Londoners because the area seldom had any public ceremony 'to brighten the normal dinginess of existence'. The decorations, explained the reporter, 'succeeded in imparting to the streets an air of brightness and gaiety which is sadly lacking in their every-day appearance'. He continued:

> Borough High-street...was a veritable avenue of artificial flowers. There was not a house or building of any kind without its piece of bunting, while in some instances the whole of the brickwork had been made to conceal its dinginess beneath a decoration of evergreens, of garlands of paper flowers, or of blue or crimson cloth artistically draped and looped. An arch, whose very lightness gave it a peculiar charm, and bearing the inscription, 'Peace and Prosperity to our Country' marked the point of entry into South London from over London Bridge. A graceful canopy of crimson plush spanned the High-street...the structure was supported on six pillars on either side, and was surmounted by the Royal Arms rising about a trophy of flags. Opposite St. George's church was a large crown, which hung suspended in mid-air in the open space formed by the junction of the High-street with Long-lane and Marshalsea-road.[175]

According to Arthur Fowler Neil, who was a sergeant at the time, Detective Inspector Godley was convinced that Chapman planned to abscond, which is why he needed to arrest him early in the day. Neil disagreed; he thought that Chapman intended to delay his departure until the evening because 'the cupidity in his mean soul made him anxious to get that day's takings first'.[176]

Several sources wrongly describe Chapman's arrest in melodramatic terms; in fact it was a very quiet and civilised affair. At 10am Godley had a meeting with Joseph Henry Vaughan Marks, the coroner's officer, then at noon he and his colleagues Sergeants Kemp and Leak battled their way through the 'seething, teeming multitude' assembling in Borough High Street until they reached the Crown, which was among the most gaudily adorned buildings. Its bar was already crammed with people. According to the *Daily Mail*:

> [The policemen] walked under the great crown that hangs in front of the public-house and the gay flags that decorated the façade and walked up

---

175 *The Times,* 27th October 1902.
176 Neil, A.F. (1932) *Forty Years of Manhunting,* Jarrolds, p7.

to the bar. A placard announced windows and seats to view the pageant, and joyous sightseers sat in the windows above. They took no notice of the two [sic] quiet men who walked into the house. Behind the bar was a small, dark man of gloomy appearance, with prominent cheek-bones and sunken jaws and sallow skin.[177]

Godley asked to speak to Chapman in private. The landlord lifted the bar flap and walked with the policemen through to the billiard room at the rear of the pub. Godley said, 'Maud Marsh, who has been living with you as your wife has been poisoned by arsenic, and from the surrounding circumstances I shall take you to the police-station while I make enquiries about the case'. Chapman feigned bewilderment: 'I know nothing about it. I don't know how she got the poison. She has been in Guy's Hospital for the same sort of sickness.'

At Godley's request, the group climbed the stairs to the second floor back bedroom in which Maud had died. Chapman unlocked it with a key from his trouser pocket. He had made no attempt to hide anything and was co-operative and helpful, even stooping to pick up three bottles of medicine from the floor, to save the policemen the effort. He passively handed over anything Godley wanted, including £268.10s kept in a locked drawer (worth nearly £27,000 today).[178] Godley took the medicines, the money and some documents, relocked the bedroom door and pocketed the key.[179]

Leaving Leak to guard the scene, Godley asked Chapman to accompany Kemp and himself to the station. They went down to the bar, where Godley told Mrs Marsh that her daughter was not legally married. This was shocking news and she immediately challenged Chapman to admit it to her face, which he did.

Before leaving the pub, Chapman asked if he might make sure that his beer was flowing correctly, especially in view of the enormous increase in custom expected that day. Godley accompanied him down into the cellar, where Chapman attended to the barrels. After asking Mrs Marsh and Miss Cole to manage the pub until his return, Chapman was ready to go to the police station:

> 'Don't handcuff me', he pleaded, as they were about to leave the house, and, rather than cause a stir among the crowd, two detectives caught hold of the prisoner's arm and marched down the bedecked street like three old friends, the other two police-officers bringing up the rear. So quietly was the whole business carried out that nothing was known of the arrest until nightfall.[180]

Chapman had waited eight long months to see his new monarch pass by his front door, but when the much-anticipated moment finally came he wasn't there. He may have read about it in the newspapers, which described the exciting events in Borough High Street in detail.

---

177 *Daily Mail,* 28th October 1902.
178 This was in the form of £110 in notes, £143.10s in gold and £15 in silver.
179 According to Neil, the till in the bar parlour contained £400 in gold, silver and copper. This was not mentioned by Godley, and as its value today would be around £40,000 Chapman is hardly likely to have left it in a till in a public bar, even had the notes actually fitted in the till! Neil, A.F. (1932) *Forty Years of Manhunting,* Jarrolds, p7.
180 *Worcestershire Chronicle,* 21st March 1903.

ARREST OF CHAPMAN.

*The arrest of Chapman and the interior of the Crown. From the Illustrated Police News.*

INTERIOR OF THE CROWN.

*George Godley (left) and Samuel Leak.*

It was nearly half-past 2 o'clock when the great gates at [London Bridge] were swung back and their Majesties commenced their progress through South London. The people occupied the pavement in dense masses from the very edge of the curb-stone right up to the shop fronts. Throughout the whole length of the High-street, from the bridge to the corner of Borough-road, there was scarcely an inch of room without its occupant. Every window was crowded with spectators, and almost every roof had its complement of sightseers. It was, altogether, a wonderful crowd. The progress of the King and his Consort was one continuous triumph. The cheering, which began at London-bridge, was carried on in unbroken volume all the way down the High-street, and it was not until the splendid cavalcade was lost to sight in Borough-road that the people's enthusiasm ceased its vocal expression.[181]

Having locked Chapman in a cell, at 4pm Inspector Godley and Sergeant Kemp, accompanied by the coroner's officer Joseph Marks and Dr John Jaquet (the divisional surgeon of police), returned to the Crown, where Sergeant Leak was in his sixth hour of guard duty. From Chapman's bedroom, and a box room across the hall, Godley and Kemp took possession of additional salient items, including photographic chemicals, medicinal powders, a pocket book, an 1893 diary, a ball syringe, part of a catheter, some papers written in a foreign script, a will, half-a-dozen medical books, a fully loaded, five-chambered American revolver (in its case), a quantity of business-related documents, a photograph of Bessie and some letters she had written to Chapman.

According to R.M. Gordon, there was also 'a series of photos Chapman had taken of Maud Marsh, which had documented her slow decline and death.'[182] However, he is the sole source of this story and did not cite its provenance. In A.F. Neil's version of events, 'a portmanteau, partly packed, lay on a couch' and a locked safe (opened with Chapman's keys) contained a bundle of £10 notes, some old letters in Russian, and 'a sheet of paper with notes of the boat-train departures from London'.[183] Leo Grex claims that police also found a single ticket to Antwerp.[184] None of these items was mentioned by Godley.

---

181 *The Times*, 27th October 1902.
182 Gordon, R.M. (2008). *The Poison Murders of Jack the Ripper*, McFarland, p110.
183 Neil, A.F. (1932) *Forty Years of Manhunting*, Jarrolds p7.
184 Grex, Leo (1985) *Detection (Stranger than Fiction)*, Ravette, p126.

When Godley finished at the Crown he returned to the station and at 7pm moved Chapman from his cell to the charge room. He was still blithely confident of returning home that evening, cheerily telling Godley, 'My brewers will bail me.' But Godley denied him bail:

> I said, 'No, I have not finished my enquiries yet, it is a very serious case of poisoning'. He said, 'She did not die suddenly; if she had been poisoned she would have done'. I had the three bismuth powders with me then. I said, 'I found these three powders on the drawers in your bedroom'. He said, 'The doctor sent them'. I said, 'I am going to see the doctor and finish my enquiries'.[185]

While Godley was interviewing Dr Stoker, Chapman asked Kemp if he might speak to him. 'Your inspector brought some white powders in just now which he said he found in the drawers in the bedroom', he said, 'has the doctor examined them yet?' Then, 'lowering his head and speaking in a low tone', he confided in Kemp: 'I would not hurt her for the world...I had a lot of trouble with my barmaids, and I took a great fancy to this one.' He told Kemp that there had been 'some jealousy lately'. Maud, he said, 'wished to be a mother', but she had also pointed out to Chapman that they had been together for over a year, and she was losing patience fast. Chapman claimed that Maud had threatened him with an ultimatum: unless she fell pregnant soon, she warned, 'You won't have me with you long'. Perhaps he was trying to plant a suspicion in Kemp's mind that Maud had committed suicide.

Inspector Godley continued his long, gruelling day by returning to Southwark police station at 10.15pm:

> I said, 'It is now my duty to charge you with the wilful murder of Maud Marsh by poisoning her with arsenic'. He said, 'I am innocent, can I have bail?' I said, 'No'.[186]

---

According to H.L. Adam, after Godley arrested Chapman his former Inspector Frederick Abberline congratulated him with the words: 'You've got Jack the Ripper at last!'[187]

185 Godley's testimony at the Old Bailey.
186 Ibid.
187 Adam, H.L. (1930) Trial of George Chapman, William Hodge, p52.

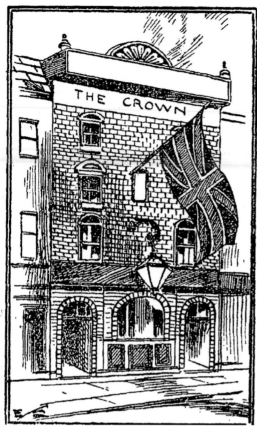

*Newspaper sketches of the Crown on the day of Chapman's arrest, decorated with a flag in honour of the royal procession later that day. From Lloyd's Weekly (above) and the Illustrated Police News.*

*The variations in the height and proportions of the building, the type of flag and the shape of the ground floor centre window are curious, considering the artists were able to visit the Crown. The IPN version is perhaps the more accurate, as the building was not bare brick but rendered, and tall and narrow.*

## INVESTIGATION AND EXECUTION

The period between Chapman's arrest and his execution was five months. This was an unusually long time. Edgar Edwards, who preceded Chapman to the gallows, killed his victims on 23rd December 1902 and was hanged just ten weeks later. After opting to plead insanity, Edwards was curious to read the fate of a fellow triple-murderer who had taken a different option. He followed Chapman's case in the newspapers with fascination, once remarking to a prison warder, 'He is a hot 'un, ain't he?'[188] Edwards never heard the outcome of Chapman's trial: he was hanged on 3rd March, a fortnight before it began.

Chapman's final months were busy and eventful. He was initially held at Brixton Prison, where he was 'compelled to don convict garb' (owing, apparently, to several small infractions of the rules). From there he was transported in a black, four-wheeled, horse-drawn police van at least fifty times to attend hearings at Southwark coroner's court, Southwark police court and, finally, the Old Bailey. Although in good health he was held in the infirmary at Brixton because prison regulations stated that all prisoners remanded on murder charges should be accommodated there. He received many visitors, among them his defence team, the prison governor, its medical officer and lay visitors, a priest and a trio of personal friends (whose identities were never revealed).

Reading the newspapers absorbed much of Chapman's day. During his first month in prison several other murder cases were reported. Milliner's assistant Kitty Byron had stabbed her married lover Arthur Baker to death on the steps of their local post office, two Jewish men had knifed a third in Whitechapel and a man had kicked his wife to death in Mortlake. Two baby farmers in Clerkenwell were up on a charge of child murder and two servant girls had smothered their victim with a pillow. In Durham a miner had shot his wife and daughter and a labourer had raped and murdered a seven-year-old girl; in Glasgow a man was hanged for slitting his wife's throat.

Although Chapman could see from press reports that much of what was being said about him was incorrect, and that the police were unaware of many important facts — such as his real name and nationality — he offered them nothing. Other than pleading ignorance or innocence, he remained silent, preferring to see what they could discover without any pointers from him. According to *The Echo*, the police were 'receiving communications from different parts of the country in

---

188 *Sunday Referee*, 29th March 1903. When Adam repeated the story 27 years later he reversed it, claiming that Chapman said, 'Edwards is a hot 'un!' Adam, H.L. (1930) *Trial of George Chapman*, William Hodge, p22.

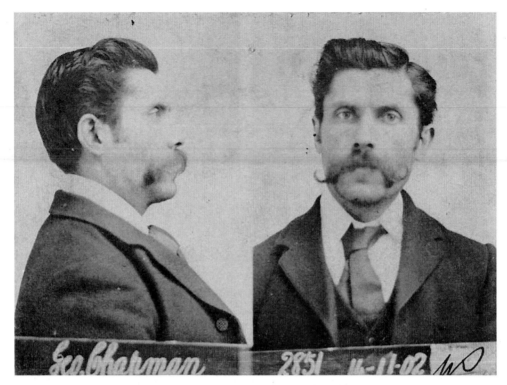

*Official police 'mugshot' photos of George Chapman, taken on 14th November 1902. Photo courtesy of the Metropolitan Police. In his 2007 book Shadow Pasts: History's Mysteries, Professor Rubinstein described Chapman as 'Truly fearsome-looking...looks as if he might well have been Jack the Ripper when he was in a good mood, and then turned really nasty when under the weather'.*

*The chapel, later a mission hall, in Collier's Rents before the first floor was converted for use as Southwark coroner's court. Anon, John Harvard Library.*

regard to the antecedents of Chapman, which are of a very remarkable character', whilst the *Daily Mail* stated that 'some of the finest brains at Scotland Yard are working almost night and day following up every shred of evidence'.[189] They were also scrutinising the many items removed from the Crown, where Godley's search had uncovered some unexpected and interesting documents, including undertakers' accounts and memorial cards pertaining to the funerals of Mrs Mary Chapman and Mrs Bessie Chapman, and a most incriminating label. 'Having bought poison at Hastings', wrote H.L. Adam, almost incredulously, 'he very carefully kept a label that recorded its purchase...Has ever a criminal been quite as helpful to the police as this man was?'[190] Adam concluded that Chapman must have considered his intelligence to be 'so superior to that of the police [that his] exposure was hardly possible'.[191] The *Daily Telegraph* concurred: having got away with murder twice, it suggested, 'he grew reckless with long impunity'.[192] However, Chapman's confidence was misplaced: he had left a trail of evidence sufficient to hang him.

His pocket-book did not reveal much. It contained a loose sheet of paper upon which was written: 'Came from America in 1893, independent', and 'Deposits £100, when from America I had £1000.' Written upon one page were the words 'February 13th, 1901, Wednesday. Bessie Taylor dead, at 1.30am [*sic: she died at 1.30pm*], with great sorrow, by G. Chapman.'

Chapman's small collection of books was — with one exception — exclusively of the medical variety. It included *The Works of Aristotle the Famous Philosopher Containing his Complete Masterpiece and Family Physician; his Experienced Midwife, his Book of Problems and his Remarks on Physiognomy*. First published in 1680, it dealt mainly with human reproduction and so was banned throughout the prudish Victorian era and indeed right up to the 1960s (although at the time of his arrest copies were being advertised for sale in the classified column of the *Illustrated Police News*). Chapman also owned two volumes of *British Pharmacopoeia,* an annual first published in 1864, containing information on drugs and recipes for medicines. There was also an old edition of Ranking and Radcliffe's *The Half Yearly Abstract of the Medical Sciences;*[193] a book in Polish entitled *Five Hundred Prescriptions for Diseases and Complaints*; Thomas's *Practice of Physic*; and all four volumes of Cassell's *Family Physician* (borrowed from Harriet Greenaway in Hastings).

Curiously, the only non-medical work in Chapman's possession was *My Experiences as an Executioner* by public hangman James Berry in 1892. The book explained in detail the precise sequence of tasks executioners performed when preparing to hang someone. Did Chapman suspect that one day he might be caught? According to H.L. Adam, when Berry read in a newspaper that Chapman owned a copy of his book, he wrote to Inspector Godley begging him to 'keep all reference to the book out of the case, explaining that he wanted to be entirely dissociated from it. He had, he said, destroyed all copies remaining in his possession and all others he could find.'[194]

189 *The Echo*, 29th October 1902; *Daily Mail*, 30th October 1902.
190 Adam, H.L. (1930) *Trial of George Chapman*, William Hodge, p38.
191 *Ibid*. p36.
192 *Daily Telegraph*, date unknown, quoted in *Southland Times* (NZ), 25th March 1903.
193 Its full title was *The Half Yearly Abstract of the Medical Sciences, Being a Practical and Analytical Digest of the Contents of the Principal British and Continental Medical Works Published in the Preceding Six Months.*
194 Adam, H.L. (1930) *Trial of George Chapman*, William Hodge, p19.

Chapman's tactic of silence delayed the Old Bailey trial by causing him to be remanded weekly at Southwark police court for sixteen weeks, which was a record then, and indeed one that was never surpassed.[195] The first hearing was on 27th October 1902; the last on 11th February 1903. Generally, Cecil Maurice Chapman was on the bench, but occasionally Paul Taylor deputised for him. George Chapman's solicitor was Henry Sydney, the same man who had acted for him during the shares scam case a few months previously. The witnesses' depositions were recorded by Harry Whitfield Coates, the second clerk of the court.

The inquest, conducted by City and Southwark Coroner Dr F.J. Waldo, was spread over four sessions: 28th October, 18th and 25th November and 18th December. Chapman attended all but the first session, Mr Sydney was present at every one, as was the jury of twenty men.[196] At both the police court and the coroner's court, Chapman was flanked by either two gaol warders or one warder and a constable, and was provided with a pencil, a sheaf of blank paper and a board upon which to rest the paper and take notes.

Southwark police court stood at 298 Borough High Street, opposite the police station and a few minutes' walk from the Crown. At the first hearing, on Monday 27th October, Inspector Godley was the only witness and his sole purpose was to get Chapman remanded for a week. Scandal-seekers in the public gallery were not disappointed. Not only had a pub landlord murdered his teenage barmaid (and probable mistress), but he was old enough to be her father. Moreover, on the very first day of the magisterial hearing, Godley (having discovered the tell-tale undertakers' bills relating to Mary and Bessie) 'uttered a sentence which created a sensation': he announced that Maud was the third woman to have died whilst living under Chapman's roof. Mr Sydney's response was nonchalantly dismissive: 'A mere coincidence, probably', he said, 'unconnected with the present charge'.

Pressmen saw Chapman for the very first time. The *Daily Mail* said he appeared 'haggard and distressed', and that his fingers 'clutched in agitation' at his nautical pilot's cap. The blue of his double-breasted, serge sailor's suit 'intensified his pallor, and he seemed to feel the full significance of the accusation'.[197] The *Daily Express* described him as 'undersized, with sunken cheeks' and 'a slight German accent', and opined that the case 'promises to be one of the most remarkable in criminal records.'[198] The reporter wrongly stated that Chapman and Maud had previously attended the same court as prosecutors in a wilful damage case on October 23rd. (She had died on the 22nd.)

Among Chapman's papers Godley had discovered a note suggesting that he had been to America, so he asked magistrate Paul Taylor not to allow bail, as there was nothing to prevent the prisoner from absconding across the Atlantic. Taylor remanded Chapman for eight days and enquired if the case might require three or

---

195 Adam claimed there were fourteen hearings; some of the press seventeen, but there were exactly sixteen: 27th October, 4th, 12th, 19th and 28th November; 5th, 12th, 17th, 24th and 31st December 1902; 7th, 14th, 21st and 28th January, and 4th and 11th February 1903.
196 Women were not permitted to serve on juries at any court, or to work as police officers, court officials, solicitors, barristers or coroners.
197 *Daily Mail*, 28th October 1902.
198 *Daily Express*, 28th October 1902.

The caption reads: 'THE ACCUSED MAN, CHAPMAN [far left], BEFORE THE MAGISTRATE, MR PAUL TAYLOR, AT THE SOUTHWARK POLICE COURT. Detective-inspector Godley [far right] giving evidence.' The inset picture depicts 'the arrest of Chapman in his billiard-room by Inspector Godley and Detective-sergeant Kemp'. From Shurey's Illustrated.

Chapman taking notes in the dock at Southwark police court, from Lloyd's Weekly.

four remands. Godley retorted, 'It may require a dozen if we have to exhume [the] bodies.' His was a good guess.

One of the multitudes avidly reading the details of Chapman's arrest for murder was Alfred Clarke, then languishing at His Majesty's Pleasure in Chelmsford Prison. He appealed to the governor, Captain Connor, arguing that, because Chapman's true character had been discovered, his own case should be re-examined. Connor did everything in his power to assist Clarke, who expected an early release. But Clarke was moved to Portland Prison, where Connor had no influence. His appeal was still processed, but more slowly.

The inquest into the death of Maud Marsh, conducted by coroner Dr Waldo, began on 28th October at Southwark coroner's court, which was housed in a former mission hall in a dingy backstreet called Collier's Rents.[199] The hall was separated from the Crown by a small public garden alongside St George-the-Martyr church. Owing to the morning papers' extensive coverage of the police court hearing and the fervent neighbourhood gossip, a large and unruly mob assembled outside, vying fiercely with one another to gain entry, eager to hear about the goings-on at the Crown, and — hopefully — to get their first ever glimpse of an actual murderer. Chapman's absence was, therefore, a huge disappointment.

The *Daily Mail* described the scene: 'In a roomy gallery facing the coroner's chair was a motley collection of tattered and battered humanity which had crowded in from the squalid approaches to Collier's-rents.'[200] Dr Waldo's chair was placed on the platform behind the rail whence preachers formerly addressed the congregation. On the wall were 'cheap Biblical pictures and scriptural texts, providing a strange setting for so gruesome a case'.[201] Solicitor Henry Sydney again represented Chapman, whilst E.H.A. Newman, who had lately defended Hilda Oxenford against Chapman's lawsuit, was engaged by the Marshes on a watching brief. The jury, having been sworn in, was taken across to the mortuary to see the corpse. Even in death Maud still looked 'young and comely'. One juryman described her as having 'dark hair and complexion, strongly marked eyebrows and aquiline nose, and a pleasing expression'.

Godley and Kemp gave evidence whilst the jury listened attentively and a gaggle of reporters took notes. The only civilian witness called was Robert Marsh. Described as a respectably dressed, 'tall stalwart man', he stated that he had identified his daughter's body. Dr Waldo set the date of the second, official post-mortem as 30th October and, to allow time for the associated report to be prepared, adjourned the inquest until 7th November (in the event, it resumed on 18th). Dr Waldo rose and left, followed by the uncalled witnesses and the jurors, and 'the tatterdemalion crowd of sightseers clattered noisily down the stairs and joined the unkempt women and dirty children in the street outside'.[202] According to one report, after the hearing Sergeant Kemp was 'closeted' at the former mission hall with 'two women who appeared very distressed'. They were anxious to tell the police some titbits about Chapman's life in Union Street, his behaviour during the Boer War and his fake wedding.[203]

---

199 Collier's Rents is now called Tennis Street.
200 *Daily Mail*, 29th October 1902.
201 *Daily Express*, 29th October 1902.
202 *Daily Mail*, 29th October 1902.
203 *The Echo*, 29th October 1902.

After news of Chapman's arrest appeared in the papers and was spread by the neighbourhood gossips, 'excited groups of sightseers' began to assemble at the Crown, obliging the police to maintain a constant presence. The pub, which was being run by a hired barman, was soon 'crowded night and day', despite its forlorn appearance: 'A tattered flag hangs from the window and the front of the house is still placarded with notices of "Seats to Let" for the royal procession.'[204]

The second post-mortem on Maud Marsh was carried out at St George's mortuary at dusk on Thursday, 30th October. It was superintended by a bushy-bearded Yorkshireman named Dr Thomas Stevenson, a toxicologist employed by the Home Office as a forensic analyst, who would one day be knighted for his services to public health. He was already a household name, having appeared as an expert witness in several high-profile murder trials involving poisoning, including those of Dr Lamson in 1882, Mrs Maybrick in 1889, Dr Thomas Neill Cream (the 'Lambeth Poisoner') in 1892 and Edward Bell in 1899. The post-mortem was conducted by James Stoker and Patrick Cotter (who had also performed the first) and Ludwig Freyberger. Freyberger was pathologist to the London County Council and had been personal physician to Friedrich Engels. Close at hand were Frank Gilbert (the mortuary keeper), Inspector Godley and Sergeant Kemp. Outside, a patient cabbie waited in attendance, seated on the bench seat of a horse-drawn four-wheeler.

The doctors could find no organic cause of death. Frank Gilbert had brought along the three glass jars given to him by Dr Stoker after the first post-mortem, and these and others were carefully placed in a large box which, after being corded and sealed, was sent in the waiting cab to Guy's Hospital for later examination by Drs Stevenson and Bodmer. After several days of tests, Stevenson was certain he knew how Maud had died: 'All the parts of her body', he later announced, 'were literally saturated with antimony. It was quite plain that a considerable dose must have been administered to her some few hours before her death.' He explained that the proportion of tartar emetic to antimony was roughly 3:1, so twenty grains of tartar emetic contained about seven grains of antimony. Two or three grains of antimony 'given repeatedly to a healthy person would eventually cause death'. Nearly four grains were found within Maud's corpse. Stevenson had analysed a bottle of brandy and water that Godley had found in Maud's bedroom and it contained enough antimony to kill someone.

The hearings at the police and coroner's courts were covered extensively by the national and provincial newspapers, whose reports were syndicated in the international press and published across the English-speaking world. The hugely popular Lloyd's Weekly devoted an entire broadsheet page of its 2nd November 1902 edition to a lengthy article that brought together everything about Chapman that had been published in other newspapers, to which it added some newly acquired anecdotes. The article was well illustrated with woodcuts, some drawn from the artist's imagination. Six days later a rival publication, Shurey's Illustrated, a low-class, sensationalist penny paper, printed a similarly splendid, double-page feature article recounting Chapman's life.[205] Both publications recounted word-for-word the same

---

204 Daily Express, 29th October 1902.
205 Launched in October 1899, it ran for 183 issues until April 1903.

*Maud Marsh's funeral cortege setting off from Messrs Alfred Smith and Co, Southwark Bridge Road, and 'disgraceful scenes' at the funeral. From the Illustrated Police News.*

anecdotes as well as printing their own exclusive tales. A week after *Shurey's* went to press, a scandal-sheet called the *Illustrated Police News* provided a host of artist's impressions depicting the *Mosquito* caught in a storm, Mary at the piano and Chapman wielding a cut-throat razor against the jowls of a customer.[206]

*Lloyd's* sold over a million copies a week, whilst the circulation of *Shurey's* and the *Illustrated Police News* fluctuated between 150,000 and 600,000. Each copy sold was, of course, read by several people. Having his case featured so prominently in these and other popular publications quickly launched Chapman into nation-wide infamy. However, most accounts of his life were littered with factual inaccuracies. This is not surprising, as the information had been hastily cobbled together from a variety of sources, including people who claimed to have known him, other inaccurate press reports and a trail of falsehoods laid by Chapman himself. The result was a hotchpotch of anecdotes, some factual, some fabricated, and some an amalgam of both, presented to a readership which lacked the resources to disentangle the truth from the lies.

The crowd that packed into the public gallery of the police court on Tuesday 4th November experienced great disappointment, for Chapman was visible for a mere five minutes, barely long enough for one reporter to note that he was 'a sallow-faced, gloomy individual',[207] and for another to comment that he 'appeared bright and cheerful, walked into the dock with a brisk step, and after bowing to the magistrate, cast a glance around the court'.[208] A policeman announced that his colleagues at Bishop's Stortford and Southwark were conducting a search for young William Spink, feared by some to have died at Chapman's hands. Although he knew where the boy was, Chapman withheld the information, causing the police unnecessary work. A florist appeared and asked Chapman to append his initials to a card that was to accompany a bespoke wreath he had ordered for Maud's funeral. That evening, her body was conveyed from the mortuary to the undertaker to be prepared and coffined, ready for her burial the following day.

Maud Marsh's funeral took place on 5th November. Although Chapman was not permitted to attend, he had readily consented to pay all the expenses. Nobody can accuse him of parsimony: her coffin was well-made and bore brass mountings. It was 'covered with a purple velvet pall, crossed with bands of gold lace and fringed with white'. Chapman had commissioned an elaborate, expensive wreath comprising lilies, tuberoses, camellias and pink chrysanthemums tied with a violet ribbon. The accompanying card bore the printed words *In Memoriam*, beneath which the florist had added — doubtless on Chapman's instructions — 'From a devoted friend.' It was signed with his initials in a shaky hand.

Owing to the substantial press coverage, hordes of 'morbid sightseers' assembled outside Alfred Smith's premises, undeterred by the 'drenching rainstorms'.[209] According to the *Angus Evening Telegraph*,

---

206 'How would they have felt,' remarked Gordon, 'if they had known they were being shaved by Jack the Ripper!' Gordon, R.M. (2000) *Alias Jack the Ripper: Beyond the Usual Whitechapel Suspects*, McFarland, p252.
207 *Shurey's Illustrated*, 8th November 1902.
208 *Manchester Courier*, 8th November 1902.
209 *Daily Express*, 6th November 1902.

> Not even the damp, grey, cheerless weather could prevent a large crowd assembling at the junction of Southwark Bridge Road and Friar Street...As early as nine o'clock eager-faced women and children were trying to peer through the windows of the room where Maude [sic] Marsh's body was.[210]

Some canny hawkers had thought of a way to profit from Chapman's notoriety: they dodged in and out of the crowd selling *In Memoriam* cards bearing the words 'In affectionate memory of Maude Marsh.' On another leaf was printed exactly the same popular verse as had appeared on Bessie Taylor's card: 'Farewell, my friends, fond and dear/Weep not for me a single tear/For all that was or could be done/You plainly see my time was come.' Below that were the additional lines: 'Past all pain forever/Done with sickness now/Those dear eyes are closed for ever/Peaceful is thy brow.'

At noon a hearse drawn by four horses appeared at the junction of Friar Street and Southwark Bridge Road to collect the coffin. About a thousand people — chiefly women — had gathered on the pavement, causing a serious obstruction at (what is still) a very busy junction. Chapman had provided quite a spectacle: 'Nothing was lacking in the way of ostentation', remarked the *Daily Express*. 'The horses had black plumes, decked with white ribbons, and black velvet trappings almost touching the ground.'[211] Chapman's generosity in providing Maud with a lavish funeral stands in stark contrast to his refusal to pay a penny towards Bessie's and his condemning Mary to a pauper's grave.

At ten past twelve, six bare-headed pallbearers carried the coffin out to the hearse. Men in the crowd removed their hats; women wept openly. Chapman's gorgeous wreath was placed upon the coffin and the procession trundled slowly southwards to the Marshes' home in Croydon. Maud's family climbed into two sombre mourning coaches, each of which was drawn by two grandly plumed horses. A mounted police inspector rode ahead of the procession and, although 'the rain descended in a pitiless manner', it seemed that the town's entire population had turned out. Thousands lined the streets leading from Longfellow Road to the chapel at Croydon Cemetery, where a 'vast assembly' had gathered, 'awaiting a new sensation'. The gawpers 'pushed and scrambled' as they 'fought madly for admission to the church' and 'women with tumbled hair and torn garments desecrated graves and overturned flowers in their determination to see the burial'.[212]

Amid such disgraceful behaviour two vicars — the Rev. Mr John Henry Crickmer, curate-in-charge of St Phillip's, Norbury, and the Rev. Mr Ernest Phillips, curate of St Saviour, Croydon — tried to impose some decorum onto the proceedings. However, as the coffin was placed in the chapel, 'many of the crowd made an unseemly rush for the doors'. After the service 'there was another unseemly rush to get a glimpse of the newly-made grave.' (It was later reported that, owing to these 'distressing scenes', the Metropolitan Police intended to keep the time and place of the burial of Edgar Edwards's victims 'as secret as possible'.)[213]

---

210 *Angus Evening Telegraph*, 6th November 1902.
211 *Daily Express*, 6th November 1902.
212 *Ibid.*
213 *Sheffield Daily Telegraph*, 7th January 1903.

Some of the mob expressed strong opinions about the presence of Chapman's showy wreath. A few days earlier, someone (H.L. Adam thinks it was Robert Marsh) had written to a newspaper promising that, if a wreath should be received from Maud's killer, it would not be allowed reach her grave. However, rather than cause a scene, or draw even more attention to the offending item by removing it, the Marsh family exhibited dignity and sagacity by leaving it atop the coffin as it was lowered into the grave; that way it was quickly out of sight rather than being allowed to upset mourners by appearing on display alongside their own floral tributes. Despite this, there were still 'indignant murmurs' from those who disapproved, and 'women permitted their tongues to carry them to strange lengths in expressing their views about the wreath'. As the coffin was lowered into the grave, 'a few girls threw modest offerings of white flowers' upon it, 'affording a touching relief to the unwholesome curiosity of the loafers and the strident women.'[214]

In his cell at Brixton Prison, Chapman read about Maud's funeral in the national newspapers. Mr Sydney told one reporter that his client was 'so bright and cheerful' that 'no one, who did not already know it, would imagine that he was on trial for his life'. He was eating and sleeping 'remarkably well' and was 'in good health and spirits'.[215] Maud and Chapman, Sydney asserted, 'lived happily together and never had an angry word'. This, he promised, 'will be confirmed by witnesses for the defence.'[216] However, although by 2nd November diligent police officers had amassed no fewer than twenty witnesses for the prosecution, Mr Sydney had not yet secured one for the defence. A few days later the police heard from a woman offering to be a witness to Chapman's innocence:

> It is stated that at the resumed inquest...a letter will be produced by the police which they this morning received from a woman who some time ago was in the employ of Chapman and the deceased woman and who also worked for the second Mrs Chapman [i.e. Bessie]. The writer alleges that she can, if necessary, prove from her own personal knowledge that both of the deceased women were in the habit of taking arsenic in small quantities for the purpose of producing a brilliancy to the eyes and hair.

The police instructed the letter-writer to present herself at the coroner's court, but she failed to put in an appearance and was never heard of again.[217]

With its licensee in prison for the foreseeable future, it was illegal for the Crown to trade, so arrangements were made for the licence to be transferred on 7th November to Arthur Charles Browne, a twenty-five-year-old barman.

Jessie Toon was arrested on 11th November for being drunk and disorderly. She told Southwark magistrates that 'certain men' had threatened to kill her if she gave evidence in the Chapman case. She was bound over to keep the peace.[218] On the same day the New York Evening Herald published the startling news that Chapman hailed from Boston, Massachusetts, where he had once been employed in a saloon. Scotland

---

214 Daily Express, 6th November 1902.
215 Manchester Courier, 8th November 1902.
216 Daily Mail, 31st October 1902.
217 Manchester Evening News, 10th November 1902.
218 Daily Mail, 12th November 1902.

Yard officials, it claimed, were in communication with Boston police in order to find out whatever they could about his life in the USA (they appear to have discovered nothing). The article made some additional erroneous statements, claiming that Maud fell sick after eating rabbit that Chapman had cooked, and that she died in a hospital, where suspicion was aroused because a doctor remembered that the previous Mrs Chapman had also died there.[219]

It was at the police court hearing of 12th November that evidence relating to the poisonings began to be heard. Archibald Bodkin KC, together with Francis John Sims, a clerk working in the Treasury Solicitor's department, appeared on behalf of the Treasury. Proceedings were brief and uneventful, and the public was excluded. Bodkin stated that, because the coroner's inquest was not yet complete, they proposed to hear only from Robert Marsh, and only on the subject of George Chapman's relationship with Maud and Chapman's reaction when Dr Grapel was consulted. Mrs Marsh, clad in deep mourning and wearing a black veil, listened in silence. Chapman was remanded for another week.

During the second sitting of the coroner's inquest, on 18th November, Collier's Rents was again swarming with gawpers, many of whom stood in the street throughout the four-hour hearing. 'The motley crowd outside were rewarded for their wait in the biting wind by a glimpse of Chapman as he was driven past in a four-wheeled cab and handcuffed to two stalwart warders', the local paper commented.[220] Superintendent Walters and Chief Inspector Richard Bonner were in court, along with Godley and Kemp, described as 'the two smart officers...who have the whole case in hand.'[221] Dr Waldo announced that he had applied to the Home Secretary for an order to exhume Bessie Taylor's remains.

Chapman entered the court 'haggard and pale, although he endeavoured to look cheerful'. When the Marshes arrived he had the barefaced impudence to give them 'a smiling nod of recognition'.[222] Their three daughters each gave evidence. Louisa revealed that Maud had never set eyes on her own marriage certificate. She admitted belabouring Maud on the subject, insisting that 'the certificate is the first thing a husband gives his wife' and repeatedly asked if she really was legally married. Eventually Maud had snapped: 'Yes I am! So there!' Louisa shared Maud's revelation that Chapman pulled her hair and banged her head.[223] She then divulged an even more distressing and deeply shocking secret — that Chapman had been in the habit of injecting Maud's womb with carbolic, because 'he did not wish to have a family until he had made enough [money] to retire'.[224]

The clerk of the court called the loquacious Jessie Toon. According to the Daily Mail, her evidence 'poured out like a river', which 'provoked loud guffaws among the crowd in the gallery'. The paper called her a 'twentieth-century Mrs Gamp'[225] and noted that even Chapman, 'seated between two giant warders', had 'leaned forward

219 The Evening Herald, 11th November 1902.
220 Southwark & Bermondsey Recorder, 22nd November 1902.
221 Ibid.
222 Manchester Courier, 22nd November 1902.
223 Ibid.
224 The Echo, 18th November 1902.
225 A Dickens character who was an alcoholic, untrained midwife and nurse.

*Lymm churchyard and the exhumation of Bessie, from the Illustrated Police News. The two coffins on the left are, presumably, those of Bessie's parents.*

## THE SOUTHWARK MYSTERY.
THE BODY OF THE SECOND MRS. CHAPMAN EXHUMED.

on the wooden form and smiled'.[226] Mrs Toon 'created a profound sensation' when she stated that one sip of the brandy Chapman had served to Maud 'burned my lips and mouth and made tears come to my eyes'. This echoed Mrs Marsh's experience, and it raises some questions. The incidents were clear evidence that Chapman had deliberately laced the drinks with poison, and yet — incredibly — neither woman told Stoker, or Grapel, or the police when they arrested Chapman. Did the women conspire to exaggerate or even invent the incidents to support the charge against Chapman?

In the police court on 19th November Chapman was charged with 'feloniously killing and slaying' Maud Marsh and remanded for a further eight days. Afterwards another Mr Chapman, who had been following the case avidly in the newspapers, entered the witness box and requested an interview with the prisoner, whom he hoped was his long-lost brother George, a hairdresser from north London who had emigrated to America twenty years previously. The man was duly taken down to the cells, but upon seeing Chapman knew instantly that he was mistaken. When told why the man had peered at him, Chapman remarked that he had no brother.

In late October, soon after details of Chapman's previous victims had been published in the press, the Manchester Courier reported that, 'In Lymm and the surrounding villages, and also in Warrington, the case is the subject of much comment.' St Mary's churchyard had suddenly become 'an object of melancholy interest to the natives of the locality and visitors'.[227] On Sunday 2nd November 'scores of bicycles lined the churchyard wall' whilst their owners assembled around the grave of Bessie and her parents.[228] Because of this, after news of Dr Waldo's request for the exhumation of her body was made public,

> Great efforts are being made to keep the proceedings secret, and perhaps to throw people off the scent the official has engaged rooms in Lymm, as though intending to stay in the village for several days. There have been so many false alarms that the public were beginning to think there would be no disinterment.[229]

However, word got out: on the evening of 21st November small groups of 'curious sightseers' began to loiter in the darkness around Bessie's grave. As the clock struck twelve, 'a large crowd collected in the neighbourhood of the picturesque churchyard, but a strong force of a dozen police constables kept all the morbid sightseers at a distance'.[230] At that time Mr Tull, shop manager to undertaker Alfred Smith, was just leaving London on the midnight train. His duties were to identify the nameplate he had attached to the coffin, and then to unfasten the lid. Whilst a cordon of police blocked the road, the exhumation began at 4am on Saturday, 22nd November. A newspaper described the proceedings:

> The grave in which the second Mrs Chapman lay beneath her mother and father was surrounded by the screen of white sheets, and at five o'clock in the morning gravediggers commenced the task of exhumation with the aid of lanterns. The morning was bitterly cold, and the ground

226 Daily Mail, 19th November 1902.
227 Manchester Courier, 31st October 1902.
228 Manchester Courier, 8th November 1902.
229 Manchester Courier, 22nd November 1902.
230 Penny Illustrated Paper, 29th November 1902.

was frozen to a depth of several inches. The work of bringing the three coffins to the surface was accomplished at eight o'clock, and they were arranged in a row by the side of the grave. As the morning wore on curious villagers gathered around the churchyard, but they were told by the police that the exhumation had taken place on Thursday, and they passed on. At ten o'clock Dr Stevenson, expert to the Home Office, drove up to the cemetery in a carriage, accompanied by two assistants. The trio immediately proceeded to a temporary mortuary, a hut at the far end of the cemetery, where the coffin containing the body of Mrs Bessie Chapman was brought for examination.

At this time those present in the cemetery were Dr Stevenson, his two assistants, the clergyman who holds the benefice of Lymm parish, Detective-inspector Godley, Mr W. Tulle [sic], assistant to undertaker Mr A. Smith of Southwark Bridge Road, two brothers of Bessie Chapman, and the husband of Bessie Chapman's sister. Mr Tulle scraped the dirt off the plate on the coffin, and displayed the simple inscription, and at once proceeded to unscrew the lid of the coffin. The body was found to be in fair condition and the two brothers easily identified it. Under the personal direction of Dr Stevenson, the two assistants removed the chief organs of the body and placed them in square glass jars. The remains of Bessie Chapman were replaced in the coffin, and the three coffins were again interred, the clergyman reading the funeral service over the fresh interment. The three gravediggers filled in the grave, and the stone was carefully replaced.[231]

Considering she had died nearly two years previously, Bessie's body was found to be extraordinarily well-preserved. This is a side effect of antimony, which speeds up mummification.

A few days later, during the 25th November sitting of the inquest, evidence was heard from Miss Cole, Frank Gilbert and William Bird, and Drs Stoker, Grapel and Targett. This sitting excited enormous public interest because the findings of the post-mortem on Maud Marsh were due to be announced. Despite knowing that his terrible crime was about to be publicly exposed, Chapman 'walked into court with an almost sprightly step'. His subsequent body language, however, 'betrayed a nervousness which was justified by the gravity of the occasion...the hand which held the morning paper trembled noticeably'. When Dr Waldo consulted with Godley, Chapman's eyes 'furtively watched the two as they talked earnestly together'.[232]

Costermonger William Bird of 88 Broadwall, New Cut, was questioned about the rabbit he had supplied to the household. Aged forty-six, he had been in the same trade for eighteen years. The customer would choose a rabbit and he'd skin it and cut it up on the spot. 'Sometimes I sell two hundred on a Saturday', he boasted. Most were frozen, imported from New Zealand, and were 'Beautiful rabbits — no better can be got!'[233] Miss Cole, the servant at the Crown, was certain that the rabbit she cooked had not caused Maud's gastric problems, because the rest of the household ate it without ill effects. She thrilled the public gallery with the revelations that Chapman used to

231 *Southwark & Bermondsey Recorder*, 29th November 1902.
232 *The Echo*, 25th November 1902.
233 *Daily Mail*, 26th November 1902.

order her out of the kitchen when he prepared items for Maud, including tumblers of mysterious, milky-white liquid.

When Dr Stoker gave evidence he disclosed that Maud and Chapman were not married. Mr and Mrs Marsh 'peered curiously at the accused, who turned his head in the opposite direction', as well he might, since the revelation brought shame on the Marsh family by exposing to the world that their daughter, a mere teenager, had agreed to live 'in sin' with a man twice her age and, apparently, with their consent. As Stoker described Maud's illness, his visits, his conversations with the accused and how Dr Grapel came to be involved, Chapman 'made copious notes on a piece of official paper, looking out from under his eyebrows at the coroner'. Stoker informed the court that Dr Bodmer, the public analyst, had found 'an appreciable amount' of arsenic in Maud's digestive system. Conscious of the gravity of that announcement, those present suddenly fell silent and 'the accused became the subject of every gaze. He fidgeted uneasily afterwards, and then he smiled grimly.'[234] The next witness, Dr Grapel, recounted his visit to Maud and explained what had led him to suspect she was being poisoned.

At the police court on 28th November, the lanky but graceful frame of Mr (later, Sir) Herbert Beerbohm Tree was seated on the bench alongside magistrate Cecil Chapman during the greater part of the proceedings. Tree was an illustrious thespian, a celebrated theatre manager and founder of the Royal Academy of Dramatic Arts, who usually hobnobbed with MPs and aristocrats. During the hearing Chapman appeared 'perfectly calm and collected'.[235] He listened carefully as Mrs Marsh and Louisa Morris — the latter described as Maud's 'not very smartly clad married sister'[236] — told the harrowing tale of Maud's gruesome illness and excruciating death. Louisa spoke of Chapman's attentiveness to Maud, but also recounted his curious remarks about giving her 'a bit like that' and 'fifty doctors could not find out'. Her deposition was followed by that of her sisters, Alice and Daisy, the former revealing Chapman's tactlessness in inviting her to take Maud's place at the Crown; the latter describing the day of the sham wedding.

A week later Chapman 'stepped briskly into the dock, dropped his cap smartly by his side, and sat down'.[237] Mrs Marsh described her bout of sickness and diarrhoea after taking a tiny sip of Maud's brandy. Jessie Toon corroborated Mrs Marsh's story and told the court that Chapman refused her a glass of spirits, because 'when she drank, she talked'. According to one report, 'There were some heated passages between this witness and Mr Sydney...concerning an alleged injection made by the nurse on the girl's arm, which the witness stoutly denied.'[238] Mrs Toon was followed by Miss Cole, Mr Gilbert, Dr Targett, Dr Grapel and the coroner's clerk.

At 2pm on 9th December at St Patrick's Cemetery, Leytonstone, with Godley and the cemetery superintendent in attendance, six gravediggers began their unenviable labours. Within just two hours daylight had disappeared and a lantern and lighted candles were placed around Mary Spink's grave whilst a canvas sheet sheltered the

---

234 All quotes in this paragraph are from *The Echo*, 25th November 1902.
235 *Lloyd's Weekly*, 30th November 1902.
236 *Southwark & Bermondsey Recorder*, 22nd November 1902.
237 *Manchester Courier*, 6th December 1903.
238 *The Penny Illustrated Paper*, 13th December, 1902. The 6th December edition of the *British Journal of Nursing* was furious at Mrs Toon, a mere *charwoman*, being described as 'a nurse.'

diggers from the icy wind. By 9pm six of the seven coffins that had been buried on top of Mary's had been hauled out. The coffin immediately above Mary's was brought to the surface the next morning, followed by Mary's. The stench from the rotting cadavers was reported to be stomach-churning.

As was the case with Bessie Taylor, Mary's corpse was extraordinarily well-preserved. Elizabeth Waymark, in attendance to identify Mary, declared that 'the face was perfect'. Sergeant Neil thought it 'the most wonderful sight I have ever seen — a corpse five years buried as fresh-looking almost as though in life'. According to Neil, Dr Stevenson exclaimed, 'Remarkable, Wonderful! Just as I expected!'[239] During the post-mortem Stevenson found no sign of phthisis, the cause of death cited by Dr Rogers. In his opinion Mary Spink, like Bessie Taylor, had died of gastroenteritis brought about by antimony poisoning.

Press coverage of the case saved the police a considerable amount of work, for people from Chapman's past came forward. The most important was William Davison, formerly a pharmacist in Hastings. The investigating officers knew his name from the poison label they had discovered hidden inside one of Chapman's books, but they could not trace him because he had moved away. Reading about the Southwark Poisoner in the newspapers, Davison — who had retired to Brighton — went to his local town hall and made a statement. At the police court on 12th December, thirty-one-year-old Detective Sergeant Charles Gilpin Bradford of Hastings police — who had been in the force for nine years and remembered Chapman's barbershop — presented the poison register from Davison's former pharmacy.[240] It had been signed by George Chapman in April 1897, recording his purchase of one ounce of tartar emetic.

The remainder of the hearing was taken up with Drs Stoker, Bodmer and Stevenson describing Maud Marsh's illness and treatment and pontificating on the finer points of arsenic and antimony. Chapman, who 'looked better in health and appeared more cheerful than formerly, listened with marked attention to the statements of the various witnesses and made copious notes, some of which he passed to his solicitor'.[241]

On 17th December, just before the police court hearing began, Godley and Kemp entered the pub opposite and requested that the landlord and all his male customers follow them. Augmented with a few more recruits enlisted from passers-by, a row of twenty assorted men was assembled in the yard of the court. Chapman was placed at random among them. Mr Davison donned his pince-nez and strode along the line. As well as selling him tartar emetic and secondhand medical books, Davison had been shaved by Chapman on numerous occasions, and they had often engaged in interesting discussions. He was, therefore, able to pick him out without the slightest hesitation.

That day the courtroom was crowded to utmost capacity. After Dr Bodmer spoke about finding antimony in Maud's body, Davison told the court exactly where and when Chapman had obtained it. This damning evidence thrilled the spectators, whose excitement was increased by hearing the next witness's juicy revelations, because these concerned Chapman's sexual immorality. An attractive young

239 Neil, A.F. (1932) *Forty Years of Manhunting*, Jarrolds, p15.
240 The shop was by then in the hands of chemist and druggist Ernest William Shipman.
241 *Southwark & Bermondsey Recorder*, 15th December 1902.

woman entered the witness box and gave her name as Florence Rayner. Chapman, who 'throughout the hearing had been very pale and nervous',[242] 'looked up from the iron rails of the dock and fixed his gaze earnestly — even eagerly — upon her'.[243] She told a hushed court about Chapman's stolen kisses and his entreaties to elope. As she recounted his promise to give Maud 'something' and there would be 'no more Mrs Chapman', she fainted. The *Daily Mail* attributed her collapse to 'the heaviness of the atmosphere', and indeed there was no fresh air in the overcrowded courtroom. Whilst she was 'tenderly carried out and cared for in an adjoining room', the prosecutor took the opportunity to grill Dr Stoker once again. On her return Miss Rayner recounted how Chapman had ejected her when she requested a reference, had her arrested on a trumped-up charge, and then visited her new workplace to inform her that she had scuppered her chances of being with him at the Crown.

At the final sitting of the coroner's inquest, on 18th December, Chapman — though 'pale, hollow-eyed and gaunt' — chatted pleasantly to his warders, referring from time to time to a newspaper which he carried.[244] He again gave a nod of recognition to the Marsh family as they entered the old mission hall, dressed in deep mourning. Dr Waldo heard from Godley, Mrs Marsh and her daughters Louisa and Alice, Miss Rayner, Mrs Toon, Miss Cole, Mr Gilbert and six doctors — Stoker, Grapel, Targett, Stevenson, Bodmer and Freyberger.

Godley produced Chapman's collection of medical books and Davison's handwritten poison label. He again described the circumstances of the arrest, and Chapman's repeated protestations of innocence. Dr Freyberger asserted that, with regard to the findings of the post-mortem, he agreed with the conclusions reached by the other doctors. The remaining witnesses repeated the evidence they had given in the police court. When Louisa Morris spoke, Chapman 'smiled and at times almost laughed, but followed each word intently and made notes'.[245]

Dr Waldo announced that the chemist Mr Davison would not be giving evidence because he had arrived late at Brighton station and missed his train. He then summed up the case for the benefit of the jury. They were obliged to conclude that Maud's death was due to antimonial poisoning; their sole task was to decide how it had entered her system. Did Maud take it herself or did someone give it to her? If they thought Chapman had deliberately killed her they should return a verdict of wilful murder. Presumably, the jurymen stood outside in the cold during their twenty-minute deliberation because, two years later, Dr Waldo was to complain that the former mission hall was not a fit place to conduct inquests, mainly because there was nowhere but the street for juries to retire and discuss the case. Whilst awaiting the verdict, Mrs Marsh and Miss Rayner engaged in 'animated converse'.[246] (One wonders what Maud's mother had to say to the young woman, knowing she had flirted with Chapman and enjoyed his kisses while Maud pulled pints downstairs.) When the jury filed back in, Chapman's gaze was 'fixed on the floor'. The foreman of the jury announced the results of their discussion: the antimony found in Maud's

---

242 *Penny Illustrated Paper*, 20th December 1902.
243 *Daily Mail*, 18th December 1902.
244 *Daily Express*, 19th December 1902.
245 *The Echo*, 18th November 1902.
246 *Daily Express*, 19th December 1902.

body had been administered by George Chapman. The coroner thanked the jurymen and exempted them from further service for five years. Later he would issue a warrant indicting Chapman to be tried at the Central Criminal Court for wilful murder once the magisterial enquiry was completed.

The jury's verdict was a devastating blow for Chapman, and it comes as no surprise that, at the ninth hearing at the police court, on Christmas Eve, he entered the dock 'trembling' and 'appeared very ill'.[247] Fortunately for him, he was obliged to stand for barely a minute, purely in order to be remanded for a further seven days. He was then whisked back to Brixton Prison in the usual police four-wheeler to celebrate his final Christmas.

## CLARKE'S RELEASE

Meanwhile, in Chelmsford Prison, Alfred Clarke spent six weeks pursuing his third attempt to obtain a release. On 4th November he sent a fresh petition to the Home Secretary claiming unfair conviction. All of Clarke's appeals cited perjury by the Chapmans, prompting a civil servant to scrawl: 'This man will go on for ever harping on this "perjury" string' on Clarke's third petition. Soon afterwards, Clarke received assistance from beyond the grave: Mr Marsh told his solicitor that, on her death-bed, Maud had confessed to perjury. This information spread quickly to all the relevant parties, including Melville Macnaghten, chief constable of the CID of the Metropolitan Police,[248] who sent a memo about the case to the Under Secretary of State at the Home Office. On 13th December, Clarke submitted a fourth appeal against his conviction.

Richard Loveland Loveland, who had overseen Clarke's case, was consulted and, on 18th December, he wrote to the Home Office to say that he still saw no grounds to release and pardon him. Although it now seemed that Chapman had indeed lied about £700 having been borrowed against defunct shares, Clarke was still guilty of the offence; it was merely the amount that was reduced. He referred the petition to the Secretary of State. Civil servants at the Home Office disagreed with Mr Loveland Loveland. One of them, Frederick Dryhurst, believed there were grounds for Clarke's release and his superior, Henry Simpson, principal clerk in the criminal department of the Home Office, annotated the petition with his own comments:

> A very difficult case. It is impossible to arrive at anything approaching certainty about the real facts, but seeing how very untrustworthy the evidence for the prosecution now appears to have been, I agree [with Dryhurst]...If Chapman's evidence was so untrue as Mr Loveland Loveland thinks it to have been, there is very little left to support the conviction. Money was no doubt obtained from Chapman, but it by no means follows that it was obtained by a false pretence. Chapman can scarcely have believed that a man would part with a £1,000 share certificate carrying 4½% in order to raise a loan of £2. It is possible that he knew that the jury would not accept a story like that and so increased a hundredfold the amount he had lent.

247 *Daily Mail*, 1st January 1903.
248 Sir Melville Macnaghten CB KPM (1853–1921) became Asst Commissioner (Crime) of the London Metropolitan Police in 1903. In 1894 Macnaghten had compiled a report on the Ripper murders.

In between the weekly police court hearings, Godley and his team had been engaged in establishing Chapman's antecedents, collecting snippets of his life and fitting them together like random pieces of a jigsaw puzzle. Now he knew that Chapman was a habitual liar, Sergeant Kemp decided to examine some banknotes belonging to Chapman, that the police still had in their possession. They were found at the Crown in October, and yet their serial numbers were those of the notes Chapman swore on oath he had given to Oxenford six months before. Kemp informed Godley, who advised the Home Office. This new information was enough to tip the scales in Clarke's favour, and on 29th December 1902 he was given an unconditional release, having served six months of a three-year sentence.

A decade later Kemp was to recall his satisfaction in being able 'to procure the release of a wrongfully-convicted man',[249] but Clarke was a career criminal and was soon back behind bars: he was sentenced at Chelmsford Assizes to fifteen months' hard labour for long firm frauds.

## POLISH ROOTS DISCOVERED

Most of Chapman's documents were written in Russian, and when Joseph Petrykowski translated them he soon discovered that 'George Chapman' was in fact a Pole called Kłosowski. Godley must have suspected something of the sort from the man's accent. Whilst the Marsh family had never doubted that he was American, they were simple folk living in a sleepy suburban town, unlikely to have ever conversed with either a Pole or an American. But Godley had heard the speech of many eastern Europeans during his years as a bobby in the East End; he had also probably conversed with a sufficient number of Americans to realise that Chapman's accent resembled the former and not the latter.

Godley and his team had been busy gathering statements from witnesses in Leytonstone, Tottenham and Hastings. By Christmas they had found Levisohn and Wicken (who had recognised Chapman from sketches in the papers). When shown Chapman's recent 'mugshot' photos, one front-facing and the other in profile, the pair were certain he was the barber they had known more than a decade previously.

To make sure the paperwork was correct and would not lead to Chapman's acquittal on a technicality, in preparation for the next police court hearing on 31st December Godley drew up a fresh charge of the wilful murder of Maud Marsh, this time against 'Severino Klosowski.' ('Severino' was a corruption created by the rendition of 'Seweryn', firstly into Russian Cyrillic script and then into English.) Chapman continued to display superb acting skills: not only was he mystified by the charge of murder, he also had no idea how it was committed. 'By what means?' he asked, seemingly perplexed: 'Stabbing, shooting, or what?' Upon hearing his birth name he declared, 'I do not know the other fellow', and when the charge was read to him a second time he enquired: 'Who is the other fellow?' Godley clarified the situation in the simplest possible terms: 'That is you,' he explained, 'we call you Severino Klosowski, otherwise George Chapman.' The accused man persisted in his feigned bewilderment: 'I do not know anything about the other name'.

---

249 'Adventures of A Detective: Scotland Yard Sleuth Tells of Odd Experiences Hunting Criminals.' *Washington Post*, 26th October 1913.

As the year drew to a close the *Daily Mail* remarked, 'The Southwark poisoning mystery, the most sensational since the trial of Mrs Maybrick, bids fair to eclipse that case in public interest.'[250] On 31st December, members of the public again vied with one another to obtain one of the few available seats inside Southwark police court, which was 'crowded in every part', as were 'the approaches thereto'. One newsman remarked: 'Though the case has now been before the public for two months, interest in it increases rather than diminishes.'[251] Among those who did manage to wangle himself a seat at Chapman's tenth hearing was a famous actor wearing a beautiful silk top hat. Harry Brodribb Irving was the thirty-two-year-old son of the internationally celebrated Sir Henry Irving, the first actor to receive a knighthood. 'H.B.', as he was always called, had trained as a barrister before opting for a career on the stage. He still took a keen interest in matters legal, was a member of various criminological societies, and attended trials in order to 'study human nature in the dock'.

Most of the morning was taken up with hearing the final pieces of evidence relating to the death of Maud Marsh. DC Frederick Pusey explained that the undertaker Alfred Smith had failed to respond to a witness summons, and so a warrant was obtained to oblige him to attend. He arrived shortly afterwards and related the events of 22nd October — the day Maud died.

During the luncheon adjournment, Chapman — who presented 'an unusually haggard appearance'[252] — was taken across the road to the police station and formally charged with the wilful murders of Mary Spink and Bessie Taylor.

Archibald Bodkin KC, Counsel for the Treasury, kicked off the afternoon session by presenting a garbled version of Chapman's — or rather, Kłosowski's — antecedents. The local paper described it as 'a story of exceptional interest, and such a one as has been seldom, if ever, heard at Southwark police-court'.[253] The defendant was 'hanging his head and moving uneasily on his seat in the dock' as Bodkin recounted his life story 'in a calm and unemotional manner'. His ninety-minute speech was awash with mistakes: Chapman was Jewish, attended military school, passed examinations in medicine and surgery, abandoned his wife in Poland and had known Levisohn in Warsaw. Bodkin got names, places and dates wrong throughout, and yet, according to *The Times*, his 'accuracy in detail was never at fault'.[254] (To be fair, he was probably relying on information collated by his colleague Francis Sims.) When Bodkin had finished, Inspector Godley injected renewed excitement into the proceedings by announcing that he had removed a fully loaded, five-chambered revolver from Chapman's bedroom.

A General Chapman and a clergyman named Chapman sat on the bench alongside magistrate Cecil Chapman.[255] One can imagine all three giving a collective sigh of relief at hearing the news that the prisoner's real surname was Kłosowski.

---

250. Found guilty of poisoning her husband with arsenic, Maybrick was at that time twelve years into her life sentence. *Daily Mail*, 30th December 1902.
251 *Sheffield Daily Telegraph*, 1st January 1903.
252 *The Echo*, 31st December 1902.
253 *Southwark & Bermondsey Recorder*, 3rd January 1903.
254 *The Times*, 3rd January 1958. The obituary of Sir Archibald Bodkin.
255 *Daily Express*, 1st January 1903.

As the final police court hearing of 1902 drew to a close, someone reported that Willie Spink had been found safe and well and living in Hornchurch Cottage Homes.[256] Chapman was remanded for yet another week and, as he climbed into a police van, 'a large crowd assembled outside the court to witness his departure'.[257]

Godley's team continued its work. Having learned something of Kłosowski's life in Poland from his translated documents, by early January officers were building up a picture of his years in London by taking statements from the Baderskis, John Ward, Joseph Renton, William Wengel and Ethel Radin in preparation for the recommencement of the police court proceedings on 7th January 1903. Just before that hearing began, there occurred what one newsman dubbed 'a sensational incident':

> A small but important drama was enacted in the courtyard. Selecting with scrupulous fairness men of about the same height as Chapman from the crowd waiting to get inside, Inspector Godley ranged them in a line and told the prisoner to stand where he liked. Chapman... stepped briskly to near the middle of the line. Then a woman came into the courtyard. Without hesitation, after a single glance, she walked up to the prisoner and, with a finger outstretched, said, 'That is my husband.'[258]

Arthur Fowler Neil, who was a police sergeant at the time, told the story quite differently in his 1932 memoirs. He claimed that Chapman immediately denied knowing Lucy and she remonstrated, in English, 'Ah Severino, don't say that! You remember the time you nearly killed me in Jersey City?'[259] Inspector Godley did not mention this incident when he gave evidence, indicating that Neil made it up. Nevertheless, several decades later R.M. Gordon embellished the story: 'This was the first time the police had heard of his attack on his wife,' he wrote, 'and they would explore that episode in later interviews with Lucy.'[260]

Chapman's appearance at the police court continued to attract huge public interest. The scene outside was described evocatively in *The Echo*:

> A large, struggling, albeit well-dressed crowd surged round the two small doors of the Court, clamouring for admission. They stood there swaying to and fro in a most uncomfortable manner for over half an hour. The tedium of the wait was suddenly broken by one of the doors opening and an officer calling out, 'Reporters first.' Immediately from in front, in the middle, and on the fringe notebooks and pencils appeared above the heads of the crowd, and, after much struggling, pushing, and shoving, the Pressmen were able to get inside the Court, and the more fortunate quickly seized upon the few available seats, Then the public were allowed to surge in, and they stood packed like the proverbial sardines in the limited space at the back of the dock.[261]

---

256 A home for unwanted or orphaned children, comprising a hamlet of eleven houses, each one in the charge of foster parents and containing about thirty children.
257 *Southwark & Bermondsey Recorder*, 3rd January 1903.
258 *Daily Mail*, 8th January 1903.
259 Neil, A.F. (1932) *Forty Years of Manhunting*, Jarrolds, p27.
260 Gordon, R.M. (2008). *The Poison Murders of Jack the Ripper*, McFarland, p110.
261 *The Echo*, 7th January 1903.

At 12.20pm Chapman stepped briskly into the dock, attired in a black morning coat and continuations, and wearing a mourning tie, as befitted a recently widowed man. He carried a large bundle of papers and sported a small pencil behind his ear. The charge sheet was read out: 'George Chapman, thirty-six, licensed victualler, did feloniously kill and slay Maud Marsh by administering arsenic [sic] to her on 22nd October 1902; Severin Klosowski, otherwise George Chapman, His Majesty's Prison, Brixton, publican, feloniously, wilfully, and of malice aforethought killing and murdering Mary Isabella Spink on 25th day of December 1897...further feloniously, wilfully, and of malice aforethought killing and murdering Elizabeth [sic] (Bessie) Taylor on 13th day of February 1901.'

Alfred Clarke's barrister, Martin O'Connor, was given permission to address the court. He explained that on 3rd January a writ had been issued against Chapman by his client, who was intent upon exacting redress for the six long, miserable months he had spent in prison owing to Chapman's perjury. O'Connor objected to Mr Sydney's application for £110 of Chapman's cash, then being held by the police, to be released, as he wanted it retained against possibly winning damages for his client. It appears that the writ failed.[262]

Proceedings then began and the first witness called was Wolff Levisohn, 'a slightly-built, middle-aged Jew'. He was extremely talkative, frequently emphatic, easily excitable, entertaining and sometimes comical — causing even Mr Sydney to laugh out loud. As his fellow Pole spoke, Chapman 'was busy taking voluminous notes, and covered several sheets of foolscap paper'.[263] From time to time he handed them to the gaoler, who passed them on to Mr Sydney.

Levisohn's verbose anecdotes used up the whole morning. (As his words were repeated at the Old Bailey, they will be included later.) The court adjourned for luncheon and as Chapman left the dock he was hissed at by the crowd. When the hearing reconvened, 'The rough scenes witnessed in the admission of the public at the opening were re-enacted...and the Court became even more uncomfortably crowded.'[264]

Amongst those present was Lucy Kłosowska, described as 'a tall, well-built woman with sallow skin and dark hair, adorned with fur and feathers'[265] (in other reports she is fair-haired). She was stylishly dressed in a black fur jacket, a brown fur boa and a hat decorated with long, white feathers. Although only thirty-one, a reporter from The Echo called her 'middle-aged'.[266] As she stepped forward to be formally identified by her brother, all eyes fell upon her. She initially stood behind Chapman, but as he turned around to look at her she swiftly stepped behind the partition of the reporters' box, where she remained throughout the hearing.[267]

Despite several authors' claims to the contrary, Lucy did not take the witness stand. A wife could not be compelled to give evidence against her husband and, in any case, she could contribute nothing in respect to the three poisonings. She apparently

262 Manchester Courier, 7th January 1903.
263 The Echo, 7th January 1903.
264 Ibid.
265 Northampton Mercury, 9th January 1903.
266 The Echo, 7th January 1903.
267 Lincolnshire Chronicle, 9th January 1903.

made a written statement to the police about her association with Chapman, but as his file has since been lost or destroyed we do not know what she told them.

Lucy's brother Stanisław Baderski and sister Stanisława Rauch each took the witness stand. Stanisław related the story of Lucy's courtship and marriage, detailing where they lived and where Chapman worked until Lucy left him in the summer of 1892. Stanisława was 'a tall, good-looking woman, dressed in a light blue serge dress, surmounted with a brown fur boa, and wearing a black semi-picture hat'. A reporter captured her broken English:

> The first day I come over I see him, before even I see my sister, and the man in the dock he is the same. Two children were born to my sister, and then she leave [with] her husband and go to America. [Mr Bodkin asked: 'did she return from America?'] Yes, she lived then with he in the dock in Scarborough-street. [Did he ever tell you anything about himself?] He tell me not much, but that he had been a feldsher in hospital of the Infant Jesus, near Warsaw. [Did you see a lot of men near the Court this morning?] Yes; and when I see him I nodded and said, 'It is him.'[268]

None of Chapman's documents contained any reference to the Hospital of the Infant Jesus, so either he lied about that, or Stanisława misremembered his words.[269] Neither of Lucy's siblings breathed a word or even hinted that Chapman ever threatened Lucy, or was unfaithful or unkind to her. Mr Sydney's cross-examination of the siblings focussed on trying to shake their confidence in Chapman's identity, but they stood firm and Mrs Rauch 'repeated emphatically that she was not mistaken'. Alfred Wicken, 'a tall, well-built, dark-haired young man', also identified Chapman as Kłosowski, the Polish barber with whom he had worked at Haddon's.[270]

Joseph Renton recounted his cousin Mary Spink's childhood and the family's move to Leytonstone. He told the court that when he last saw Mary in 1896, she was using Chapman's surname, but the two men had never met.

The following week, 14th January, the court was 'again packed, whilst the press was represented by nearly a score of artists and reporters'. Once again men passing on the street were picked at random to form an identity parade. The witnesses that day were Mrs Ethel Radin; a Hastings contingent comprising Mrs Annie Helsdown, Mrs Harriet Greenaway, Miss Alice Penfold, Mrs Elizabeth Martin and Mr Alfred Constable; Mr Bray; Mr George Schumann; Mrs Martha Doubleday and Inspector George Godley. Chapman was 'complacently wearing now and then just a shadow of a smile' as he 'viewed the scene with the imperturbability of a distinguished spectator'.[271]

Mrs Radin and Mr Schumann identified George Chapman as Kłosowski, as did Mr Bray, though he was so short-sighted that the magistrate permitted him to leave the witness box and approach the dock. After squinting at Chapman, Mr Bray told the court about Annie Chapman, whom he described as a 'young girl', and

268 The Echo, 7th January 1903.
269 Ignatius Knaster, in a letter published in the Southwark & Bermondsey Recorder on 31st January 1903, claimed that his brother, a house physician at the Infant Jesus Hospital in the 1880s, had checked the records and discovered that no Seweryn Kłosowski was ever employed there.
270 The Echo, 7th January 1903.
271 The Echo, 14th January 1903.

Chapman taking notes in the dock at Southwark police court, from Lloyd's Weekly.

A sample of Chapman's handwriting. The words 'This statement is true' and his signature, from his witness statement during the shares scam case. From the National Archives.

A drawing from the Penny Illustrated Paper. The caption reads: '"Chapman" entering the prison van at Southwark police court before being committed for trial on the charge of murder. (From a Snap-Shot taken by R. Shield.)' Chapman was depicted as taller than he was. He appears to be the same height as the policemen, but he was 5ft 5, and no man was recruited to the police if he was under 5ft 10.

*this statement is true*

*george chapman*

revealed that Chapman had got her 'into trouble' — by which he meant pregnant outside of marriage. Mesdames Helsdown and Greenaway, who had each lived in the same house as Chapman in Hastings, recounted their respective recollections. Mrs Helsdown remembered Mary's cries, bruises and green vomit and her words were corroborated by Elizabeth Martin and Alfred Constable. Mrs Greenaway recalled that Mary Spink had shown her Chapman's revolver and that she had lent the couple her costly set of Cassell's *Family Physician*, which had never been returned.

Alice Penfold described how Chapman had shamelessly courted her whilst, unknown to her, he was married to one woman and living in sin with another. She also revealed that he had continued pursuing her even after he and Mary had moved back to London. Mrs Doubleday's disclosures were equally scandalous: Chapman would order her to leave the bedroom each time he dosed Mary with medicine, and when he gave Mary brandy she would vomit.

Inspector Godley was next on the witness stand. He read out Mary's death certificate and told the court that her estranged husband Shadrach Spink — then living in Eastbourne — had learned of her death only from following the Maud Marsh murder mystery in the press. Seeing his wife's name in print had prompted him to contact the police and make a statement, the contents of which were not publicised. He did not appear in court; he had left Mary long before she met Chapman, and could not contribute anything useful to the case.

Although the police were in possession of his Russian documents and being identified by the Baderski family, with whom he had conversed in his native Polish, Chapman remained unwavering in his insistence that he was a true-born American. In January 1903 he wrote to Consul General Henry Clay Evans at the US Embassy to apply for his protection, maintaining that each of his three wives had died from natural causes.[272] When asked for more details he penned a lengthy reply detailing his life story. This found its way into the hands of a *Daily Mail* reporter, who used it as the basis of a lengthy article published on 14th January.

### THE POISON CASE
### CHAPMAN'S CAREER
### THE THINGS HE FORGETS.

Despite the fact that at the Southwark police court, George Chapman... was identified by a Polish woman as her husband, Severino Klosowski, a Polish Jew, he now declares that he is an American citizen. He denies that his name is Klosowski or that he ever resided in Warsaw. He first communicated by letter with the American authorities in London, stating that he is an American citizen, without living relatives or friends, and asserting his innocence of all the crimes of which he is accused. Subsequently he placed information in the hands of the American authorities to the effect that he was born in America. His father, he alleges, was born in England. Chapman has no witnesses to substantiate his story, and is even unable to remember the name of a single person or family who is mentioned in what he sets forth as his life history.

---

272 *Montana Anaconda*, 15th January 1903.

## HIS BIRTHPLACE.

It is a remarkable story that Chapman recounts of his career. It was on a farm near a small town in the State of Michigan, USA, that, thirty-seven years ago, he states, he was born. His mother died when he was but eleven months old, and his father, who bore the name of Alfred Chapman and was a carpenter by trade, moved to New York, when Chapman was still a baby. Chapman's first recollection goes back to his sixth or seventh year. It was then that his father died, and though he remembers the incident of his death, his memory of his father is very vague. Most of his information on the subject of his parents was gathered from a German family in Hoboken, New York, in whose care he was left at the time of his father's death. This family kept a general and grocery store in what Chapman describes as the main road near the Hoboken ferry. Among other early memories are his duties as errand boy in this store, which he left to take a similar position in another German grocery store in Thirty-fourth street, New York City. Later he worked also as an errand boy at a grocery between Sixteenth and Eighteenth streets east. When 12 or 13 years of age Chapman fell in with an American who dealt in horses and lived in Jersey City Heights. He took employment with this man as a sort of general utility boy and hostler, and stayed with him for three or four years. At first he enjoyed the work, as the man went about New York State trading and selling horses, an occupation which was productive of sufficient change to fascinate Chapman until the novelty wore off and he decided to learn hairdressing. He was by this time about sixteen years of age, and had had no schooling whatever. He had no knowledge of any living relatives, and had come to regard himself as the only member of his family left since his father's death.

## BECAME A BARBER.

He started his hairdressing experiences in a shop in Ninth avenue, between Thirty-fourth and Fortieth streets, New York. This shop was owned by a German, whose Christian name — Friedrich — is all Chapman can recall. Here he remained for six months, and then went to another German barber in Fourteenth street west, where he stayed for a year. Later he worked for a barber whose shop was at the corner of Bleeker street and Seventh avenue. Thus, we are told, he spent his young manhood. He did not drink or smoke, never went with any set companions, never frequented any particular places of amusement, and lived with private families, sometimes German, sometimes not. He formed no attachments, and had no close friends among either sex. Generally he went by the name of George Chapman, but on some occasions he used the name of Smith. In addition to his work as a barber, Chapman sold such articles as appertain to the hairdresser's business, and thus made some extra money. He was economical and saved all he could, and his expenses were of the lowest. One of the best known places in which he claims to have been employed was in Fulton street, just round the corner from Broadway. This was in 1890. The man who kept this shop was, he states, a dark-complexioned German, short of stature.

## CAME TO ENGLAND.

In 1893, having gathered together some £300, Chapman decided to come to England. He crossed the Atlantic in a cattle-boat, the Westerland, he thinks her name was, paying £2 and doing some odd work for his passage. Shortly after his arrival in London he attempted to return on the same boat, but was unable to do so, and before he found a way of getting back to America that suited him he was induced to invest his little capital and remain in this country.

Such is Chapman's account of his life, and although he admits that the fact that he can remember no names is no inconsiderable bar to any substantiation of it, he asserts his confidence that if the story is given sufficiently wide publicity some of the people who knew him in America will come forward and prove its truth. Chapman's description is as follows: Age, 37; height, 5ft. 5in; weight, 10st 3lb; blue eyes, brown hair and heavy brown moustache; high and slightly receding forehead; nose slightly turned up, and features generally small. The American authorities have given Chapman to understand clearly that should he be found guilty of the commission of any crime in England the fact that he was born in the United States, and was therefore an American citizen, even if clearly proven, would have no effect whatever upon the course of justice.

On 14th January *The Echo* announced that the Exchange Telegraph Company had forwarded Chapman's citizenship claim to the State Department at Washington, adding that the US embassy attached no importance to it. Meanwhile, Evans asked Chapman to supply documentary proof to support his claim, but Chapman did not reply, which comes as no surprise as he had none to offer.

Chapman's letter to the consul ensured that his case again aroused the interest of newspapers across the USA, which published statements conveying the news that the murderer Chapman — dubbed 'the Southwark saloonkeeper' and the 'East End rum-seller' — was a true-born American. Some printed his photo because, 'He thinks if his picture were published some of the many folk he knew in America but whose names he has forgotten will identify him.'[273] Thenceforth, transatlantic readers were kept up to date with Chapman's case until his execution.

But it was Londoners who hungered most for all the gory details of 'the most notable murder trial of modern times'.[274] As early as December 1902 the owner of a waxwork show in Islington had pre-judged his guilt and began displaying models of 'Chapman and his Victims.'[275] Chapman was furious. He instructed Mr Sydney to take legal proceedings against the owner and, while he was at it, against the publisher of some doggerel rhymes entitled 'The Southwark Poisoning Case'.[276]

On 21st January the police court heard from Henry Dacre, who recounted meeting the Chapmans in 1896 to discuss Mary's trust money; from William

---

273 *Atlanta Constitution*, 29th January 1903.
274 *Illustrated Police News*, quoted in Freeman, N. in Moore, G. and Maunder, A. (2004) *Victorian Crime, Madness and Sensation*, Ashgate, p231.
275 Later, Madame Tussaud's artists were to create a masterpiece that had pride of place in the Chamber of Horrors for over sixty years.
276 *The Echo*, 1st January 1903.

Clilverd, manager of the London, City & Midland Bank; from Hastings solicitors Mr Langham and Mr Jones; and from Francis H. Owen of Lloyds Bank, Hastings. Other witnesses included Petrykowski (the police interpreter); officers from both Dr Barnardo's and Shoreditch Workhouse, who related Chapman's attempts to get rid of Willie; and Mesdames Mumford, Pagett and Waymark, who spoke about Mary Spink's alcoholism and Chapman's attempts to cure it with a 'special medicine' he had read about in his 'doctors' books'. Whilst describing Mary's illness and death, Mrs Waymark fainted.

The hearing resumed seven days later. It was a day of dense fog, but it seems nothing could deter the eager spectators, since 'the Court was again crowded by those anxious to obtain a glimpse of Chapman'.[277] The proceedings focussed mainly upon Mary Spink and Bessie Taylor. Their killer entered the dock, 'his hair carefully brushed, a new tie neatly adjusted, and wearing his frockcoat'. He appeared 'cadaverous but self-possessed', and as each witness spoke he scribbled feverishly. A gaoler was, as usual, standing by the dock and 'giving him fresh supplies of foolscap for his ever-increasing mass of notes'.[278] Inspector Godley produced a photograph of Bessie and her death certificate. Sergeant Neil reported finding no record of Chapman's purported marriages to either Mary or Bessie. Elizabeth Painter, Martha Stevens and Sister Martha Ibbs recounted Bessie's agony during her final weeks. As Miss Painter spoke, Chapman 'buried his face in his hands and wept freely'.[279]

According to his biographer, Home Office toxicologist Dr Stevenson was 'an admirable witness. His evidence was so clearly expressed that even those without scientific knowledge never failed to grasp its true meaning.'[280] Stevenson described his findings at the post-mortem of 9th December. Although interred for five years, the condition of Mary's body was 'quite remarkable': it looked like 'a corpse that had been coffined that day'. He pointed out that the bodies of Mary and Bessie had also been 'preserved by that very poison which robbed them of life'.[281] Mary's face was pallid and her hands were pink; her skin felt like soft leather and her muscles were firm. Her stomach showed signs of 'inflammatory mischief', but was neither perforated nor ulcerated. It was of a cinnabar red colour, and so were her bowels, which were 'coated inside with a substance resembling yellow paint, such as an antimonial compound would produce'. Stevenson found antimony in all of her vital organs. There was, he stated, no evidence of alcoholism.[282] During the expert's evidence Chapman 'sat with his eyes fixed upon the ground'. Looking 'pale and worn', he 'sighed frequently'.[283]

Because it had dragged on for so long without a climax, by mid-January interest in the case was beginning to wane. Even the Marshes had ceased to attend and in early February employed Britain's first black barrister, Henry Sylvester Williams, to attend the hearings on their behalf.

---

277 Southwark & Bermondsey Recorder, 17th January 1903.
278 Daily Mail, 29th January 1903.
279 Daily Express, 5th February 1903.
280 Rolleston, H.D. (2004) 'Stevenson, Sir Thomas.' www.oxforddnb.com (accessed 16th May 2013).
281 Daily Mail, 17th March 1903.
282 Southwark & Bermondsey Recorder, 31st January 1903.
283 Lincolnshire Chronicle, 30th January 1903.

At the police court on 4th February, Chapman, 'pale but self-possessed', 'stepped with a firm, military step into the dock'. When he smiled it 'had the effect of heightening his haggard appearance to a most repulsive degree'. The day was devoted to Bessie Taylor. Her brother William gave evidence, as did a family friend from Altrincham named William Kelsall, Mr Sanderson from Bishop's Stortford, Inspector Godley and William Tull. Dr Stoker was called once again, this time to recount how he had invited three other physicians to give their expert opinions on Bessie's mystery illness. Dr Stevenson reported the findings of his post-mortem. Bessie was, like Chapman's other deceased lady-friends, chock-full of antimony, administered in the form of tartar emetic. The substance was formerly used as the main ingredient in certain quack medicines sold as cures for alcohol addiction, he said, but 'these remedies have not been sold for that purpose for some years'.[284] There had not, to his knowledge, been a criminal case involving antimony since 1876.

Courtesy of magistrate Cecil Chapman, Hargrave Lee Adam managed to get a seat on the bench in order to watch 'that alien assassin...very closely for a few hours'.

> I thought him a particularly sinister-looking individual, with his swarthy complexion, piercing shifty brown eyes, high cheek bones and cruel mouth. His Tartar origin was clearly depicted on his face. That he was inconceivably callous I had striking proof. It came about in a curious manner. During the whole time the prisoner was in the dock he was making notes on slips of paper at frequent intervals. The slips he held down low beneath the dock rail, and while writing, his face was averted from the bench...A brother of one of his victims [William Taylor] was giving evidence of a very revolting and damning character, and in silent comment, as it were, on one of the witness's statements a cynical smile overspread the countenance of the prisoner. At the same time, he slowly raised his face and his eyes caught mine watching him closely. Suddenly the smile ceased and with an effort he straightened his countenance. It was a small incident, but it spoke volumes.[285]

At the sixteenth and final magisterial hearing, on 11th February 1903, Chapman seemed anxious and his movements 'lacked their customary elasticity'.[286] The prosecution called for his committal on the three charges of murder. Magistrate Cecil Chapman asked the accused if he had anything to say, but received no response. Mr Sydney said his client pleaded not guilty, reserved his defence and would call no witnesses at this stage. Cecil Chapman noted this, committed the prisoner for trial on a magistrate's warrant, and wrote on the charge sheet: 'I think Inspector Godley and Sergeants Kemp and Neil, and the other officers engaged in this case, deserve special credit for the pains taken and skill shown in obtaining evidence.'

As Chapman left the police court for the final time, accompanied as ever by a brace of warders, he was again hissed at by a waiting crowd. He said nothing, but his angry glare conveyed his feelings.

284 Adam, H.L. (1930) *Trial of George Chapman*, William Hodge, p218.
285 Adam, H.L. (1908) *The Story of Crime*, T.W. Laurie, p198–199
286 *Manchester Courier*, 12th February, 1903.

From mid-February, having no more court hearings to report, the newspapers fell silent on the Chapman case. He received a brief mention in *The Echo*, which announced that, ever since poison had been lobbed over the wall into the exercise yard at Brixton Prison, he had been put on suicide watch. Chapman had taken 'a certain man' into his confidence, and asked him to 'purchase a phial of prussic acid, seal it up in a rubber ball, and bounce the ball over the Brixton Prison wall' whilst Chapman was at exercise. But instead of performing this service (for which he was, apparently, well paid) the man reported the request to the authorities.[287]

Chapman had over a month to wait until his next public appearance. He passed much of it reading and consulting his solicitor. On 2nd March, Mr Sydney applied to Southwark magistrates for the restoration of £110 in banknotes, confiscated by police from the Crown and still in their possession. About £150 in gold and silver (worth about £15,000 today) had been returned to Chapman to pay for his defence costs, but this was almost exhausted. The magistrate told Mr Sydney to apply at the Old Bailey. In case he was sentenced to death and there was anything left from the £110 after his costs were paid, Chapman made a will in favour of Bessie's siblings Eliza and William.

This is the last will and testament of me, George Chapman, now detained at H.M.'s Prison, Brixton, licensed victualler. I hereby revoke all wills heretofore made by me and declare this to be my last will and testament. I give devise and bequeath the whole of my estate, consisting of £110 in the hands of the Commissioner of Police for the Metropolitan district, and further, the wearing apparel and jewellery at the Crown public-house Borough High-street, to Eliza Taylor, of Hall Farm, Preston-park [sic], Cheshire, and William Taylor, of 62, Lausanne-road, Hornsey, thereout to pay my just debts and funeral and testamentary expenses, and after paying thereof to divide the balance equally between them, share and share alike. I hereby appoint the said Eliza Taylor and William Taylor executrix and executor of this my will. In witness whereof I, the said George Chapman, have to this, my last will and testament, set my name this fourteenth day of March 1903.[288]

The witnesses were Mr Sydney's young clerks Reynold Oswald Sholl and George Baker, the address for both was given as Mr Sydney's office at 2 Renfrew Road, Lambeth.[289]

In the event, all of Chapman's £110 was needed for his legal fees, bringing the cost of his defence to £260, the equivalent to about £26,000 today. The Taylors inherited only garments and jewellery. Valued at about £140, the items included three mantles, for which Chapman had paid the enormous sum of £87 (worth £8,700 today), which suggests that each was made of an expensive fur. Some sources say he

---

287 *Daily Express*, 20th March 1903.
288 Quoted in full in *The Echo*, 4th April 1903. Eliza was Bessie's sister; she lived not at Preston Park but Preston Brook.
289 The 1901 census shows Sholl (as 'Shole' 'solicitor's clerk') and his family living at 300 Borough High Street, above Mr Sydney's Southwark offices.

also left a ring and some of Maud's clothing to the Marsh family. These items were likely to have been equally valuable: one photograph shows Maud wearing a beautiful silk gown that was way beyond her means, doubtless a gift from Chapman.

Once it was clear that he would never be returning to the Crown, Chapman gave Mr Sydney power of attorney and instructions to sell its lease. Nothing is known about the money raised from the sale. In November 1901, Chapman had paid £258 for the lease, £60 for fittings and £160 for utensils, a total of £478, worth almost £48,000 today. He had named the Taylors as beneficiaries of anything that might be left of his £110 but, strangely, there was no mention of the pub, his biggest asset.

## THE OLD BAILEY

The Central Criminal Court acquired its nickname from the street on which it stands. This was called 'Old Bailey' because it follows the line of the city's bailey (i.e. wall). The court was erected alongside Newgate Prison in the 1500s and had been reconstructed several times. Three months before Chapman's trial commenced, yet another rebuild was inaugurated by the ceremonial laying of a foundation stone by the Lord Mayor of London. The new building was finished in 1907 and officially opened by Edward VII.

At the time grand juries of twenty-four 'good and loyal men' (which, in practice, meant those of sound financial and social standing) were appointed at the beginning of each monthly session. After convening for two days at the Guildhall, the London grand jury moved to the Old Bailey, where it had to decide which cases had sufficient evidence to merit sending the defendant to trial by jury. This was called 'finding a true bill'. If a true bill were found, the case was passed to the clerk of arraigns, who called upon the accused to plead and empanelled a jury of twelve men to decide if the prisoner was guilty or not.

Chapman had been committed for trial on both a coroner's warrant and a magistrate's warrant. The former bypassed the need for the grand jury's approval, but the latter did not, and so, when the March Sessions opened at the Old Bailey, Sir Forrest Fulton KC, the Recorder of London, addressed the grand jury on the subject of the prisoner George Chapman.[290] Just one month previously, Sir Forrest had railed against 'the number of disreputable foreigners' the court was obliged to deal with.[291] He remarked that he was 'not very sorry' to discover that Chapman was 'either a Polish or a Russian Jew' who carried on in his own country — 'whatever that was' — the occupation of 'a barber-surgeon'. Although he initially asserted that it was impossible to think of a motive to explain Chapman's crimes, Sir Forrest nevertheless offered one: 'Having gratified his desires with these women, he thought it better to get rid of them without any further trouble.' He added that, in any case, the members of the grand jury 'need not trouble themselves with motive'. A true bill was returned upon each of the three murder charges.[292]

The usual sequence of a trial was as follows: the prosecution made an opening statement, brought its witnesses and examined them. They could be cross-examined by the defence and then re-examined by the prosecution. The defence would then

---

290 The recorder was the most senior permanent judge of the Central Criminal Court.
291 *The Times*, 10th February 1903.
292 *The Echo*, 9th March 1903; *Daily Mail*, 10th March 1903; *Southwark & Bermondsey Recorder*, 14th March 1903.

introduce and examine their own witnesses, who could be cross-examined by the prosecution and then re-examined by the defence. Closing speeches were made, firstly by the prosecution and then by the defence. (The procedure was slightly different at Chapman's trial: the prosecution would have the last word because of a traditional privilege enjoyed by the Solicitor General in the cases he prosecuted.) The judge summed up, the jury retired and deliberated, its foreman announced the verdict and the judge either pronounced the sentence or liberated the prisoner.

The trial of George Chapman began on Monday, 16th March 1903 and ran for four days. Present in court on the first day were Mr Justice Grantham; Sir Joseph Savory, Bart, the former Lord Mayor of London; Hamilton Cuffe, 5th Earl of Desart KCB, PC, Director of Public Prosecutions; the prosecution and defence teams; Chapman (flanked by his warders); a large number of journalists, including George R. Sims, who 'followed the case with close attention'; and as many eager spectators as could possibly be squeezed into the courtroom. The public's fervour had been provoked by the press. The *Daily Express* expected it to be 'one of the most sensational murder trials ever recorded in all [the Old Bailey's] grim old history';[293] whilst *The Echo* said it 'promises to be one of the most remarkable cases on the crime-list of the Metropolis'.[294] The provincial newspapers were equally animated: one proclaimed: 'No criminal trial has excited such widespread interest since Neill Cream was convicted in 1891.'[295]

Hundreds had turned out to watch the trial, but by the time the doors opened every seat in the public gallery had already been reserved, because tickets of admission had been issued in advance by the under-sheriff to 'privileged persons', among them some famous names including the popular actor H.B. Irving, music hall star (later, Sir) Arthur Seymour Hicks, and the celebrated gentleman jockey Arthur Coventry, a cousin of the Earl of Coventry.[296]

> The galleries were filled with those who set out with the intention of devoting their attention for a week to the intricacies of the case. It is strange what a fascination these 'big' cases seem to have for all classes alike. Men and women — and there were several ladies occupying the front seats near the judge's bench — came prepared to sit in a stuffy Court for hours.[297]

'People flocked to the first day's hearing in much the same way as they do to the theatre',[298] and some of the ladies were clearly seasoned theatre-goers, for they came equipped with opera glasses and even arranged for refreshments to be brought in. An overspill of about a hundred people gathered in the courtyard outside, some of whom loitered in the vicinity all day, hoping for a chance to gain admittance.

No. 1 court was scheduled for demolition. Dating back to 1774, it was poorly constructed and ill-lighted, and yet was a little less dismal than it had been a few months previously, when Newgate still stood next door, blocking out the daylight.

293 *Daily Express,* 16th March 1903.
294 *The Echo,* 16th March 1903.
295 *Lincolnshire Chronicle,* 20th March 1903. Cream, the 'Lambeth Poisoner', was convicted in 1892.
296 Arthur Coventry 1852–1925, official Jockey Club Starter until 1902.
297 *The Echo,* 16th March 1903.
298 Adam, H.L. (1930) *Trial of George Chapman,* William Hodge, p28.

The small Court has improved greatly in the matter of lighting since the dark and grim buildings outside were pulled down. It almost looked cheerful in comparison, and as if affected by the changed appearance, the jurors in waiting chatted pleasantly with one another, and the barristers — young and old — discussed the case, sometimes not from a purely legal point of view.[299]

Mr Justice Grantham was sixty-seven years old and (said *The Times*) he possessed a refined, eager face, a genial manner, manly frankness, courage, and cheery audacity.[300] Gordon Honeycombe described him as 'an imperious figure, with a resonant voice, whose preconceived ideas about a prisoner's guilt tended not to be concealed.'[301] A member of the Sussex landed gentry, he had been a Conservative MP for eleven years, resigning his seat on his appointment to the judiciary. He was famous for riding to the Courts of Justice on horseback, booted and spurred, and with hunting-crop in hand.[302]

The prosecuting counsel comprised the solicitor-general Sir Edward Carson KC, MP, Henry Sutton, Charles W. Mathews and Archibald Bodkin. Carson had 'a long, lean figure and a long, lean face'. Eager, tense and determined, he spoke with a noticeable Dublin accent. He was one of the most brilliant advocates of his era and had gained fame in 1895 for defending the Marquess of Queensberry against Oscar Wilde's libel action.[303] Carson was later to become an appeal judge, attorney-general, cabinet member and leader of the Ulster Unionist Party, and in due course was elevated to the House of Lords as Baron Carson of Duncairn. In contrast, Henry Sutton was a man whose 'diffidence and timidity even in simple matters were almost touching'. Sutton wrote *The Law of Tramways & Light Railways* and later became a judge (of whom *The Times* remarked: 'there was perhaps no judge in recent years who left so little mark on our legal history').[304] Charles Mathews (known as Willie) was a small, spare man with a keen, alert face and a prim, artificial manner. Born in New York in 1850, he was the stepson of a comedian so successful that he could afford to send him to be educated at Eton College. Mathews would succeed Lord Desart as Director of Public Prosecutions and, on Mathews's death in 1920, that lofty position would be filled by Archibald Bodkin, the fourth member of the prosecution team. He was a tall, broad-shouldered man with a clean-shaven, rugged countenance and commanding aspect, whose large, grey eyes were reputed to express a wonderful depth of retrospection. He was also recorded as being an intolerant killjoy, with no interests outside of his career, who only prosecuted (never defended) and later gunned for suffragettes, spies and indecent publications (as DPP he famously banned *Ulysses* and *The Well of Loneliness*).[305] In due course Sutton, Mathews and Bodkin would each receive a knighthood.

---

299 *The Echo*, 16th March 1903.
300 *The Times*, 1st and 4th December 1911.
301 Honeycombe, G. (1993) *More Murders of the Black Museum*, Hutchinson, p163.
302 *Illustrated London News*, 9th December 1911.
303 When Carson threatened to bring several male prostitutes to prove Wilde a 'depraved sodomite', Wilde abandoned the case.
304 *The Times*, 1st June 1920.
305 *Ulysses* for sexual innuendo and *The Well of Loneliness* for its lesbian theme.

Chapman's defence team was considerably less illustrious. It was led by George Elliott KC, 'a short, stubby little man with rosy cheeks'. Described as 'the picture of geniality', he had a 'rubicund, beaming face' which looked 'as if nothing were too difficult for him to handle'. He possessed an irrepressible sense of humour, he was noted for smiling contemplatively at his own witticisms. Elliott was assisted by thirty-year-old, Oxford-educated Vyvyan Ashleigh Lyons and Arthur Hutton, a tall gent who always wore a monocle and who had been Chapman's prosecuting counsel during the shares scam case. Mr Sydney continued as Chapman's solicitor, and the court interpreter, Mr A.H. Louis, was on hand should his services be required.

Above the dock in which Chapman would be sitting, the gallery was crowded to utmost capacity. At 11am, as the eager spectators looked down,

> The prisoner entered the dock via a trap-door, having had to walk along a stone-paved passage called 'Birdcage Walk'. Under the flagstones of this passage were the men who had been hanged in Newgate, so every man who left the court sentenced to death had to walk over his own imminent grave.[306]

Chapman's facial hair had been severely trimmed. 'His eyes have a haunted, peculiar look,' said *The Echo,* 'the hollow of the cheeks was accentuated by the shaving of his "mutton chops" and the clipping of the moustache.' His hair was 'neatly brushed' but by now his clothes looked 'very shabby' and his tie was 'negligently done up'; he wore a 'wrinkled frock-coat, with a new linen collar turned back in front'.[307] As the jury was sworn in he stroked his attenuated moustache thoughtfully. Beside the 'broad-shouldered warder he appeared a very little man indeed', wrote the *Daily Express*.[308] He was twice asked to plead by the clerk of arraigns, but his responses were inaudible, 'as if he had already given up hope'.[309] Eventually his hushed plea of 'not guilty' was heard. 'One detected,' remarked the *Daily Mail,* 'no foreign accent in those few words.'[310]

According to the *Daily Express*, the trial would last a fortnight:

> The magistrate's depositions fill 560 folios, and over 100 witnesses are to be called by the Treasury. These include seventeen doctors and experts, thirteen solicitors, five registrars, six undertakers, and three superintendents of cemeteries. In their cosmopolitan ranks will be represented Warsaw, Hamburg, Cayenne and eleven different English counties. Four interpreters will be required for the foreign evidence.[311]

Each point was overstated. The trial lasted four days and the prosecution presented forty-three witnesses from seven counties. None was brought from another country, and the few foreign-born witnesses needed no interpreter.

The trial centred on the death of Maud Marsh. Evidence with regard to the deaths of Bessie and Mary was to be given only as confirmation of Chapman's 'habits

---

306 Marriner, B. (1993) *Murder with Venom,* True Crime Library, p19.
307 *Daily Express,* 17th March 1903.
308 *Ibid.*
309 Adam, H.L. (1930) *Trial of George Chapman,* William Hodge, p28.
310 *The Echo,* 16th March 1903; *Daily Mail,* 17th March 1903.
311 *Daily Express,* 21st February 1903. Cayenne is the capital of French Guiana in South America.

*Cameos: Lord Desart, from Vanity Fair (VF); Arthur Hutton, from Trial of George Chapman; Willie Mathews, from VF. Full-length portraits: Justice Grantham, from VF; Archibald Bodkin, by George Belcher.*

and methods' and to help prove that Maud's death could not have been accidental or caused by anyone else. The case against him was entirely circumstantial but the facts were irrefutable: he had purchased antimony; three women with whom he cohabited had died of antimonial poisoning; nobody but he had access to all three victims.

Chapman declined to speak and brought no witnesses. His unwillingness either to present a defence or to admit guilt was puzzling, intriguing but ultimately deeply unsatisfying. Press and public alike relish a lively courtroom drama, but that is created by the cut-and-thrust of each side battling it out vigorously with witnesses on both sides, fierce cross-examination by both prosecution and defence, the breaking of alibis and the bamboozling of hapless witnesses. Chapman's trial lacked these elements; nevertheless it gripped the nation. Harry Furniss recalled that, at the same time as the Chapman case was in the news,

> there were several important cases prominently before the minds of the populace...But was it of these that the public talked most? No; it was the death of Maud Marsh...of the identity of George Chapman...of the details of the exhumations...For a moment the reading folk of Great Britain might consider the other sensational 'attractions'...but the main interest centred on the doings of the landlord of the Crown pub.[312]

Sir Edward Carson's opening speech, delivered in 'slow, cold, deliberate sentences', included a brief but inaccurate synopsis of Chapman's life story. Faced with a man who had worked as a *barber* after (apparently) training as a *surgeon*, he found it irresistible to combine the two words to create a phrase that sounded familiar. Barber-surgeons had existed from the Middle Ages, but in 1745 the two trades had become independent of each other. The last barber-surgeon to practise in London was Mr Middleditch of Great Suffolk Street, Southwark, who died in 1821. The phrase 'barber-surgeon' was revived in the public consciousness during the mid-1800s by a short story featuring Sweeney Todd, the Demon Barber of Fleet Street. Why Carson's team asserted that the word 'feldsher' meant 'barber-surgeon' is a mystery, because one of their own witnesses, Wolff Levisohn, who had been a feldsher in Poland, described it as 'an assistant to a doctor, what you call here a practical nurse, who put on bandages and that sort of thing'.[313]

Sir Edward presented a brief overview of the deaths of all three women, and enlightened the jury on the subject of the realities of death by poisoning:

> If a distinction can be made in degrees of murder, I submit that no murder is more determined and more malicious than that by poison, such as the one we are enquiring into. Certainly no murder could be more demonstrative of the cruelty of the person perpetrating it, than that of a man, standing by a bedside, day after day, of the person he professed to love and seeing her suffering torture and gradually sinking away, from what he had by his own hand administered under the pretext of treating that person for maladies with which he professed to be acquainted.[314]

312 Furniss, H. (ed) *Famous Crimes Past and Present*, Vol. IX, No. 109, c. 1908. Caxton House.
313 *Daily Mail*, 8th January 1903; *Northampton Mercury*, 9th January 1903.
314 Adam, H.L. (1930) *Trial of George Chapman*, William Hodge, p62. Oddly, the *Daily Mail*, 17th March 1903, ends the speech: 'for maladies which his treatment alone had produced'.

The first witnesses called were Wolff Levisohn, Ethel Radin, Stanisław Baderski and his sister Mrs Rauch; hairdressers Alfred Wicken and George Schumann; legal clerk William Bray, Inspector Godley and pharmacist William Davison.

*The Echo* described Levisohn as 'A short man, his features almost hidden in long grey hair'. Having 'walked clumsily to the witness-box', he recounted his version of the antecedents of George Chapman.[315] Levisohn's deposition at the police court two months previously had been long-winded and he repeated it, although nothing he said had the slightest bearing on who poisoned Maud Marsh. In the 1880s and 1890s, Levisohn explained, he had been a hawker of barbers' and hairdressers' requisites and he recognised the man in the dock as one of his former customers, Ludwik Zagowski. Zagowski had been an army feldsher in Warsaw and by 1888 was working in a barbershop beneath the White Hart in Whitechapel, becoming its proprietor in 1889. That year, Zagowski's wife and children arrived from Poland but he had refused to support them, and so Levisohn and another man gave the woman a few pennies. Labelling him 'a brute and a scoundrel', Levisohn stated that, had Zagowski had not left Whitechapel in 1890, he and other men 'would have given him a good, sound thrashing'.[316] When asked to describe Zagowski, Levisohn became very animated and 'pointed dramatically' at Chapman:

> There he sits! That is his description. He has not altered from the day he
> came to England; he has not even a grey hair. Always the same — same
> la-di-da, 'igh 'at, and umbrella.[317]

Mr Sydney accused Levisohn of having 'a lot of feeling in this matter'. Levisohn denied this, but 'became excited once more' when he added, 'Why, bless your heart, the moment I see the name Chapman I know this is the man, but I don't want to push myself forward, so I wait till the police come to me.'[318] He explained later that a barber called George Chapman had also suddenly disappeared from Tottenham, and he suspected that Zagowski had taken the man's name.[319]

The other witnesses repeated the statements they had made in the police court. Chapman's brother-in-law, Stanisław Baderski, was described as a 'smartly dressed tailor'; his sister-in-law, Stanisława Rauch, was 'a tall woman, gorgeously attired in a large black hat and veil, blue-and-white costume, and big, heavy brown fur boa, which seemed to require a big effort to support'. She caused a flutter of excitement as she 'seemed to glide across the well of the gloomy old Court'. Clearly relishing her moment in the limelight, after she mounted the steps to the witness box she 'turned around and smiled broadly at the Court as she lifted up her veil, disclosing her clear, pleasant features'.[320] Mrs Rauch was followed by sixty-year-old William Davison. 'Adjusting his steel-rimmed pince-nez, with methodical deliberation he took a good long look at the prisoner — who negligently returned

---

315 *The Echo*, 16th March 1903.
316 *The Echo*, 7th January 1903.
317 *Northampton Mercury*, 9th January 1903. Adam quoted Levisohn as saying 'a black coat, patent boots and high hat'; the *Daily Mail*: 'frock coat and high hat'; *The Echo*: 'a high hat and black bag'.
318 *Ibid.*
319 Perhaps the same George Chapman whose brother turned up at Southwark police court (see page 112).
320 *The Echo*, 16th March 1903.

his gaze.'[321] Davison confirmed that he had sold Chapman sufficient tartar emetic to kill forty people. The following morning the *Daily Mail* remarked that there was 'something grotesque about the suggestion' that Chapman had 'brought three women to their graves with the aid of less than an ounce of tartar emetic, which cost him tuppence'.[322]

The foreman of the jury asked if they might compare the 1885 signature of S. Kłosowski in the book *Five Hundred Prescriptions for Diseases and Complaints* with the 1895 specimen on the lease of 518 Tottenham High Road. They matched.

When the court adjourned at 4pm, Chapman left the dock 'with an air of relief', returning briefly to hand back to the gaoler the borrowed remnant of lead pencil as he murmured a word of thanks. Then, 'with one last look at the curious crowd, he passed to the cells below'.[323] The jury was whisked off to spend the night at a hotel, under the care of the ushers of the court.

Outside the Old Bailey on the morning of Tuesday 17th March, people queued in the vain hope of getting a seat in court No. 1, where proceedings began at 10.30. Mr Elliott asked for Chapman's money to be returned so he could pay for his defence. Chapman had requested this during the magisterial hearing, but the prosecution counsel had objected on the grounds that some of the money probably belonged to Mary Spink, whose husband and sons, as next-of-kin, had legal claim to it. The police were still holding £110 in notes, one of which bore the same serial number as a note paid out of Mary Spink's bank account. Mr Elliott promised that they would not quibble about one ten-pound note if Chapman could have the remaining £100. The judge assented.

Mrs Marsh, 'a little woman, dressed wholly in black, glided by the side of the dock and mounted the steps leading to the witness box'. Chapman 'craned forward to get a better view' of her, whilst she 'turned her head...and gave him a piercing look'. In response, and 'contemptuously tossing his head back', Chapman 'returned the gaze with interest, then dropped his head'. Mrs Marsh replied to questions in monosyllables, and sometimes so weakly that 'every ear was strained to catch the broken sentences'. She 'bared her simple soul to the court' when she described how adroitly Chapman had overruled her moral objection to Maud's living alone with him. Recounting the tragic story of her daughter's illness and death caused her to break down; she only just managed to continue 'through her heavy sobbing'.[324] She glared at Chapman as she described his crocodile tears when Maud died, but this time he did not meet her gaze, preferring to keep his head bent down and to scribble copious notes. Members of the jury were also reported to be 'very busy with their quills'.[325]

321 *The Echo*, 16th March 1903.
322 *Daily Mail*, 17th March 1903.
323 *Daily Express*, 17th March 1903.
324 *The Echo*, 18th March 1903.
325 *Daily Express*, 18th March 1903.

*Image: Sir Edward Carson, from Trial of George Chapman.*

The examination of Mrs Marsh took up most of the morning. She was followed by her spouse and her daughters Louisa and Alice, who repeated the statements they had given at the police court. When Mr Justice Grantham heard that Maud had been in Guy's Hospital for a month he remarked, 'I am not surprised at the hospitals asking for charity when they take care of the wives of licensed victuallers.' A man in Chapman's financial position was expected to pay for medical treatment; it was bad form for the solvent to take advantage of hospital services intended only for the poor.

When the afternoon session began, 'the mass of humanity packed into the little gallery between the two squat pillars over the dock craned their necks forward eagerly in their anxiety to get a view of the prisoner, and the front rank (mostly females) seemed in some danger of toppling over on to him'.[326] Those who 'craned' effectively were rewarded with a view of Chapman, and those who did not could read about his appearance and demeanour in the press:

> His bright eyes are the most striking feature of his face, being set quite close under the brows...As he leaned back in his chair, as he often did, with his head well lifted, looking confident and at ease, his face bore an expression of quick intelligence. His head is a little small, but the brow is wide, and the dark hair, brushed back neatly, gives a smart touch. The cheekbones are slightly prominent. A firm chin is nearly hidden by a large curly moustache.[327]

Jessie Toon, the chatterbox whose silence Chapman had attempted to buy, stepped into the witness box wearing a black sailor hat (the current fashion fad) and a thick fur necklet tightly fastened at her throat. She recalled Chapman using a stethoscope to listen to Maud's lungs and heart. When the instrument in question was placed on the counsel's table, 'an unpleasant thrill ran through the court, and many people half-rose in their seats to get a glimpse of it'. Mrs Toon described how a sip of Maud's brandy had burned her mouth, and revealed that Chapman had dubbed Mrs Marsh an 'old cat' whose sole interest in having a post-mortem was 'to show him up'.[328] Next came Miss Cole, the servant at the Crown, who related the 'poisoned rabbit' story. She was followed by obstetrician Dr Targett, a 'clean shaven, sharp-featured looking man with a professional air'.

Those in the public gallery listened with increased relish as two attractive young women supplied juicy evidence of Chapman's philandering. Florence Rayner 'came to the witness-box in a black picture hat and with keen reminiscences'.[329] She recalled Chapman's flirting and asking her to elope. Asked if she objected to his kisses, she giggled as she admitted: 'I could not help myself.'

Annie Chapman, a 'large-featured woman of small stature, aged about thirty, with dark hair and eyes', wearing a black dress and a large hat adorned with a big brown feather, was described as 'a pathetic human document' and a 'faded little woman, with tired eyes and plaintive voice'.[330] With an 'unhappy expression', she

---

326 *The Echo,* 17th March 1903.
327 *Daily Mail,* 17th March 1903.
328 *Daily Express,* 18th March 1903.
329 *Ibid.*
330 *Ibid.*

recounted the details of how, ten years hence, she had been persuaded to live in sin with the accused, who at that point was leaning forward, balancing his chair on its two front legs. His chin was almost resting on the edge of the dock as he stared fixedly at Annie, who broke down in tears and hid her face in a handkerchief as she recalled his uncaring attitude towards her pregnancy. The judge asked if Chapman ever did anything for his child. Annie's reply was brief: 'No, never.' She did not mention that the boy had died as a baby. Chapman had returned to making notes. The *Daily Express* wrote:

> Calmly writing, Chapman occasionally glanced at her with the grave concern of a clerk who is anxious to accurately report the statement of a witness in whom he has no other interest...Even at the dramatic climax to this recital, when the former mistress faced the wife...Chapman appeared but mildly curious — nothing more. He leaned forward a little, the better to view his wife as she stood just under the dock. Then he selected a fresh slip of blue paper without further noticing her.[331]

The appearance of Lucy Kłosowska caused a sensation, said *The Echo*, and 'none looked at her more narrowly' than Chapman.[332] Wearing a chic black sailor hat, from which fell a thin, white veil, she was brought forward into the well of the court so that Annie could identify her. How must these two women have felt, meeting each other's gaze, after hearing that, after they left him, Chapman had murdered three of his mistresses? The realisation that they were the only women known to have cohabited with George Chapman and survived must surely have made their blood run cold.

By then Lucy had been with her new partner, Polish cabinetmaker Frank Szymański, for at least five years. They had produced two children and, for outward respectability, she passed as his wife. Lucy and Cecilia (her daughter by George Chapman) had adopted Frank's surname, which was not revealed in court. This may have helped the family to continue daily life without neighbours, colleagues and acquaintances discovering Lucy and Cecilia's connection to the infamous Southwark Poisoner.[333]

As the second day drew to a close and the court-room 'grew darker and dingier in the lengthening shadows,' Chapman 'put aside his pencil wearily and leaned back in his chair as though anxious for the sitting to end.'[334]

On Wednesday, 18th March, 'The gallery near the roof at the back of the dock was not more than comfortably filled and there was a marked falling-off in the number of gaily-attired ladies.' According to *The Echo*, Chapman seemed disappointed that his audience had diminished.

> The giant proportions of the two warders made Chapman appear a strangely-miserable specimen of humanity. He clutched convulsively at the lapel of his seedy frock-coat and gazed around the court with a weary air...contracted his brows, and then lifted his eyebrows as though a little surprised at the number of empty seats.[335]

---

331 *Daily Express,* 18th March 1903.
332 *The Echo,* 17th March 1903.
333 In the 1901 census they are recorded as Lucja and Cecylya Szymański.
334 *Daily Express,* 18th March 1903.
335 *The Echo,* 18th March 1903.

*Artists' impressions of court No. 1 at the Old Bailey. Top: Archibald Bodkin (left) and Wolff Levisohn, from Lloyd's Weekly. Centre: Chapman in the dock. (As he did not give evidence it presumably depicts the clerk of arraigns asking him to plead.) From Thomson's Weekly. Bottom: Mrs Rauch (left) and Lucy Kłosowska, from Lloyd's Weekly.*

*Sir Edward Carson (left) and Dr Thomas Stevenson, from Vanity Fair.*

*Mr Justice Grantham (left ) and George Elliott KC, from Trial of George Chapman.*

Twenty-three witnesses gave evidence, of whom four were called more than once. Dr Stoker was followed by Dr Bodmer, Mr Gilbert, Mr Marks and Dr Stevenson. Described as 'a white-haired analyst, suggesting a Dissenting evangelist rather than a poison expert', Stevenson had found 3.83 grains of tartar emetic containing 1.37 grains of antimony in Mary's remains after four years' burial. Bessie's corpse had 29.12 grains, containing 10.49 grains of antimony after two years. A week after her death, Maud's body had 20.12 grains of tartar emetic containing 3.83 grains of antimony. There were signs that a large dose had been given to each woman shortly before death.

Dr Stevenson caused a 'sensational incident' when he held up three long, thin glass tubes containing antimony sulphite extracted from Maud's stomach and liver. The judge took hold of it and Stevenson drew his attention to 'the glistening, shining part'. It was passed around amongst the barristers and, as Mr Elliott inspected 'the fearful thing', Chapman 'craned his neck forward, as though unable to remove his gaze from the piece of evidence so suddenly produced'.[336] 'While antimony held the floor,' remarked the *Daily Express*, 'the atmosphere of a chemist's shop filled the Old Bailey...the sinister intent of these elaborate preparations was forgotten [and] instead of a trial for murder the scene suggested to more than one onlooker a hospital lecture before rows of interested students.'[337] The trial transcript provides a synopsis of Stevenson's testimony, omitting counsel's questions:

> When tartar emetic or antimony is administered as a rule the greater part of it is very quickly ejected — purging relieves it — the effect of the poison itself generally takes a very considerable time before it causes death — death has occurred in many cases where it is given in repeated moderate doses — vomiting and purging makes people waste away — it produces gastro-enteritis and they also appear to die from failure of the heart — antimony depresses the circulation — it quickens the pulse, but gives it a very feeble power — two grains of tartar emetic has killed, but that is not ordinary — I should put the ordinary fatal dose at probably 15 grains — others put it at 10 — even that might not be fatal if the greater portion of it is vomited...I am of the opinion if two or three grains were given repeatedly to a healthy person that it would eventually cause death — when doses of antimony are given from time to time the symptoms are great depression, profuse perspiration, followed by nausea and vomiting — purging is set up with pain in the abdomen, and usually after a time there is a burning or metallic sensation in the throat and stomach — there is a great thirst — spasms are quite common.[338]

Elliott asked Stevenson if tartar emetic was used to cure alcoholism. He replied that it once was, but added that he had no reason to believe that Maud was addicted to drink. Carson recalled Mrs Marsh and asked her if Maud had been intemperate. Choking back her tears, she managed to give an emphatic reply in the negative. If any of the team made the connection between Elliott's question and Mary Spink's reputed fondness for drink, he seems to have kept the thought to himself.

336 *The Echo*, 18th March 1903.
337 *Daily Express*, 19th March 1903.
338 OldBaileyonline.org, retrieved 16th May 2013.

Seventeen more figures stood in the witness box that day: Dr Freyberger; police officers Godley and Neil; friends and family of the deceased, including Joseph Renton, Martha Doubleday, Jane Mumford, Elizabeth Waymark, William Taylor, William Kelsall, Elizabeth Painter and Martha Stevens; employers, landlords and neighbours, including John Ward, William Wengel, Annie Helsdown, Harriet Greenaway; and two undertakers — Henry Pierce (re: Mary Spink) and William Tull (re: Bessie Taylor and Maud Marsh). After the public laughed at a humorous misunderstanding during the testimony of one of the witnesses,

> The behaviour of the Court jarred on the prisoner. He glowered angrily at the persons in the well of the Court; twisted the remnant of his once magnificent moustache with an impatient movement, and shifted in his seat uneasily. The circumstance seemed to annoy him, and he took refuge in burying his face under the ledge to resume his writing.[339]

In between the actions that gave occasional glimpses into his thoughts, Chapman was strangely inconspicuous:

> As a rule prisoners of the first magnitude are worth close attention by Old Bailey habitués. They usually exhibit emotion of some sort. But this man is always the same. Quiet, unobtrusive, half-hidden by the warder on his right, he has attracted comparatively little attention from the spectators. When he is engrossed in his notes there is really nothing to see but a section of his glistening, carefully-brushed hair.[340]

Chapman's constant, profuse and at times feverish note-taking was mysterious. Of what might the ever-growing, scribble-strewn pile of foolscap have comprised? Perhaps it was a charade, a mere ruse to provide him with a reason to keep his head down and look as though he were doing 'something', rather than sitting passively as the evidence against him mounted up. Maybe he thought he could intimidate the witnesses by pretending to be writing something which would challenge their testimony, lead to incisive cross-examination and expose them as liars. Only occasionally did he send a note — via a warder — to one of his defence team, and sometimes this led to a question being asked of a witness. But even in these instances the query failed to challenge that witness's testimony or prove him or her to be lying or mistaken. They seem to have been pointless questions that, for all the difference they made, were not worth the breath spent in asking.

On the fourth and final day of the trial, Thursday, 19th March, the eyes of the pressmen were focussed firmly on Chapman. 'When he entered the dock he was ghastly pale...The restless movements of the hands, the twitchings of the mouth, all betrayed the emotion which he would fain conceal.'[341] He 'sighed heavily, and sat down, or rather tumbled into his seat'. Chapman's nonchalance had deserted him: twice during the day he shed tears. George R. Sims called him 'a miserable object', adding 'I have seen many men and women tried for their lives, but I never saw one who from the first to the last showed so plainly all the symptoms of abject terror.'[342]

---

339 *The Echo*, 18th March 1903.
340 *Daily Express*, 18th March 1903.
341 *South London Press*, n.d., quoted in Gordon, R.M. (2000) *Alias Jack the Ripper,* p300.
342 George R. Sims, *NZ Truth* (New Zealand), 25th January 1908.

Dr Stevenson resumed his lengthy evidence, during which 'a pained expression overspread Chapman's haggard countenance'.[343] Stevenson gave way to Bodmer, who was followed by Godley, who exhibited Chapman's long-barrelled American revolver in its leather holster. Those present 'saw the rays of light streaming through the window behind flash on the bright nickel'. 'This', announced Godley, 'was found in the prisoner's box.[344] It was loaded in every chamber'. He offered it to Mr Justice Grantham, who initially waved it away fearfully, but accepted it into his hands after Godley reassured him that it was no longer loaded. The final witness at the trial was William Kemp, on temporary promotion from sergeant to acting inspector.

The prosecution having completed its case, it was time for Chapman's barrister to sum up. Few of the forty-three prosecution witnesses had been cross-examined, and none with rigour or shrewdness. When the defence did at one point look as though it was getting its teeth into a piece of weak evidence, it transpired to be something that was, in fact, cast-iron. According to the *Daily Mail,*

> Day by day the evidence connecting him with the murder of his three 'wives' had slowly but relentlessly gathered force, so that when his counsel rose to present the defence the case for the Crown was absolutely overwhelming. Klosowski shook with terror when he took his seat and cast a furtive glance eloquent of fear at the jury.[345]

At 11.50am George Elliott KC began his final attempt to save his client from the gallows. Although his counsel spoke of nothing geographical, Chapman was 'nervously examining the small map of London which he held on his knees, and which he turned round and round, bending his head down so as to avoid observation'. At one point he 'turned and discussed the map with one of the warders then faced round, and with a distrustful look at the jury took out a clean handkerchief and held it up to his eyes'.[346] Elliott began his summing-up by admitting 'the magnitude of the task before me'. He paid tribute to Sir Edward Carson for the 'conspicuous fairness' with which the prosecution was carried out, and thanked Professor William Smith of King's College, London, for his advice and assistance.[347] Chapman took notes but 'sat there, heedless, apparently, of the words uttered on his behalf'.[348]

As news spread that the Chapman trial had reached its final stages and that the verdict would shortly be announced, people made a scramble for No. 1 court, which 'became increasingly crowded until there was not an inch of room left. Even the gangways were packed to stifling excess'. A number of 'fashionably-attired ladies' were in attendance, and 'the bench was crowded with civic officials and their friends'.[349] The court was airless because, after a juryman complained of a draught, all the doors and windows had been tightly closed.

---

343 *The Echo,* 19th March 1903.
344 In those days most working-class people owned so few possessions they could all be placed in one trunk, which they carried with them each time they moved lodgings. This trunk was colloquially known as one's 'box'.
345 *Daily Mail,* 20th March 1903.
346 *Ibid.*
347 William George Smith 1866–1918, lecturer in Experimental Psychology at King's College.
348 *Manchester Evening News,* 19th March 1903.
349 *Lloyd's Weekly,* 22nd March 1903.

Through the afternoon fresh spectators were constantly arriving, squeezing into the narrow passages when all the seats were full. A fringe of morbidly curious listeners — unwilling to lose the prisoner's slightest gesture — hung over the gallery above the dock. The alleyway behind counsel's table was choked with young barristers intently studying the Solicitor-General. A line of aldermen, with sheriffs, under-sheriffs, a chaplain, and a coroner, stretched across the court at the judge's right. Seldom has the Old Bailey been so solidly packed with men and women. They stood for hours on one side of the dock, taking turns in climbing on a bench for mental snapshots of Klosowski, and usually mistaking the principal warder for the prisoner...To these people the prisoner, absorbed in his own future, paid not the slightest heed.[350]

Elliott reminded jurors that the case was 'surrounded by a storm of prejudice' and pleaded with them to overcome any bias engendered by 'the fact that throughout the land there was a sense of distrust and suspicion with regard to the number of aliens poured upon these shores'. Elliott was quite correct: a few weeks earlier an American newspaper had remarked:

> The cost of this constantly growing colony of worse than worthless foreign dregs to London is very great, both to the municipal authorities and the government, to say nothing of the comfort and safety of the general public. The police records for the past twelve months disclose about 3,000 arrests of this class...a large number of these people at once adopt purely English names...the community, for instance, has recently been deeply interested in the case of a public house keeper named George Chapman...[his] real name is Severino Slosowski [sic], and he is a Pole. All of his victims have been Englishwomen.[351]

Everyone 'looked in vain for any motive in this case', continued Elliott, because Chapman 'had but to tell Maud Marsh to go, and she must have left, for she had no claim upon him'. And if Chapman was indeed Kłosowski, this was a point in his favour, for Annie and Lucy were alive and well: 'If he had made no attempts on the lives of these women, why should he have sought to take the lives of the three women mentioned on the charge?' What is more, Chapman 'Had courted investigation by the readiness with which he had consented to other medical men...being summoned.'

Elliott made a half-hearted attempt to discredit the expert witnesses. With reference to Dr Stevenson, the jury should 'pause before they condemned a man merely upon the scientific evidence of a gentleman, no matter how eminent he might be'. He addressed the solid evidence of Davison the chemist, his poison book and the label found in Chapman's possession and dismissed them with one sweeping comment: Davison's memory 'must be somewhat defective'. Furthermore,

> If the prisoner is a man possessing more than average intelligence, a man of special knowledge, how can you suppose that he would have been such an utter idiot, so very, very foolish, as to have purchased this murderous product in such quantities from a man who knew him, knew

350 *Daily Express*, 20th March 1903.
351 *Philadelphia Enquirer*, 23rd January 1903.

his name, his occupation, where he was working…It was absurd, and the Hastings chemist was mistaken in his identity.

But Chapman *was* that 'utter idiot', and it was futile for Elliott to attempt to persuade the jury that Chapman had not purchased the poison: the evidence was watertight.

Chapman listened to Elliott's speech impassively until he uttered the word 'antimony'. At that juncture he borrowed a fragment of pencil from the gaoler and began to scribble copiously on slips of blue paper provided by the court. These notes were handed to Mr Elliott every few moments, after which Chapman peered anxiously at him 'to observe their effect'. However, as his defence counsel's speech grew longer, Chapman appeared bored, stifled a yawn and gazed out of the window. Scaffolding and other signs of construction work were visible through the grimy glass. Having turned his chair so he could see outside, Chapman 'watched the travels of an iron bucket suspended from a rope, which travelled backwards and forwards from a crane in the yard beyond'.[352] A *Daily Express* correspondent described how the prisoner's demeanour changed over the course of the day:

> From upright impassiveness, which he resolutely assumed upon beginning this last day in public, Klosowski bent in his chair inch by inch, so that at last his head was below the top of the dock; his body shook with a peculiar tremor, and his black brows were contracted in a nervous frown as though trying to suppress a great emotion. He had no appetite for luncheon, and as the afternoon waned he grew more limp and lachrymose.[353]

That afternoon Chapman 'carried a handkerchief, sniffed repeatedly, and seemed to be striving hard to keep back a flood of tears'. As Mr Elliott continued his summing up, 'the prisoner's sniffs were again heard throughout the Court, and big tears were seen tumbling down his sunken cheeks'. When Elliott pointed out to the jury that, if they erred, the accused would be hanged and 'it will be impossible to repair the mistake', Chapman 'broke down in earnest, and buried his face in his handkerchief'.[354] Before long, he was 'sobbing freely',[355] but H.L. Adam felt that Chapman's tears were 'of much the same kind as he had been wont to shed after slaughtering his victims'.[356]

Mr Elliott's oration, which had taken two-and-a-half hours, was 'slightly applauded by those in Court as he resumed his seat'.[357] One reporter sympathised with his unenviable task, remarking that his speech was 'as good as anyone could have made in the hopeless circumstances.'[358]

At 3pm Sir Edward Carson began his closing speech for the Treasury by congratulating Mr Elliott on his 'able defence' of Chapman, and assuring him that the prosecution harboured no prejudice against the accused man for being an alien.

352 *Daily Express*, 20th March 1903.
353 *Ibid*.
354 *The Echo*, 19th March 1903.
355 *Manchester Evening News*, 19th March 1903.
356 Adam, H.L. (1930) *Trial of George Chapman*, William Hodge, p28.
357 *Manchester Evening News*, 19th March 1903.
358 *The Advertiser* (Adelaide), 27th April 1903.

Then, 'with unimpassioned voice, but dogged, deliberate manner',[359] he got into his stride, asking: 'What am I to say of motive in a case of this kind?' Chapman had 'a most ample motive...a history of unbridled, heartless, and cruel lust'. He entreated the jurors to:

> Look at that poor, wretched grave, and that disinterred coffin, where the woman who went through pangs of suffering and cruel pains still lies, the victim of a foul murder, and well may her body appeal to us to do justice!

He pointed out that Chapman ran very little risk in calling in a series of doctors: after all, he had managed to deceive them all. He concluded by imploring the jury to 'do your duty like men'. According to Sir Edward's biographer, his eyes 'occasionally had fallen upon the man in the dock, whose eyes in turn were fixed upon his prosecutor with sullen malice. "I have never seen such a villain", asserted Carson, "He looked like some evil wild beast, I almost expected him to leap over the dock and attack me".'[360]

Mr Justice Grantham's forty-five-minute summing-up was described by one writer as 'practically a continuation of the speech for the prosecution'.[361] He complimented both sides on their 'eloquent addresses' and impressed upon the jurymen the gravity of the task before them, reminding them that their job was to decide only whether Chapman had killed Maud Marsh, not Mary Spink or Bessie Taylor. The judge stated that the case was unique from three points of view: legally, chemically and medically. Legally, because it was the first time the antecedents of a prisoner had been investigated in the way they had been in this case, and also in the way two previous deaths were admitted as evidence. This was inconsistent with the usual rules, but was allowed because the evidence against Chapman had been wholly circumstantial. (The judge was mistaken. Similar evidence was given in Neill Cream's trial in 1892.) Chemically, because it enabled Dr Stevenson to observe how antimony preserved the tissues of the body in an almost perfect state of embalmment. Medically, it was a sad reflection that a man who had only been a hairdresser's assistant should be able to defy doctors, and to murder women under their very noses without the slightest fear of being found out. He referred to Chapman as a 'surgeon'.

> It is very sad to think that one whose position as surgeon was such that he could not follow it, or did not wish to follow it, and he came over here to act as an assistant hairdresser for many years, and yet his knowledge of poison and medicine should enable him to baffle the surgeons for five or six long years.

Chapman, the judge continued, seemed 'perfectly indifferent to any doctor' and had even boasted that he could give Maud a pinch of something no one could detect. Mary's symptoms had clearly been those of poison, and are well known to every doctor, so and he found it strange that Rogers did not recognise them. He issued Rogers with a posthumous rebuke for issuing a death certificate which blamed 'something that

---

359 *Daily Mail*, 20th March 1903.
360 Marjoribanks, E. (1932) *Carson the Advocate*, 2005 edition, Kessinger, p304. Sugden has remarked that although Carson's reminiscence is much quoted, that does not make it accurate.
361 Freeman, N. (2004). In Moore, G. and Maunder, A. *Victorian Crime, Madness and Sensation*, Ashgate, p219.

could not, by any possibility, have been the cause of her death'. The judge was sorry to be obliged to comment on the medics' shortcomings, but criticised Dr Sunderland's opinion on Bessie's illness as 'not worth what was being paid for it', adding that bringing in Dr Elliman 'was like going from the frying-pan into the fire', because he had all but accused the patient of inventing her symptoms.

Grantham thought Stoker and Cotter better than the two specialists, but still labelled Stoker 'not equal to his position'. He hauled him over the coals for not realising his patient was being poisoned, and for issuing a death certificate for Bessie that was 'founded on his ignorance'. He asked, incredulously, 'Have you ever known a case where four doctors gave four different opinions, and when the patient died still there was no post-mortem?' Stoker also saw Maud 'dying by inches in the greatest agony from an irritant poison' and yet did not inquire into it, and administered to her the same 'remedies' that had failed to work on Bessie. 'If it had not been for poor old Mr and Mrs Marsh,' he observed, 'I do not believe there would have been the slightest chance of detecting the cause of death.' This eventuality would, of course, have left Chapman free to kill further victims.

When the Marshes had sent for Dr Grapel, Grantham remarked, that was 'the first time in all these long years that any intelligence has been brought in.' He suggested that Grapel's suspicions of poisoning may have provoked Chapman to administer the fatal dose, because 'he got frightened and thought it would not be wise to hesitate any longer'. The doctors should have removed Maud from his care, or at the very least they could have surreptitiously sneaked from her bedroom some vomit, excrement, and the brandy Chapman had placed by Maud's bed, and sent them for analysis. Had the doctors acted more swiftly, they may have saved Maud's life or, failing that, Chapman could have been arrested before he disposed of his stockpile of tartar emetic. The judge also thought it odd that nobody noticed that Maud recovered when away from Chapman and relapsed when she returned to him.

The doctors at Guy's Hospital were next in the firing line. Grantham called it 'abominable' that 'one of the finest institutions in the world' was unable to discover what ailed Maud.[362] This was partly because Targett, the eminent surgeon whose patient she was, failed to examine Maud or even speak to her, but accepted the diagnosis reached by his juniors. 'The actions of all the medical men', the judge concluded, was 'a sad series of misadventures'.

Mr Justice Grantham asserted that there was no doubt that each woman had died of antimonial poisoning. When he cited Davison's poison register, and announced: 'There you have the prisoner's own handwriting as the purchaser of this tartar emetic', Chapman became noticeably distressed:

> For the first time the wretched man began to realise the overwhelming strength of the chain of circumstantial evidence which had been laboriously forged against him. Then he broke down, collapsed both mentally and physically, his forbidding features twitched convulsively, his cruel, claw-like hands pawed the air, and ever and anon were used to wipe the perspiration which streamed down his evil face.

362 *Manchester Courier*, 21st March 1903.

In the case of an ordinary murderer some pity might have been aroused in the crowded court by these evidences of suffering, but for this criminal, convicted already in the minds of everybody of three of the foulest and cruellest crimes of recent years, there could be no feelings of sympathy.[363]

The judge admitted that Chapman was a class of alien 'against whom there is a strong feeling that we have too many', but warned the jury that they must not allow such sentiments to have any bearing on their verdict.

The jury retired at five o'clock and returned after twelve minutes. Chapman 'was again conducted weeping into the dock', where he 'had to be assisted to the rail'. After the foreman of the jury pronounced him guilty of murder, the clerk of arraigns asked him: 'Have you anything to say why sentence of death should not be passed upon you, according to law?' Chapman 'turned a leaden face to the stern representative of the majesty of the law, and his lips moved, but never a word came from them'. He 'would have fallen in a heap to the floor of the dock had not two stalwart warders, each of a stature and physique which seemed to dwarf the creature in their charge, seized hold of him by the arms and helped to hold him upright'.[364]

The judge donned the customary black cap and addressed Chapman directly: 'Severino Klosowski, for I decline to call you by the English name you have assumed, the only satisfactory feature in the case...is that I am able to address you as a foreigner and not as an Englishman.'[365] Referring to Chapman's 'frightful cruelty', he described the three victims as 'women on whose bodies you gratified your vile lust'. He then proceeded to deliver the death sentence with 'impressive solemnity':[366]

> I have now only one duty to perform and that is to pass upon you the sentence of the law, which is — that you be taken hence to the place from whence you came, and that from thence you be taken to some lawful place of execution, and that there you be hanged by the neck until you be dead, and that your body be buried within the precincts of the gaol within which you have been last confined after your conviction, and may the Lord have mercy on your soul.[367]

To this, the chaplain added, 'Amen', and Chapman 'sobbed bitterly with his head against the panelling of the dock'.

> Weeping for himself with far more sincerity than he ever wept for his victims, the man who reduced slow poisoning to a science bade farewell to the world at the Old Bailey yesterday...Condemnation brought a great change in this remarkable murderer. In the shadow of the gallows he lost his reserve and wept silently, hopelessly, as a man weeps who is possessed by utter despair.[368]

As daylight ebbed away, the court became very gloomy:

363 *Worcestershire Chronicle*, 21st March 1903.
364 All quotes in this paragraph *Worcestershire Chronicle*, 21st March 1903.
365 Adam, H.L. (1930) *Trial of George Chapman*, William Hodge, p164–5.
366 *Worcestershire Chronicle*, 21st March 1903.
367 *Ibid.*
368 *Daily Express*, 20th March 1903.

On a spring morning, with a welcome light streaming in through the dusty windows from the site of vanished Newgate, the Old Bailey presents a fairly cheerful appearance. But at dusk, with dim gas lamps emphasising every grim detail, even to a wrinkle in the black cap and the tear on the prisoner's cheek, it is a picture, once seen, never to be forgotten.[369]

The *Daily Mail* continued to disparage Chapman for being an alien. In one edition, it described him as 'the cowering Russian Pole' and remarked:

Klosowski is not in appearance a typical Russian Pole. He is an under-sized man, with small, sharp features, and in repose his face does not suggest a foreigner. It was not until, huddled and terror-stricken, he was being half-lifted from the dock after hearing his death sentence that one noted in his upturned face, and particularly his eyes, a clearly foreign look.[370]

Later the paper remarked that Chapman 'had entered the dock looking like an Englishman' and 'left it looking like a Pole.'[371]

When it was time for Chapman to leave the court, he was 'still in a dazed condition, and trembling in every limb'.[372] Supported by two prison officers, he stumbled down the steps leading from the dock. Years later Jack While (the reporter who had enraged Chapman with his comments about the fire at the Monument) claimed to have lifted Mrs Marsh up so she could watch the murderer's final exit.[373]

Chapman was locked in a temporary cell for forty-five minutes whilst his death warrant was prepared and signed. After being handcuffed, he was escorted outside into the yard where, observed by Colonel Henry Bevan Isaacson, governor of Brixton Prison, and Major Knox, his counterpart at Wandsworth, he climbed into a prison van, accompanied by Wandsworth's chief warder Charles Hazell and two of his staff. According to a man who later claimed to have been one of the warders, as the vehicle emerged from the precincts of the court to begin its journey to Wandsworth Prison,

A huge crowd awaited him outside the court, and cheers and hoots were strangely intermingled. Chapman shuddered time and again as angry, excited faces pressed forward to the windows of the cab, which had to be guarded by mounted police until we were well out of the neighbourhood of the court. By the time we reached Wandsworth he was like a limp rag.[374]

'Thus ended', commented the *Angus Evening Telegraph*, 'in the triumphant vindication of the law the most sensational poisoning trial of the present generation.'[375]

---

369 *Daily Express*, 20th March 1903.
370 *Daily Mail*, 20th March 1903.
371 *Daily Mail*, 8th April 1903.
372 *Angus Evening Telegraph*, 20th March 1903.
373 *Sunday Express*, n.d., 1931.
374 *Weekly News*, 17th October 1919. The warder either misremembered the van as a cab, or (as is more likely in my opinion) the entire scenario was a figment of his imagination.
375 *Angus Evening Telegraph*, 20th March 1903.

## THE BIRTH OF THE CHAPMAN–RIPPER THEORY

On 23rd March the *Daily Chronicle* reported that police investigating Chapman's past had begun to suspect him of being Jack the Ripper. The article was despatched by cable across the English-speaking world, and newspapers in Australia, Canada and the USA repeated the news; some even claimed that the original source had announced that Chapman was definitely the elusive Whitechapel Murderer. Some American papers were particularly bold, running headlines such as 'He Is Jack the Ripper', 'Original Jack the Ripper under sentence of death' and 'Jack the Ripper to die on the gallows.'[376] Others exhibited scepticism and one of the few British papers to mention the story was of the opinion that 'the grounds for this curious theory are very slender.'[377]

Meanwhile, as Chapman spent much of his time reading newspapers and magazines, this startling development cannot have evaded his notice. If he made any comment it was not recorded for posterity. The morning that the *Daily Chronicle* article was published, he was purportedly thrice told that his wife was waiting to speak with him, but he refused to see her. Lucy's visit may have been prompted by the article: perhaps she intended to ask him to admit or deny his involvement. (I shall return to the Chapman–Ripper theory in Part Six.)

## THE CONDEMNED MAN

As soon as Chapman's death sentence was passed, the owners of the world-famous Madame Tussaud's Waxworks set about creating a strikingly lifelike model of him. It was put on display in a prominent position in its Chamber of Horrors and, by 28th March, advertisements in the national papers announced its presence. (The model was viewed by millions over six decades until it was removed in the 1960s, having been damaged by fire.)

Whilst awaiting execution Chapman occupied the condemned cell that Edgar Edwards had vacated on 3rd March. The thought of death 'paralysed him physically and mentally',[378] his appetite increased or decreased (according to which reporter one believes) and he was 'restless' and 'uneasy', especially at night. 'Precautions were taken to prevent any attempt at self-destruction: two warders are constantly in his cell', stated one pressman.[379] Another claimed that 'What little food he takes he is unable to retain. His appearance is wretched in the extreme, and at times he cries bitterly.' The warders revealed that 'in the whole course of their experience, they had never seen a more dejected prisoner'. To keep up his spirits he was encouraged to exercise outdoors twice daily, but only when the other inmates were at breakfast or lunch, to avoid meeting them.

Chapman was deeply offended at being described in court as a Jew, calling the label 'a stigma'. To emphasise the point he specified that he wanted a Roman Catholic priest, not a rabbi. However, he declined the Lenten diet, opting for the normal prison infirmary fare.

---

376 *Fort Wayne Weekly Sentinel*, 23rd March 1903; *Atlanta Constitution*, 24th March 1903 and 5th April 1903.
377 *Manchester Courier*, 24th March 1903.
378 George R. Sims, *NZ Truth* (New Zealand), 25th January 1908.
379 *Worcestershire Chronicle*, 28th March 1903.

*From the Daily Mail.*

It was a singular characteristic of Klosowski — we will not commit the indignity to Englishmen of using his assumed English name — that in his very last hours he was perturbed by a trifling point altogether apart from the enormity of the tragedies in which he had a hand. He was 'annoyed' that he should have been termed a Polish Jew, and we are told that he did his utmost, latterly, in the way of eating pork, to refute the Judge's 'aspersion' on his character.[380]

Unsurprisingly, the Jewish community felt stigmatised at being associated with a serial murderer. The Rev. Frank L. Cohen of Brixton Prison reassured readers of the *Jewish Chronicle* that Chapman was definitely a Gentile.[381] The RC priest assigned to Wandsworth Prison was twenty-nine-year-old Father Aloysius Hawarden, the first Salesian priest to be ordained in England. He took care of Chapman's spiritual needs, was a frequent visitor to his cell, and would be present at his execution.

Chapman also received visits from the other three men who were responsible for his well-being: the governor, sixty-five-year-old James Knox, a retired army major; the prison doctor, Irish-born George Beamish and the chief warder, Charles George Hazell, who were in their fifties.[382]

The condemned man's foreign birth continued to rankle on some people. One correspondent to the *Morning Advertiser* wrote, under the heading 'Aliens and Full Licences':

> Sir, now that the Chapman case is over, I should like to know how it has been possible for such a man — an alien — to come from goodness knows where and obtain the various full licences in London and elsewhere which he has managed to secure. My brethren in the trade know as well as I do the difficulties which an Englishman desirous of becoming a fully-licensed victualler has to surmount. First he must supply the police with the names and addresses of two or three most respectable people who have known him for 10, 15, or 20 years. Finally, if at any time, however remote, he has had the misfortune to be summoned for some paltry offence — coverable by a half-crown fine or merely a caution — the chances are his application for a licence will be refused.

380 *Coventry Evening Telegraph*, 7th April 1903.
381 *Southwark & Bermondsey Recorder*, 17th January 1903.
382 These officials and their wives all lived within the prison.

Here is a foreigner and a criminal who was able to hold licences with impunity! — I am, Sir, yours, &c., East Ham.[383]

'East Ham' was mistaken; until he was charged with murder, there was no indication that George Chapman was a criminal, and therefore no reason to bar him from holding a licence.

Chapman continued to protest his innocence. He also criticised the conduct of the trial and complained that Mrs Toon and Miss Rayner should have been cross-examined more rigorously. He insisted that he was American, that the police had got the wrong man and had falsified evidence, and that the witnesses had committed perjury. No court of appeal existed in those days; a prisoner could, however, send a petition to the Home Secretary. On Chapman's instructions, Mr Sydney drew up such a document, citing two reasons to support Chapman's appeal for a royal pardon. The first was that the deaths of Mary and Bessie should not have been admitted as evidence towards the murder of Maud because 'Evidence of such a character has never before been admitted in a criminal trial.' The second reason related to the chemical evidence and had two parts: firstly, Chapman was 'convicted almost entirely on the evidence of the Medical and Chemical witnesses' and secondly, that this evidence may have been faulty. Sydney cited the case of Thomas Smethurst ('the Richmond Poisoner'), who in 1859 was sentenced to death for murder but pardoned when it was discovered that a senior toxicologist and an eminent chemist had made errors whilst testing for arsenic and antimony.

The petition was sent to the Home Office on Saturday, 28th March. Two days later, civil servant Charles Troup,[384] the recently appointed assistant under-secretary, annotated it with a comment pointing out that both of Sydney's grounds for appeal were based on incorrect information. Regarding the first point, Troup noted that it was 'a well established rule' to admit evidence of previous poisonings, and cited the cases of *R v Geering*, *R v Flannagan & Higgins*, and *R v Thomas Neill Cream*. With regard to the second point, it was 'incorrect on both heads'. Not only was there 'strong evidence independent of the scientific evidence', but the scientific evidence 'was so complete as to leave no possibility of questioning it'. The petition and Troup's comments were read by Sir Kenelm Digby, the permanent under-secretary.[385] He returned it to Troup, who wrote on it: 'Nothing further in this case. Send out the usual "no interference" letters.' Troup wrote to the under-sheriff, Frederick Kynaston Metcalfe, to let him know that the death sentence was to be carried out. (Among his duties, an under-sheriff was responsible for making arrangements for executions and was one of the officials obliged to be present.) The following day Chapman's petition was read by the Home Secretary, Aretas Akers-Douglas, who wrote upon it, 'There can be no possible ground for interference in this case.'[386]

Meanwhile, in Wandsworth Prison, Chapman waited anxiously for the outcome of his petition. One newsman reported that he 'sleeps little, pacing the cell

---

383 *Morning Advertiser*, 23rd March 1903. A search at the London Metropolitan Archives revealed that no testimonials for Chapman survive.
384 (Later Sir) Charles Edward Troup, KCB, KCVO, 1857–1941.
385 Sir Kenelm Edward Digby KCB, GCB, 1836–1916.
386 National Archives, file HO 144/680/101992/12.

# CHAPMAN'S PETITION FOR A ROYAL PARDON

THAT YOUR PETITIONER was tried on the 12th of March [*The trial ran from 16th to 19th March.*] at the Central Criminal Court before Mr. Justice Grantham and a Jury for the Murder of Maud Marsh, by the administration of Antimony, found guilty and sentenced to death.

That at the Trial evidence was received regarding the deaths of Mary Isabella Spink and Bessie Taylor. That this evidence though objected by your Petitioners Counsel was admitted by the Judge, and was used to shew that your Petitioner having lived with Mary Isabella Spink and Bessie Taylor at the time of their death, and Antimony having been found in their bodies, his must have been the hand that administered it. The learned Solicitor General so laid the Case before the Court.

YOUR PETITIONER is informed that evidence of such a character has never before been admitted in a Criminal Trial and never before so used; that the whole weight of legal authority is against it. Its effect was not to show that your Petitioner was guilty of the crime with which he was charged but to prejudice his Trial by the suggestion that he might have been guilty of two other crimes and that he was a bad man and likely to commit crime.

The result was to confuse the issue before the Jury and to prejudice your Petitioner who was not tried only on the one indictment then before the Court but had to simultaneously defend himself against two other charges, and without any notice in the indictment that he was to be charged, a thing contrary to the very foundation of the Criminal Law. Had your Petitioner been involved in a civil trial, had he been tried for a lesser Criminal offence Your Petitioner is informed that he would have had the right of appeal, and a very great probability of prosecuting such appeal successfully. His life being at stake it appears that Your Majestys Courts can give him no redress for a wrongful procedure, however great the hardship inflicted on him. Therefore it is, no other course being open to him, Your Petitioner ventures to bring the matter before His Majesty. Further that Your Petitioner was convicted almost entirely on the evidence of the Medical and Chemical witnesses, and would humbly call attention to the fallibility of such testimony and to the difficulty of being sure that all possibility of mistake has been eliminated to show the danger of a conviction chiefly in Scientific testimony.

YOUR PETITIONER would crave leave to refer to the Case of Doctor [*Thomas*] Smethurst trial at the Old Bailey in 1859. In that Case the greatest Medico-forensic authority of the day, Doctor Taylor [*Dr Alfred Swaine Taylor, Professor of Chemistry at Guy's Hospital, Fellow of the Royal College of Physicians, Fellow of the Royal Society*] and Doctor Odling [*Dr William Odling, physician, Fellow of the Royal Society, Professor of Practical Chemistry*] gave evidence on oath before the Coroner that having first tested their apparatus and found no arsenic or antimony in them they then examined by Reinschs test a certain bottle which has been traced to the Prisoner, and that in it they found arsenic and antimony. This evidence they repeated at the police court, and the Prisoner was committed for trial. It was then discovered that their experiment was unreliable, that in fact there had been no arsenic or antimony in the bottle but that what was found there had been introduced by the Witnesses in the course of their test.

YOUR PETITIONER would draw attention to the fact that in that Case the Medical men had done everything in accordance with the scientific knowledge of that time. That it was believed that their results were accurate. It was on the fortunate accident of a new discovery in science that demonstrated their fallibility. Mr Brande a very eminent chemist said he would have fallen into the same error. 'The fact, he said is new to the Chemical world.' The Prisoner in that Case was pardoned, the Home Secretary expressing himself as follows: 'The necessity which I have felt for advising Her Majesty to grant a free pardon in this Case has not as it appears to me arisen from any defect in the Constitution or proceedings of any Criminal Tribunals; it has arisen from the imperfections of Medical Science and from this fallibility of Judgment in an obscure malady even of skilful and experienced practitioners.'

YOUR PETITIONER therefore most humbly prays His Majesty to take Your Petitioners Case into your Royal consideration and that His Majesty will be greatly pleased to issue your Royal warrant for YOUR PETITIONERS pardon.

[Signed] Henry I. Sydney, Solr. for and on behalf of George Chapman committed as Severino Klosowski.

*The main entrance to Wandsworth Prison.*

for the greater part of the night';[387] another opined that Chapman 'really believed almost to the last that he would be able to escape the grasp of the law.'[388] Chapman may have read in the newspapers that three other men facing execution had petitioned successfully and been reprieved. Joseph Abbott's suicide-by-poison pact with his wife had gone awry: she died and he survived; Grocer George Pepperdine shot his wife dead in a pub and Andrew Moore murdered a vicar. These men were, apparently, all British-born, which probably made Chapman feel even more acutely that he was a 'persecuted alien' when his petition failed. The *Manchester Evening News* wrote that he 'showed signs of great disappointment and practically collapsed'.

> In this condition he remained for some days, suffering great depression of spirits and exhibiting a peculiar restlessness, particularly at night, so that the most vigilant observation was kept by the warders to guard against an attempt at self-destruction.[389]

A slightly different report appeared in the *Manchester Courier*:

> [He] flew into a violent passion, reiterating his assertions of innocence, and alleging perjury on the part of witnesses. He expressed his determination to appeal to the King direct, and declared he would never allow himself to be hanged branded as an alien of Polish extraction. Asked if he desired to see anyone, he replied, 'yes; I'd like to see the Home Secretary, and lay my case before him.' When left by Major Knox in the custody of the warders he was still talking of seeing the King.[390]

## FINAL DAYS

Even though his appeal had failed and his execution was now an unavoidable certainty, Chapman stubbornly and pointlessly continued to insist that he was an American and that he was innocent of any crime. One newspaper revealed that an unnamed 'famous psychologist' had declared that Chapman would 'most assuredly confess his undoubted crimes before execution'. After he made no confession, the psychologist backpedalled, saying 'there are phases of human character which absolutely defy analysis'.[391]

In his final few days, Chapman received his solicitor and priest, but his only personal visitors were three unnamed friends (two men and a woman). None had been witnesses and the woman was not Lucy. Perhaps they included Mr and Mrs Bushell, the couple Chapman had employed to run the pub until it was sold.[392]

Chapman spent most of the day before his execution corresponding with friends. His letters were written on official notepaper which bore his prison number, 14,293, alongside his Polish name (which must have annoyed him). Some or all of his outgoing letters were leaked to the press. They revealed that, whilst over the years

---

387 *Daily Mail,* 2nd April 1903.
388 *Worcestershire Chronicle,* 21st March 1903.
389 *Manchester Evening News,* 7th April 1903.
390 *Manchester Courier,* 11th April 1903.
391 *Gloucester Citizen,* 8th April 1903. The psychologist may have been Dr Smith of King's College. See p144.
392 *Sheffield Evening Telegraph,* 16th April 1903, stated that Mr Bushell was 'formerly in Chapman's employ at the Crown Inn, and, upon his arrest, manager on his behalf until the property changed hands.'

his spoken English had become increasingly fluent through constant interaction with native speakers, he never reached equal proficiency in written English. George R. Sims remarked:

> Before his trial he would speak and write English fairly well. His last letters...showed that the knowledge of English he once possessed had been almost obliterated. His more recent mental equipment seemed to have peeled off. His last letter written in English was unintelligible.[393]

The *Daily Mail* published the following snippets from Chapman's letters, without revealing their recipients or how it obtained them.

> Just a line as promised. I am better than I have been, but I don't feel werry good in ability. I felt as I could have streng enough to do anything but realy I do not have strength as I expected. It is too much for me... Believe me, I remain to you all, yours faithfully G. Chapman.

> I regret to say and to find as have been unfortunately in this, so Dredfull blow to me. Bellive me I am surprise of this after I should be find as gilty of the Dredfull crime.

> But I only got to say is this as I am here charged innocently and condemt in this sivilased seposed country of wich I am Perfectly having no knolege of this accused act against me.

A letter dated 3rd April and sent to Frank and Emma Bushell reads as follows:

> Yurs to hand and I am very Pleased to here from you and I must tel you as I had not answer of my patitn [*petition*] from the Home Secy and I had no notice of any sort till nuow. I hop I shell Recive notice soon o the decision as bn not know to me yet. Xxxxx. But styl Let it be once settled. You can see Playn or nuf as there is no secret and a floor in wholl the scandals Representatn o my case. Therefore Please do as I my want you to do for me if I send you my paper and statement which I made up and offered to the consel which the was not Represented and I will give you the instruction whod to do so it can be make kno to my bruther-in-law W. taylor and you my be a little halpe to hint then He will do anything he can for me and my Benefit if it not to the Benefit if it not to the present state but layter one. You may see if you be at trafalge square. You see the corner of trafalge street and strant [*The Strand*] on the Left hand side in an shiping offices just before you get to Parlement Street and there you will find an American papers for sale. You ask him if you can have my wish and instruke him as I Refere to be widly reinstale in America and you may be a good enuf and ask him if this is just as Refere to belive me as dos statements are truth as God is in Haven and on this the may Reley upon and Demand just and not critasetion and scandlization as was brought by the Police in the gret city of this country. Belive me as the[y] have made biggest Pergery as ever been know before in Regards the Polishe witness. I can not write any more. Be good. Remanbe me to you all and Good Baye to you all from me yours George Chapman.

---

393 *NZ Truth* (New Zealand), 25th January 1908.

> Mr Petts please give up my two frame glased and in perfect order as the[y] are my own Private property an on behalf of my society as certificates one Refering to star outfelows no 2 and one Refering to London Carmen trade union no 6 I Requested you to be given up to my Representif Mr Bushell. George Chapman.[394]

The final paragraph was a request to the Crown's new tenant, Mr Petts, that two glass-framed friendly society emblems — depicting the Star Oddfellows and the London Carmen — that Chapman left behind be handed to Frank Bushell. They may have been a token of gratitude for running the pub after his arrest.

Chapman's longest letter, dated 6th April at 4pm, was also addressed to the Bushells, who presumably sold it to the press, since snippets of different lengths ended up in various newspapers across Britain, and, decades later, in *Trial of George Chapman*. Collating the various excerpts I have attempted to piece together the letter in its entirety.

> I have to prepare myself for the dredfull death which is so close. It is only a few hours to weit for. My dear frients believe me, I cannot express my sorrow to you of my posision, but yet I wish it was over as the time is dredful long waiting for it...I am innocent of this accusetion of Poisoning them. And therefore Believe me, be careful in your own life of dangers of other ememis whom are unknow to you. As you see on your own expirence in my case how I was unjustly criticised and falsly Represented. Also you can see I am not Belived. Therefore you see where there is Justice. Belive me it is last letter to you, and you will never have the chance to see me or receive any more letters from me. It is not good to me [to] deny. If I was gilty I would say. But as I am not, therefore, I must insist upon to my last, as I cannot accuse myself of which I am innocent of. They can take my life but they cannot kil my soul and tak it from me. God is my judge, and I pray to have mercy on my soul for my sins which I have dun during my Life. But, as to crime, I am innocent, and I have clear conscious of it. Therefore you my jest tell you as there is circumstensioll avidence so far of the true evidence and Belive me is it no good to come to this diteels [*details*]. But do take care of yourself and be prepared agist your amenis [*enemies*]. I pray God for siners who are suffering unjustly in this country. Belive me I am werry grievously sorry but it could not be help now...I therefore thank you for you kindness and good fileing [*feeling*] having to me, I only wish I could so sumting for you but you see how I am fixed and how I am dineyde of everything, and with gret crisisasetion [*criticism?*] and it [*is*] all most barbarios and cruell represented without any direct proov [*proof*] or other Direct secomstensiol evidence. It is Barbarios thing to condemned a man but you see it is done Therefore my dear friends, be Humen to all living critioc [*creatures?*] in this world as I have been, but you must forgive and forget if I have dun eny unjust to you. Please be merciful and forgive me. Shall be now starting preparing for my Deth as it is past four o'clock afternoon. I enclose this letter with great sorrow and I cannot express it any more. Therefore, good bye to you Mrs. F. Bushell

394 *Sheffield Daily Telegraph*, 8th April 1903.

and Mr. F. Bushell and Frankie and Doris and all your friends. Good bye for ever from yours faithfully Frent. — George Chapman.

It is noteworthy that, although the Bushells were his 'dear friends' (indeed his only friends) Chapman addressed them with starchy formality — by title, initial and surname, even in the shadow of the gallows. In another letter, quoted by H.L. Adam, he continued his absurd fiction that he was a US citizen:

> One thing whod I wish is this to be Remembered as I am an American orphend of good family and I left my foster father, against his wish, and I took to erning my living at age of ten. And since that time I worked the best I could get.[395]

Predictably, perhaps, reporters commented on the pitiful state of Chapman's written English. One remarked that his 'calligraphy was fair, but the spelling and punctuation was so bad that the document was almost unintelligible'.[396] The *Daily Mail* described his letters as 'a strange jumble of words which exhibits him clearly as an alien entirely baffled by the language which a few weeks ago he spoke as well as an Englishman', and continued:

> The theory was never more clearly borne out that an ignorant, illiterate man of low type who has during his later years put on a veneer of education and social polish will, if condemned to death...entirely relapse into his original condition of illiteracy and stupidity.[397]

Provincial newsmen were no less taken aback:

> Chapman's last letters, with their revelation of strange illiteracy and incoherent thought, came as a surprise to the public, which had certainly attributed to him greater cunning and strength of mind. Rightly viewed, however, they are only an index to the meanness and cowardice plainly traceable throughout the unhappy man's career.[398]

One reporter wondered how Chapman had secured a public house licence despite his 'complete ignorance of the written language'.[399] Another expressed surprise that, despite being 'almost illiterate', he was 'able to defeat...several doctors'.[400]

Prison staff reminded Chapman that, on the day prior to his execution, a condemned man traditionally said goodbye to his loved ones, but Chapman loved no one, and had either driven away or murdered all those who had loved him. Governor James Knox visited Chapman's cell and suggested allowing his friends to visit again, but he replied curtly, 'I have none' and asked only for Fr Hawarden. Mass was celebrated in the chapel, where Chapman partook of Holy Communion. He was seated near the organ, which, 'screened by curtains, shielded him from observation by other prisoners'.[401]

395 Adam, H.L. (1930) *Trial of George Chapman*, William Hodge, p44.
396 *South London Chronicle*, 11th April 1903.
397 *Daily Mail*, 8th April 1903.
398 *Gloucester Citizen*, 8th April 1903.
399 *Coventry Looker-On*, 11th April 1903.
400 *South London Chronicle*, 11th April 1903.
401 *Sheffield Daily Telegraph*, 8th April 1903.

Although Lucy had recently borne a daughter, whom she named Helena, according to the *Daily Express* she visited every day but Chapman refused to see her. On 6th April she 'sent three consecutive messages to the condemned cell that she was waiting outside. There was no answer.'[402] Her purpose in calling was never established. Perhaps she wanted to give Cecilia the opportunity to meet her biological father for the last time. According to the press, Chapman never relented, but many years later Cecilia claimed that she and her mother were admitted to the prison infirmary, where Chapman was 'hiding under the bedsheets', mimicking an American accent and claiming to be a US citizen.[403] A sketch in the *Illustrated Police News,* captioned 'The Last Interview', depicts a man, a woman and a girl peering at Chapman through prison bars. The woman could be Lucy Kłosowska or Emma Bushell, the man Frank Szymański or Frank Bushell, and the child Cecilia Kłosowska or Doris Bushell, who were at that time both ten years old.

The evening before his death, and after a private mass, Chapman was visited by Major Knox and Dr Beamish. He thanked them for their kind attentions. Then the hangman and his assistant arrived at the prison and made the usual preparations. Chapman was taken to be weighed, to enable them to compute the correct drop. Both rope and machinery were then thoroughly tested. The executioner, William 'Billie' Billington, was twenty-eight. His father and brothers performed the same role; indeed, he had recently succeeded his father as Britain's principal executioner. He was assisted by twenty-five-year-old Henry 'Harry' Pierrepoint, also the son of an executioner, who would take over as principal on Billington's resignation in 1905. The job of public executioner was neither a full-time post nor a paid one. Billington was a blacksmith and Pierrepoint managed a furniture shop. Like all of Britain's hangmen they had volunteered to execute people in the name of the monarch in their spare time, for nothing more than expenses. In total, Billington hanged fifty-seven people, and assisted at fifteen other executions. Pierrepoint hanged seventy and assisted thirty-five times. In accordance with tradition, on the night of 6th April, the pair slept within the prison walls.

THE LAST INTERVIEW.

Chapman stayed up late, reportedly reading the Bible. Then his prison clothes were removed for the final time, for he would be hanged in his tail-coated suit. He put on his prison nightshirt and retired to his Spartan bed.

402 *Daily Express,* 7th April 1903.
403 O'Donnell, K., Parlour, A. and Parlour, S. (1997) *Jack the Ripper Whitechapel murders.* Ten Bells Publishing.

## EXECUTION

On 7th April 1903 Chapman became the twenty-fifth person to be executed at Wandsworth. The 135th (and last), hanged in 1961, was also a Pole, Henryk Niemasz.

One newspaper claimed that Chapman had passed 'a broken and restless night'; another stated that he 'slept fairly well'. After being roused by the chief warder at 6am, he washed but was not shaved, then dressed himself in the costume which he had worn during his trial: 'frock coat, a fancy waistcoat, nondescript trousers, and a much-worn blue-and-white print shirt'.[404] Another newsman remarked that Chapman's demeanour that morning was 'in marked contrast to the bravado assumed at the police-court and the inquest, where he joked with his warders and nodded pleasantly and defiantly to the relatives of his victims'.[405] Now he was moody and depressed, and so nervous that he started at the slightest sound.

At 7am Chapman was escorted to the chapel, where the rites of Roman Catholicism were celebrated for his sole benefit by Fr Hawarden but, according to one report, the condemned man 'did not manifest any interest in the proceedings.'[406] After escorting him back to his cell, some sources claimed that warders brought him a breakfast comprising bread, butter and coffee, which he barely touched. Other sources said he was given ham and eggs, bread and butter and toast and coffee, followed by a fried sole, all of which he merely picked at. The veracity of these reports is questioned by Stewart McLaughlin of Wandsworth Prison Museum, because fish was never served at breakfast and coffee was not available in those days, the choice being between tea and cocoa.

The gallows at Wandsworth Prison had been transferred in 1878 from Horsemonger Lane Gaol, where they had been used for 135 public executions. They were housed in a specially built room, known as the Cold Meat Shed, near the coal yard at the end of A wing. The cross beam was eleven feet above the trap doors, which opened into a brick-lined pit, dug twelve feet deep into the ground.

> The traps are formed of two hinged leaves held in position from below by bolts, which are withdrawn when the lever is pulled, allowing the leaves to drop on their hinges. Above the trap a rope of standard length is attached to a strong chain, which is fitted to the overhead beam in such a way that it can be raised and lowered and secured at any desired height by means of a cotter slipped into one of the links and a bracket fixed to the beam. This enables the length of chain to be adjusted to make the drop accord with the height and weight of the prisoner.[407]

All hangings at Wandsworth were scheduled for 9am and could take place only after the executioner had received an official 'authority to hang' from the sheriff of the county of London. This was delivered in person at 8.40am by Frederick Kynaston Metcalfe, the under-sheriff, accompanied by his twenty-year-old son Percy, a recent Cambridge law graduate and future under-sheriff.

---

404 *Daily Express*, 8th April 1903.
405 *London Evening News*, date unknown, c. 10th April, quoted in the *Manchester Courier*, 11th April 1903.
406 *Daily Express*, 8th April 1903.
407 Fielding, S. (2008) *Pierrepoint: A Family of Executioners*. Amazon Kindle Edition, no page numbers.

The convicts due for release that day were allowed out half an hour earlier than the usual time on account of the execution. They were entertained to a breakfast of tea, coffee, bread and butter — courtesy of the Surrey and South London Discharged Prisoners' Aid Society — in a small pine-wood and corrugated-iron shed near the gates, from which emanated the 'merry clatter of cups and saucers'. Leaving before the predictable (and less palatable) sermon began, many joined the small groups beginning to assemble in the vicinity of the prison. Some were discussing the case in subdued tones; others approached the gate in order to peer at a notice on the blackboard outside the entrance, which announced:

> Capital Punishment Amendment Act 1868. 31–32 Vict., c.24, s.7. The sentence of the law passed on Severino Klosowski (or) George Chapman, found guilty of murder, will be carried into execution at nine o'clock tomorrow. (Signed) R. Kynaston Metcalfe, Acting Under-Sheriff of the County of London. James Knox, Governor. Wandsworth Prison, 6th April 1903.

Newcomers — most of them women — arrived in dribs and drabs. As the small groups grew larger they became increasingly loud as individuals raised their voices to ensure that their opinion of Chapman and his murderous activities could be clearly heard. Eventually about two hundred amateur criminologists had assembled, and the consensus was that 'hanging was too good for him' — indeed, some proclaimed that he deserved to have every conceivable torture inflicted upon his person. On the periphery stood a smaller group, comprised of some of the witnesses who gave evidence in the case. Among them, it was rumoured, were members of the Baderski family, including Lucy. Wilder rumours circulated among the crowd: Chapman had confessed; he was 'wanted for lots of murders in Russia'; he had been 'proved to be Jack the Ripper'.[408]

At the Grapes in Bishop's Stortford, the house flag was hoisted at half-mast.[409] In Southwark, a ragged flag still hung forlornly from the Crown, a leftover from the royal procession. 'Originally a dark brown, but now a dirty black,' wrote the *Daily Express*, 'passers by will see in it to-day a grim appropriateness'.[410] Chapman's erstwhile neighbours and customers were acutely aware that his execution was scheduled to take place that morning:

> As nine o'clock drew near, groups, mainly composed of women, assembled at the end of all the many courts which abut on the Borough High-street, from which a view of the clock of St. George's Church could be obtained. The majority of these people had known the criminal personally...When the hands of the clock pointed to the hour of nine, the majority of the women assembled in the street indulged in a shrill cheer.[411]

Inside the prison the atmosphere was one of sombre decorum. At 8.30am Fr Hawarden said prayers in the condemned cell. As nine o'clock approached, Chapman 'appeared to feel his position acutely' and suffered the greatest mental anguish. When

---

408 *Manchester Courier*, 11th April 1903.
409 *Falkirk Herald*, 15th April 1903.
410 *Daily Express*, 7th April 1903.
411 *Manchester Courier*, 11th April 1903.

Pierrepoint visited his cell and pinioned his arms, Chapman trembled violently, broke into a cold sweat and appeared faint; he had to be revived with brandy and water. According to the *Daily Mail* he 'went to his death the perfect type of the degraded, illiterate, cowering alien'.[412]

At three minutes to nine, the 'melancholy procession' began. Accompanied by Fr Hawarden, and with Major Knox, Dr Beamish, the chief warder Charles Hazell and Pierrepoint and Billington following, Chapman — 'although pale and trembling' — was able to walk unassisted.[413] Wearing his frock-coat, but hatless and collarless, he moved 'with a faltering, nervous step; in fact, almost shuffled, along the 150-yard route, moaning and muttering to himself'.[414] Once in the open air, the first sight that greeted him was his own grave, freshly dug by fellow convicts. Descending a flight of stone steps, he had to turn firstly to the right, then to the left, and then to the right again. His final view of the outside world was of a beautiful flower-garden full of hyacinths, primroses and wallflowers in bloom. He then entered the shed containing the dreaded gallows. As Fr Hawarden read the service for the burial of the dead Chapman muttered inaudibly; perhaps he was saying his own private prayers.

Billington placed the customary white hood over Chapman's hair, pinioned his legs just below the knees, and then pulled the hood down over his face. Assisted by Pierrepoint, he positioned Chapman under the beam with his feet on the wooden trap doors. He was 5 ft 5¾ and weighed 146 pounds, and so a drop of 7ft 3 was chosen, the length being adjusted by a chain. Billington slipped the noose over Chapman's head, adjusted it to fit his neck, and then immediately pulled the lever that released the

SCENE AT THE EXECUTION

bolt which allowed the trap doors to fall open. (This sequence of actions was always performed without a pause, because any dawdling would inflict unnecessary distress upon the prisoner.) As Chapman dropped into the pit, the rope dislocated his vertebrae, causing instant death. Harry Furniss described the sound as 'falling doors followed by the dull squelch of the constricting rope'.[415]

Meanwhile, outside the prison, those among the crowd who were habitual attendees of executions — and who doubtless deplored the abolition of public hanging in 1868 — led the novices towards the left-hand side of the gate to the walls of the prison and 'stood there with heads cast down, listening'.

412 *Daily Mail*, 8th April 1903.
413 *Essex Newsman*, 11th April 1903.
414 *South London Chronicle*, 11th April 1903.
415 Furniss, H. (ed) *Famous Crimes Past and Present*, Vol. IX, No. 109, c. 1908. Caxton House.

*Image: 'Scene at the execution', from the Illustrated Police News.*

# Jack the Ripper Will Go to the Gallows, Today.

## Believed That He Will First Confess His Many Murders.

### Writing Statement Which May Solve Whitechapel Mysteries.

London, April 5—Before Severino Klosowski, known as George Chapman, an East End rumseller, goes to the gallows on Monday, it is believed he will sign a confession not only of the poisoning of three common law wives in quick succession, but also will admit he committed the atrocious Whitechapel murders and similar crimes in America— that, in fact, he is the unspeakably savage human bloodhound notorious the world over as "Jack the Ripper."

# DOOMED MAN BROKE DOWN.

## Murderer, Thought to Be Jack the Ripper, Hanged in London Today.

### Sight of the Gallows, and Black Cap Caused Him to Lose His Nerve Completely.
### End of a Long Chapter of Crime.

*Chapman's execution, as reported in the American press. Left: Daily Kennebec Journal, 6th April 1903. Above: Lima Times Democrat, 7th April 1903. Below left: Atlanta Constitution, 8th April 1903. Below: New York Daily People, 8th April 1903.*

# RIPPING JACK AT ROPE'S END

## Man Believed To Have Been Whitechapel Murderer in London.

London, April 7—Klowshowishi, alias Chapman, the Southwark saloonkeeper, who murdered by poison three women who lived with him as his wives in different parts of London, was hanged in Wandsworth jail. He was in a state of complet collapse and had to be supported by warders. He protested his innocence to the end and declaring his real name was Chapman and said he was an American by birth.

The London detectives are of the opinion that the man hanged today was "Jack the Ripper," who butchered so many women in the Whitechapel district.

# HANGED AT LAST

## LONDON SURE THAT "JACK THE RIPPER" IS FINISHED THIS TIME.

### Condemned Man Dies Protesting Innocence—Claimed to Be An American— Answered Description of Fiend of Whitechapel.

London, April 7.—Protesting his innocence to the spring of the drop, declaring that he was an American and his real name Chapman, Severino Kloshowski, the Southwark public house keeper, who was more than suspected by the London police of being the long sought and notorious "Jack the Ripper," was hanged this morning in Wandsworth jail.

He was convicted at the Old Bailey on March 19 of the murder of three women who had lived with him as his wives at different times, and who, it was proved, he had killed by poison.

164

Suddenly the prison clock could be heard chiming the hour — eight — nine. A moment's creepy silence and then a heavy, muffled thud was heard and a dull deep-throated bell tolled once. 'He's gone', one big, heavy-jawed man amongst the crowd remarked, following with the explanation that the thud one heard was the noise of the doors of the trap falling against the sides of the pit the moment the condemned man was launched into eternity.[416]

'It's a good job done!' remarked one little old lady, and similar sentiments were expressed by others. In accordance with the prison's procedures at that time, no black flag was hoisted, but a single bell tolled for fifteen minutes. After being left to hang for an hour, Chapman's corpse was released from the noose and lowered into a coffin. Dr Beamish declared Chapman dead and Inspector Godley gave formal identification of the body. Dr Freyberger conducted a post-mortem which concluded that death was caused by the fracture of the fifth cervical vertebrae and breakage of the spinal cord. As there was no suspicion of insanity his brain was not examined.

Outside the gaol about two hundred people 'leaned against the paling of a nursery garden and looked up at the walls'. After an hour an official notice was posted on the doors, announcing that the execution had been successful. It was signed by all those present at the hanging and accompanied by a certificate issued by Dr Beamish. Upon reading it the crowd left, 'gloomily satisfied'.[417] John Troutbeck, coroner for the south-western district of London, arrived with his jurymen in time to commence the inquest at noon. After hearing the evidence, the jury returned the verdict that the death sentence had been carried out in accordance with the law.

Chapman's remains were buried in the prison grounds, along with those of over twenty other executed criminals, including Kate Webster and Dr Lamson.[418] His grave was the first of a new row. The prison had recently introduced a numbering policy and Chapman's was to be grave No. 2. The first row contained twenty-four graves, the last of which contained the body of Edgar Edwards. 'Twenty-four initials graven on a wall were the only visible sign of the fact,' explained the *Daily Express*, 'everywhere else all round was sweet, fresh unbroken grass.'[419] 'There Severino Klosowski lies till the Day of Judgment,' wrote Harry Furniss, 'his memory detested by the living, his name handed down from generation to generation as that of the foulest criminal of the early twentieth century.'[420]

## AFTERMATH

Just as they had covered Chapman's trial, so the press across the English-speaking world reported his death. These quotes from three provincial British newspapers are typical of the tone of the comments:

---

416 *The Echo*, 7th April 1903.
417 *Daily Mail,* 8th April 1903.
418 Webster was the only woman hanged at Wandsworth. She was executed in 1879 for murdering and dismembering her employer. Her effigy also stood in Tussaud's Chamber of Horrors for some years. Lamson was an American, hanged in 1882 for murdering his brother-in-law with poisoned Dundee cake.
419 *Daily Express*, 8th April 1903.
420 Furniss, H. (ed) *Famous Crimes Past and Present*, Vol. IX, No. 109, c. 1908. Caxton House.

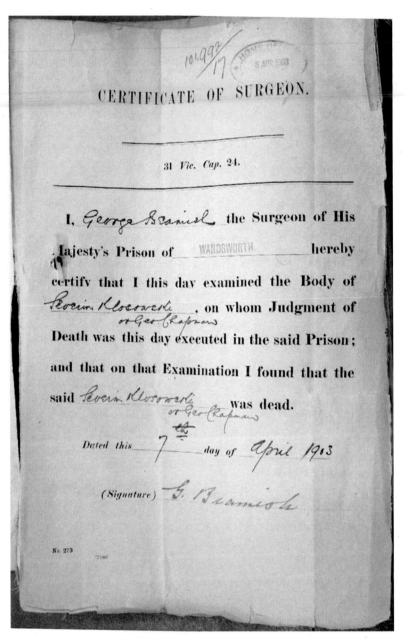

# CERTIFICATE OF SURGEON.

31 *Vic. Cap.* 24.

I, *George Beamish* the Surgeon of His Majesty's Prison of _____ WANDSWORTH _____ hereby certify that I this day examined the Body of *Severin Klosowski or Geo Chapman*, on whom Judgment of Death was this day executed in the said Prison; and that on that Examination I found that the said *Severin Klosowski or Geo Chapman* was dead.

Dated this 7th day of *April 1903*

(Signature) *G. Beamish*

No. 275

Chapman's death certificate, signed by Dr George Beamish.

Few men have gone to the scaffold with less public regret, or with a greater feeling that his sentence was richly deserved...He was one of the most merciless murderers who ever lived; he appeared to have little more remorse in betraying and afterwards killing a helpless woman than a man would have in trapping and then knocking on the head a noxious reptile.[421]

It was a particularly sordid crime, and the man who will calmly watch the effects of slow poison administered by himself to a fellow-being cannot hope for that mercy he himself denied. The world is well rid of such a miscreant as Klosowski, and his fate should serve as a salutary lesson to those who are prepared to go to any length to satisfy their lustful craving.[422]

The most sentimental of our humanitarians must find it difficult to force tears over the fate of [Chapman]...From beginning to end his career is a revelation of meanness and cowardice.[423]

The US press, having reported a few weeks previously that Jack the Ripper had been arrested, continued that theme when they received word that he had been hanged. One stated that 'London detectives are of the opinion' that Chapman was the Ripper; another declared that he also committed Ripper-style crimes in America.

Presumably someone was trying to gain either notoriety or hard cash by claiming to have Maud's bedroom furniture in his or her possession, for the day following the execution an announcement in a London paper stated that the proprietor of the Crown 'wishes to notify the public that the rooms occupied by the late Maude [sic] Marsh and Severino Klosowski are still in their original condition, and therefore any furniture shown elsewhere is a fraud'.[424] A few days later another newspaper reported that 'the bedroom which Maud Marsh occupied during her fatal illness remains now practically as on the day of her death, in so far as the furniture is there without rearrangement'.[425]

Just days after Chapman's death, Dr Stoker was given an opportunity to respond publicly to what he termed 'the unfair and unjust remarks' of Mr Justice Grantham. Within a piece on deaths from tartar emetic, written by the eminent toxicologist Dr Stevenson and published in the British Medical Journal, Stoker remarked:

> It would be a dreadful thing, both from a medical and social point of view, if doctors went about looking for irritant poison in every case presenting symptoms of gastro-enteritis, and no medical man in full possession of his senses would think of pursuing such an insane course. In the two cases under consideration [Bessie and Maud] there was nothing whatever to suggest poison; the symptoms and signs were identical with what we find every day, especially in the summer months, when gastrointestinal troubles are prevalent; there was no hint of

---

421 Coventry Evening Telegraph, 7th April 1903.
422 Manchester Evening News, 7th April 1903.
423 Coventry Looker-On, 11th April 1903.
424 Quoted in the Edinburgh Evening News, 9th April 1903.
425 Manchester Courier, 11th April 1903.

any accidental contamination of their food; there was nothing in the demeanour, history, or circumstances of either of them suggesting a desire on their part to take their own lives; and nobody could suspect the husband, who was at all times unremitting in his attentions to them, willing, even anxious, to carry out any suggestion of the doctor regardless of considerations of trouble or expense, full of sympathy and apparent concern of their sufferings and frequently in tears. I was at all times given to understand that the nurse administered the nutrient enemata. I never once heard during the illness that Chapman prepared the food.

It was not brought to my notice that the nurse and mother suffered after partaking of some of the patient's drinks, though I should imagine the doctor would be the first person to whom they should complain. The judge ignored logic, reason, and facts in his desire to give blame to those who assisted in the course of justice, and but for whose initiative justice would have been baffled, and the body of Maud Marsh would, with her sister victims, be now hiding a terrible crime deep in some lonely cemetery.[426]

During his summing-up, Mr Justice Grantham had commented on the trend for cremation. He worried that, if exhumation was no longer possible, deaths by poisoning would increase. The Chapman case should be taken as a warning, he declared. Henry Thompson, president of the Cremation Society of England, refuted Grantham's assertions, but John Ellis, MP for Rushcliffe, cited Chapman's crimes when he asked the Home Secretary to take steps to ensure that cremation could not be used to conceal evidence of murder. The following month a New Zealand newspaper also referred to the Chapman case in an article about cremation.[427]

In mid-April a subscription fund was inaugurated at Croydon for the erection of a suitable memorial to Maud Marsh.[428] It was never built and to this day she has no headstone. Bessie's kinfolk had her headstone reworked in order to erase the surname Chapman and replace it with Taylor.

Chapman had sent a written message to Mr Petts, the new landlord of the Crown, authorising him to let Frank Bushell take two framed emblems which were hanging on the wall in the bar. But when Bushell called for them, Petts refused to hand them over, obliging Bushell to apply to a magistrate to decide on ownership. Enquiries revealed that 'the letter which contained the alleged authority had been detained by a solicitor's clerk.'[429] Presumably, once the letter was examined, the magistrate found in Bushell's favour.

In June 1903 a firm from Redhill held a midnight auction in the yard of the Horseshoe Inn, 7 Newington Causeway, close by Southwark police station, to dispose of Chapman's household belongings on behalf of Mr Petts. Dubbed by one newsman 'a gruesome sale', it was intended to take place at the Crown, but the venue was changed at the last moment. The auctioneer received a telegram from the proprietor of a 'dime

426 *British Medical Journal*, 11th April 1903.
427 *Nelson Evening Mail*, 11th May 1903.
428 *Western Times*, 18th April 1903.
429 *Manchester Evening News*, 15th April 1903.

show' in Tunbridge Wells offering £120 for the lot, the equivalent to £12,000 today; however, the 'large crowd of morbid sightseers and grim relic-hunters' objected: they demanded the opportunity to secure mementoes according to their individual budgets. He conceded to their wishes and the bidding commenced. The entire contents of Maud's bedroom (described as her 'death-chamber') was offered, featuring a green plush chair and the bedstead — and indeed the bedding — upon which she had died, as well as over a hundred other 'souvenirs of the poisoner fiend', including framed bar notices designed by him and the suit he was wearing when arrested. The rosewood piano Chapman brought from Hastings sold for £5; a (by then desiccated) bouquet he had presented to Maud shortly before he killed her went for 15s (the equivalent of £75 today); the four volumes of Cassell's *Family Physician* fetched £2.2s; a pair of 'his and hers' bicycles ('hers' having been ridden by all three victims) raised £6 (£600 today). For the more cost-conscious, quart pots from the Crown were 3s, while 4s would secure something bearing Chapman's signature.[430] It would be interesting to know whether all of these once-prized items were discarded long ago by the purchasers' descendants, unaware of their provenance, or if any are mouldering in cobweb-strewn attics.

After giving evidence at Chapman's trial, Jessie Toon moved to Osborn Street, Whitechapel (close to the White Hart), but in June 1903 she appeared before a Southwark magistrate on a charge of disorderly conduct. Denying an accusation of drunkenness she explained that, on her first visit to the area since Chapman's execution, she had been physically attacked in Borough High Street. Pointing to the bruising on her face, she claimed that Mary Corby and another woman had thumped her because they believed that she had poisoned Maud Marsh herself and 'got the man hung innocent.' According to Mrs Toon, since giving evidence against Chapman she had been 'frequently insulted and assaulted'. Just a week previously, she would have been 'stabbed by some Jews' but for the intervention of kindly bystanders. Magistrate Ernest Baggallay doubted the veracity of her tales and, because of her two previous convictions for similar offences, Toon was fined ten shillings (or seven days in default). Corby was merely bound over to keep the peace. As she left court Jessie again made reference to the Chapman trial, asking: 'Am I to be murdered through being a witness?'[431]

Even after his death, Chapman's foreignness continued to be the focus of disparaging comments. Under the headline 'Cost of Hanging an Alien', the *Daily Mirror* remarked that his trial had cost the country £1,128.17s 1d, whereas that of the home-grown villain Edgar Edwards amounted to just £207.13s 6d, and that of Annie Walters and Amelia Sach, the infamous Finchley baby farmers, a mere £154.11s 11d. 'It cost the country,' the reporter concluded, 'eight times as much to convict and hang the alien Klosowski as two British women.'[432]

In February 1904 Dr Waldo presented the Chapman case during a public lecture he gave at Lincoln's Inn, titled: 'Illustrative Cases of Poisonings'.

At Chelmsford Assizes in June 1905, Alfred Clarke was sentenced to fifteen months' hard labour for long firm frauds. He seemed to relish his association with the

---

430 *The Echo*, 12th June 1903.
431 *Angus Evening Telegraph*, 29th June 1903; *Nottingham Evening Post*, 27th June 1903. Jessie's age was given as 31 and her occupation as charwoman. The 1901 census lists a Mary Corby, aged twenty-seven, born in Ireland, married to a fish-curer and living just off Borough High Street.
432 *Daily Mirror*, 11th August 1904.

infamous murderer, for he told the court that Chapman had killed Maud because she had threatened to reveal his perjury during the shares scam case.[433]

About 1908 Harry Furniss published the ninth part of his *Famous Crimes Past and Present* series, a twentieth-century 'Penny Dreadful'. The front cover image was an artist's impression of Chapman's facial expression upon hearing his death sentence and within a splendid, ten-page illustrated feature recounted his life story. Sketches depicted the victims and the Marsh family, and also Chapman in various settings: in his billiard room, in the dock at Southwark, and in the gallows shed, about to be hanged.[434] Furniss made a few errors with names ('Marshall' Doubleday; Lucy 'Paderski'; 'Elizabeth' Taylor) but his narrative was mostly faithful to the facts and, although a few conversations and scenarios were fabricated, their content is acceptably truthful. The article was certainly more accurate than the story published in the BPP and closer to the truth than most biographies that followed.

## THE FATE OF LUCY AND CECILIA

From (at latest) the end of 1897, Chapman's wife Lucy had been cohabiting with Franciszek (Frank) Szymański, a Polish cabinetmaker five years her junior. Having adopted his surname, when the first of their five children were born (Henry in 1899 and Helena in 1902) she told the registrar that she was married to Frank, giving her previous surnames as 'late Kłosowski, formerly Baderska'. When completing the 1911 census, Lucy claimed to have been married for thirteen years, but in fact their wedding took place ten weeks after Chapman's execution, on 20th June 1903, at the Polish Roman Catholic church of St Joseph and St Casimir on Cambridge Heath Road, Bethnal Green. Three years later the church moved to Mercer Street, a turning south off Cable Street, close to Lucy's first marital home, and changed its name to Our Lady and St Casimir. Just five years after Lucy's wedding, Cecilia, her daughter by Chapman, married there on 4th October 1908. She was sixteen and her Polish husband, Albert Przygodziński, was at least twice her age. In May 1910 their first child (also named Cecilia) was born whilst Lucy was pregnant with her fifth child, Frankie, giving baby Cecilia an uncle who was four months her junior.

Since at least 1901 the Szymańskis and their growing brood had lived in Limehouse. Their various homes were located in the same grid of mean streets, half a mile from West India Dock Road (where Chapman had once worked for the Radins). By 1911 they had five children and were living in severely overcrowded conditions at 23 Latham St. They occupied just two rooms in a very humble and compact two-storey terraced house; the other four rooms housed nine members of a Russian/Polish family. According to Lucy's great-grandson, Cecilia's son David J. Brown, Lucy worked in a factory making men's trousers and, because of difficulties faced after her father was executed, Cecilia left school aged twelve (instead of the usual fourteen) and worked for her mother, sewing on buttons. Later, Lucy became the caretaker of a Polish Club and, at some point after the 1911 census, the family moved to São Paulo, Brazil, where there are currently a number of Szymańskis, presumably Lucy's descendants.[435]

433 *Daily Express*, 24th June 1905.
434 Furniss, H. (ed) *Famous Crimes Past and Present*, Vol. IX, No. 109, c. 1908. Caxton House.
435 In the 1911 census, Frank Szymański is absent from home. He may have gone to Brazil to research the feasibility of emigrating there.

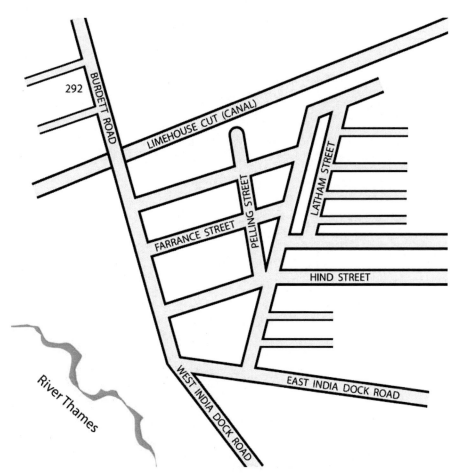

*Street plan of Limehouse c. 1900, just north of West India Docks and the River Thames. Lucy and Frank lived variously in Pelling St (1899/1901); Farrance St (1903); Hind St (1908) and Latham St (1911). Lucy's sister Josephine and family lived in Farrance Street (1901) and Stanisława (Mrs Rauch) and family lived at 292 Burdett Rd for at least fifteen years. None of Lucy's homes survive (the whole area has since been covered by modern housing) but the Rauches' house remains intact. Map by the author.*

David J. Brown claimed that Cecilia married young because she disliked her stepfather and refused to accompany him to Brazil; however, her wedding predated the family's emigration by at least three years. Brown also stated that Chapman's daughter Cecilia did not tell her six children who her father was until her daughter Cecilia became engaged, whereupon she asked the fiancé, Arthur Brown, 'Do you realise that you'll be marrying the granddaughter of a murderer?'[436]

Cecilia and Albert lived for several decades in an upper flat at 21 Leman St, Whitechapel, just metres (as the crow flies) from Scarborough Street, where Cecilia had been born. Of their six children, four produced offspring, giving Seweryn Kłosowski a number of living descendants in Australia and the UK. Links to the surname Kłosowski were lost by women marrying and men changing their Polish surname for English ones, and so only in March 2013 did some of Kłosowski's descendants discover that they were related by blood to a notorious serial killer.

---

436 David J. Brown, quoted in O'Donnell, K., Parlour, A. and Parlour, S. (1997) *Jack the Ripper Whitechapel murders.* Ten Bells Publishing.

*Seweryn Kłosowski resplendent in a black frock-coat, white shirt with standing collar and folding wings, plain cravat, buttonhole, slight quiff, and walrus moustache. He was known to take his own photographs using a camera with a timer, so perhaps this is a self-portrait. From Trial of George Chapman.*

# 4

## MOTIVE

When a killer is caught, a definite motive generally emerges, either during the investigation or the trial. This was not the case with Chapman. If he was aware of his reason for killing he never revealed it, except, perhaps, to Fr Hawarden, who was duty-bound to maintain lifelong silence. This aspect of the case remains a mystery. Nobody knows if Chapman felt the urge to murder and then picked three women at random, or if there was something about each of his three victims as individuals that prompted him to kill them.

Over the years various motives have been suggested. In 1903 Sir Edward Carson blamed Chapman's 'unbridled, heartless, and cruel lust'. Thirty years on, Arthur Fowler Neil ascribed the murders to Chapman's 'diabolical cunning, or some insane idea or urge to satisfy his inordinate vanity'.[437] More recently, Terry Lynch has suggested that the 'change in profession [from barber to publican] brought about an alteration in the personality of Chapman, as...he proceeded to murder three women'.[438] According to Mohd Yaakob Yusof, an (unnamed) crime writer proposed that 'Chapman murdered his women when his pub business began to drop off, believing they were bringing him bad luck'.[439] Most researchers who pass comment on the matter propose that Chapman killed for a practical reason: for money, to prevent exposure or to get his victims out of his life; others have argued that his motive had a psychological basis, such as misogyny or sadism.

### MONEY

The most frequently cited motive for Chapman's crimes is the financial one. It is a long-held notion: as early as 1930 Sir Archibald Bodkin declared that Chapman 'got a little monetary advantage' each time he killed;[440] and it continues to this day; for example, web author David J. Schow states that Chapman was 'devoted to the pursuit of murdering four [sic] of his assorted wives [sic] for settlement and trust monies'.[441]

In fact Chapman gained financial benefit only from Mary, and she had transferred her inheritance to him months before her death, removing Chapman's motive to kill her, unless, as Emsley has speculated, it was a loan and, to evade repaying it, Chapman did away with her and destroyed any incriminating paperwork. There is no evidence that the money was not a gift, although Mary doubtless expected Chapman to utilise it to provide for herself and her son for the foreseeable future.

437 Neil, A.F. (1932) *Forty Years of Manhunting*, Jarrolds, p26.
438 Lynch, T. (2008) *Jack the Ripper*, Wordsworth, p158–9, p327, p329.
439 www.crimerack.com/2012/05/george-chapman-case-file/ (accessed 16th May 2013).
440 *BPP* 1930, Select Committee on Capital Punishment.
441 www.davidjschow.com/hid/hid_fromhell.html (accessed 16th May 2013).

In the case of Bessie Taylor, it is true that her family was comfortably-off; she had some good jewellery and expectations of inheritance. Her employment was not well-paid, but she was reputed to have built up a nest-egg. We know that Chapman wanted her to make a will in his favour; however, had she done so, William Taylor would surely have mentioned it when he gave evidence at the Old Bailey and, in any case, Chapman could not have told the Taylors that he had no funds to pay for Bessie's funeral. There could not have been a pecuniary motive to kill Maud. Her parents were in poorly-paid jobs and, as a teenager earning only a few shillings a week, she cannot have accumulated any substantial savings. It is possible that he took out an insurance policy on her life, but there is no supporting evidence.

## TO PREVENT EXPOSURE

Alfred Clarke was convinced that Chapman murdered Maud Marsh to ensure she could not reveal his perjury during the shares case. R.M. Gordon proposed that Chapman feared she would expose his arson and false insurance claim.[442] These theories do not explain the deaths of Mary or Bessie. They must have been killed for other reasons; in Mary's case, this could be in order to retain her inheritance for himself. This line of thought leaves us floundering to find a reason for his ending Bessie's life.

Could it be that each woman in turn worked out that he was poisoning her, and intended to speak out? This theory fails to explain why he was administering the tartar emetic in the first place, and it falls apart because all three died surrounded by friends or family and, even though Chapman was absent much of the time, none of his victims pointed the finger of suspicion at him. On her death-bed Maud confessed her perjury but said nothing about being poisoned. If Mary or Bessie spoke out he could have been prosecuted for attempted murder, but if they died he might get away with it. This would provide a motive for finishing them off, but Maud's case was different: Chapman knew that Stoker planned a post-mortem, and so the only way to avoid being caught was to cease poisoning her and let her recover. Instead he gave Maud one large, fatal dose, prompting the post-mortem that exposed his poisoning and which led, eventually, to his execution.

## LIBIDO AND PROMISCUITY

Sir Forrest Fulton remarked in 1903 that, 'Having gratified his desires with these women, [Chapman] thought it better to get rid of them without any further trouble.'[443] Similarly, in 1930 H.L. Adam wrote: 'As soon as his primitive desires were satisfied, Chapman became indifferent, taking no trouble to make the woman believe that he still had any affection for her.'[444] These comments are contradicted by the facts: Chapman remained with his girlfriends for two years, three years, and fourteen months respectively, and he feigned affection until the moment each one died (and even after). Other writers have theorised that, after having sex with one woman for a while, Chapman became bored and hankered after fresh conquests. Although this suggests a reason to change partners, it fails to provide a motive for three murders.

---

442 Gordon, R.M. (2008) *The Poison Murders of Jack the Ripper*, McFarland, p88.
443 *The Echo*, 9th March 1903; *Daily Mail*, 10th March 1903.
444 Adam, H.L. (1930) *Trial of George Chapman*, William Hodge, p39.

Brian Marriner suggested that Chapman's (alleged) promiscuity stemmed from his misogyny:

> I am convinced that the answer is that he secretly despised women. Time and again it has been noted in studies of promiscuous people that although they engage in abundant sex, they do not really like it. For them, the act is not an expression of love, but a means of expressing contempt for their eager victims.[445]

Apart from the fact that promiscuity does not equate to abundant sex,[446] there is not a shred of evidence to show that Chapman was more libidinous than the average man. Even if he was, that still provides no motive for murder. Quite the reverse: having overcome the strict sexual morality of the era and secured a willing partner, surely he would want to retain that regular sexual outlet. Chapman deliberately took sex off the agenda by making his lovers ill for long periods of time — strange behaviour indeed for a man whom several writers have labelled as highly-sexed. If anything, the poisonings look like an excuse to avoid sexual activity.

## TO GET RID OF THEM

Martin Fido opined that Chapman seemed 'hopelessly incapable of bringing a romantic relationship to a clean end'.[447] Similarly, Jakubowski and Braund asserted that he had 'decided that breaking up with wives was now as redundant as marrying them'.[448] Stratmann was confident that his motive for murdering Mary is 'not hard to fathom': he was 'tired of her drunken ways, and had extracted all her money'. She sounds vaguer in her assessment of his next killing: 'Perhaps he tired of Bessie, too.' She argued that he had tried abandoning Lucy and Annie, but they came to him for support, so he took 'desperate steps to avoid his responsibilities'. But Lucy sought no support and he easily rebuffed Annie, so this suggestion does not hold water. Stratmann continued: 'Maud, fatally for her, had been hinting that she wanted to start a family'; in other words, that her longing for a baby had prompted him to kill her.[449] Norma Buddle suggested that Chapman killed his girlfriends because he 'didn't want them in the way' when he brought other victims home to his pub to kill them. But if domestic privacy was Chapman's goal, buying a public house, engaging residential staff and inviting three women to cohabit with him seems the wrong way to go about it.

Although these theories provide reasons why Chapman might end each relationship, they fail to explain why he preferred to murder his discarded mistresses instead of throwing them onto the street (as many men did in those days). If he was too spineless or polite to do so, he could have left. He was, after all, footloose, having neither property nor family ties to keep him fixed in any specific area, town, or even country; it would have been quick and easy for him to have found lodgings and employment elsewhere. He could have made a new life in the USA, though the other side of the great metropolis would have done just as well: in those days a London man

445 Marriner, B. (1993) *Murder with Venom*, True Crime Library, p27.
446 A person can have abundant sex with just one partner, or infrequent sex with a number of them.
447 Fido, M. (1993) *Murder Guide to London*, Academy Chicago, p193.
448 Jakubowski, M., and Braund, N. (2008) *The Mammoth Book of Jack the Ripper*, Robinson, p460.
449 Stratmann, L. (2010) *Greater London Murders*, History Press, p238.

could render himself untraceable simply by crossing the River Thames, changing his job and adopting a pseudonym.

Chapman moved home at least once whilst living with each of his victims, and every upheaval offered all parties an ideal opportunity to reflect upon the relationship. Without exception, each woman opted to accompany him to the new premises, although only one was under financial pressure to do so. Bessie and Maud did not need him: they had families who would have welcomed them home, and both were accustomed to earning their own living. Mary's choices were more restricted because Chapman had appropriated all of her capital, she had no parents, little work experience, and a small son to support. Instead of seizing the opportunity afforded by the house-move to offload his (supposedly unwanted) girlfriends, Chapman chose to continue each relationship. In the case of Maud his means of escape could hardly have been easier: while she was in hospital for a month he could simply have packed her belongings and engaged a local carter to convey them to her parents' home.

The coward's way to end a relationship is to behave obnoxiously until the other party leaves. Though there is no evidence that Chapman was habitually cruel to Lucy or Annie whilst living with them, we must bear in mind that, in those days, women did not walk out on men they were married to, or cohabiting with, on a mere whim, most especially if a child was involved. In fact, powerful social norms and religious and patriarchal indoctrination caused women to remain with men even when they were being abused. That Lucy and Annie left hints at ill-treatment on his part. Court witnesses gave evidence that he hit Mary and Maud, ranted at Bessie and forced abortions on Maud. Maybe he killed them because abuse failed to drive them away. As H.L. Adam pointed out, neither Mary, Bessie or Maud 'made the slightest attempt to leave him, which each was at liberty to do.'[450] Perhaps Lucy and Annie escaped with their lives because they walked out on him. The three who died were the ones who stuck by him.

If Chapman killed his girlfriends to rid himself of them, then it is curious that he *three times* chose a path that would keep them with him for as long as possible. A path, moreover, that would cause him the maximum amount of inconvenience, sexual frustration, expense and risk. Causing someone to suffer constant diarrhoea and vomiting brings in its wake horrible, messy clean-up work. It is a daunting task to take on the responsibility of a helpless, bedridden person's food, drink, medicine, welfare, comfort and hygiene whilst simultaneously running a pub and liaising with visiting doctors, nurses, concerned friends, neighbours and customers, and family members who stay for days or weeks. Continuously faking worry is emotionally draining, as is never letting it slip that one is deliberately inducing the illness.

Slow-poisoning was costly. It is true that the tartar emetic cost only tuppence, but using it caused Chapman to incur doctors' fees, nurses' and cleaners' wages, medicine bills and funeral expenses. The women's long periods of illness left him a barmaid short, adding to his workload. Keeping his girlfriends ill meant no sexual activity for weeks at a time, and yet little or no freedom or privacy to pursue other women. Last but certainly not least, he chose a method of getting free from his women that risked his own life.

---

450 Adam, H.L. (1930) *Trial of George Chapman,* William Hodge, p39.

If Chapman's motive for murder was to be rid of his women, why did he bother to feign loving concern? Had he displayed callous indifference when Bessie and Maud were ill, their families would have whisked them away, and he would have been rid of them painlessly and swiftly, and without any expense or danger to himself.

## TO PREVENT THEM LEAVING

The evidence seems to suggest that, rather than killing his girlfriends to get rid of them, Chapman made them ill in order to keep them with him. He had already been abandoned by Lucy (twice) and by Annie. Alice Penfold had cold-shouldered him and Florence Rayner had walked out. Maybe Mary, Bessie and Maud had each begun to voice unhappiness and to talk of leaving. Like the scenario depicted in the film *Misery*, perhaps he incapacitated them and made them bedridden as a ruse to force them to stay. Whilst their plans to leave were on the back burner, he took the opportunity to play the loving husband in order to regain their affections and perhaps to convince them of their dependence upon him. Each time the woman recovered sufficiently to revive her plans to leave, Chapman again prevented her from doing so by inflicting another mysterious bout of gastric illness.

This theory makes logical sense, covers all three murders, and is supported by certain anecdotes relating to Maud and Lucy. Chapman told Sergeant Kemp that Maud wanted a child, was losing patience, and had said that, unless she fell pregnant soon, 'You won't have me with you long' — in other words, that she intended to leave him. The BPP's account of the incident in Jersey City stated that Chapman's threat to kill Lucy was provoked by her threat to leave him.

Chapman's flirtations with Alice and Florence may have been pre-emptive: Mary and Maud intended to leave, prompting him to seek a replacement. In each case, it was only after his dalliances came to an end that he recommended poisoning his girlfriends.

This theory may appear to have quite a serious flaw, in that none of his victims' families reported that they were planning to leave; but each woman may only have reached the stage of voicing their discontent privately to Chapman. It is even possible that the notion that they were planning to leave him was an irrational fear of Chapman's, borne of an abandonment complex stemming from a related childhood trauma.

## A CURE GONE WRONG

Another theory is that Chapman murdered for two different reasons: one appertaining to Mary; the other to Bessie and Maud, and that his intention — at least initially — was to cure rather than kill.

The medical training that Chapman received in Poland was similar to that offered in England and the USA half a century earlier. Although his certificates mentioned only blood-letting, a related practice was purging, which meant emptying the entire digestive tract, usually in the downwards direction, although upwards was also popular. Vomiting was thought 'cleansing and beneficial in a whole variety of illnesses'[451] from mumps to melancholia. The 2007 edition of Goldfrank's *Manual of Toxicologic Emergencies*, while describing tartar emetic as 'outdated and dangerous', acknowledges its 'long history of use as an emetic, as well as a sedative, expectorant, cathartic, and diaphoretic'. Many mid-nineteenth-century American patent medicines were comprised simply of tartar emetic mixed with sugar, and could be obtained easily and cheaply.[452]

According to Chapman, Mary Spink was physically dependent on alcohol and, when deprived of it, suffered delirium tremens. When he was being trained as a feldsher, tartar emetic had long been used as a standard cure for alcoholism. Indeed, Chambers's Remedy for Intemperance, first marketed in New York in 1827, successfully cured thousands of 'the most obstinate drunkards'. Its phenomenal popularity prompted investigation by the Committee on Quack Medicines, which revealed its active ingredient to be tartar emetic.[453] Shortly afterwards an American medical journal described what was later referred to as aversion therapy:

> We have known several instances, where drunken stewards of mess-rooms, and tipling [sic] butlers, have been cured — at least for a time, of their intemperate habits, by the admixture of tartar emetic with the wine and spirits that were purposely left in their way...the antimony must be given by stealth, and in the drunkard's favourite beverage, otherwise the charm will be ineffectual, and the antipathy will not be engendered against the inebriating material.[454]

As early as 1829 Dr J.H. Kain was warning that tartar emetic 'must always be used with caution' and, 'if severe vomiting and purging ensue', the dose should be diminished'.[455] In 1830s Britain tartar emetic was also being used to treat delirium tremens, and in 1845 a popular dictionary of practical medicine explained:

> When violent delirium follows drunkenness...frequent repetition of tartar emetic will often calm the patient...The distressing sickness thus induced, and which may, in the helpless state of such persons, easily be prolonged, has occasioned such disgust at, and dread of, all intoxicating beverages, as to cause them to be shunned for a long time afterwards.[456]

In 1855 an article entitled: 'Tartar Emetic: A Remedy for Drunkenness' appeared in *The Lancet* and, by the 1870s, a patented cure was available. All of Chapman's medical books, whether brought from Poland or bought in Hastings, were old editions. One was a copy of Ranking and Radcliffe's *Half Yearly Abstract of the Medical Sciences*.[457] Could it have been the early 1863 edition, in which Professor Laycock of Edinburgh stated that tartar emetic 'has been administered in large doses in delirium tremens'?

451 Moss, K. (1999) *Southern Folk Medicine 1750-1820*, University of South Carolina Press, p33–74.
452 Among them were Horry's Sugar Powder for the Fevers and Dorothea Christina Schmidt's Emetic to be Given in the Fever. Marriott's Dry Vomit, Dr Collier's Saline and Dixon's Antibilious Pills.
453 *The New York Medical and Physical Journal*, Vol. 6, 1827, p430.
454 *Ibid.*
455 'On Intemperance, considered as a Disease, and as susceptible to Cure', from the *American Journal of the Medical Sciences* and reviewed by Johnson, J. (1829) *The Medico-chirurgical Review*, Vol. 14, p195.
456 Copland, James, M.D. (1845) *A Dictionary of Practical Medicine*, Vol. 2. Harper, p688.
457 Its full title was *The Half Yearly Abstract of the Medical Sciences, Being a Practical and Analytical Digest of the Contents of the Principal British and Continental Medical Works Published in the Preceding Six Months*.

When Mary first became ill with gastric trouble, Chapman had been perfectly frank with people, telling them that she had delirium tremens, that he was consulting medical books in order to find out 'how to stop her drinking', and that he was secretly giving her 'stuff to make her the better of the drink', adding that 'when she gets better I will tell her what I have done to stop it.' That Chapman gave Mary 'something' to cure her alcoholism was mentioned twice at the police court and again at the Old Bailey. At one point, Dr Stevenson stated that tartar emetic was a cure for alcohol addiction. Unfortunately he was discussing Maud Marsh, and so the relevance of his remark to Mary Spink went unnoticed.

The intention to cure Mary of alcoholism provides a rational motive to give her tartar emetic, but what caused Chapman to administer it to Bessie and Maud? Did he fear that, being pub landladies, the easy availability of alcohol might cause them to become addicts? Or did they suffer from other maladies that could be cured with the drug? In 1846 an American, A.J. Cooley, explained that it could cure persons who 'eat enormously from a mere vicious habit',[458] an idea that was still in circulation in 1897, when an American newspaper published this anecdote:

> A patient at one time had much too good an appetite, to his thinking; he was getting stout and pursy, and by no ordinary means could he keep the demands of his clamorous stomach within reasonable bounds...a slight dose of tartar emetic was taken a short time before every meal. This succeeded admirably; the appetite lessened; the 'too solid flesh' began to melt and the patient was quite satisfied.[459]

Bessie was described as 'plump', which might point to a fondness for plenty of food. But what about Maud? In his 1860 *Treatise on Therapeutics and Pharmacology, or Materia Medica*, George B. Wood wrote:

> In nervous diseases there are now and then paroxysms of high excitement, in which tartar emetic proves very useful, by the sedative and relaxing effects which attend its nauseating operation...I have used it very happily in controlling the violent paroxysms of hysteria.[460]

Maud had been treated by Dr Grapel for 'hysteria'. At the time, girls and women who were headstrong or disobedient were often labelled 'hysterical'. If Maud initially rebelled against Chapman's attempts to dominate and control her, he may have 'treated' her 'illness' with what was fast becoming his favourite cure-all: tartar emetic. The drug could also be used to assist with abortions: Dr Wood noted its efficacy in relaxing the aperture of the cervix, so Chapman may have used it to facilitate the insertion of the catheter of a ball-syringe into the womb.

The use of tartar emetic in treating a range of conditions provides a logical reason for Chapman to administer it to each woman, but falls short of explaining why he continued to dose them after it became clear that they would die if he did not desist. He may have ignored the dosages recommended in the book, in the arrogant belief that his judgment was superior to that of the author. Whilst this theory may

458 Cooley, A.J. (1846) *A Cyclopædia of Several Thousand Practical Receipts*. Appleton.
459 *Daily Gazette* (Ohio), 19th November 1897.
460 Wood, G.B. (1860) *A Treatise on Therapeutics and Pharmacology, or Materia Medica*, Vol. 2.

account for one death, it does not explain three. The post-mortems showed that each woman had been given a massive dose just before death, which indicates a deliberate rather than accidental overdose.

Chapman may have started out with the rational motive of attempting to cure Mary of alcoholism, but something psychopathological — hitherto dormant — was awoken within him, driving him to repeatedly poison her, beyond the therapeutic doses, until she died. Perhaps he discovered that he secretly enjoyed making Mary ill, gained pleasure from her suffering, liked removing her autonomy and freedom of movement by confining her to bed, and derived gratification from having her sickness or health, her life or death, entirely under his control.

He may also have relished the intellectual superiority that the drug bestowed upon him. Although he had told those around him that he was 'giving Mary something', when she became ill most failed to notice the connection. Only the pub's staff, Susan Robinson and Richard Pagett, suspected foul play, leading Richard to make a direct, blatant accusation that Chapman seemingly wanted to kill Mary. But they moved out, leaving Chapman free to concentrate on deriving pleasure from watching Mesdames Doubleday, Waymark and Mumford become increasingly worried and puzzled by Mary's mystery illness. All three women were ill-educated members of the labouring class. The real test came when he consulted a physician. When Dr Rogers failed to deduce what was going on, Chapman felt a deep sense of gratification from having outwitted someone medically qualified. The climax of his triumph came when Rogers issued a death certificate without a post-mortem — Chapman had literally got away with murder whilst his victim was under the care of a qualified medic! Having found a substance that enabled him to kill with impunity, he became enamoured with it. By the time he was dosing his third victim, he could barely contain his fascination and certain gleeful remarks leaked out: he could give Maud 'a pinch' and 'fifty doctors could not find out'.

This theory suggests that Chapman's sole reason for dosing Bessie and Maud with tartar emetic was the pleasure he derived from showing off how clever he was by baffling doctors. It explains why he had no objection when Dr Stoker brought in three colleagues to examine Bessie. Quite the opposite: the more medical men were involved, the greater the boost to his ego. The arrival of each new expert presented a further opportunity for him to pit his wits against someone university educated, and to demonstrate his intellectual superiority over them. His victims were mere pawns in a macabre game.

Chapman became increasingly daring, as though obsessed with his ability to create illness and death right under the noses of staff, friends, neighbours, family and doctors without arousing suspicion. He flirted with carelessness, even became reckless at times by insisting on preparing his victims' food and drink away from prying eyes. He progressed from dosing Mary behind a locked door to allowing people to be present when he administered the drug, to giving visitors deadly concoctions with which to feed the victim themselves. He even placed brandy and water, both laced with deadly poison, on a night table, so that Mrs Marsh might unwittingly administer the lethal dose and kill her own daughter — or, indeed, herself. It seems that his game was not to avoid detection, but to find out just how many clues he could give before somebody joined the dots. As one contributor to jtrforums remarked:

[He] had them go through months of projectile vomit, torrential diarrhoea and all the while having a stream of doctors and relatives visiting...It's hardly subterfuge. Short of making their heads explode I cannot think of more in-your-face poisoning.[461]

Chapman's poison murders were similar to progressing through levels of a game. The first objective was to discover how many fully qualified physicians a humble ex-feldsher could outwit. The next was to delay the legal process with passivity without co-operation, using tactics such as refusing to confess and offering no assistance in discovering his identity or antecedents, diversionary tactics such as pretending to be American and petitioning for a reprieve. Finally, how long could a murderer delay his execution? At this he fared quite well: the interval from his arrest to his hanging was a little over five months, twice as long as the comparable murderer Edgar Edwards, whose 'guilty but insane' plea ensured that his life was ended by the noose just ten weeks after his crimes.

## MISOGYNY

Hatred of women was first proposed in 1930, when H.L. Adam wrote that the 'primary purpose' of Chapman's poisonings was 'the pursuit, the capture, and the destruction of women'.[462] Although described as 'a sallow-faced, gloomy individual',[463] George R. Sims observed that Chapman nevertheless 'had the power of fascinating women'.[464] He certainly got whatever he wanted from them: money, obedience, sex, toleration of violence and other ill-treatment, even blind devotion to the point of perjury. Stratmann suggested that, to 'charm them into unquestioning devotion', Chapman used 'flattery, and extravagant gifts...pretended to be wealthier than he was, and constantly boasted about his adventures, travels and medical qualifications'.[465] The misogyny theory proposes that, having deliberately induced a series of women to fall in love with him, he abused the power this gave him, firstly by ill-treating them and then by inflicting a long, slow torturous death. According to crime writer Gordon Honeycombe:

> Chapman wanted his women to be useful but passive and decorous doormats, submitting fully to his every professional and personal need. Fear and hatred of women were probably deeply embedded within his psyche. But he needed them for domestic and sexual purposes, and to constantly reassert his own, and others', high opinion of himself.[466]

Honeycombe failed to explain why, if Chapman needed his girlfriends for sex and housework, he killed them. Another problem with his assessment is that being 'passive and decorous doormats' used for 'domestic and sexual purposes' is an accurate description of how women were regarded and treated by the majority of ordinary

461 'Mr Poster', jtrforums.com, 12th May 2009.
462 Adam, H.L. (1930) *Trial of George Chapman*, William Hodge, p5.
463 *Taranaki Herald* (NZ), 22nd December 1902.
464 *NZ Truth* (New Zealand), 25th January 1908.
465 Stratmann, L. (2010) *Greater London Murders*, History Press, p231.
466 Honeycombe, G. (1993) *More Murders of the Black Museum*, Hutchinson, p158.

men at that time. When placed in their historic context, and excluding the murders, Chapman's behaviour towards his women was perfectly normal, and less brutal than that of many of his peers. 'Fear and hatred of women' ran like a thread throughout Victorian society, and the dominance and control of his female partner, including the administration of moderate physical chastisement, if he deemed it 'necessary', was accepted — even expected — of every man. There is no evidence that Chapman was a misogynist as an individual, only that he was the product of a profoundly misogynistic society.

## RELIGIOUS MANIA

Perhaps Chapman, having been raised to view his sexual urges as dirty, immoral, wicked or animalistic, projected his self-disgust onto the sex responsible for provoking them. He persuaded four women, each one raised in the sexually repressive Victorian era, which indoctrinated them to be virginal before marriage and faithful within it, to cohabit with him 'in sin'. Perhaps he was driven by a perverted religious fervour to test 'decent' women's moral fibre. When they agreed to sex outside of wedlock he was so disgusted by their immorality that he punished three of them by making them endure the longest, slowest, most painful death that was possible for him to inflict. (Perhaps he would also have poisoned Annie, had she not moved out.)

## SADISM AND PSYCHOPATHY

Some researchers have theorised that Chapman killed because he had a mental derangement which caused him to enjoy seeing others suffer. George R. Sims was perhaps the first to suggest this when he wrote in 1907: 'To watch the long agony of the women with whom [Chapman] had cohabited...was the gratification of an instinct which is a form of insanity.' In 1930 Norman Hastings claimed that Chapman poisoned women 'simply to gloat over their agony' and opined that, 'In his own way' he cared more for his victims than for 'any other women who came into his eventful life, yet he could watch them slowly dying without the slightest compunction'.[467] A Canadian journalist writing in the 1960s believed that Chapman killed his girlfriends purely 'for the pleasure of watching them die.'[468] Linda Stratmann conjectured that he 'may have got a thrill from committing murder, the exercise of power over a helpless victim, and slow poisoning enabled him to enjoy the process over a long period of time'.[469]

The only sort of person who is capable of inflicting torture on others, whilst remaining unaffected and unremorseful, is a clinical psychopath. This term is used to describe someone who is unable to form normal emotional attachments, has no empathy, feels no remorse, and yet appears decent and even charming. Many of the characteristics of psychopaths that neurologist Dr Gordon Banks has described dovetail neatly with what we know about Chapman.[470]

---

467 Hastings, N. *Thomson's Weekly News*, 21st June 1930, quoted in Norder, D. (ed.) *Ripper Notes, The International Journal for Ripper Studies*, #21: How the Newspapers Covered the Jack the Ripper Murders (2005), p84.
468 *Winnipeg Free Press*, 25th October 1969.
469 Stratmann, L. (2010) *Greater London Murders*, History Press, p238
470 Gordon Banks PhD, MD. Gordonbanks.com (accessed 16th May 2013).

| Banks's description of a psychopath | George Chapman's behaviour |
|---|---|
| Knows intellectually what punishment is decreed for certain crimes, yet when caught puts up rationalisations and defences, and seems surprised when he is punished. | Knew that murder carried a penalty, was surprised at his arrest, bewildered at being charged and shocked at receiving the death sentence. |
| His inability to love or to show any but the most superficial kindness to others prevents him from forming meaningful relationships. | Appears to have felt no love for, or attachment to his girlfriends, his wife or his children. |
| Enjoys being in a position of power over others, especially women. | Rendered victims bedridden, giving him complete power over them. |
| Plays jokes and tricks on others to humiliate them or to assert dominance. | Told Bessie's friend Elizabeth Painter: 'Your friend is dead.' |
| Often found in positions of imposture. | Lived under an assumed name; lied about his past. |
| Attracted to vocations that give opportunities for exerting power, such as...medicine. | Trained as a feldsher. Enjoyed acting as nurse to his victims. |
| Charming and makes friends easily, but those who rely upon him soon find out that he has no sense of responsibility. | Charmed women into intimacy but felt no responsibility towards them or his children. |
| Can solemnly lie while looking the victim in the eye, showing no anxiety whatever. | Interacted closely with his victims, without giving himself away. |
| Gives no real love, but capable of inspiring love, sometimes to a fanatical degree, in others. | Inspired at least five women to love him. |
| Oblivious to the consequences of risk-taking [which] leads to being found out. | Took risks; boasted about fooling doctors; retained incriminating paperwork. Was found out. |

If Chapman was indeed a psychopath or sadist, he concealed it with a convincing veneer of normality. He was sufficiently charming to woo a series of women, and affable enough to engage with customers as a barber and a pub landlord.

## MSbAP

Chapman's game of 'Outwit the Doctors' suggests that he may have had a condition known as Munchausen Syndrome by Adult Proxy (MSbAP). Munchausen Syndrome, first described in 1951, is a personality disorder in which a person feigns illness in order to gain attention. It is called Munchausen Syndrome by Proxy (MSbP) when the illness is fabricated or induced in another (i.e. the proxy).[471] In most documented cases

---

471 MSbP was first named by paediatrician Roy Meadow in 1977. Since 2002 the term Fabricated or Induced Illness (FII) has increasingly been preferred in the UK. Cases of MSbP had been reported prior to Meadow's classic description, although they did not use the term. The first published case of MSbP via poisoning appears to be that reported by Dine in 1965. Dine, M.S. 'Tranquiliser poisoning: An example of child abuse., *Pediatrics,* 1965;36:782–785.

the proxy has been a child but could be an adult, hence MSbAP.[472] The perpetrator derives emotional satisfaction from receiving attention and sympathy and, above all, a narcissistic ego-stroke from deceiving and outwitting medical professionals. The following aspects of the syndrome dovetail perfectly with Chapman's actions:[473]

➢ induces vomiting and diarrhoea (the commonest illness in the proxy)

➢ is attentive to his victims, even though he is harming them

➢ earns praise from others for his devotion to the victim's care

➢ appears concerned about the victim

➢ maintains a high degree of involvement in the care of the victim

➢ is very friendly and co-operative with doctors

➢ appears to be medically knowledgeable and/or fascinated with medical details; discussing in detail symptoms and care

➢ welcomes medical tests

➢ appears to be unusually calm in the face of the victim's worsening symptoms

➢ when caught, gives a convincing display of innocence

➢ continues to deny guilt, even when confronted with proof

According to expert Myrna R. Nieves, perpetrators experience 'gleefulness in being able to fool powerful, sought-after parental figures'. Although 'constantly giving clues' to their behaviour, she explained, they have 'an ability to organize the perceptions of doctors so that they miss or ignore such clues'. In this 'dramatic play', the victim matters little to the perpetrator, despite 'an appearance of deeply caring'.[474] Another expert, Tim Field, explained that,

> the intent is to induce illness and injury, rather than commit murder, for the death...would take away the object which he repeatedly manipulates for his gratification...However, the injury or illness must be severe enough to warrant the need for medical intervention.[475]

---

472 A case in which the proxy was an adult was first documented by Mircea Sigal, David Altmark and I. Carmel in *The Journal of Nervous and Mental Disease*, 1986. Altmark and Sigal, this time with Marc Gelkopf, published 'Munchausen Syndrome by Adult Proxy Revisited' in 1991 in *Israel Journal of Psychiatry and Related Sciences*, 1991; 28(1): 33–6.
473 The list was compiled from the work of Tim Field, Robert G. Zylstra, LCSW, Karl E. Miller MD, Walter E. Stephens MD and Myrna R. Nieves MD FAAP.
474 Myrna R. Nieves MD. 'Munchausen by Proxy Syndrome', 2005. home.coqui.net/myrna/munch.htm
475 Tim Field, www.bullyonline.org/workbully/munchaus.htm (accessed 16th May 2013).

Satisfying those two requirements would entail maintaining a fine balance for prolonged periods of time between keeping each victim alive and yet severely ill. Field stated that if, 'as often happens' he miscalculates, and the victim dies, the sympathy he receives 'becomes another opportune vehicle for gaining attention'. If suspicion is aroused, explained Dr Nieves, medical staff and family members are reluctant to believe that perpetrators who 'appear to be so caring can perform horrendously cruel acts'. Similarly, Tim Field asked: 'How many people would dare to think that this wonderful, kind, caring, compassionate person…is, in reality, a murderer? Or, given the repeat nature of the crime, a serial killer?'

Neither Munchausen Syndrome nor its variations had been identified in Chapman's era, and yet several commentators seem to have recognised its symptoms in him. Mr Justice Grantham remarked that Chapman had been able to 'defy the doctors', and had for years been making people ill 'without the slightest fear of their being able to discover it'. One reporter labelled Stoker 'the doctor he so daringly baffled';[476] another commented that Chapman had 'hoodwinked the doctors with the greatest ease'.[477] George R. Sims remarked that Chapman's ability to outwit doctors was 'the astounding feature of the case'.[478]

If this theory is correct, then perhaps what happened is this: Chapman started out with the intention to cure Mary of alcoholism. His administration of tartar emetic was initially therapeutic, which explains why he bought it from someone who knew him, signed the chemist's register clearly and in the name he normally went by, and told his staff frankly that he was giving 'something' to Mary to cure her of the drink. When Dr Rogers could not understand the cause of her gastric illness, Chapman gained a deep, intoxicating pleasure from baffling such an experienced medic, and these feelings awakened within him the syndrome we now call MSbAP.

This theory seems more convincing than others because Chapman's behaviour matches exactly the description of MSbAP as provided by experts in that condition.

476 *The Echo,* 18th March 1903.
477 *Lloyd's Weekly,* 9th August 1907.
478 *NZ Truth* (New Zealand), 25th January 1908.

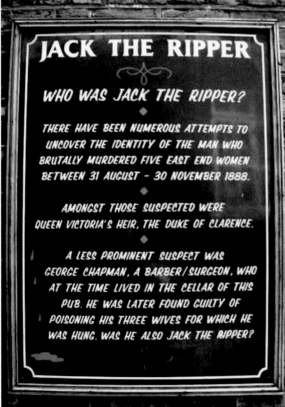

The White Hart today, and the alley leading to George Yard (now Gunthorpe St). The cellar barbershop was accessed via a door in the alley, opposite the cart. Source of photo unknown.

A large placard currently on the side wall of the White Hart announces confidently that Chapman lived in the cellar during the Ripper murders. Those responsible for the notice have no evidence to support that claim. Photo by Mark Ripper.

## UNCORROBORATED TALES, INVENTIONS AND MYTHS

When author Philip Sugden remarked that 'Faulty primary sources, dishonest research and the sheepish repetition of printed folklore have taken us very far from the truth',[479] he was referring to Jack the Ripper, but his words apply equally to Chapman: even trusted and respected authors and journalists have repeated errors and retold myths, and some have even fabricated events and conversations.

Myths about George Chapman have existed for 111 years. They began to arise during the investigation into his poison murders. Some arose from misunderstandings about his past life in Poland, for example the *Daily Express* reported that he attended military school in Warsaw 'for five years from October, 1873' (when he was seven years old)[480] and during his court hearings he was described as Jewish, and as a surgeon (or barber-surgeon) who had served in the Russian Army.

A number of anecdotes that are accepted as indisputable facts about George Chapman can be traced back to just one person. These include the beliefs that he had once tried to obtain an illegal medicine, had a wife and children in Poland, worked at the White Hart in 1888 and used the pseudonym Zagowski. Norma Buddle even derived the title of her dissertation 'The Cable Street Dandy' from Levisohn's description of Zagowski as a 'la-di-da'.[481] However, each one of those tales derives solely from a man whose memory was less than reliable: Wolff Levisohn.

### WOLFF LEVISOHN

Levisohn was a witness at both the police court and the Old Bailey. His purpose was to identify Chapman as Kłosowski (which he failed to do). However, he regaled the courts with a stream of anecdotes which have influenced every retelling of Chapman's life story right up to the present day. Unfortunately neither a verbatim transcript of his words, nor a story of his life exists. The book *Trial of George Chapman*, the Old Bailey website and various newspapers offer abbreviated versions of Levisohn's testimony, as notated by court clerks and reporters, and I have utilised these, plus official records, to assemble the following information.

A Jew born in the Russian-occupied section of Poland about 1849, Levisohn moved to London as a teenager and returned to Poland aged twenty-one to perform his national service, serving as a feldsher in the Russian Army for seven years. He was back in London in time to be included in the 1881 census, and in 1887, whilst living in Whitechapel, married Alice Sutton, an Englishwoman twelve years his

---

479 Sugden, P. (2002) *Complete History of Jack the Ripper*, Constable Robinson, Kindle Edition 2012, p11–12.
480 *Daily Express*, 7th February 1903.
481 La-di-da: pretentious; foppish; dandyish; affectedly refined in manners or tastes.

junior. It is curious that Alice should marry a Jew, because her father was a vicar and her great-grandfather was chaplain to the Lord Mayor of London. Whilst she raised their two sons, Levisohn eked out a modest living as a hawker of supplies to east London barbers and hairdressers.[482]

As a court witness in 1903, Levisohn cast his mind back fifteen years to recall one of the many customers he used to call upon now and then: a Varsovian named Ludwik Zagowski. Like Levisohn, he had been a feldsher in the army and later in a Warsaw hospital, and asked him to obtain 'a certain medicine'. Levisohn declined because, 'I did not wish to get twelve years', indicating that the drug was an illegal one. Some researchers have lately suggested that it was an abortifacient, but in fact, as Chapman later proved, abortions could be performed using substances and equipment that were legal.

Although he could not speak English, only Polish mixed with Yiddish, Zagowski worked in a barbershop beneath the White Hart pub in 1888 and became its proprietor in 1889. That year a woman arrived from Poland with two children in tow, walked into the cellar barbershop and announced in Polish: 'That is Ludwik, my husband.' They were 'big children — a girl and a boy', Levisohn recalled.[483] His story becomes a little vague at this stage: Zagowski either shunned his family or took them in but neglected them, and so Levisohn and another charitable man gave Mrs Zagowska a few pennies to buy food. Zagowski left Whitechapel in 1890. 'We called him a brute and a scoundrel,' said Levisohn, 'if he had not disappeared when he did we would have given him a good, sound thrashing for it.'[484]

Four years later, whilst calling at Haddon's barbershop in Tottenham, Levisohn spotted a moustachioed Pole working there and took him for Zagowski. Remembering how Zagowski had spurned his wife and children, Levisohn probably treated the man frostily and restricted communication to the minimum, but seeing an Englishwoman bringing the barber's dinner to the shop, was provoked to ask the whereabouts of the 'first wife'. The barber replied: 'Ach, she has gone.'[485] Levisohn later ran into him in another barbershop, where he had two wives: 'a tall, fair, foreign lady' and 'a little, dark Englishwoman', but neither was Mrs Zagowska. Levisohn lost touch with the barber about 1895 (and, he grumbled, lost 13s 6d as well, presumably the amount outstanding on his account). Later he heard the man had 'gone to Brighton'.

In November 1902, police officers investigating Chapman's past encountered Levisohn who, in court the following month, stated that the man sitting in the dock who called himself George Chapman was Ludwik Zagowski.[486] At no point did Levisohn identify Chapman as Kłosowski; in fact it seems he had never heard the name before. He told police that Zagowski obtained his English name from a hairdresser called George Chapman, who had disappeared.

---

482 During another court case, on 19th May 1890, Levisohn said, 'I have got hairdressing tools at home. I hawk them about.' Oldbaileyonline.org (his name is given as William 'Levishon').
483 *Lincolnshire Chronicle*, 9th January 1903.
484 *The Echo*, 7th January 1903. In 1890 there was 'a prosecution' (he did not give details) which led to Levisohn's ceasing to supply clients in Whitechapel.
485 *Daily Mail*, 8th January 1903.
486 On 7th January 1903 Levisohn said that the police had approached him 'about six weeks ago' and that he had identified Kłosowski at the police court 'three weeks ago'.

Levisohn's anecdotes, although long accepted as facts, are full of holes.

➤ Levisohn stated that the barber he knew between 1888 and 1890 and again between 1894 and 1895 was named Zagowski. He never heard him called any other name. However, witnesses who knew Kłosowski in 1888 and 1889 (Ethel Radin and the Baderskis), around 1891 (Schumann) and between 1893 and 1895 (Annie Chapman, Alfred Wicken and William Bray) made no mention of his ever using a pseudonym. (Wicken stated in 1903 that he had only just discovered that Levisohn knew Kłosowski as Zagowski; moreover, Wicken had never heard the name Zagowski until Levisohn used it in court in 1903.) In addition to all these witnesses, two Post Office directories, his marriage certificate and his son's birth certificate confirm that Kłosowski was using his own name from late 1888, during 1889 and 1890, and until 1895.

➤ Kłosowski could not have worked at the White Hart barbershop from 1888 to 1890, as Levisohn claimed. Witness statements, two Post Office directories and a marriage certificate indicate that he lived and worked at Cable Street for the latter part of 1888, the whole of 1889, and the first few months of 1890.

➤ Levisohn stated that Zagowski *left* Whitechapel in 1890. Other witnesses said that Kłosowski *arrived* there in 1890 (which fits perfectly with his leaving Cable Street).

➤ Kłosowski did not 'disappear' from the scene in 1890, as Levisohn claims. He married Lucy in October 1889 and documentary evidence (in the form of his son's birth certificate and the census) shows that he was living and working in Whitechapel in September 1890 and April 1891.

➤ No other witness who knew Kłosowski between 1888 and 1890 mentioned a wife and children arriving from Poland in 1889.

➤ Levisohn described Zagowski's offspring as 'big'. In 1889 Kłosowski was just twenty-three, too young to be the father of two 'big' children.

One theory can explain every discrepancy between Wolff Levisohn's recollections and those of other witnesses and the documentary evidence, and settle all six problems listed above: Zagowski and Kłosowski were two different people. One was a Varsovian who dressed as a la-di-da and worked at the White Hart from 1888 to 1890. There are two indicators that he was older than Kłosowski: firstly, his children were 'big'; secondly, before coming to England, Zagowski had performed military service — which began at age twenty-one — and then subsequently worked as a feldsher before coming to London, whereas Kłosowski was already in London at age twenty-two. Levisohn stated that Zagowski spoke only Polish and Yiddish, but Kłosowski was fluent in Russian.[487] Kłosowski was a Roman Catholic, but Zagowski was Jewish: in official records from that time, everyone with the surname Zagowski had a Jewish forename. Zagowski's disappearance from Whitechapel in 1890 dovetails perfectly with Kłosowski's arrival that same year — at exactly the right time to take up the vacancy at the White Hart created by Zagowski's departure.

---

487 In Poland, all education from elementary school through hospital teaching and university lectures took place in Russian.

After Zagowski left Whitechapel in 1890, Levisohn never saw him again. His memory of the man faded, and his work brought him into contact with many Polish and Jewish barbers. When in 1894 he saw a moustachioed Pole working for Haddon, he mistook him for Zagowski. Because he disapproved of Zagowski's behaviour towards his family, Levisohn doubtless acknowledged the 'brute' with a cold, formal nod and had no desire to engage him in convivial banter. But when he saw that the 'scoundrel' had acquired a new spouse (in reality, Annie Chapman), Levisohn could hold his tongue no longer: he enquired about the first wife in an acid manner designed to remind the man that he remembered his shameful conduct towards her in 1889. Although Levisohn was referring to Mrs Zagowska, when the man — actually, Kłosowski — replied, 'Ach, she's gone', he meant Lucy.

On Levisohn's subsequent encounter with 'Zagowski' (actually, Kłosowski) he had 'two wives', and, as Levisohn correctly stated, neither was Mrs Z. They were Lucy and Annie. Levisohn's description matches them perfectly: Lucy was foreign, tall and fair; Annie was English, short and dark. His timeline fits a six-week period in late 1894 when Annie, Lucy and Kłosowski lived together above Haddon's. Could Levisohn's recollection that the missing barber had 'gone to Brighton' stem from a vague memory of hearing that he had moved to Hastings, along the coast from Brighton?

Levisohn can be forgiven for his mistake in believing that the barber he met between 1888 and 1890 and the one he met between 1894 and 1895 were one person. When he shared his recollections, he was harking back fifteen years and trying to remember inconsequential people and mundane events which had no personal impact on him. Moreover, he does not appear to have possessed the sharpest of minds. Although in his early fifties, *The Echo* said his features were 'almost hidden in long grey hair' and that he 'walked clumsily up the steps leading to the witness box'. He was to die of throat cancer just six years later. Was he an alcoholic, or suffering from another condition that adversely affects mental clarity?

Although Levisohn's unlikely tale of the abandoned wife and children traipsing across Europe, somehow tracking down Zagowski (like a needle in a haystack) to a cellar in Whitechapel, and depositing themselves, penniless, on his doorstep, is uncorroborated, it has not only been repeated by later writers as if fact, but also altered and, on occasion, mercilessly embroidered. The BPP started the ball rolling in 1903:

> Towards the end of 1888 [Kłosowski] came to England with a young Jewess, to whom he had promised marriage, and who had borne him a child. The couple resided together for some time in the East-end of London, and the prisoner then persuaded the young woman to go to some relatives in America, promising to follow her in a short time. This promise, however, he did not fulfil, and in October of 1889 he was married to a woman named Lucya Baderski...and resided with her for some time in a barber's shop in Cable Street, where a child was born to them [*sic*]. Subsequently they moved to another shop in the Whitechapel Road, and while there the young Jewess returned from America with her child and claimed the prisoner as her husband.[488]

488 Return showing the Working of the Regulations for carrying out the Prosecution of Offences Act 1879 & 1884. British Parliamentary Papers, Vol. 56, HMSO, 1902. Pub as the *Blue Book*, 1903, p12–16.

By 1919 another of Chapman's *ad hoc* biographers decided that two children was insufficient, and increased it to three. Since then, many authors (including Fabian, Emsley, Marjoribanks, Marriner, Honeycombe and Gordon) have published their own version of the 'wife from Poland' tale, adding to it whatever twist took their fancy. The number of children varies from one to three, and the fate of their mother also changes. Some authors assert that she died at Kłosowski's hands. Edward Marjoribanks appears to be the source of this myth: in 1932 he announced, rather boldly, that Kłosowski had 'beheaded' her.[489] Although he offered neither source nor evidence to support this startling claim, in 1957 it was not only repeated as fact but also embellished by a man from whom we expect better: retired Scotland Yard Detective Superintendent Robert Fabian. If Kłosowski tired of a woman, he claimed, 'he could think only of cutting off her head. He did this to his first wife, when he was 22 years old, and she was 19.' For good measure, Fabian then added a fabrication of his own: 'The local police felt so strongly about it that [he] fled to England.'[490] Obviously, a beheaded wife cannot have taken her child(ren) to Whitechapel, and yet, when Brian Marriner retold the tale of spousal decapitation in Poland, he stated later that the wife subsequently travelled to England.[491] In 2002 R.M. Gordon suggested that Kłosowski fled Poland because he was 'running for his very life', adding later that 'murder would seem to be the best motive for running as fast as he could.'[492] However, Gordon must have been referring to an earlier murder, because later he suggested that Kłosowski killed and dismembered his first wife not in Poland but in London, and that her remains are now known as the Pinchin Street torso.[493] Most of these writers forgot to account for the fate of the offspring, but at least Honeycombe remembered them: he speculated that Kłosowski may have killed them (and their mother) with poison.[494]

There is another tale involving Levisohn, though it did not originate from him. H.L. Adam, Gordon and others have claimed that he and Kłosowski knew one another in Poland. This is impossible: Kłosowski moved to Warsaw from rural Poland in 1885, at least four years after Levisohn had left Poland and settled in England permanently.

## A CENTURY OF ERRATA

The aforementioned British Parliamentary Papers of 1902 were published in the government's *Blue Book* in the summer of 1903. A brief summary of Chapman's life appears within a report on recent serious crimes, but it contains so many definite errors and dubious facts that it is of scant use to historians searching for the truth. The usual myths were presented (e.g. Chapman had 'studied surgery with a surgeon') and some fresh anecdotes received their first airing. For example, in

489 Marjoribanks, E. (1932) *Carson the Advocate*, Macmillan. 2005 edition, Kessinger, p304. The MP for Eastbourne, Marjoribanks committed suicide at the age of thirty-two, whilst writing that book.
490 *Corpus Christi Caller-Times*, 8th December 1957.
491 Marriner, B. (1993) *Murder with Venom*, True Crime Library, p11.
492 Gordon, R.M. (2002) *The Thames Torso Murders*, McFarland, p181–2.
493 'Rippercast: The Whitechapel murders Podcast. The Chapman-Ripper Theory', 6th April 2009.
The torso was part of a long series of dismembered bodies that were found near the River Thames in 1873, 1874, 1884, and between 1887 and 1902. No arrests were made in connection with the 'Thames Torso murders', as they are often called.
494 Honeycombe, G. (1993) *More Murders of the Black Museum*, Hutchinson, p148.

America Kłosowski was unfaithful and threatened Lucy with a revolver. The story of his subsequent life is more accurate, though many details are incorrect.[495] George R. Sims published another version of Chapman's life story in two lengthy press articles in 1907 and 1908, and in doing so introduced further inaccuracies, for example stating that Lucy — who Sims described as Chapman's 'second wife' — was a Jewess whom he had married in a synagogue.[496]

Chapman seems to have fallen out of the spotlight for about ten years, until in 1919 'My experiences as a Prison Warder' appeared. It is possibly the first full-length account of Chapman's life in which the (anonymous) writer himself fabricated events, rather than simply repeating uncorroborated tales or making unintentional errors. The warder claims to have attended 'Leverino Kloshoffski' at Holloway — a women's prison in which Chapman was never incarcerated! The prisoner, he stated, was born and raised in Warsaw, where he 'passed many examinations in medicine and surgery'. He married there 'eventually' and fathered three children (which would take at least five years, assuming no multiple births). Having achieved all the foregoing by the tender age of twenty-two, Kloshoffski abandoned his family, sailed to London and opened a barber's shop in Whitechapel. A year later his family turned up, but he spurned them, moved to Tottenham and lived with Annie Chapman, taking her surname. Mary Spink's husband left her 'in consequence of her connection with Chapman' and, two months later, she gave birth to a son. (As Willie was born in 1888 that places Chapman with Mary before the abandoned wife caught up with him.) Chapman pretended to marry Mary 'according to the Jewish law'. He was suspected of the deaths of 'many more women' than the three he killed 'with arsenic'. The abandoned Polish wife appeared in 1903 at the Old Bailey (this identifies her as Lucy, who was only seventeen when she was, supposedly, a mother of three in Poland). Lastly, the warder claimed that, at his execution, Chapman's final act before the trap doors fell open was to nod goodbye to him and his colleague. A tall tale, reminiscent of that told in the *Mikado*.[497]

An anecdote about Chapman appeared in an Australian newspaper in 1921. While it seems far-fetched, there may be some elements of truth in it.

> There is a little story of him in his early wander years of hairdressing. It is also the story of a girl who seems to have had a narrow escape. The incident, one account relates, took place in London; according to another version it was in Scheveningen, where he certainly appears to have had a job through one summer season. He made friends with a local family, and presently declared himself violently in love with one of the daughters. To add to his importance, he was accustomed to dazzle this simple family with accounts of his scientific acquirements, telling them that he merely followed a humble calling until it became financially possible for him to resume the studies needed for him to become a qualified surgeon. They fell into the habit of consulting him about their ailments, until one day he started boasting of the power of

495 Return showing the Working of the Regulations for carrying out the Prosecution of Offences Act 1879 & 1884. British Parliamentary Papers, Vol. 56, HMSO, 1902. Pub as the *Blue Book*, 1903, p12–16.
496 *Lloyd's Weekly*, 9th August 1907 and *NZ Truth* (New Zealand), 25th January 1908.
497 *Weekly News*, 17th October 1919.

life and death which science placed in medical hands. One of the sons laughed. Perhaps he said that doctors were no different from anybody else who could buy two pennyworth of poison; that they were just as open to suspicion and punishment. Chapman snapped his fingers — a favourite trick of his — and ended the discussion with the remark, 'You will see.' A few days later, after a couple of glasses of beer at a cafe, taken in company with the Pole, the young fellow experienced a mild attack of vomiting and diarrhoea. It passed off, but the parents, not unnaturally, decided that the foreign gentleman was rather too knowledgeable an individual to have near their food.[498]

Chapman again faded into the shadows until 1930, when London journalist Hargrave Lee Adam published his *Trial of George Chapman* as part of the Notable British Trials series. Most of the book consists of heavily abbreviated transcripts of what witnesses said at the police and coroner's courts and the Old Bailey. These are preceded by a short biography of Chapman which is littered from start to finish with factual errors which have been repeated by many subsequent writers.

Shortly after Adam's book appeared, former police superintendent Arthur Fowler Neil devoted a chapter of his 1932 memoirs, *Forty Years of Manhunting,* to presenting his version of Chapman's life story. It, too, was full of errors, but none were copied from Adam. He called Mary Spink 'Catherine Spinks' and stated on one page that she died in 1895 but on the next that it was 1897. He also got Bessie's death-year wrong. Neil did not even spell his subject's Polish name correctly, rendering it as 'Kloskovski'.

Neil was far from alone in citing erroneous dates and names. Honeycombe suggested that Bessie's sister Mary was her twin (*they were born four years apart*). Begg dated Chapman's stay in America as 1890 to 1895 whilst Neil gave it as 1888 to 1892 (*it was 1891-2*). Stratmann says that Chapman's Old Bailey trial began on 11th February (*16th March*); Thurgood claims that it ended on 20th March (*19th*) and Lynch gave the year of his year of execution as 1901 (*1903*). Meirion Trow has recently told his readers that Chapman worked in Praga in 1897 (*it was 1885-86*) and moved to London in July 1897 (*1887-88*).

With regard to Chapman's professional life, there is the ubiquitous myth that he was a surgeon, an article in the *BMJ* that refers to him as 'Dr George Chapman',[499] repeated claims by many authors that he served in the Russian Army, and Trow's assertion that he ran the White Hart pub.

Chapman's private life is also misrepresented. Emsley asserted that he, Lucy 'and the baby' set off for the USA in May 1890'[500] (*the baby died before they left London — and it was 1891*). Stratmann and Eddleston say that the baby died in the USA. Leo Grex stated that Chapman went to the USA in 1888, accompanied by 'the Polish woman who claimed to be his English wife'. She returned in 1891 and he 'followed her two years later.'[501] Chapman's victims are habitually referred to as 'wives' and he is often accused of bigamy. Rubinstein referred to Lucy as 'his first common-

498 *The Register* (Adelaide), 28th July 1921.
499 'Serial Homicide by Doctors', *British Medical Journal*, 23rd December 2000.
500 Emsley, J. (2006) *The Elements of Murder*, OUP, p241–242.
501 Grex, Leo (1985) *Detection (Stranger than Fiction)*, Ravette, p117.

law wife, May Baderski'.[502] Grex claims that Chapman married Lucy using 'forged certificates'. Thurgood wrongly thinks that Mary was a divorcee whose fortune consisted of £6,000 (*it was £570*) and that the Marshes called in the same doctor as Chapman. Nash alleged that Chapman 'ran around with other women' whilst living with Bessie,[503] Freeman claimed that Annie 'suffered frequent abuse at his hands'[504] and Paul Roland stated that when Lucy confronted him about his philandering he 'beat her in a fit of temper'. There are no data to support any of these authors' assertions, nor to back up the *Observer* in its claim that Chapman was arrested because Maud's relatives 'became suspicious upon his making love to her sister.'[505] Grex, Jakubowski and Braund argued that Chapman never killed until he had found a replacement; however, this was not true in any of the three cases.

According to Grex, Chapman acquired his name from 'Betsy Chapman'. After being under Abberline's surveillance he moved to Hastings to avoid him, opened a barbershop (using money earned in the USA) and met 'Catherine' Spink. When she died there was no one but him in the room, and he returned to London because he thought Abberline had given up looking for Jack the Ripper.[506]

The frequency and diversity of Chapman's sexual activities is another secret he took to his grave, but that has failed to prevent certain authors from making emphatic statements on the subject. Brian Marriner, whose biographical essay on Chapman was subtitled 'The Cruel Casanova',[507] resorted to hyperbole to justify that label. Chapman's 'long line of lovers', he wrote, was 'seemingly endless.' We know of one wife and four or five mistresses plus brief flirtations with two women, five years apart, neither of which resulted in seduction. Hardly 'endless.'

Peter Thurgood recently claimed that it was 'a well-known fact' that Chapman had 'an enormous sexual appetite';[508] similarly, casebook.org's official biography of Chapman cites his 'outrageous sexual drive', while Roland went so far as to label it 'insatiable'.[509] None has explained the provenance of this highly personal information. How can it be 'a well known fact' when none of the primary source material (either documents or witnesses) makes reference to Chapman's libido?

There is confusion not only in relation to whom Chapman killed but also how, where and when. Gordon and Thurgood incorrectly refer to him as 'a known mass murderer', but that is defined as killing four or more people at the same time and place. Trevor Marriott claimed that he was 'convicted of killing his wife and several other women';[510] Begg, Whitehead and Rivett incorrectly date the poison murders as between 1895 and 1901. Paul Roland claims that Kłosowski assumed the name Chapman in 1895 'in a belated attempt to evade the unwanted attentions of the British authorities, who were beginning to suspect him of having murdered several of his

---

502 Rubinstein, W.D. (2008) *Shadow Pasts: History's Mysteries,* Pearson, p56.
503 Nash, J.R. (1990) *Encyclopaedia of World Crime,* p682.
504  Freeman, N. (2004) in Moore, G. and Maunder, A. *Victorian Crime, Madness and Sensation,* Ashgate, p220.
505 *The Observer,* 14th November 1920.
506 Grex, Leo (1985) *Detection (Stranger than Fiction),* Ravette, p118.
507 A chapter within Marriner, B. (1993) *Murder with Venom,* True Crime Library.
508 Thurgood, P. (2013) *Abberline: The Man who Hunted Jack the Ripper,* History Press, p140.
509 Roland, P. (2007) *The Crimes of Jack the Ripper,* Capella, p121.
510 Marriott, T. (2007) *Jack the Ripper: The 21st Century Investigation,* Blake, p248.

former wives'.[511] The Fanthorpes believed that the poison he used was arsenic. After the fire at the Monument, writes Thurgood, Chapman 'obtained the lease on another pub, as far away as possible'.[512] In fact, the Crown was less than half a mile away.

John J. Eddleston, in the preface to his book *Jack the Ripper: An Encyclopaedia* correctly observes that many writers 'have perpetuated myths, errors, sloppy research, and downright invention'. He wanted his book viewed 'as a trustworthy, accurate, and interesting work that may be relied upon to give the facts and that will not, like so many others, perpetuate myths'.[513] His entry on Chapman begins: 'At 12:30am [*it was p.m.*]...Maud Marsh died at the Crown public house, High Street, Islington' (*it was Borough High Street, Southwark*). He makes further mistakes with names, dates and sequences of events, and — ironically — perpetuated myths. 'Lucy was dismayed', he writes, 'when, within a few weeks of the wedding, a woman turned up...from Poland.' Eddleston states that Lucy returned to England in February 1892 'after an argument' (*speculation*), and Chapman followed 'two weeks later' (*it was several months later*). He calls Bessie 'Elizabeth' and dates Chapman's move to the Crown as June 1902 (*it was January*).[514] Eddleston's greatest blunder is the inclusion of Chapman's murders in his 2010 book *Foul Deeds in Islington*. Including Mary Spink is cheeky but just about excusable if one is in a generous frame of mind (she died in nearby Finsbury). However, Bessie and Maud were murdered in Southwark, on the other side of the River Thames. Eddleston's mistake is particularly bizarre because it is impossible to research Chapman's murders without being constantly reminded of the borough in which they occurred: Chapman was the *Southwark* Poisoner; he was arrested in *Southwark* by the police of *Southwark* Division and taken to *Southwark* police station. Eddleston even cites as his source transcripts of depositions made at *Southwark* police court and *Southwark* coroner's court![515]

In his 2011 biography *Inspector Frederick George Abberline and Jack the Ripper*, Peter Thurgood promised in his subtitle to give readers *The Reality behind the Myth*, and yet his two chapters on George Chapman repeated the usual myths and errors.[516] He also introduced some new ones: in Warsaw, writes Thurgood, Kłosowski 'met and married his first wife, who almost immediately became pregnant', so he 'promptly finished his studies and started to look for a full time job in order to provide for his new family'. However, he abandoned them, went to London and married Lucy. Somehow, his first wife found out and rushed from Poland 'in an attempt to reclaim her marriage and get rid of this other woman', and

> [F]or a while both women cohabited with Klosowski. This happy threesome ended, however, when Baderski bore Klosowski a son in September 1890. This was too much for his first wife to bear, and after a blazing argument, she walked out and returned to Poland.[517]

---

511 Roland, P. (2007) *The Crimes of Jack the Ripper*, Capella, p119, p 121.

512 *Abberline: The Man who Hunted Jack the Ripper*, History Press, p133. Thurgood is the author of books on London's history and states online that he has lived in London all his life.

513 Eddleston, J. (2001) *Jack the Ripper: An Encyclopedia*, ABC-Clio. pxi–xii.

514 *Ibid.* p202–204.

515 Eddleston, J. (2010) *Foul Deeds in Islington*, Wharncliffe Books, p116–128.

516 This was a self-published Kindle book which has since been withdrawn and, after being given a fresh title, was re-issued in a paper edition by the History Press (see the next footnote).

517 Thurgood, P. (2013) *Abberline: The Man who Hunted Jack the Ripper*. History Press, p128–129.

This is yet another rehash of the 'Polish wife' myth, to which Thurgood has added a few extra details, such as her early pregnancy, the 'happy threesome' and the 'blazing argument'. None of these details appear in the primary sources, and I challenge Mr Thurgood to substantiate them.

Perhaps he would also like to offer some justification for contradicting the sworn testimony of three female witnesses: Mrs Radin, Miss Rayner and Miss Chapman. The testimony of each is easily accessible in *Trial of George Chapman* and online, both on the Old Bailey website and within newspaper archives. However, Thurgood has added many details that do not appear in the transcript, without explaining the provenance of his additions. Firstly, he claims:

> Shortly after arriving in London, Klosowski introduced himself to a Polish barber as a hairdresser and qualified doctor, using the alias Ludwig Zagowski. [When his son was ill] Klosowski pretended to care for him. This arrangement didn't last long however when the Pole found out that his son was actually getting worse under Klosowski's supposed care. Klosowski was undaunted by this rejection, and soon found himself another job...[518]

The man Thurgood refers to as 'the Pole' must be Abraham Radin, a Russian Lithuanian (he was the only person who employed our man as a barber and had a sick child). Mrs Radin's court testimony is the sole source of information about Kłosowski's time with them. She swore that the man called himself *Kłosowski* and said he had been a doctor's *assistant*. She did not say that her son grew worse under his care, nor that she and her husband rejected him. Thurgood offers no reason for misrepresenting Mrs Radin's testimony.

Turning to Florence Rayner, Thurgood states that Chapman took her 'upstairs to his flat where they made love', and that she claimed to have 'heard Maud's screams when he beat her.' These statements run contrary to Florence's sworn testimony. It is the same story with Annie Chapman:

> He brought home another woman, telling [Annie] Chapman that she was to share their bed, [Annie] grew impatient and angry, and consequently left him. [When pregnant, Annie] gave Klosowski two options, either he married her and threw the other woman out, or he should support her and the baby when it was born. Klosowski simply refused either, denying that the baby was his, and telling her that he was moving out of London soon anyway...[519]

In fact, Annie said nothing about sharing a bed, being impatient or angry, or wanting Chapman to marry her, nor that Chapman denied the baby was his. Where, then, did Mr Thurgood obtain all these details?

In light of all the foregoing, it was most curious to learn recently that Professor David Wilson believes that Chapman's life story has been 'analysed extensively' and 'diligently researched', and deeply ironic that he includes errors and tall tales in his own retelling.[520]

---

518 Thurgood, P. (2013) *Abberline: The Man who Hunted Jack the Ripper,* History Press, p128.
519 *Ibid.* p130.
520 Wilson, D.A. (2011) *History of British Serial Killing,* Amazon Kindle, no page numbers.

## JACK THE RIPPER AT LAST?

Between 1888 and 1891 eleven women were murdered in the East End of London. Collectively these crimes are called the Whitechapel murders and whoever committed them was never caught. Many researchers agree that not all the women were killed by one person, but that the same culprit — nicknamed Jack the Ripper — was responsible for five deaths which occurred in a ten-week period in the autumn of 1888. This group is now known as the Canonical Five (C5); all were attacked in the early hours of the morning, all except one were killed outdoors and some were gruesomely mutilated and eviscerated.

| WHITECHAPEL MURDERS PRIOR TO THE CANONICAL 5 | | |
|---|---|---|
| Emma Smith | 3 Apr 1888 | Osborn Street/Brick Lane |
| Martha Tabram | 7 Aug 1888 | George Yard (now Gunthorpe St) |
| THE CANONICAL FIVE | | |
| Mary Ann Nichols | 31 Aug 1888 | Buck's Row (now Durward Street) |
| Annie Chapman | 8 Sept 1888 | Hanbury Street, Spitalfields |
| Elizabeth Stride | 30 Sept 1888 | Berner St (now Henriques St) |
| Catherine Eddowes | 30 Sept 1888 | Mitre Square, City of London |
| Mary Jane Kelly | 9 Nov 1888 | Dorset Street, Spitalfields |
| WHITECHAPEL MURDERS FOLLOWING THE CANONICAL 5 | | |
| Rose Mylett | 20 Dec 1888 | Poplar High Street |
| Unidentified torso | 10 Sept 1889 | Under railway arch, Pinchin Street |
| Alice McKenzie | 17 July 1889 | Castle Alley, Whitechapel |
| Frances Coles | 13 Feb 1891 | Swallow Gardens, Whitechapel |

Martha Tabram is sometimes counted amongst the victims of Jack the Ripper and, indeed, her death — owing to its location and timing — was investigated in parallel with the C5 murders. She is often supposed to be particularly pertinent to Chapman's candidacy because she was killed on the landing of a tenement block in a gloomy backstreet, at the other end of which stands a pub called the White Hart, beneath which Chapman once worked in a cellar barbershop.[521]

---

521 By strange coincidence, Tabram was born in Marshall Street, Southwark, just a couple of minutes' walk from the Crown.

## THE FIFTEEN POINTS

Fifteen points have been cited as reasons to support the notion that George Chapman was responsible for (at least some of) the Whitechapel or Jack the Ripper murders.

1. He was a convicted murderer.

2. He had a history of violence, especially against women, and attacked Lucy with a knife.

3. He was a skilled surgeon. He knew how to cut open bodies and remove organs, like the Ripper.

4. His arrival in London coincided with the beginning of the murders.

5. He worked (and possibly lived) at George Yard when Mrs Tabram was murdered there.

6. He lived and worked in the East End throughout the murders.

7. Lucy stated that, in 1888, he stayed out till the early hours of the morning.

8. In 1888 police believed Chapman was the Ripper.

9. He matched witness descriptions of the Ripper.

10. Both Chapman and the Ripper were ambidextrous.

11. The Whitechapel murders ceased when Chapman went to the USA.

12. A series of Ripper-style murders occurred whilst he was in the USA and ended when he left.

13. In 1902/1903 police believed Chapman was the Ripper.

14. Abberline congratulated Godley on catching Jack the Ripper 'at last'.

15. After his death, police continued to believe he was the Ripper.

These points, when listed together in this fashion, do seem to provide excellent — some would say conclusive — reasons to name Chapman as Jack the Ripper. But do they stand up to scrutiny?

### 1. HE WAS A CONVICTED MURDERER

About this point there can be no mistake. He was hanged for killing Maud Marsh and compelling circumstantial evidence strongly suggests that nobody but he could have been responsible for the deaths of Mary Spink and Bessie Taylor.

### 2. HE HAD A HISTORY OF VIOLENCE, ESPECIALLY AGAINST WOMEN, AND ATTACKED LUCY WITH A KNIFE

R.M. Gordon has claimed that Chapman 'grew up amid violence', was 'suspected of criminal activity at a young age', threatened many women, was a 'violent misogynist' and was 'violent continuously' to women.[522] His first point is probably a reference

---

522 Gordon, R.M. (2000) *Alias Jack the Ripper: Beyond the Usual Whitechapel Suspects.* McFarland, p313–6.

to the insurrections in some areas of Poland against the Russian occupation of their country, but there is no evidence that Chapman's family was involved. Nor is there any reason to think that Chapman was suspected of crimes in Poland. Gordon's assertion that he threatened many women with violence is misleading. It implies that he bullied women in general, when in fact he was a domestic tyrant. Wife-beating was commonplace amongst the working classes in those days; it does not indicate that a man was Jack the Ripper. Chapman wasn't violent 'continuously' but sporadically, nor did he attack women randomly; his aggressive outbursts were restricted to specific, individual women with whom he was sexually and emotionally involved.

The anecdote that Chapman attempted to stab, murder or behead Lucy with a knife — the Ripper's trademark weapon — has been repeated so many times that people assume it is true. Those who cite the incident as evidence to support the Chapman–Ripper theory are either unaware, or are failing to disclose, that the *two* sources from which the story originates contradict one another. The version most commonly quoted was published in the *Daily Chronicle* of 23rd March 1903 and purports to have derived from a statement made by Lucy:

> [Kłosowski] held [Lucy] down on the bed, and pressed his face against her mouth to keep her from screaming. At that moment a customer entered the shop immediately in front of the room, and Klosowski got up to attend him. [Lucy] chanced to see a handle protruding from underneath the pillow. She found, to her horror, that it was a sharp and formidable knife, which she promptly hid. Later, Klosowski deliberately told her that he meant to have cut her head off, and pointed to a place in the room where he meant to have buried her.[523]

The second version appeared in a report compiled by the staff of the Director of Public Prosecutions for the British Parliamentary Papers of 1902, and published within the *Blue Book* in June 1903 as part of a short biography of Chapman:

> While [in Jersey City] the prisoner treated his wife very badly and his infidelity was of such a character as to cause her to threaten to leave him. In return he threatened her with a revolver and showed her a grave he had dug in the floor of the shop into which he said he intended to put her body.

A revolver. Not a knife. At most, only one version can be correct — but which? If the source for both was Lucy, did she give conflicting accounts, or did somebody change her words before they were published? The *Chronicle* claimed that Lucy made a 'statement', but did not say whether she told her tale to a reporter, the police, her family, a solicitor or the prosecution team. If it was the police, then the BPP version is the more reliable, because its author, a civil servant, would have had access to the police file (a reporter probably would not). The *Chronicle* version would have been filtered through a policeman and a reporter, making it vulnerable to tampering. Perhaps one of them leaked the story to the *Chronicle,* but changed the revolver into a knife to support the theory that Chapman was the Ripper — a suspicion that first saw the light of day in the same article.

---

523 *Daily Chronicle,* 23rd March 1903. The paper was absorbed by the *Daily Mail* in 1960.

The knife version of the tale is better known not because it was more likely, but merely because it had the good fortune to be printed within a newspaper article, which made it more accessible. Moreover, the article was despatched by cable across the English-speaking world and published in the press in North America and the Antipodes.[524] By sheer bad luck, the revolver version appeared only in a government report, and therefore reached a much smaller readership.

Whilst the revolver version is either unknown or conveniently suppressed, the knife version is repeatedly cited by supporters of the Chapman–Ripper theory as pretty much conclusive proof that Chapman was a knife-wielding maniac. What is more, it is habitually exaggerated, embellished and misrepresented. The incident was a verbal threat, and one that Chapman never carried out, despite having numerous opportunities to do so during his marriage to Lucy. Most retellings from 1903 to the present day ignore this fact and inflate mere words into an actual, physical attempt to kill. Even Sugden states that Chapman 'attacked Lucy with a knife'. The distortion continues to this day, even though the *Chronicle* article is posted on casebook.org and available to anyone with internet access. Strangely, casebook's Chapman biography states that he 'attacked Lucy with a knife' and cites the *Chronicle* article in support, yet it does not support that statement. R.M. Gordon claims that the 'knife attack' appears in Adam's *Trial of George Chapman*.[525] Although Adam mentioned Jersey City, his book contains nothing about any incident involving a knife (or a revolver).

The most recent exaggeration of the knife version of the tale appears in Peter Thurgood's biography of Abberline. Describing the incident as an 'attempted stabbing', he states that Lucy claimed that her husband threatened her 'on numerous occasions', and that fights between the couple led to 'serious violence' by Chapman. Lucy said none of these things, and nor did any other witness, and yet, again, Thurgood offers nothing to corroborate his assertions.[526]

Ironically, it is the revolver version of the story that should be favoured, because Chapman was repeatedly associated with firearms. According to the sworn statements of court witnesses, he carried a revolver around Leytonstone (in a black bag) and Mary showed it to a neighbour in Hastings. A photo of Chapman and Bessie reveals several guns on the wall behind them; Miss Painter recalled that Chapman threatened Bessie with a gun; he had a shooting gallery in the Grapes and was reported to have fired shots from the Monument. Lastly, Inspector Godley found a revolver at the Crown and presented it in court. In contrast, no witness mentioned Chapman either possessing or using a knife.

Even if the weapon Chapman had cited in his verbal threat to Lucy was a knife, it would illustrate merely that, when sufficiently angry, Chapman was capable of making empty verbal threats. This, as researcher Gareth Williams has pointed out, 'puts him in the company of millions of other men and does not signify that he was of the "cutting" type of killer at all, still less the "cutting-and-eviscerating" type'.[527]

Ultimately, the revolver/knife tale is of little value to historians. The impossibility of verification makes it more a source of frustration than elucidation.

524 One US newspaper falsely stated that Lucy had reported the incident to the US police.
525 Gordon, R.M. (2002) *The Thames Torso Murders of Victorian London,* McFarland, p200.
526 Thurgood, P. (2013) *Abberline: The Man who Hunted Jack the Ripper,* History Press, p129.
527 As 'Sam Flynn', casebook.org, 28th February 2008.

The police file that might have contained Lucy Klosowska's statement — if it ever existed — has been lost, stolen or destroyed. The two versions of the tale contradict one another and, as much of the other information published in each source is incorrect, they are both unreliable.

Lucy's tale was published in the same issue of the *Daily Chronicle* that suggested Chapman was Jack the Ripper. Did the reporter hear the revolver version from Lucy (or from having access to the civil servant's report before it was published in the *Blue Book*) and change it to a knife to strengthen Chapman's candidature for Jack the Ripper?

The tale of the threat to kill (whether by knife or gun) may even have been fabricated by Lucy. She did not have an unblemished record of truthfulness: she twice lied in the census and to a registrar of births, even though these were criminal offences.[528] Perhaps she refused to give evidence at the Old Bailey because she felt more comfortable fibbing to a bobby over a cup of tea and behind closed doors than telling tall tales in the witness box in front of lofty legal personages, crowds of nosy spectators and a gaggle of Fleet Street reporters eagerly recording her every word, most especially after publicly swearing on the Bible to tell the truth.

Incidentally, some writers have misinterpreted the introductory sentence of the *Daily Chronicle* article. It read: 'Lucy Klosowski, who was present in the Central Criminal Court last week, has made a startling statement'.[529] This phrasing has led people to believe that Lucy testified on oath in the witness box at the Old Bailey, an error that is still being perpetuated today.

**3. HE WAS A SKILLED SURGEON. HE KNEW HOW TO CUT OPEN BODIES AND REMOVE ORGANS, LIKE THE RIPPER**

This assertion raises two questions: did Chapman possess surgical skills, and did the Ripper need them? As explained in Part One, the incorrect notion that Chapman had been trained to cut into bodies originates from a mistranslation of the Russian word фельдшер (feldsher) as 'surgeon', a mistake that arose because the interpreter, a Pole called Petrykowski, did not know an English word that conveyed the meaning of the word feldsher. It seems that Petrykowski was not a qualified translator or professional police interpreter. He described himself as someone 'acquainted with' the Russian language. Attempts to locate him giving evidence at other trials, in the census and other official government records drew a blank. Perhaps he was nothing more than a drinking pal of Godley's, one of the many thousands of Poles who had washed up in London.

Thanks to Petrykowski's poor choice of words, it has been accepted as fact for over a century that Chapman had been trained in 'surgery', possessed 'surgical' skills and worked as a junior 'surgeon'. But he was not trained in 'surgery' according to the meaning of the word in the English language today, i.e. cutting into bodies and removing or otherwise interfering with internal organs.

---

528 In the 1901 census she claimed to be married to Frank Szymański. In the 1911 census she claimed to have been married to him for thirteen years. The couple married in 1903. Under the Census (Great Britain) Act, 1900 she was liable to a fine not exceeding five pounds.
529 *Daily Chronicle*, 23rd March 1903.

R.M. Gordon boldly claims that there is 'evidence' that Chapman 'qualified as a Junior Surgeon',[530] but we can see that this is incorrect on two counts. Firstly, 'junior surgeon' is a mistranslation of 'surgeon's assistant', a post in which Chapman had worked in Warsaw. Secondly, although Chapman applied for admission to the exam, no record exists that he sat it, let alone passed it.

A lack of training in surgery may weaken the Chapman–Ripper theory but it does not demolish it, because it is not universally agreed that the Ripper needed such training. Some doctors who examined the Whitechapel murder victims thought that medical knowledge was displayed, but police surgeon Dr Thomas Bond, after studying the reports of the injuries, concluded:

> In each case the mutilation was inflicted by a person who had no scientific nor anatomical knowledge. In my opinion he does not even possess the technical knowledge of a butcher or horse slaughterer or any person accustomed to cut up dead animals.[531]

A feldsher's knife skills were confined to lancing carbuncles, furuncles and boils, and removing moles and warts. Had later researchers been able to obtain Chapman's original Russian documents and commission a fresh translation from a properly qualified interpreter, the 'surgeon' myth would have died years ago.

## 4. CHAPMAN'S ARRIVAL IN LONDON COINCIDED WITH THE BEGINNING OF THE MURDERS

Nobody knows exactly when he arrived in London. A receipt issued in Poland at the end of February 1887 was found in his possession. He appeared in an 1889 London street directory for which the deadline for applications for inclusion was December 1888. According to Ethel Radin he was in London by 6th August 1888. He may have arrived before Emma Smith (the first of the Whitechapel murder victims) was killed in April 1888, but she was attacked by a group of men and there is no reason to believe that Chapman was among them.

## 5. HE LIVED AND WORKED IN THE EAST END THROUGHOUT THE MURDERS

This is true. Chapman lived in the East End and within easy walking distance of the sites. Until he married Lucy in October 1889, he probably enjoyed enough privacy to be able to come and go in the early hours unobserved and to deal with blood-stained clothing and knives.

## 6. HE WORKED (AND POSSIBLY LIVED) AT GEORGE YARD WHEN MRS TABRAM WAS MURDERED THERE

Mrs Tabram's body was found on the landing of a block of flats in George Yard on 7th August 1888. She had been stabbed thirty-nine times. Chapman worked in a barbershop at the White Hart, on the corner of George Yard. According to Wolff Levisohn, Chapman was there from 1888 to 1890. This was contradicted by two other witnesses: Stanisław Baderski and George Schumann. Neither placed Chapman at the White Hart before 1890.[532] Whilst the timeline of Baderski and Schumann has been

---

530 Gordon, R.M. (2000) *Alias Jack the Ripper: Beyond the Usual Whitechapel Suspects*, McFarland, p314.
531 Bond's letter to Assistant Commissioner Robert Anderson, 10th November 1888.
532 In 1903 Schumann said Chapman worked at the White Hart 'twelve years ago', i.e. early 1891.

ignored or dismissed, that of Levisohn has been seized upon and elevated to a fact by those who wish to put Chapman in the frame for Tabram's demise.

The promotion of Levisohn's timeline began in March 1903, when the *Daily Chronicle* stated that in 1888 Chapman 'was undoubtedly occupying a lodging in George Yard'. The source given is 'the police', but their source was Wolff Levisohn. Abberline read it in the *Chronicle* and repeated it, giving the information the weight of his endorsement. A number of researchers continue to assert that Chapman worked (some say also resided) at the White Hart in 1888, citing Levisohn's testimony. Levisohn did not say that Chapman worked there in 1888, but *from 1888 to 1890*. Levisohn's timeline is easily disproved, not only by the evidence of other witnesses but by the aforementioned Post Office street directory and Chapman's marriage certificate, both of which place him in Cable Street in 1889. As Levisohn was wrong about Chapman's whereabouts in 1889 and 1890, why should we believe what he said about 1888?

Even if Levisohn's timeline was correct, it still would not prove that Chapman attacked Martha Tabram. A murderer need not live or work in a particular area in order to kill someone there, and it is absurd to argue that, if a knife murder was committed in George Yard in 1888, of the half-a-million men who lived in the East End, the culprit must be the one who, nearly fifteen years later, was convicted of a poison murder.

### 7. LUCY STATED THAT, IN 1888, HE STAYED OUT TILL THE EARLY HOURS OF THE MORNING

A number of authors have offered versions of this myth. None seems to have realised that, as Lucy did not meet Chapman until 1889, she was unable to witness his movements during 1888. The date the couple met appears in the transcript of Chapman's Old Bailey trial, which was published in 1930 within H.L. Adam's *Trial of George Chapman*. It is therefore puzzling to find, within the same book, Adam claiming that, in 1903:

> Abberline...closely questioned...Lucy Baderski about Chapman's nightly habits at the time of the [Ripper] murders. She said that he was often out until three or four o'clock in the morning but she could throw little light upon these absences.[533]

Having left the police in 1892, Abberline had no authority to question Lucy a decade later; however, Godley may have bent the rules for his former colleague and allowed him to interview her informally about Chapman's lifestyle during the 'Autumn of Terror' in 1888.[534] But such an interview would have been pointless: Lucy married Chapman in late October 1889, after meeting him only 'four or five weeks' previously.

The inclusion of the trial transcript in Adam's book means it was available to Marjoribanks during the research for his 1932 biography of Carson. However, this did not stop him from wondering whether Chapman, whilst living with Lucy, was 'abroad in the street at night, with his surgeon's knife concealed under his coat, taking unholy pleasure in hunting down the poor unfortunates for mutilation and murder'.[535]

---

533 Adam, H.L. (1930) *Trial of George Chapman*, William Hodge, p52.
534 Abberline was living in London at the time: his home until he retired to Bournemouth in 1904 was in Stockwell, near Southwark.
535 Marjoribanks, E. (1932) *Carson the Advocate*, quoted in *Nottingham Evening Post*, 11th July 1932.

Nowadays researchers need not even obtain Adam's book to peruse Chapman's trial transcript: it has been on display on the Old Bailey website for a number of years. Despite this, Gordon, Gosling, Milne and Thurgood claim that, in 1903, Lucy told police about Chapman's mysterious night-time absences in 1888. Peter Thurgood couched the assertion in these terms: 'At Klosowski's trial, his first wife, Lucy Baderski, brought up the fact that her husband had been in the habit of staying out into the early hours of the morning.'[536] The words *At Klosowski's trial* could be construed as meaning that Lucy gave testimony. Robert Milne eschews such ambiguity, stating emphatically that Lucy 'testified at his trial that when he lived in Whitechapel he would go out carrying a small bag, not coming home until 4:30am'. Milne cites his source as 'transcripts of witness evidence' from the trial, the very transcripts that make it clear that Lucy did not testify, and did not know Chapman during the Ripper murders.[537]

## 8. IN 1888 POLICE BELIEVED CHAPMAN WAS THE RIPPER

A number of authors have claimed that in 1888, or shortly thereafter, Chapman was a suspect for the Whitechapel or Jack the Ripper murders. In 1946, for example, Justin Atholl stated that Sir Edward Carson had suspected him in 1888.[538] According to Trevor Marriott, a former police detective constable, 'witnesses placed Chapman...near the scenes of some of the [Whitechapel] murders at the time they occurred'. Marriott's phrasing is annoyingly ambiguous: did he mean that Chapman was seen near to a murder scene in 1888, or that court witnesses said in 1903 that Chapman had lived near a murder scene in 1888? Later, Marriott claims that Chapman was 'always looked on by the police officers who investigated the Ripper murders as a prime suspect', but is puzzled by the police's failure to arrest him in 1888:

> I can't understand why they didn't. Maybe they thought there was no prospect of a conviction but I would have thought, given the fears which stalked the streets of the East End at that time, that they would at least have questioned him.[539]

According to some, they did: both R.M. Gordon and Debra Gosling assert that in 1888 Godley and Abberline knew Chapman, suspected him of being the Ripper and interviewed him, a myth that Peter Thurgood has recently repeated:

> The murder [of Tabram] occurred within yards of Klosowski's place of work, and when he was questioned by the police, they found out that at the time of this murder, Klosowski had rented rooms in George Yard Buildings; the very building in which Tabram was found murdered... The police questioned a number of local people regarding the Tabram murder, including Klosowski on a number of occasions. Despite regular questioning, nothing ever came of the investigation surrounding the murder. Klosowski was allowed to walk free.[540]

536 Thurgood, P. (2013) *Abberline: The Man who Hunted Jack the Ripper,* History Press, p140.
537 www.thestar.com/news/world/article/1056621--was-a-polish-surgeon-the-real-Jack the Ripper (accessed 16th May 2013).
538 Justin Atholl, 'Who Was Jack the Ripper?' *Reynold's News,* 15th September 1946.
539 *Daily Mail,* 9th March 2004; *Evening Standard,* 9th March 2004.
540 Thurgood, P. (2013) *Abberline: The Man who Hunted Jack the Ripper,* History Press, p128. Thurgood believed that Kłosowski was using the surname Zagowski when he was questioned.

There is not a shred of evidence that Kłosowski was investigated or questioned even *once*, nor that he was suspected of the Whitechapel or Ripper murders at the time they happened, nor that he was known to the police prior to 1902.

### 9. HE MATCHED WITNESS DESCRIPTIONS OF THE RIPPER

In 1932 Arthur Fowler Neil wrote that 'the only living description' of the Ripper 'tallied exactly with Chapman, even to the height, deep sunk black eyes, sallow complexion and thick, black moustache'.[541] Several others have made similar claims, but in fact at least twelve people gave descriptions and none fits Chapman exactly, although parts of some do. The traits reported are sufficiently broad to apply to many thousands of men: the age ranges from twenty-five to over forty, the build slim to stout, the height between 5ft 5 and 6ft. The suspect sported a fair, grey, fawn, carroty or black moustache; sometimes side whiskers; sometimes a beard. One would be hard-pressed to find an East End man in the 1880s without any of those characteristics.

George Hutchinson's description is the best match to Chapman. The 'surly looking' man he saw with Mary Jane Kelly[542] was about thirty-five, 5ft 6, of Jewish appearance, with a pale complexion, dark hair, eyes and eyelashes and a slight moustache, curled up each end. H.L. Adam called this 'a most faithful description of Chapman' — without mentioning that the age was thirteen years adrift.[543]

The *Daily Chronicle* stated with confidence that both Chapman and the Ripper 'carried a black bag and wore a P & O cap'. In fact not one of the twelve who provided (contradictory) descriptions of the Ripper mentioned a P & O cap (though one cited a sailor's cap and another a grey cloth cap). Several people mentioned a black bag, but such bags were common and the descriptions were vague.

### 10. BOTH CHAPMAN AND THE RIPPER WERE AMBIDEXTROUS

This was an uncorroborated claim made by A.F. Neil in 1932. There is no evidence that either Chapman or the Ripper were ambidextrous.

### 11. THE WHITECHAPEL MURDERS CEASED WHEN CHAPMAN WENT TO THE USA

The word 'when' implies that knife-murders of women in east London continued until the day Chapman left England and ended abruptly on his departure. That is not what happened. The final murder in the C5 Jack the Ripper series occurred in November 1888. After that, a torso was found in Pinchin Street in September 1889 and Frances Coles was murdered by an unknown assailant in February 1891. Chapman went to the USA in May or June 1891.

### 12. A SERIES OF RIPPER-STYLE MURDERS OCCURRED WHILST CHAPMAN WAS IN THE USA AND ENDED WHEN HE LEFT

The *Daily Chronicle* of 23rd March 1903 stated that, after the London Ripper murders ceased, 'crimes of a similar character were committed in America.' Abberline read this, believed it and endorsed it by repeating it to other pressmen. Shortly afterwards,

---

541 Neil, A.F. (1932) *Forty Years of Manhunting*, Jarrolds, p17.
542 Mary Jane Kelly was the fifth of the C5 Ripper victims.
543 Adam, H.L. (1930) *Trial of George Chapman*, William Hodge, p51.

police in Jersey City — where Chapman supposedly lived — announced that no Ripper-style crimes had been committed there, and their words were published in some US newspapers.[544] Aficionados of the Chapman–Ripper theory — and, indeed, many unbiased researchers — habitually cite this imaginary 'series' (which has also been described as 'an outbreak', 'a reign of terror', and even an 'epidemic'!) All bar one have felt under no obligation to present any details or sources, let alone proof; they seem to expect readers to take their word for it that such a series occurred.

The exception is R.M. Gordon, who has identified four specific murders perpetrated in and around the New York/New Jersey area in 1891 and 1892. However, the only one conducted in 'Ripper-style' was the first: the murder of Carrie Brown in New York on the night of 23rd April 1891. The other three victims were Hannah Robinson, strangled in New York in August 1891; Elizabeth Senior, stabbed by an intruder in New Jersey in January 1892; and Herta Mary Anderson, who was shot dead and had her throat cut in New Jersey on 8th June 1892.

We do not know when Chapman and Lucy went to the US. One ship's record shows a couple like them arriving in New York on 28th July, but Lucy's sister stated that they left London in May. However, in order to place Chapman in New York in time to kill Carrie Brown on 23rd April, Gordon searched ships' records and reported in 2003 that he had found a 'Sveri' or 'Sverni' Koslowsky on board the *S.S. Waesland*, which sailed from Hamburg on 13th April and arrived in New York on 23rd, just hours before the murder.[545] Wolf Vanderlinden later pointed out that Gordon had made a mistake: the man was *Yuri* Koslowsky, and the ship was the *S.S. Wieland*, which arrived in New York on 22nd April. Gordon accepted the correction. But Yuri was unlike Chapman in every particular: he was a thirty-year-old unmarried labourer, travelling with a group of workmates from Wilkowice in southern Poland to Chicago, via Hamburg.[546]

Chapman was almost certainly in the USA at the time of the second and third murders, one of which was in New York and the other in New Jersey. However, these killings involved strangling and shooting, neither of which fits the modus operandi of either Chapman the poisoner or Jack the Ripper. His presence for the fourth murder, in New Jersey on 8th June, is doubtful. Although no ship's record has been found relating to his return to London, according to Lucy's sister he was back by the end of May, which would rule him out. Even if she was mistaken, official records place him in London on 20th June,[547] so he could still have been in New Jersey as late as 8th, provided there was a fast ship leaving New York in the next two days.

Women were murdered in the US before Chapman arrived, while he was there, and after he left. At that time thirty million men lived in the US, of which a million-and-a-half were in the New York/New Jersey area, and there is no good reason to single out Chapman from this multitude, other than his later poison murders (i.e. that he was 'a murderer at heart'). Despite this, the story that there was a distinct set of murders, for which only he could have been responsible, continues to be repeated and embellished. For example, Thurgood recently wrote:

---

544 See for example the *Arizona Republican*, 24th March 1903.
545 Gordon, R.M. (2003) *The American Murders of Jack the Ripper*, Greenwood, p26.
546 Gordon later admitted his error: he had meant Yuri Koslowsky and the *Wieland*. 'Rippercast: The Whitechapel murders Podcast. The Chapman-Ripper Theory', 6th April 2009.
547 He registered his daughter's birth on that date.

The American police didn't have any reason at the time to look into Klosowski as a potential suspect. It wasn't until some years later, when he was being investigated regarding the murders of his wives/partners, that the police realised he was a possible suspect.[548]

Neither the British nor the American police ever treated him as a suspect for any murders in the US. It may come as a surprise to some readers to hear that there is no evidence that Chapman and Lucy lived in New Jersey. The unreliable revolver/knife anecdote detailed earlier is the sole source of that information; court witnesses stated only that the couple went to the US. Enquiries made in 1903 by reporters working for various newspapers found no evidence that Chapman and Lucy had lived in New Jersey.[549]

> No evidence can be found that George Chapman, who a cable despatch printed in this city yesterday says, is declared by the London police to be the original 'Jack the Ripper', ever lived in Jersey City, as his wife is said to have declared. Inquiry by the police and others yesterday failed to give any trace of him, and Chief Murphy is satisfied that the story that he once kept a barber shop in Jersey City is not correct. Poles who lived there at the time Chapman is supposed to have made it his home, when his wife is represented as saying that he once tried to murder her in a room back of his shop, said yesterday that they never had heard of the man and added that in 1893 [sic] when Chapman says he was a barber there, there were no Polish barber shops in the city.[550]

### 13. IN 1902/1903 POLICE BELIEVED CHAPMAN WAS THE RIPPER

Chapman's name was first publicly linked with that of Jack the Ripper in the aforementioned *Daily Chronicle* of 23rd March 1903:

> The police officers who have been engaged in tracing Klosowski's movements in connection with the three murders with which he was charged, are forming some rather startling theories as to the antecedent history of the criminal. These theories are connected with the Whitechapel murders which startled the world some fifteen years ago and were attributed to 'Jack the Ripper'.

The officers were not named. Those known to have investigated Chapman's poison murders were Inspector Godley and Sergeants William Kemp, Samuel Leak and Arthur Fowler Neil. According to Philip Sugden, Godley was 'struck by the similarities between Chapman and the Ripper and considered the possibility that they were one and the same man'.[551] Sugden gave no source for this information. R.M. Gordon claims that it was Godley who leaked the information to the press. In fact, of the four policemen, only one ever stated publicly that he believed Chapman was the Ripper. (This was Neil, and he did not do so until 1932.)

---

548 Thurgood, P. (2013) *Abberline: The Man who Hunted Jack the Ripper*, History Press, p129.
549 *Atlanta Constitution*, 24th March 1903; *Arizona Republican*, 24th March 1903.
550 Chapman visited the USA in 1891–2; the date 1893 was probably derived from his fake autobiography. *Gleaner* (Jamaica), 3rd April 1903.
551 Sugden, P. (2002) *Complete History of Jack the Ripper*, Constable Robinson, 2012 Kindle Edition, p441.

The *Chronicle* article prompted the *Pall Mall Gazette (PMG)* to interview Frederick Abberline, who had investigated the Whitechapel murders in 1888 and retired from the police in 1892.[552] His thoughts appeared in the *PMG* the following day:

Should Klosowski, the wretched man now lying under sentence of death for wife-poisoning, go to the scaffold without a 'last dying speech and confession,' a great mystery may for ever remain unsolved, but the conviction that 'Chapman' and 'Jack the Ripper' were one and the same person will not in the least be weakened in the mind of the man who is, perhaps, better qualified than anyone else in this country to express an opinion in this matter. We allude to Mr. F.G. Abberline, formerly Chief Detective Inspector of Scotland Yard, the official who had full charge of the criminal investigations at the time of the terrible murders in Whitechapel.

When a representative of the Pall Mall Gazette called on Mr. Abberline yesterday [23rd] and asked for his views on the startling theory set up by [the *Daily Chronicle*], the retired detective said: 'What an extraordinary thing it is that you should just have called upon me now. I had just commenced, not knowing anything about the report in the newspaper, to write to the Assistant Commissioner of Police, Mr. Macnaghten, to say how strongly I was impressed with the opinion that "Chapman" was also the author of the Whitechapel murders. Your appearance saves me the trouble. I intended to write on Friday [20th], but a fall in the garden, injuring my hand and shoulder, prevented my doing so until today.'

Mr. Abberline had already covered a page and a half of foolscap, and was surrounded with a sheaf of documents and newspaper cuttings dealing with the ghastly outrages of 1888.

'I have been so struck with the remarkable coincidences in the two series of murders,' he continued, 'that I have not been able to think of anything else for several days past — not, in fact, since the Attorney-General [*sic*] made his opening statement at the recent trial, and traced the antecedents of Chapman before he came to this country in 1888. [*Abberline was referring to Solicitor General Sir Edward Carson's speech on 16th March.*] Since then the idea has taken full possession of me, and everything fits in and dovetails so well that I cannot help feeling that this is the man we struggled so hard to capture fifteen years ago.

My interest in the Ripper cases was especially deep. I had for fourteen years previously been an inspector of police in Whitechapel, but when the murders began I was at the Central Office at Scotland Yard. On the application of Superintendent Arnold I went back to the East End just before Annie Chapman was found mutilated, and as chief of the detective corps I gave myself up to the study of the cases...

[T]here are a score of things which make one believe that Chapman is the man...

---

552 In the 1901 census John Collins (1871–1954), a member of the *PMG* staff for twenty years, was lodging with Abberline in Stockwell, south London. Perhaps he was still in residence in 1903, and conducted the interview with Abberline.

# INFAMOUS WHITECHAPEL FIEND "JACK THE RIPPER" IS INMATE OF CONDEMNED CELL

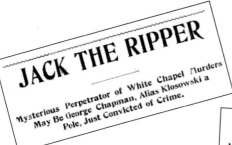

## JACK THE RIPPER

Mysterious Perpetrator of White Chapel Murders
May Be George Chapman, Alias Klosowski a
Pole, Just Convicted of Crime.

### "JACK THE RIPPER."

Whitechapel Murderer Said to Have
Been a Resident of America.

NEW YORK, March 23.—A London
dispatch was printed here today alleg-
ing that George Chapman, who was
convicted of the murder of several women in London, is the original "Jack
the Ripper."

# JACK THE RIPPER.

## Mystery of Fifteen Years Ago Believed to Have Been Solved.

By Scripps-McRae Press Association.

London, March 23—Police have unearthed circumstantial evidence tending
to prove that George Chapman, convicted of murder last Thursday, is
"Jack the-Ripper," mysterious perpetrator of revolting Whitechapel murders of 1888.

---

*A selection of American press headlines published after the Daily Chronicle revealed that some English police officers suspected Chapman of being Jack the Ripper. Top to bottom: San Jose Evening News, 23rd March 1903; Newark Advocate, 24th March 1903; Washington Morning Olympian, 24th March 1903; Elyria Chronicle, 23rd March 1903. A sketch of Jack the Ripper, based on Hutchinson's description. From the Illustrated Police News.*

Although he claimed to have 'a score of reasons' to suspect Chapman, a careful perusal of the reporter's two interviews with him unearthed only seven, of which four were incorrect and two were vague.

| | ASSESSMENT OF ABBERLINE'S SEVEN REASONS | |
|---|---|---|
| 1. | Chapman arrived in London shortly before the murders began. | Correct. |
| 2. | Ripper murders ceased when he went to America. | Vague. |
| 3. | Fitted witness descriptions. | Vague. |
| 4. | In the USA he tried to kill Lucy with a knife. | Incorrect. |
| 5. | Lived and/or worked at George Yard in 1888. | Incorrect. |
| 6. | Skilled surgeon; knew how to cut open bodies and remove organs. | Incorrect. |
| 7. | A series of Ripper murders occurred whilst he was in the USA. | Incorrect. |

Mr Abberline continued:

We have never believed all those stories about Jack the Ripper being dead, or that he was a lunatic, or anything of that kind. For instance, the date of the arrival in England coincides with the beginning of the series of murders in Whitechapel; there is a coincidence also in the fact that the murders ceased in London when 'Chapman' went to America, while similar murders began to be perpetrated in America after he landed there. The fact that he studied medicine and surgery in Russia before he came here is well established, and it is curious to note that the first series of murders was the work of an expert surgeon.[553]

Carson had not mentioned any murders in America, so Abberline must have learned of them from the same *Daily Chronicle* article, which had suggested a connection between Chapman's transatlantic movements and some purported unsolved murders in the USA. In his weekly column in the *Sunday Referee,* journalist and amateur criminologist George R. Sims addressed Abberline's theory as published in the *PMG*:

I was rather surprised to find high-class newspapers suggesting Chapman as 'Jack the Ripper'. 'Jack' was a homicidal maniac. Each crime that he committed was marked with greater ferocity during the progress of his insanity. How could a man in the mental condition of 'Jack' have suddenly settled down into a cool, calculating poisoner? 'Jack the Ripper' committed suicide after his last murder — a murder so maniacal that it was accepted at once as the deed of a furious madman. It is perfectly well known at Scotland Yard who 'Jack' was, and the reasons for the police conclusions were given in the report to the Home Office, which was considered by the authorities to be final and conclusive.

How the ex-Inspector can say 'We never believed "Jack" was dead or a lunatic' in face of the report made by the Commissioner of

---

553 *Pall Mall Gazette*, 24th March 1903.

*(Left) Frederick G. Abberline, from the Evans-Skinner Crime Archive.*
*George R. Sims from My First Book, the Experiences of W. Besant and Others.*

Police is a mystery to me. It is a curious coincidence, however, that for a long time a Russian Pole resident in Whitechapel was suspected at the Yard. But his name was not Klosowski. The genuine 'Jack' was a doctor. His body was found in the Thames on December 31, 1888.[554]

This unattributed quote in the *Westminster Gazette* could also have derived from Sims's pen:

I have every proof — of a circumstantial and private character, of course — in my possession that Klosowski and Jack the Ripper are not identical personages...it is quite certain that the heads of the Detective Department at Scotland Yard have not authorised or inspired this suggestion as to Klosowski's implication in the Whitechapel horrors... the series of crimes in the two cases are so distinct that I should scarcely suppose any student of criminology could accept the conclusion that with the capture of Klosowski the mystery of the Whitechapel murders has at last been solved.[555]

Three days later the *PMG* countered the above assertions:

Since the Pall Mall Gazette a few days ago gave a series of coincidences supporting the theory that [Chapman was Jack the Ripper] it has been interesting to note how many amateur criminologists have come forward with statements to the effect that it is useless to attempt to link Chapman with the Whitechapel atrocities. This cannot possibly be the same man, it is said, because, first of all, Chapman is not the miscreant who could have done the previous deeds, and, secondly, it is contended that the Whitechapel murderer has long been known to be beyond the reach of earthly justice.

---

554 The Russian Pole alluded to was Kosminski and the doctor was Montague Druitt (although he was not a doctor). *Sunday Referee,* 29th March 1903.
555 *Westminster Gazette,* c. 28th March 1903, quoted in the *West Australian,* 19th May 1903. Neither paper named Sims but there is no doubt that it was he who spoke to the *Westminster Gazette.*

In order, if possible, to clear the ground with respect to the latter statement particularly, a representative of the Pall Mall Gazette again called on [Abberline] yesterday, and elicited the following statement from him: 'You can state most emphatically', said Mr. Abberline, 'that Scotland Yard is really no wiser on the subject than it was fifteen years ago. It is simple nonsense to talk of the police having proof that the man is dead. I am, and always have been, in the closest touch with Scotland Yard, and it would have been next to impossible for me not to have known all about it. Besides, the authorities would have been only too glad to make an end of such a mystery, if only for their own credit.'

To convince those who have any doubts on the point, Mr. Abberline produced recent documentary evidence which put the ignorance of Scotland Yard as to the perpetrator beyond the shadow of a doubt.

'I know,' continued the well-known detective, 'that it has been stated in several quarters that "Jack the Ripper" was a man who died in a lunatic asylum a few years ago, but there is nothing at all of a tangible nature to support such a theory.'

Our representative called Mr. Abberline's attention to a statement made in a well-known Sunday paper [*i.e. Sims's column in the Referee*], in which it was made out that the author was a young medical student who was found drowned in the Thames. 'Yes,' said Mr. Abberline, 'I know all about that story. But what does it amount to? Simply this. Soon after the last murder in Whitechapel the body of a young doctor was found in the Thames, but there is absolutely nothing beyond the fact that he was found at that time to incriminate him. A report was made to the Home Office about the matter, but that it was "considered final and conclusive" is going altogether beyond the truth. Seeing that the same kind of murders began in America afterwards, there is much more reason to think the man emigrated. Then again, the fact that several months after December, 1888, when the student's body was found, the detectives were told still to hold themselves in readiness for further investigations seems to point to the conclusion that Scotland Yard did not in any way consider the evidence as final.'

'As to the question of the dissimilarity of character in the crimes which one hears so much about,' continued the expert, 'I cannot see why one man should not have done both, provided he had the professional knowledge, and this is admitted in Chapman's case. A man who could watch his wives being slowly tortured to death by poison, as he did, was capable of anything; and the fact that he should have attempted, in such a cold-blooded manner to murder his first wife with a knife in New Jersey, makes one more inclined to believe in the theory that he was mixed up in the two series of crimes. What, indeed, is more likely than that a man to some extent skilled in medicine and surgery should discontinue the use of a knife when his commission — and I still believe Chapman had a commission from America — came to an end, and then for the remainder of his ghastly deeds put into practice his knowledge of poisons?' [556]

---

556 *Pall Mall Gazette*, 31st March 1903.

By 'his commission', Abberline was referring to the theory that George Chapman had been engaged by an eccentric American collector of internal organs to supply uteri, and that this was (at least part of) Chapman's motive for committing the Whitechapel murders. In the earlier *Pall Mall Gazette* article (published 24th March) Abberline had referred to the comments of Mr Wynne Baxter, the coroner who oversaw the inquest into the death of Annie Chapman at the hands of Jack the Ripper. Dr Baxter, summing up the evidence for the inquest jury, noted that Dr George Bagster Phillips, the police divisional surgeon, saw signs of specific intent in the murderer's work, as though he had sought to possess a particular organ. In addition, Dr Baxter said that he himself had been contacted by the sub-curator of a pathological museum, who had been visited by an American wishing to procure a number of uteri, for which he offered £20 each. Rumour had it that there was a black market for these macabre trophies. Abberline observed that he found it curious that 'after the Whitechapel horrors America should have been the place where a similar kind of murder began, as though the miscreant had not fully supplied the demand' for uteri. (This comment helped to spread the myth that there was a series of Ripper-style murders in the USA.) The identity of the American collector was never confirmed, and it is possible that he never existed and the market for fresh but useless organs was a matter of speculation, rather than fact.

I now return to the *PMG* of 31st March, in which Abberline continued:

'Indeed, if the theory be accepted that a man who takes life on a wholesale scale never ceases his accursed habit until he is either arrested or dies, there is much to be said for Chapman's consistency. You see, incentive changes; but the fiendishness is not eradicated. The victims, too, you will notice, continue to be women; but they are of different classes, and obviously call for different methods of despatch.'

In his column in the *Referee* of Sunday 5th April, Sims continued to refute Abberline's contentions:

It is argued that 'Jack' could not have drowned himself in 1888, because there were murders in Whitechapel in 1891. The last of the Ripper series was the Miller's-court horror, which occurred on November 9, 1888. The East End murders of later years were not in the same 'handwriting'. No one who saw the victim of Miller's-court [*Mary Jane Kelly*] as she was found ever doubted that the deed was that of a man in the last stage of a terrible form of insanity.

[It] is an absolute absurdity to argue that a cool, calculating poisoner like Klosowski could have lived with half a dozen [*sic*] women and put them quietly out of the way by a slow and calculated process after being in 1888 a man so maniacal in his homicidal fury that he committed the foul and fiendish horror of Miller's-court. A furious madman does not suddenly become a slow poisoner. 'Jack the Ripper' was known, was identified, and is dead. Let him rest.

In the words of Abberline and Sims we see clearly the beginning of the two polarised theories which still co-exist today. Abberline focussed on the practicalities and the coincidences that put Chapman in the frame. Sims applied an early form of criminal profiling, citing the radically differing signature as proof that, regardless of how many coincidences there were, Chapman cannot have been Jack the Ripper.

## 14. ABBERLINE CONGRATULATED GODLEY ON CATCHING JACK THE RIPPER 'AT LAST'

This anecdote first appeared in H.L. Adam's 1930 book *Trial of George Chapman*: 'When Godley arrested Chapman Abberline said to his confrere "You've got Jack the Ripper at last!"' It has become firmly embedded in Chapman's story by being repeated over the course of eighty-three years by various authors — most recently by Peter Thurgood in 2013 — and is quoted as fact on numerous websites. Variations have infiltrated some retellings: Gosling has Abberline making the comment when Chapman was hanged; Atholl thought Chapman had said it of himself upon his arrest, but on the whole it has survived relatively unscathed.[557]

The story leaves several questions unanswered. For example, Adam did not say whether Abberline's words were conveyed to Godley in person, or by telephone, letter or telegram. In the 1880s Godley had been a sergeant in Whitechapel Division where, as a chief inspector, Frederick Abberline headed the hunt for Jack the Ripper, so the pair probably knew one another; but Abberline left the police in 1892 (he worked for Pinkerton's until 1904), and there is no evidence that the pair were personal friends, or that they were in touch when Chapman was arrested in 1902.

Abberline died in 1929, a year before the anecdote was published in Adam's book, but Godley was still alive and Adam thanked him 'for much information'. This adds weight to the anecdote, but does not indicate that Godley was permitted to read the book prior to publication. On the other hand, knowing Godley would read it, Adam could hardly have penned a complete fabrication.

The problem with the anecdote is that the information which caused Abberline to suspect that Chapman was the Ripper was not known at the time of his arrest in October 1902. Abberline himself made it clear that his suspicions were awakened by Sir Edward Carson's speech at Chapman's trial on 16th March 1903; therefore he cannot have congratulated Godley five months previously. Philip Sugden has suggested that Abberline did indeed make the comment to Godley, but not until March 1903, and Adam simply got the dates muddled.[558]

## 15. AFTER HIS DEATH, POLICE CONTINUED TO BELIEVE HE WAS THE RIPPER

Several diverse sources (a US newspaper in 1938; Dean and Hyde in 1953; Thomas Noguchi in 1985; Debra Gosling in 2003) have claimed that, after Chapman was hanged, Scotland Yard, or Abberline, or Neil and Godley, went on believing for many years that Chapman was the Ripper.[559] 'Scotland Yard', in the sense of the highest echelons of the Metropolitan Police, never commented on the suggestion; Neil said nothing on the subject until 1932 and then returned to silence.

Godley seems never to have espoused the Chapman–Ripper theory. Having helped to investigate the Whitechapel murders case earlier in his career, his knowledge

---

557 See the section on Gosling on page 222. Justin Atholl, 'Who Was Jack the Ripper?' *Reynold's News*, 15th September 1946.
558 Sugden, P. (2002) *Complete History of Jack the Ripper*, Constable Robinson, 2012 Kindle Edition, p446.
559 *Olean Times Herald*, 20th September 1938; Noguchi, T. (1985) *Coroner at Large*; *Calgary Herald* (Canada), 13th October 1953 (Noguchi was coroner for Los Angeles); Hyde, H.M. (1953) *Carson*, Heinemann.

of them, according to the *Police Review,* was 'perhaps as complete as that of any officer concerned'.[560] H.L. Adam said the same thing about Godley's knowledge of Chapman. And yet Godley said nothing publicly about Chapman being the Ripper, even after Abberline's suspicions appeared in the press. Godley later gave Adam information for his book *Trial of George Chapman*; surely, if Godley had believed Chapman was the Ripper, Adam would have said so in the book (even if Adam himself did not agree).

After 1903 — and until his death in 1929 — Abberline seems to have said nothing on the subject of Chapman's candidacy. It seems that his suspicion was nothing more than a two-week-wonder, a half-formed (some might say half-baked) hypothesis which he soon discarded. In 1960 E. Spencer Shew claimed that, although Abberline 'firmly believed at one time' that Chapman was the Ripper, he later 'changed his mind'; others have made similar comments, but whether they were guessing or derived the information from Abberline himself has yet to be established.[561] Most significantly of all, Abberline made no reference to George Chapman in his forty-page, hand-penned reminiscences, which strongly suggests (some might say proves) that he no longer believed him to be the Ripper.[562]

Despite this, Abberline's former position as a chief inspector on the Ripper investigation has caused great significance to be placed on his suspicion of Chapman. Without his endorsement, the vague remark in the *Daily Chronicle* that some (unnamed) police had casually wondered whether Chapman was the Ripper would have been forgotten by the time copies of the newspaper were being used to wrap up the next day's fish-and-chip suppers. Abberline's seal of approval transformed a throwaway comment into a serious theory, and it is entirely due to him that Ripperologists today include Chapman in their lists of suspects.

## THE CHAPMAN–RIPPER THEORY 1903–2013

Following Chapman's execution, only one British newspaper mentioned the theory that he was Jack the Ripper, calling it a 'wild rumour'. In America, however, the *Los Angeles Times* printed the headline: 'RIPPER JACK JUST HANGED. Executed Pole Connected with Whitechapel Horrors'.[563] The New York *Daily People* was similarly emphatic: 'Hanged at last. London sure that "Jack the Ripper" is finished this time.' The latter claimed that Chapman was 'more than suspected' by the London police.[564]

Abberline's theory was refuted again by George R. Sims in articles in 1907 and 1908 and, by 1919, a lengthy piece about Chapman's poisoning crimes, purportedly penned by a former prison warder, made no mention of the Ripper connection.

In his 1930 book *Trial of George Chapman* H.L. Adam observed that Chapman's 'career coincides exactly with the movements and operations of Jack the Ripper'. Soon afterwards, he was far more emphatic in the *Daily Mail,* in response to Frederick Wensley (recently retired as chief constable of Scotland Yard CID), who had stated publicly that Chapman was not the Ripper. 'Mr. Wensley's dissent,' wrote Adam, 'does not shake my faith in the least.' He even issued a challenge: 'We have produced

560 The *Police Review*, 1908, quoted in Begg, P. (2006) *Jack the Ripper: The Facts,* Robson, p103.
561 Shew, E. S. (1960) *A Companion to Murder*, Knopf.
562 This was confirmed by Paul Begg, who owns the hard copy of Abberline's reminiscences.
563 *Los Angeles Times*, 19th April 1903.
564 *Daily People*, 8th April 1903.

certain evidence in support of our contention that Chapman was Jack-the-Ripper. Let those...who differ also produce evidence in support of their theory.'[565] The 'evidence' Adam had amassed was:

> Mr Godley has at the present time a long statement taken from [Lucy] which was not put in evidence at the trial, but which almost definitely connects Chapman with the Ripper murders...It was pretty certainly known to the prosecution that Chapman had committed more murders than those contained in the indictment. We know that the late George Elliott...was of the opinion that he was Jack-the-Ripper.

On the letters page Mr Seymour Cocks MP confirmed that, in 1903, Chapman's defence counsel George Elliott KC had told him that he believed Chapman was the Ripper.

Two years later, however, Adam contradicted himself: 'That Chapman committed crimes of which we have no present knowledge I can well believe,' he remarked, 'That he was Jack the Ripper is another matter.'[566] Adam's comment about Lucy's statement is too vague to be labelled 'evidence'; moreover, I fear that what he claimed 'definitely connects' Chapman to the Ripper murders is Lucy's tale that he was out till the early hours in the autumn of 1888, nearly a year before she met him.

The publication of Adam's book caused the Chapman–Ripper theory to be discussed in the press, and it influenced two books published in 1932 (Neil and Marjoribanks). In one article, Norman Hastings claimed to have contacted witnesses soon after Chapman's execution. In his view, Chapman was not the Ripper: he lacked medical abilities beyond the most basic 'basin and towel' level; his appearance, whilst similar to the description given by Hutchinson, was identical to thousands of men who chose to sport curled moustaches; he was never known to associate with prostitutes, and the MO was too different. Lastly, Hastings mentions that the Ripper executed his crimes efficiently and in silence, and contrasts this with Chapman's clumsiness:

> People who knew [Chapman] well, told me that to see him running was a comical sight. While his wives were lying seriously ill he could never manage to tip-toe silently into the room, and he was forever apologising for the disturbance he caused. I simply cannot imagine such a man in the role of Jack the Ripper...Despite all his boasting, [Chapman] was a coward, and did not like to venture out alone into the dark alleys of ill-repute where all the Ripper murders took place.[567]

Godley's former sergeant, Arthur Fowler Neil, progressed through the ranks to superintendent and retired in 1927. He declared in his 1932 memoirs that Chapman was the Ripper, citing the five facts that had convinced him. Although Neil was confident that they 'bear the cold searchlight of reason' and had 'evidence to support them', only one 'fact' was correct: Chapman had lived in the East End in 1888.[568]

---

565 *Daily Mail* 7th May 1930. As a young constable in 1888, Wensley had been attached to Whitechapel Division and so would have been involved in the hunt for Jack the Ripper.

566 Adam, H.L. 'My Forty Years as a Crime Investigator', *Thomson's Weekly News*, 26th November 1932, quoted in Sugden, P. (2002) *The Complete History of Jack the Ripper*, Constable Robinson, pxxii.

567 *Thomson's Weekly News*, 21st June 1930.

568 Neil's other facts were: Chapman and the Ripper were ambidextrous; a series of Ripper murders occurred whilst Chapman was in the USA; four doctors testified that the Ripper must have had surgical knowledge and Chapman had that knowledge, and 'the only living description ever given by an eyewitness tallied exactly with Chapman'.

In 1934 Benjamin Charles Leeson, a former detective sergeant with the Metropolitan Police, admitted in his memoirs that he could not 'throw any light on the problem of the Ripper's identity', but Chapman's poisoning MO was far too different to consider him a serious candidate. He concluded: 'nobody knows and nobody ever will know' who "Jack" was'. Recently, however, Larry Barbee has claimed that Leeson believed Chapman was the Ripper.[569]

For the next two decades the theory received a public airing now and again, both in print and on radio. However, many of the 'facts' presented were, in reality, myths.

## RADIO DRAMAS

Nearly half a century after his death, Chapman's life story was presented in two radio dramatisations. Both focussed on his candidacy as the Ripper. The first was part of a series called 'The Secrets of Scotland Yard', created by the Towers of London syndicate and recorded in England for worldwide distribution. The one hundred episodes were broadcast between 1949 and 1951. Episode 29, titled 'Jack the Ripper', first aired on 23rd May 1949.[570] Its account of Chapman's life and his poison murders was mostly faithful to the facts, although the actor playing Chapman spoke in a thick, Cockney accent, despite the narrator, Clive Brook, having told listeners that Chapman was Polish. Other mistakes included his informing Annie in 1892 (the year before he met her) that he was taking her surname, and the old canard that a series of murders occurred when he was in the USA. After Chapman's arrest Godley runs into Abberline (Dorset-born, but acted with a heavy Scottish accent), who tells him that Chapman was Jack the Ripper. The narrator concluded that this was 'plausible', before injecting some intrigue with the cliff hanger '...but we shall never know'.

Chapman's story was dramatised again less than two years later, in a 1951 radio series called 'The Black Museum', syndicated throughout the English-speaking world. Episode 44 (of 51) was entitled 'The Straight Razor' (an American term for a cut-throat). It was produced by Harry Alan Towers, scripted by Ira Marion, narrated by Orson Welles and punctuated with ludicrously melodramatic music composed by Sidney Torch. Towers claimed that all the stories in the series were derived from the CID of the Metropolitan Police, leading listeners to believe they were true; however, 'The Straight Razor' bore scant resemblance to reality.

In this version, Chapman is called 'Larry Wilson' and is not identified as a Pole, just as an unspecified foreigner whose birth name was 'Wilmet'. He married dress-shop owner Daisy Alistair, used her money to buy a tavern, then killed her in 1894. His next bride was Belle Davies, a flower-shop owner whose savings he inherited after he murdered her in 1895. Lastly he wed Mabel Dill and did away with her in 1896 in a pub called the Statue. The same elderly doctor treated all three wives and became suspicious only when the third died. Finding all three bodies full of antimony, the police called at 'drugstores' and chemists' shops until they tracked down the pharmacist who had sold Wilson the tartar emetic in order to 'cure dandruff'.

569 Leeson, B. (1934) *Lost London: The Memoirs of an East End Detective*, Stanley Paul & Co, p45–46; Barbee, L. (1997) 'An Investigation into the Carrie Brown Murder'. Casebook.org (accessed 16th May 2013).
570 This programme can be heard at http://archive.org/details/OTRR_Secrets_Of_Scotland_Yard_Singles (accessed 16th May 2013).

Five pieces of 'evidence' prompted the investigating inspector to suspect that Wilson was Jack the Ripper: 1) a case of cut-throat razors found hidden in his home; 2) his arrival in London in 1888; 3) three Ripper-style murders in New Jersey when he was there; 4) he matched *exactly* the *only* witness description of the Ripper; 5) after his arrest for the poisonings there were no more Ripper murders.

As the story is supposed to be one of true crime, and to have derived from the Black Museum, it is a mystery why the identities of Chapman and his victims were hidden, and the timeline and other details changed.

Orson Welles began the episode by announcing that a razor belonging to Chapman was on display at the Black Museum. He concluded it by suggesting that there was 'more than a reasonable chance' that 'Wilson' was the Ripper and that, therefore, the 'case of razors' (sic) deserves its 'place of honour'. The museum has no record of any razor(s) of Chapman's ever having been among its exhibits,[571] and none of the weapons used by Jack the Ripper resembled a cut-throat razor.

## THE O'DONNELL MANUSCRIPT

In 1958 crime writer Bernard O'Donnell wrote a manuscript called *This Man Was Jack the Ripper*, which was never published. He devoted a section to demolishing what he mistakenly believed was H.L. Adam's theory — that Chapman was the Ripper. To his credit, O'Donnell correctly called Chapman a feldsher, not a surgeon, and lamented that 'a great deal of emphasis has been placed upon the "surgical knowledge" of Chapman...when in fact his experience in such things was of a very meagre nature'.

O'Donnell wondered how 'Klowsowski', having just arrived in London, could have acquired the Ripper's intimate knowledge of the area 'with its warren of murky courts and tortuous alleys', and how he could 'thread his way about them night after night, plying his knife in the darkness with complete immunity from capture'. He also pointed out that someone with the 'cunning and subtlety of mind' of the Ripper would never have made Chapman's 'stupid blunder' of calling the same doctor to two of his poison victims. O'Donnell concluded that Chapman could not have been the Ripper because the two sets of crimes were 'poles apart in method, selection of victims, scenes of crimes, and period over which they were committed'.

## DONALD MCCORMICK

In 1959 journalist Donald McCormick published *The Identity of Jack the Ripper.* The book ostensibly drew upon *The Chronicles of Crime*, a three-volume, unpublished manuscript written in the 1890s by Dr Thomas Dutton. McCormick named the Ripper as Alexander Pedachenko, a Russian doctor and secret service agent who lived in Walworth, south London. According to McCormick, in 1888 Dutton told Abberline that the Ripper was an eastern European Gentile. Abberline then saw Kłosowski working at the White Hart, and Wolff Levisohn fed him information about Kłosowski's background as a feldsher and informed him that Kłosowski and Pedachenko were doppelgängers who might sometimes have switched identities. Taking fright after being questioned by police, Kłosowski absconded to Tottenham, but Abberline tracked him down. He fled again, thwarting the police's plan to place him under surveillance.

---

571 The programme (episode 80) is at archive.org/details/otr_blackmuseum (accessed 16th May 2013).

There is no corroborative evidence that Dutton's book existed and McCormick's entire story is nowadays discounted by most Ripperologists. In the 1990s Melvin Harris, a researcher who specialised in exposing hoaxes and frauds, demonstrated that McCormick did not obtain his information from the Dutton papers, but from H.L. Adam's *Trial of George Chapman*, published forty years later. McCormick exposed his own fakery by repeating information from that book, 'without realising that Adam had lapsed into inaccuracy'. Harris concluded: 'McCormick has relied on Adam's sloppy and misleading summary of the Chapman trial and trapped himself.'[572]

## KEEPING THE THEORY ALIVE

It is over a century since Abberline suspected Chapman. We now have access to many resources that he lacked, including censuses, ships' manifests, birth, death and marriage records, street directories, and American and British newspaper archives. Scientists have provided us with expert knowledge of the habits and mentality of serial killers, about MO and signature and geographical and psychological profiling. Researchers have investigated Chapman's life story by poring over trial transcripts, examining official records, pinpointing his residences, constructing and arguing about his timeline and speculating on his childhood and his psychology, in their hunt for any clue, no matter how small, that he was the fiend of Whitechapel. But decades of research, pontification and debate have failed to uncover anything fresh to support Abberline's theory. Instead of more, we now have *fewer* reasons than the seven he presented in 1903. When we omit the reasons based on mistranslation, exaggeration and speculation, only four remain:

1. During the Whitechapel murders he was living in east London.
2. Some eyewitness descriptions vaguely fit his appearance.
3. He was subsequently convicted of serial murder, so was a murderer 'at heart'.
4. He had anatomical knowledge.

Although the first two are factual, they are coincidental, not evidential. Nearly half a million men lived within walking distance of the Whitechapel murder scenes. Whether they were twenty-five or fifty, fair or dark, Jewish or Gentile, tall, short, stout, thin, smart, shabby, moustachioed or bearded, the majority matched one or more aspects of the widely differing eyewitness descriptions of men seen near the crime scenes or with the victims around the times of the murders. Anyone can gain anatomical knowledge from studying text-books. Chapman's poison murders, which were committed fourteen years later, are the only factors that makes him stand out from the crowd.

Despite this, George Chapman's name has been linked with that of Jack the Ripper in countless printed books, articles, university dissertations and assignments, in television and video documentaries, at conferences and public talks, and on the Ripper-dedicated internet groups jtrforums.com and casebook.org, as well as other websites which scrutinise and assess Ripper suspects. The new century has seen the

---

572 Harris, M. (c. 1999) 'The Maybrick Hoax: Donald McCormick's Legacy', casebook.org. Harris also wrote *The True Face of Jack the Ripper* in 1994. www.strangehistory.net/tag/donald-mccormick (accessed 16th May 2013).

publication of four books which argue that he was the Ripper and others that present him as a prime candidate. In the past three years, two novels about the Whitechapel murders depict Chapman as the culprit.[573] The author of one, Nicholas Nicastro PhD, erstwhile lecturer in history, psychology and anthropology at Cornell University, declares that, although his book is fictional, he believes that Abberline was right. A recent exercise in criminal profiling names Chapman the second most likely suspect.

Philip Sugden does not discount Chapman, but remarks that the 'coincidences in opportunity, medical qualifications, appearance, social circumstances and character, however intriguing, inevitably fail to persuade by themselves'. He concludes:

> I have little hesitation in declaring Druitt, Kosminski and Ostrog 'Not Guilty.' In the case of Chapman I prefer recourse to a verdict long recognized only in Scottish law — 'Not Proven.'[574]

Other researchers are more convinced. The most hard-boiled is undoubtedly R. Michael Gordon, an American who has written prolifically on the subject, but always with the assumption that Chapman was the Ripper. Debra Gosling and Norma Buddle also favour Chapman, whilst Robert Milne and Peter Thurgood believe that he is still a viable suspect.

## R. MICHAEL GORDON

Between 2000 and 2008 Gordon produced four books which argue that Chapman was responsible not only for the Whitechapel murders but also for all the Thames Torso killings and four homicides in the USA.[575]

The twenty-two killings for which Gordon has Chapman in the frame differ widely in MO. To concur with Gordon's theory, one has to believe that a killer can switch from dismembering to ripping to strangling to shooting to slow poisoning, then return briefly to dismembering before reverting to poisoning to despatch his final victim. Sugden has called this 'frankly preposterous', adding: 'We cannot seriously accuse anyone — not even a man as bad and dead as Chapman...without clear and positive evidence to back us up.'[576] Despite immersing himself in researching and writing about Chapman for a decade, Gordon has failed to unearth a single piece of evidence to prove that he committed any murder but the poisonings.

Gordon interlaces speculation and invention with information that is fully referenced to trusted sources or official documents, without giving readers any clue that might enable them to discern between his facts and his fictions. He writes as though he knows the thoughts, motivations and secrets of people he has never met, and who lived in another country a century ago. Worse, he makes numerous

573 Nicastro, N. (2010) *The Passion of the Ripper*, Createspace; Webb, S. (2012) *Severin*, Langley Press.
574 Sugden, P. (2002) *Complete History of Jack the Ripper*, Constable Robinson, 2012 Kindle Edition, p458.
575 *Alias Jack the Ripper: Beyond the Usual Whitechapel Suspects* (2000); *The Thames Torso Murders of Victorian London* (2002); *The American Murders of Jack the Ripper: Tantalizing Evidence of the Gruesome American Interlude of the Prime Ripper Suspect* (2003); *The Poison Murders of Jack the Ripper: His Final Crimes, Trial and Execution* (2008).
576 Sugden, P. (2002) *Complete History of Jack the Ripper*, Constable Robinson. 2012 Kindle Edition, introduction.

emphatic assertions that he cannot substantiate; for example, he claims that Chapman 'threatened to murder women several times' and that, when he moved to Cable Street, he took 'his hard earned body parts with him.'[577]

According to Mr Gordon, Martha Tabram was found dead 'literally on Kłosowski's front steps'.[578] He even provides a hand-drawn map indicating precisely where in George Yard Buildings Kłosowski supposedly lived. He also claims that Kłosowski knew Ripper victim Mary Jane Kelly, who (he says) lived in George Yard Buildings until March 1888. Their acquaintanceship, says Gordon, led her to trust him enough to invite him into her room in Dorset Street (where she was murdered in November 1888). There is no evidence that Kłosowski ever lodged in George Yard Buildings. He may have lived nearby (at the White Hart) but only Levisohn placed him there in 1888. According to Gordon, those who disagree with Levisohn do so purely to advance the candidature of their own pet suspect. However, the only document that links Kłosowski with the White Hart (his son's birth certificate) places him there two years later, in September 1890.

All four of Gordon's books contain numerous mistakes with names, dates, places and house numbers. Despite spending about a decade embroiled in Seweryn Kłosowski's life, he never once uses the correct spelling of his forename. Sequences of events are muddled and facts that could easily be verified in a few minutes online were not checked. He refers to 1903 as 'Georgian England' and believes not only that Kłosowski was questioned in relation to the Pinchin Street torso, but also that Pinchin Street could be seen from the window of 126 Cable Street; in fact, a massive railway viaduct blocked the view. Gordon repeats myths that have been perpetuated for over a century and adds a number of inventions and inaccuracies of his own, among them the nonsense that, in 1880s London, 'the jobs of assistant surgeon and hairdresser were mixed in an ancient position known as a felcher' [sic].[579] He also claims that Cecilia only ever saw her father for a few days (when she was a newborn), forgetting that she lived with him again as a toddler when he, Lucy and Annie shared a flat.

Gordon feels the need to repeatedly remind his readers that Kłosowski was trained to cut up bodies. In The Poison Murders, he claims that 'History records that Severin had learned to use a knife with great skill' but the only 'historical record' of this comes from his own previous books. His argument seems to be entirely circular: because Kłosowski was the Ripper, he must have possessed knife skills and, because he possessed knife skills, he must have been the Ripper.

Harold W. Johnson, in a review posted on Amazon.com, opined that The American Murders contains 'arguments based on rumour, hearsay, wildly inaccurate newspaper accounts, and (in what I think is his most misleading, self-deluded exercise in investigative journalism) his previous books on the subject!' The book, he concluded, is a 'sensationalistic, misinformed, over-reaching, fictional novel dressed-up as a true crime account'.

Unfortunately, Gordon's books have sometimes been cited as though they are factually and historically accurate. His American Murders was even listed as a source-

---

577 Gordon, R.M. (2000) Alias Jack the Ripper: Beyond the Usual Whitechapel Suspects, McFarland, p313–316 and Gordon, R.M. (2003) The American Murders of Jack the Ripper, Greenwood, pxvi.
578 Gordon, R.M. (2002) The Thames Torso Murders of Victorian London, McFarland, p186.
579 Ibid. p181.

book by the University of Tulsa for its course 'Jack the Ripper's London', causing it to be referenced in academic papers and bibliographies. One student's dissertation cited Gordon five times and so it comes as no surprise that she concluded, 'It is hardly debatable that Klosowski was indeed the infamous Jack the Ripper.'[580]

Christopher T. George, editor of the journal *Ripperologist*, describes Gordon as 'very intent on placing the mantle of the Ripper on George Chapman, often at the expense of the truth and in the face of the verifiable evidence'.[581] He traced the antecedents of Gordon's books all the way back to Abberline:

> Because the top detective on the Ripper case was reported to have speculated that Chapman was the Ripper, it was simple for Hargrave Adam in *Trial of George Chapman* to take Abberline's apparent ideas about the man arrested by his former subordinate, Inspector George Godley, and trumpet them as if the mistruths were fact, e.g., that Chapman did live in George Yard at the time of Tabram's murder, that the Ripper murders ceased in London and that a similar series of crimes began in the United States when Chapman got there. For Donald McCormick to go even further and write in his 1959 *The Identity of Jack the Ripper* that Godley and Abberline had actually *investigated* Chapman in 1888 (apparently basing this claim on notes in Dr. Dutton's probably fictitious 'diaries'). And for R. Michael Gordon to take all this skein of misinformation and untruths and to publish a series of books on the suspect adding additional speculations about Chapman being responsible for the torso murders and crimes in his native Poland and America. And so it goes on.[582]

It does indeed go on, as the remainder of this section illustrates.

### DEBRA GOSLING

The *Southwark News* published two double-page-spread articles that link Chapman to Jack the Ripper, the first on 17th February 2000 (about George Chapman) and the other on 24th April 2003 (about Inspector Godley). Their author was Debra Gosling who, at the head of the first article, proclaimed her credentials for writing on true crime: she was once a clerical officer at Southwark police station.[583] To give further validity to her writings, beneath the 2003 article — and in eye-catching bold type — she thanks the Metropolitan Crime Museum[584] and the Crime Museum at New Scotland Yard for their 'invaluable help'. Clearly, her intention in presenting these *bona fides* was to establish that her article was serious and properly researched, and yet it is a mixture of myths, errors, and inventions.

Firstly, in the 2003 article, Gosling cannot settle on one spelling of the name of the man she purports to have researched so thoroughly: 'Kłosowski' is rendered four different ways. She erroneously states that Chapman was a qualified doctor,

580 Paper by 'hillarytu08', 2008, University of Tulsa's 'Jack the Ripper's London' website. jtrslondon. wordpress.com (accessed 16th May 2013).

581 Christopher T. George, jtrforums.com, 2nd December 2003.

582 Casebook.org, 8th June 2012.

583 Amberley Publishing's website says she was a crime analyst.

584 The Metropolitan Crime Museum does not exist. She (probably) means the Metropolitan Police Heritage Centre, which holds police service records.

was arrested on the day of the king's coronation [*the two events were nine weeks apart*] and was hanged in March [*April*]; and that Godley attended Hendon Police College [*which opened twenty-six years after he retired!*] Her typos went to press uncorrected: 213 Borough High Street is mistyped as 231; Chapman became 'tried of' Mary; regarding Maud's suspected food 'poisioning' [*sic*] we are told that 'no other diners wer taken il'.

Gosling repeats the myth that, back in 1888, Godley and Abberline knew Kłosowski, suspected he was the Ripper and interviewed him. She then moves on to creating some fresh ones, and even has the gall to quote more than once from conversations that she has fabricated. In the spring of 1902, Gosling alleges, 'a familiar face' appeared at 'Southwark nick'. Godley asked the man: 'Don't I know you from somewhere?...Isn't your name Severin Klosowski, you used to live in the East End?' This is impossible: Godley did not discover Chapman's real surname till the end of that year. Gosling also claims that, in the summer of 1902, Godley 'joined his old mucker Fred Abberline for a pint of best' and said:

> 'You know, Fred that bloomin' Klosowksi's [*sic*] up to no good. He was a slippery customer all those years ago and he's still at it now. I'm going to be watching him.' 'I still think he is the Ripper, George', replied Abberline. 'Do your best on this one, mate, he's got away with it for far too long.'

This is, again, sheer fabrication. Poetic licence might excuse Gosling for making up a sequence of words which, although fictional in itself, reflects the content of a conversation that genuinely happened. However, even the gist of this alleged chat is a factual impossibility: Abberline himself stated that he did not begin to suspect Chapman was the Ripper until the March of the following year. Former police clerical officer Gosling does not offer any justification for contradicting the words of a former chief inspector.[585]

Miss Gosling told her readers that the shares scam was about 'bonds that had gone missing' from George Chapman's pub, when in fact it was about money loaned by him, and she states that both thieves were sentenced to 'five years hard labour', when in fact only one person was convicted, and he received three years without hard labour. How Gosling managed to get even the basic outline of the case so wrong despite having access to the local and national press which covered the story remains a mystery. Months after the thief had been imprisoned, police officers searched the Crown, where, according to Gosling,

> Godley opened a box high up on a shelf and had a rummage through it. 'Blimey, sarge, look what we have here.' The bonds that Chapman had alleged were stolen were inside. Godley took out his pocket book and matched the serial numbers. Bingo. Lying little toad. The two so-called swindlers were given a royal pardon and released from their rock-breaking hell, all thanks to George Godley's keen eye and dedication.

'Lying little toad', indeed. The above interaction between Godley and Kemp is another figment of Gosling's imagination served up as fact. No bonds were found at the Crown; only one person, not two, had been imprisoned, and he was released after Sergeant

---

585 And, moreover, one who retired with eighty-four commendations and awards.

Kemp matched the serial numbers of banknotes, not bonds. Clarke did not receive a royal pardon, nor was he breaking rocks (and, in any case, had Oxenford been imprisoned, as a woman she would have been spared such punishment).

Gosling also mispresents Chapman's arrest to an outrageous degree. Despite her eulogistic praise of Godley, whom she calls 'the Met's finest officer', she blatantly ignores his sworn testimony, which was: 'I went with him into his cellar, where he did some cellar work, and then took him to the police station', and substituted two sensationalistic versions. In the first, published in 2000, Godley entered the Crown and shouted 'Oi, Klowsowski [sic], we want a word with you', at which Chapman 'legged it through the bar into the cellar' where he produced a gun and 'a shot blinded the pair'. 'As Kloswoski [sic — Gosling's third misspelling of his name] appeared from behind a barrel...the detectives jumped on him, wresting the revolver from his hand.' Not only is this account untrue, it does even not tally with her 2003 version of the same event.

When writing her second description of the arrest, Gosling evidently decided that one gun was insufficient, so she gave Chapman another and had him pull both triggers:

> DI Godley and Police Sergeant Kemp went to the Crown to arrest Chapman. On seeing them he dashed down to the cellar via a trap door. The officers pursued him but lost him momentarily. They saw a beam of light from behind a door, broke it down and found him behind some barrels. He had a loaded revolver in each hand directed at them. He threatened both officers who managed to wrestle him to the ground even though both revolvers were discharged during the struggle.[586]

Gosling cites no sources for her two different descriptions of the arrest, but her second account is uncannily similar to the following (untrue) version, printed in a Canadian newspaper in 1908. She even repeats some of the same phrasing:

> Directly the officers asked for him, Chapman, who was in the bar, dashed down a trap-door into the cellar. The officers quickly followed, only to find that for the moment their quarry had eluded them. A slight beam of light from behind a door led them to break it down, and they found Chapman standing behind some barrels, a loaded revolver in each hand. He threatened both officers, but a quick and plucky dash made him their prisoner, although both revolvers were discharged as Chapman was seized.[587]

Gosling contradicts herself several more times. In 2000 she claimed that Abberline had said, 'I see you've got Jack the Ripper at last' whilst Chapman was in prison, but three years later she changes her mind and has him speak the words after Chapman was hanged:

> Retiring to The Ship for a well-earned pint after the execution, Fred Abberline appeared. 'I see you've got Jack the Ripper at last', he shouted to Godley. Or had he???

(The piece went to press with three consecutive question marks.)

586 *Southwark News*, 24th April 2003.
587 *Ottawa Citizen*, 15th February 1908.

In 2000 Gosling stated that there was 'no evidence of Godley agreeing or disagreeing' with Abberline's idea that Chapman was the Ripper. In 2003 she claimed the exact opposite: 'Until his dying day George Godley believed that Severin Klosowski was the infamous Jack the Ripper.' Likewise, in 2000 she admitted: 'There is thought to be no evidence of Godley questioning Klosowski in connection with the Ripper murders', but in 2003 she performed another volte-face when she depicted Godley in a reverie in 1902:

> His mind drifted back to those desperate times on the mean streets of Whitechapel — all those poor toms only out to make a living. Ripped to pieces by some maniac. He'd lost count of the amount of suspects he and Inspector Abberline had interviewed. Dockers, butchers, hairdressers: so many statements and no good evidence against any of them. Bloomin' Klosowski — that's who they'd got their money on. A Polish barber-surgeon who always turned up in the right place at the right time. Arrogant as well. He'd never liked that one.

Gosling declared in her 2000 article that Abberline's suspicion that Chapman was the Ripper appeared in the *Pall Mall Gazette* 'after Chapman was hung [*sic*].' In fact the *PMG* report appeared two weeks before his execution. She also falsely claimed that the following two quotes were taken from the *PMG*.

> Chapman was single and free of family responsibility, as was the Ripper (he was out at all hours of the night). Lucy Baderski (his wife while living at Whitechapel) even goes so far as to say that her previous husband was in the habit of staying out in the early hours of the morning.

How confusing: during the murders Chapman was single, but he was also married, and his wife Lucy knew what his night-time habits were in the year before she met him. Gosling continues, still purporting to be quoting Abberline's words in the *PMG*:

> Chapman had an outrageous sexual drive, if his many affairs and relationships are any guide to go by (The Ripper was also a sexual serial murderer). He was also a misogynist (as the Ripper must have been), having beaten at least four of his lovers and killed three.

These two quotes did not originate from either Abberline or the *PMG*, as Gosling claims. They were, in fact, lifted word-for-word from the Chapman biography on casebook.org.[588]

## NORMA BUDDLE

Mrs Buddle is a prolific contributor to the online Ripper discussion boards casebook. org and jtrforums.com. She has taken a special interest in George Chapman, and is the author of 'The Cable Street Dandy', a dissertation in support of the Chapman–Ripper theory that was published in *Ripperologist* in 2009.[589] The purpose of the dissertation, she says, is 'to reconsider his candidacy by looking a little more closely at some of

---

588 I emailed Debra Gosling in June 2012 to ask about the various inventions and discrepancies within her two articles. She replied: 'Go. Away.'
589 It can also be read on casebook.org (accessed 16th May 2013).

the contested areas of his candidature'.[590] In my opinion, she has failed to achieve this goal. Far from examining the contested areas, she has repeated the same old myths and errors (Chapman was a surgeon; his deserted wife arrived from Poland; he attacked Lucy with a knife; Godley believed he was the Ripper), without looking 'more closely' at them, and she has also introduced some new ones.

In her dissertation, Norma Buddle claims that Wolff Levisohn said he met George Chapman 'in 1890 in the basement of the Whitehart [sic]'. But on casebook. org she argued that it was 1888 (which was what Levisohn actually said). Chapman's brother-in-law Stanisław Baderski testified that Chapman worked there from 1890, which does not suit Buddle's theory at all, so she simply accuses Baderski of perjury, arguing that he wanted to conceal Chapman's presence at the White Hart in 1888 because he suspected he was Jack the Ripper and wanted to protect his sister and her child from public scandal.[591] But this is both illogical and impossible: illogical because working at the White Hart in 1888 does not make anyone Jack the Ripper; impossible because the earliest press speculation that Chapman was the Ripper dates from late March 1903, whereas Baderski gave his deposition to the police court in January. Furthermore, he did not meet Chapman until 1889 and could not have known his whereabouts, movements or residence in 1888.

Mrs Buddle's piece contains ten thousand words, but about four thousand are spent dwelling on peripheral subjects such as an overview of medical services and practices across nineteenth-century Europe, and on relating that a man who attacked a group of impoverished London women looked like Chapman. (When a description failed to match his colouring, Buddle suggested that he dyed his hair and moustache.)

Whilst Buddle endorses Wolff Levisohn's testimony when it is favourable to the Chapman–Ripper theory, she rejects his description of the humble tasks carried out by feldshers and instead repeatedly insists that Chapman 'studied as a surgeon' and therefore possessed 'knowledge of how to use a knife to sever body parts'.[592]

Her suspicion that Chapman was Jack the Ripper is based partly on his subsequent behaviour: 'Would he really have waited 20 odd years before he committed his first act of violence against women?' she asks, revealing her assumption that a man who poisoned his girlfriends between 1897 and 1902 was probably knifing and eviscerating strangers back in 1882. She suspects that human remains may have been found, had Chapman's public houses and other premises been searched more thoroughly:

> The likelihood is that he continued to collect victims, from 1888 up until his arrest [in 1902], and to bring them back to his pub whenever possible, where he could murder and possibly mutilate them, disposing of their remains by burying them in such places as underneath floor boards or in the garden or in the sea — or indeed wherever he happened to be.[593]

Chapman lived in pubs for only five of the fourteen years Buddle cites and, during those five years, did not seek privacy. On the contrary, he invited a string of mistresses

590 'The Cable Street Dandy', Ripperologist, May 2009.
591 'Questions about the Cable Street Dandy', casebook.org, January–February 2012.
592 Norma Buddle (Natalie Severn), jtrforums.com, 5th October 2009.
593 Norma Buddle (Natalie Severn), casebook.org, January–February 2012.

to cohabit with him, accommodated their relations and friends and engaged day and residential staff. All had access to the cellar, kitchen, wash-house, WC and outdoor space. During the opening hours — dawn till late — members of the public were constantly coming and going and in some cases staying for several hours. Mrs Buddle is asking us to believe that, under such relentless scrutiny, Chapman managed to bring victims home and murder them, carry out blood-drenched mutilations and dismemberments, store portions of bodies for later dispersal or dig up gardens in order to hide dismembered limbs, all without his partners, staff or customers becoming aware of his actions. The notion that he left body parts under floorboards for years without anyone noticing the putrid stench of rotting human flesh is absurd. And, surely, if Chapman had wished to stalk the streets at night searching for victims, he would have remained both single and a barber, giving him domestic privacy and evenings free from work.

Although Chapman was neither a thief nor a rapist, nor known to commit crime in collusion with others, Norma Buddle suspects him of the murder of Emma Smith, who was robbed and raped by four men in April 1888. Buddle thinks that Chapman was involved purely because, prior to the attack, Miss Smith was seen in the vicinity of West India Dock Road. Even if (as Buddle believes) Chapman was working there at that time, it amounts to nothing, because it was a densely overpopulated area containing tens of thousands of other men.[594]

Norma Buddle concludes her dissertation by addressing the sticky problem of the different MOs of the Southwark Poisoner and Jack the Ripper with a slick and cleverly constructed rhetorical question:

> The history of Chapman's/Klosowski's life, was one of constant upheaval with multiple wives, multiple jobs, multiple names and addresses — why not more than one modus operandi?

This all sounds highly suspicious — until we look more closely. Chapman did not have multiple names; he changed his only once (though he did at one point tell Miss Penfold that his name was Smith). His upheavals were not 'constant', nor were they unusual. They appear so in comparison with how we live today, tied down by mortgages and long leases, but it was normal for the *fin-de-siècle* East End poor to abandon their weekly rented lodgings and blue-collar jobs quite casually (by today's standards) in search of small improvements to their domestic and working lives.

Whilst Norma Buddle admits that Chapman's MO 'is the real stumbling block' to his candidacy as the Ripper, she does not think it rules him out, because he had a rational reason to alter his methods:

> His wives [sic] had relatives who cared about them and visited them regularly.[595] He could hardly have murdered them by strangulation or throat cutting and got away with it in such circumstances. As it was, he chose a method of poison that would arouse the least suspicion.[596]

---

594 Norma Buddle (Natalie Severn), jtrforums.com, 5th May 2009. Mrs Radin said Chapman worked at her husband's barbershop in West India Dock Road for five months about 1888, but she did not say which months.
595 Mary Spink does not appear to have received visits from her family.
596 'The Cable Street Dandy', *Ripperologist*, May 2009.

If, as Buddle claims, Chapman was the Ripper, and could change MO at will to avoid detection, why did he kill all the C5 victims the same way, and his three poison victims the same way? It was partly due to the uniformity of his poisoning MO that he was executed. Had the prosecution not been able to cite the similar deaths of Mary and Bessie, Chapman may not have been convicted of murdering Maud.

## ROBERT MILNE

Robert Milne retired from the Metropolitan Police in 2008 after forty years' service with the Forensic Services Directorate at Scotland Yard. He has since written a book, *Forensic Intelligence*,[597] and has been giving Powerpoint presentations about the identity of Jack the Ripper to audiences in the UK and abroad. Mr Milne has very kindly sent me his slideshow and accompanying speaker's notes.

Milne considers Chapman a viable Ripper suspect because 'he has far more factors circumstantially surrounding him' than others.[598] He lists twenty. Some seem insignificant (he worked during the week; had a small income; appeared respectable). Others are oft-repeated myths (trained surgeon; Ripper-style murder in New Jersey). Three factors refer to the poison murders and the remainder are vague, debatable or disputed (the threat to kill Lucy; his match to witness descriptions). Three correctly cite Chapman's residence in the East End during the murders (although Milne repeats the solecism that he lived in George Yard in 1888). The final point, that Chapman 'passed himself off as Polish, Jewish, Catholic, an Englishman and an American — Irish?' is incorrect: Chapman's sole lie about his nationality or religion was his claim to have been born in the USA. The reference to 'Irish' relates to the infamous 'Lusk letter'. Milne's presentation emphasises an incident in 1888 in which George Lusk received a piece of kidney and a letter purporting to be from the killer of Catherine Eddowes (i.e. Jack the Ripper). The previous day, a strange man had asked a shop assistant for Lusk's address. Milne tells his audiences that the man was 'of similar appearance to Chapman', but does not include the wording of the witnesses' description. Newspapers in 1888 give it as around forty-five, 6ft, slimly built, clerical collar, dark beard and moustache and Irish accent.[599] As Chapman was twenty-two, 5ft 5 and freshly arrived from Poland, the similarity of which Milne speaks is hard to discern.

Unfortunately, the slide describing Chapman's life is riddled with errors; for example, that he committed bigamy four times and took his English surname from the Annie Chapman who was the Ripper victim.[600]

At the beginning of his presentation Milne correctly points out that we cannot expect the police in 1888 to have had 'the knowledge we now have today concerning geographical profiling, modus operandi and studied behaviours of serial offenders.' These modern resources should, therefore, shed new light on Chapman's candidacy. But after eliminating the incorrect, disputed and irrelevant points, Milne's 'twenty factors' boil down to this: Chapman lived in the East End when the Whitechapel

---

597 Published by Taylor and Francis in 2012.
598 Email correspondence with Robert Milne, 2012.
599 *Daily Telegraph*, 20th October 1888. The man's description was also published in the *Evening News*, 20th October 1888 and *The Sunday Times*, 21st October 1888. It was given to police by Mile End leather shop workers Emily Marsh and John Cormack. The man was also seen by Miss Marsh's father, William.
600 www.thestar.com/news/world/article/1056621--was-a-polish-surgeon-the-real-Jack the Ripper (accessed 16th May 2013).

murders occurred, and he sometimes had violent tendencies towards individual, specific women. In other words, nothing more than was known back in 1903.

## PETER THURGOOD

Mr Thurgood's biography of Frederick Abberline is the most recent book to promote the Chapman–Ripper theory. In the two chapters devoted to George Chapman, Thurgood not only endorses the anecdote that Abberline congratulated Godley on catching 'Jack the Ripper at last', but also claims that Chapman 'had always been Abberline's number one suspect' — and then contradicts himself on the very next page, stating that Abberline did not suspect Chapman until 1903.[601]

Peter Thurgood believes that, 'If a modern profiler were to try to paint us a picture of the man known as Jack the Ripper, Klosowski would fit that picture almost perfectly.'[602] By coincidence, criminal profilers have applied their skill to that very subject, so let us take a look at what they have to say.

## CRIMINAL PROFILING

Now that most of the fifteen reasons to believe Chapman was the Ripper have been found to be incorrect, does his candidature retain any validity? He certainly lived near the scenes of all the Whitechapel murders, had anatomical knowledge and was a murderer. But working against those factors is the radical difference between the modus operandi and the signature of Chapman and those of the Ripper.

As we have seen, this issue was raised as early as 1903 by George R. Sims. In response to Abberline's suspicion that Chapman was the Ripper, he asked: 'How could a man in the mental condition of "Jack" have suddenly settled down into a cool, calculating poisoner?'[603] Edmund Pearson, writing in 1936, agreed:

> Would the monster who raged through Whitechapel, with his great knife, like a Malay running amuck, afterwards content himself with stealthy poisonings? The probable answer is no; and this difference between the Ripper and Chapman seems to me practically destructive of the theory that they were the same.[604]

Nearly six decades later Philip Sugden, having pointed out that Chapman had 'the medical qualifications [sic], the opportunity, the appearance, the cunning and the cruelty to have been Jack the Ripper', concluded:

> At this point it would give me immense satisfaction to announce that we had unmasked the killer. Unfortunately I can't...[because] perhaps it is stretching credibility too far to believe that the man who committed six horrific, often frenzied, knife murders in just three months in 1888 could have quietly gone into retirement and then re-emerged a decade later in the covert guise of domestic poisoner.[605]

601 Thurgood, P. (2013) Abberline: The Man who Hunted Jack the Ripper. History Press, p135–6.
602 Ibid. p127.
603 Sunday Referee, 29th March 1903.
604 Pearson, E.L. (1936) More Studies in Murder, Harrison Smith & Robert Haas.
605 Sugden, P. (2002) Complete History of Jack the Ripper, Constable Robinson, 2012 Kindle Edition, p455.

| DIFFERENCES IN MO | | | |
|---|---|---|---|
| | | Jack the Ripper | George Chapman |
| 1 | Victims | Strangers | Partners |
| 2 | Speed of attack | Hit and run | Stay and savour |
| 3 | Speed of death | Swift | Slow |
| 4 | Mutilated | Yes | No |
| 5 | Tortured | No | Yes |
| 6 | Method | Frenzied | Calculated |
| 7 | Company | Alone | People around |
| 8 | Location | Outside (one exception) | Indoors |
| 9 | Compulsion | To rip apart | To torture slowly |
| 10 | Time of attack | Early hours | 24/7 |

Supervisory Special Agent John E. Douglas, the first full-time profiler at the United States FBI Behavioral Science Unit, described Jack the Ripper as the product of a domineering, promiscuous mother and a weak or absent father. He probably set fires and tortured small animals as a child, learning how to be destructive and violent with impunity and, as an adult, carried a knife. He worked weekdays, possibly as a hospital attendant or medical examiner's assistant, was aged between twenty-eight and thirty-six, and probably had some kind of physical abnormality. Having no consistent adult role model as a child he became asocial and preferred his own company. He was unmarried, slightly withdrawn, quiet, shy, a loner and socially inept. His physical contact with women was restricted to using prostitutes, from whom he very likely acquired a sexually transmitted disease. Police investigating the Whitechapel murders probably interviewed him many times.[606]

The kind of occupation Douglas suggested is an excellent match to Chapman's early career as a feldsher (although during the Ripper murders he was working as a barber). However, nothing else tallies. We have no data on his parents' traits or his childhood activities; he was only twenty-two during the murders; he was not known to carry a knife; he had no physical abnormalities. Most contradictory of all, Chapman was not a loner: there are few occupations more sociable than those of barber and pub landlord. Nor was he socially inept, but a confident, outgoing, even charming man who married at age twenty-three and subsequently had close, sexual relationships with several women. He was neither quiet nor shy: he liked to dominate and control his female partners, keeping them firmly in line with scoldings and threats. Far from seeking solitude, everything in his life story points to his seemingly never wanting to be alone. There is no evidence that he consorted with prostitutes or had a sexually transmitted disease. Lastly, he was not interviewed in connection with the Whitechapel murders. Although Douglas believed the myth that Chapman was a trained surgeon, he still did not support his candidacy as the Ripper:

606 Douglas, J. (1988) *UNSUB: AKA Jack the Ripper; Series of Homicides, London, England, 1888*, NCAVA Homicide (Criminal Investigative Analysis), Washington, DC: Federal Bureau of Investigation.

[T]here is no way a man hacks apart five or six women, lies low for ten years with no one noticing anything about him, then resumes his homicidal career as a poisoner...It just doesn't happen that way in real life.[607]

When Erin Sigler posted an analysis of the Chapman–Ripper theory on jtrforums.com in 2003, she drew attention to Douglas's emphasis on the difference between MO and signature. The MO is *how* a series of murders is carried out: the method; whereas the signature is *why*, what Douglas described as 'the thing that fulfils him emotionally'. Therefore the MO of a series of murders can change due to circumstances, or as the killer devises a better technique, but the signature, the psychological force that drives that killer, does not change. Sigler explained:

Both the Ripper and Chapman killed women. That much is certain. One used a knife and another used poison. That's MO. However, the signatures are vastly different. Jack 'got off', in one manner or another, by mutilating his victims. That's his signature. That's what distinguishes him from, say, a guy who cuts a woman's throat as part of a robbery gone bad. The MO is similar, but the signatures are completely different. The robber just needed to neutralize his victim in some way. He could have just as easily taken a baseball bat to her...And he's going to want to get away as quickly and as cleanly as possible. Sticking around to tear the lady's uterus out is not part of the equation.

That's just not the case with Jack. The mutilations were accomplished at great personal risk, which indicates that they were his primary focus, and the murders themselves were [more] of a means to an end than anything else. He's not a sadist — he dispatched his victims too quickly and quietly, and rather than get away while he had the chance, he instead feels the need to cut them open and see what's inside, which would have delayed his escape. A guy like that couldn't (according to Douglas, at least) just 'change his style to avoid detection'. That would defeat the entire purpose of the crimes for him.

As a poisoner, Chapman is all wrong...If he'd been the Ripper, and for some reason opted to use poison, I would have expected him to get rid of the women quickly and open them up as soon as he had the chance. The fact that he didn't, and the fact that Chapman's victims died slow, agonizing deaths, after which he made no attempt to escape and very little to avoid detection, should be very telling if you're a student of Douglas's.[608]

In 2006 Laura Richards, head of analysis for Scotland Yard's Violent Crime Command, revisited the Ripper mystery using modern criminal profiling techniques. Her assessment of his psychology was that he was 'perfectly sane, frighteningly normal, and yet capable of extraordinary cruelty'. He was socially skilled, but beneath the surface lay a complete lack of normal emotion. This fits what we know of Chapman. The team's geographical profilers computed Jack the Ripper's residence as Flower and Dean Street, Whitechapel, and Chapman lived within walking distance. Analysing

607 Douglas, J. (2000) *The Cases That Haunt Us*, Lisa Drew, p71.
608 Erin Sigler, jtrforums.com, 4th December 2003.

witness descriptions of men seen with the victims or at or near the crime scenes shortly before the murders, Richards and her team concluded that the Ripper was between 5ft 5ins to 5ft 7ins, twenty-five to thirty-five and of stocky build. At the time of the murders Chapman was 5ft 5ins, twenty-two, and almost certainly slender (in 1903 he weighed 146 lb). The team also produced an e-fit image of the Ripper, which some have dubbed the 'Freddie Mercury e-fit'.[609]

In 2012 Inspector Larry Wilson of the Royal Canadian Mounted Police studied Chapman and nine other current suspects to see if his Persons of Interest Priority Assessment Tool (POIPAT) could help identify the Whitechapel murderer. He measured each suspect against criteria which previous profilers like Douglas have cited as the killer's key traits. Chapman emerged as the second most likely suspect with a score of 220. (The top suspect scored 245 and the third 210.) But Wilson's reliance on the usual unreliable sources about Chapman led him to assign twenty points for carrying a knife, based on the dubious New Jersey 'knife attack' story. If we deduct those points, Chapman's ranking slips down to fourth place, but he is still ahead of the other six.[610]

Whether Chapman could convert from a knife-wielding slasher to a cold, calculating poisoner was the subject of a lengthy, lively and well-attended debate on casebook.org during the summer of 2011. Some posters agreed with Norma Buddle's argument that he decided to change his MO because using the Ripper's methods to murder women who lived with him would have led to his immediate arrest, and so he adopted a new, stealthier way of despatching them. Echoing the sentiments of Erin Sigler, 'Errata' pointed out that the change of method is irrelevant; it is the differing psychologies of the two killers that negates George Chapman's candidacy:

> It's not really the shift to poisoning that bothers me, but the shift towards incredible sadism that seems odd. Clearly Jack the Ripper was brutal. But he didn't drag it out. Chapman got a great deal of pleasure from slowly poisoning these women, and taunting them with their impending death. If Jack the Ripper had killed his victims slowly, with a maximum amount of pain and damage being inflicted while still living, then a shift to that kind of poisoning would make sense to me...There is something very goal oriented about Jack the Ripper, and something very game oriented about Chapman... Changing weapons doesn't bother me. Changing method of gratification does.[611]

Another poster, Wolf Vanderlinden, seemed incredulous that anyone could consider Chapman a viable Ripper suspect:

> [Some] seem to believe that a serial killer like the Whitechapel Murderer just wakes up one day and decides that he is going to kill and mutilate several women and remove organs and take them away with him. Then, on another day, he apparently just decides to stop doing that and then,

609 'Has profiling discovered the real face of Jack the Ripper?' *The Independent*, 20th November 2006. 'Jack the Ripper: The First Serial Killer', Channel Five.
610 Wilson, L. (2012) *Criminal Major Case Management: Persons of Interest Priority Assessment Tool (POIPAT)*, CRC Press.
611 Casebook.org, 15th June 2011.

Image: e-fit of Jack the Ripper, from The Independent.

later, decides to start up again but this time using poison. They seem to think that it's as simple as changing your coat. The complex mental problems, complicated psychopathology and powerful demons which drive an individual to do what the Ripper did, and which were unique to him, simply don't exist [in Chapman].[612]

The problem of the differing signatures seems to be insurmountable. If a murderer's signature cannot change as radically as it would need to in George Chapman's case, then regardless of whether or not he was trained in surgery, lived in George Yard in 1888, wore a peaked cap, was ambidextrous, dyed his moustache blond, owned a black bag, threatened Lucy with a knife, matched witness descriptions or police e-fits, or could change his MO at will, it is impossible for him to have been Jack the Ripper.

## WOLFF THE RIPPER

Four important factors that detract from Chapman's candidacy as the Ripper — his age, poor English language skills, lack of knowledge of East End geography and, most important of all, his known criminal signature (established during the poison murders) — do not apply to Wolff Levisohn. In 1888 he was in his thirties (which matches Douglas's profile), he was Jewish, and he may have had a moustache (he certainly sported one fifteen years later), which fits some eyewitness descriptions. Unlike Chapman, he was fluent in spoken English, having lived in London since his teenage years (save for a seven-year sojourn in Poland) and, as a hawker, was well acquainted with the back alleys of the East End. Levisohn was never convicted of any murder, so there is no problem of a change in either MO or signature.

Having served as a feldsher in the Russian Army for seven years, Levisohn's anatomical and surgical knowledge possibly surpassed Chapman's. In the 1880s he sold barbers' requisites, giving him contacts with manufacturers and wholesalers of cut-throat razors, scissors, and knives of every shape and size; indeed, by 1901 he had switched to selling knives. His trade furnished him with a legitimate reason to carry a black leather bag full of assorted sharp implements.

Profilers believe the Ripper was single. Although Levisohn married Alice Sutton in the spring of 1887, their first son was not conceived until the summer of 1889. Most newlyweds at that time produced a child within a year, so perhaps they lived apart for the first two years of married life. Alice may have been in a convalescent home or sanatorium, for instance, leaving Levisohn living alone in the heart of Whitechapel during the Ripper murders. His marriage certificate gives his address as 24 Great Garden Street,[613] just 200 metres from Flower and Dean Street, pinpointed by geographical profilers as the Ripper's probable residence. By the end of November 1888, just after the final C5 murder, he had moved to Tottenham. Did he move away from Whitechapel to avoid being followed home after a killing, or to evade local questioning?

Levisohn was once publicly accused of being Jack the Ripper. In November 1888, although he lived at Tottenham, he was walking (should that be 'stalking'?) the

---

612 Casebook.org, 7th July 2011.
613 Now Greatorex Street.

streets of Whitechapel alone and late at night. This places him in the very epicentre of the Ripper's killing field in the same month as the final C5 victim, Mary Jane Kelly, was murdered. About 11.30pm, Levisohn was approached by two prostitutes, Christine de Grasse and Mary Ann Johnson. The latter 'made a proposition' and, when he declined, she shrieked: 'You are Jack the Ripper!' Her companion joined in the cry, an excited crowd soon collected and Levisohn fled to nearby Commercial Street police station, where he sought refuge. His accusers were arrested and the next morning at Worship Street police court they were charged with 'molesting a Polish Jew'. Their defence was that he looked like Jack the Ripper because he carried a shiny black bag (which was, apparently, even then considered to be one of the Ripper's trademarks). Magistrate Henry Bushby, remarking that 'the public must be protected from this kind of molestation', fined the prisoners 20s each.[614] Perhaps Levisohn was on his way to commit yet another gory murder; maybe his black bag contained the requisite knives. Did the Ripper murders cease because being publicly accused was the 'wake-up call' that convinced him to stop?

Did Levisohn insist that Chapman was working at the White Hart in 1888 in order to link him to the murder of Martha Tabram, who he himself had killed? Did he claim that, back in the 1880s, Chapman had dressed as a 'la-di-da' because he had read in the newspapers that the Ripper was a smartly-dressed man? Was it Levisohn that told the press reporters that the police suspected Chapman of being the Ripper?

Kłosowski's solitary name change to Chapman is thought by some to be highly suspicious, and yet Levisohn repeatedly changed his name or its spelling, and his date of birth. In the 1891 census he was Adolff W. Lewisohn; in that of 1901, William Levison; when giving evidence for the prosecution of Chapman he was Wolff Levisohn. After he died his widow and sons changed their surname to Leveson.

Had Levisohn been on trial for murder in 1903, Abberline would have been able to cite 'a score of reasons' for naming him as Jack and Ripperologists today would be debating the 'Levisohn–Ripper theory'.

✦

And what about this mysterious 'Zagowski' fellow? An ex-feldsher who had access to knives and razors, he was foreign-looking, sported a moustache, and worked at the White Hart pub in 1888, when Martha Tabram was murdered just a few metres away. What is more, he disappeared from Whitechapel suddenly and mysteriously in 1890, shortly after the murders ended...

---

614 The equivalent to about £100 today. It seems they served fourteen days in default. *Illustrated Police News*, 24th November 1888.

# EPILOGUE: THE SOUTHWARK POISONER AND JACK THE RIPPER

I have no hesitation in placing the poisoner at the head of the list of different kinds of crimes in the degree of gravity and heinousness. For callousness, dissimulation, brutality and hypocrisy, the poisoner is without equal in all the annals of crime. He is also the greatest danger to the community at large in consequence of the subtlety of his methods, and the difficulty generally experienced in bringing his crimes to light...Secret poisoning is the very worst form of murder. And when it is perpetrated by a criminal upon his or her near relations for possible financial gain, or for motives of lust, the depth of the infamy exhibited cannot adequately be plumbed by any healthy-minded man. He can only stand shuddering and execrating at the bare contemplation of it. It would seem that such criminals as these must have been reared from the spawn of a serpent. How a man or woman, husband, wife, mother or father, can calmly inflict a painful and lingering death upon those with whom they have ties of kinship and should have of affection, the while they are using endearing terms towards them and ostensibly ministering to their sufferings, passes one's comprehension.

Hargrave Lee Adam (1908) *The Story of Crime.*

After first reading about Chapman twenty years ago, I filed him away in the back of my mind under 'domestic poisoner', a category that long-forgotten novels and dramas had led me to believe conducted clean, painless, peaceful killings: their victims simply fell asleep and didn't wake up. The Southwark Poisoner seemed tame — almost homely — compared to the Ripper, who stabbed, slashed, ripped, mutilated and eviscerated his vicious and bloodthirsty way through the mean streets of Whitechapel.

Two decades later Chapman again came onto my radar and I soon discovered that his killing method did not involve inducing peaceful slumber in the cosy comfort of his victims' own beds, but the merciless torture of three innocent women, one a mere teenager, who were forced to endure a drawn-out, painful death from relentless diarrhoea and unremitting vomiting — day after ghastly day and night after gruesome night. In addition, Chapman tormented his victims' relatives and friends, forcing them to watch helplessly as he put their loved ones through a living hell, and inflicted upon a small child the trauma of watching his mother's lengthy illness and death. A series of well-meaning doctors was also put through the mill whilst Chapman pretended to join in with their bewilderment. Eventually he drove one to his wits' end by forcing him to stand by, powerless, as his patient inched slowly towards an agonising death.

All this misery and cruelty was inflicted on good, decent people who had never done him any harm and against whom he could have no possible grudge. He was able to observe, for long periods of time, the emotional anguish he was deliberately causing without feeling guilt, shame or remorse.

The mutilations Jack the Ripper inflicted on his prey were grisly beyond words, but they were carried out only on the dead — his victims lost consciousness within seconds. Jack killed quickly in order to cut. Chapman killed slowly in order to torture. In the final assessment of the two killers, it is Jack the Ripper who emerges as the more merciful.

# AUTHOR'S NOTE: CURIOUS COINCIDENCES

Having spent most of my childhood and all of my twenties in London, by 1993 I was living in Hastings. Hurrying to catch a train one day I grabbed a book at random, off my flatmate's shelf. It was about Jack the Ripper and, although Chapman was mentioned, I took no greater interest in him than in the other suspects. Nearly two decades later I learned that he had once lived in Hastings. This local connection intrigued me, prompting me to enquire further into his life and crimes, and the research I subsequently undertook uncovered a number of curious coincidences.

As a child Chapman had resided and attended school in a village just eight miles from my father's family home near Lublin, in Russian-occupied Poland. My grandfather, born in 1889, had been forcibly conscripted into the Russian Army, an obligation which, according to one school of thought, Chapman may have left Poland to avoid. My father and Chapman both came to England at the age of twenty-two and each was married in London to a woman from the Kalisz area. I have only one photo of my father and myself in Poland and, digging it out recently, I was astonished to find it had been taken directly outside Praga Hospital, where Chapman worked and studied. I must have walked in his footsteps, and not for the first time — or indeed the last.

After his move to England, Chapman resided in three areas that have also been my home: the East End, Southwark and Hastings. My family tree includes Polish Jews who were living in Cambridge Heath Road, Bethnal Green, the very year that Lucy remarried in a church there. As a child I lived for a while on a housing estate built on the site of Nichol's Square, Stanisław Baderski's one-time home. Later, in Southwark, I attended a secondary school which stood roughly halfway between the Crown (which was still functioning as a pub) and Dr Stoker's former surgery. My classmates and I would buy bags of chips to consume whilst sitting on the swings in the park alongside Newington Sessions, where Maud and Chapman committed perjury. We did not know that the park occupied the site of Horsemonger Lane Gaol, nor that it once housed the gallows upon which George Chapman was hanged.

At age sixteen I was working in Queen Victoria Street, where Chapman once searched for the offices of the Caledonian Gold Mining Company. Three years later, whilst employed at Waterloo station, I spent most lunch breaks browsing the shops and the market stalls at The Cut and Lower Marsh, where Miss Cole bought the suspect rabbit and Maud visited with her sister shortly before her death.

My father resided in Southwark for forty years. He spent his retirement living near the Crown pub and I would take my stepmother to lunchtime concerts at St George-the-Martyr church. She was later an in-patient at Guy's Hospital, where Maud Marsh once spent a month. Both she and my father are buried in Kalisz, less than thirty miles from the Baderski family home.

In 2002 I set up a small publishing imprint in Hastings and, whilst delivering my local history publications to a nearby bookseller, I would sometimes linger to chat with the owner — Mr George, whose shop is in George Street — unaware that I was standing on the very floorboards of George Chapman's former barbershop.

What is arguably the most extraordinary coincidence came to light shortly after the first edition of this book went to print. I was informed that Chapman's great-great-great-great grandson currently attends my former primary school.

# APPENDIX I: KŁOSOWSKI'S RUSSIAN DOCUMENTS

The only existing record of Kłosowski's Russian-language documents appears in H.L. Adam's book *Trial of George Chapman*. It consists of an English translation carried out by Joseph Petrykowski, an interpreter engaged by the police. (His surname appears in the primary sources as 'Betrikowski' or 'Petrickowski'.) Petrykowski converted Polish place and personal names from Russian Cyrillic script into English, bypassing the Polish versions; then, before his translation found its way into Adam's book, it was doubtless copied and recopied. This has resulted in a plethora of misspellings.

| PHONETIC TRANSLATIONS FROM RUSSIAN, WITH THE CORRECT POLISH SPELLINGS | |
|---|---|
| *Severin* — **Seweryn** | *Nagornak* — **Nagórna** |
| *Antonio* — **Antoni** | *Emilie* — **Emilia** |
| *Zvolen* — **Zwoleń** | *Kalish* — **Kalisz** |
| *Krasseminsk/Krassenin* — **Krasienin** | *Tyminitsa, Tyshenitsa Nova* — **Tymienica Nowa** |
| *Khotche, Nodga* — **Chotcza** | *Iltetsk, Ilshetsk* — **Iłża** |
| *Moshkovski* — **Moszkowski** | *Brodnitski* — **Brodinski** |
| *Colimowski* — **Skolimowski (?)** | *Zyanski* — **Żywański (?)** |
| *Krynick* — **Krynicki** | *Olshanski* — **Olszański** |

The following is a verbatim transcription from Adam's book. Please note that *Antonovich* means 'son of Antoni' and *Nagornak* means 'a man from Nagórna'.

(1) "*Extract from birth certificate, Civil Register, Roman Catholic denomination, issued from Parish Register of Kolo.* "On the 15th day of December, 1865, at ten o'clock in the morning, there appeared Antonio Klosowski, 30 years of age, a carpenter by trade, native of the village of Nagornak, together with two witnesses, Ludwika Zywanski, aged 32, and Jacob Rozinski, aged 56, both of Nagornak, and employed there. They stated that Emilie, the wife of Antonio Klosowski, *née* Ulatowski, aged 29, had given birth to a child the previous morning. The child was named Severin and that his parents are Polish subjects. The godfather of the child was Ludwig Zyanski and the godmother's name was Marianna Colimowski. That they were present at the birth and that they affixed their signatures hereto in testimony thereof." (Then follow the signatures of the Clerical Registrar of Kolo, the Chief of the Parochial Registry of Kolo, and a magistrate of Kolo.)

(2) "This is given by the teacher of the Krasseminsk rural public primary school, consisting of one Standard, to the effect that Severin Klosowski, son of Antonio, attended the Krasseminsk School from October 17–29, 1873, till June 6–13, 1880, and completed the full term of studies of the first department, and that his conduct throughout his attendance at the school was very good.—In witness thereof I affix my own signature, Merkish, teacher, village of Krassenin, December 7–19, 1880." (The authenticity of the signature of Merkish is attested by two witnesses.)

(3) "Receipt for one rouble, paid by Rappaport to the Treasury of the Society of Surgeons of the town of Radom on behalf of the surgical apprentice, Severin Klosowski. "Radom, October 23–November 5, 1882.—N. Brodnitski, Senior Surgeon.""

(4) "The magistrate of the County of Zvolen hereby certifies that Severin Klosowski, resident of the village Zvolen, is a well-behaved man, and was never found guilty of any crime whatever. To which effect he bears testimony by his own signature and official seal.—Dushevitch, Magistrate of the County, Village Zvolen, November 16, 1882."

(5) "Certificate issued to the surgical apprentice, Severin Antonio Klosowski, to the effect that he, Severin Klosowski, was in my surgery for the purpose of studying surgery from December 1, 1880, till June 1, 1885, and during the whole of the time he, Severin Klosowski, discharged accurately all his duties. He was diligent, of exemplary conduct, and studied with zeal the science of surgery.—In testimony thereof I affix my signature, Moshko Rappaport, Senior Surgeon and proprietor of the surgery in the village Zvolen, June 1, 1885."

(6) "Certificate issued to Severin Klosowski, residing in the village of Tyminitsa, county of Nodga, district of Iltetsk, Government of Radom, to the effect that he was employed for a period of four-and-a-half years by the local surgeon, Moshko Rappaport, in the capacity of a practising surgery pupil, and under the doctor's instructions rendered very skilful assistance to patients—*i.e.*, in cupping by means of glasses, leeches, and other assistance comprised in the science of surgery. To all the above I am able to testify as an eye-witness.—(Signed) O. P. Olstetski, medical practitioner in village of Zvolen, October 10–22, 1885."

(7) "October 23–November 4, 1885.—The Radom Surgical Society, of the town of Radom, hereby certifies that the surgical pupil, Severin Klosowski, was entered at the registry of surgical pupils by the Senior Surgeon, Moshko Rappaport, in the town of Radom, November 22–December 3, 1882. Subject No. 8, and in accordance with Article 17, letter b, of the Surgical Society one rouble in silver was paid by him into the Treasury of the said Society.— In witness whereof, Brodinski, the Chief of the Society, testifies by affixing his signature and the seal of the Surgical Society."

(8) "This is given to Severin Klosowski, surgery pupil, to the effect that from October 1, 1885, till January 1, 1886, he received instructions in practical surgery at the Hospital of Praga, Warsaw, and his general conduct was good. (Signed) Krynick, Senior Surgeon.

"In accordance with the application of Severin Klosowski, and in consequence of inquiries ordered to be made the present certificate is issued from the office of the Chief of Police of Warsaw to the effect that the applicant whilst residing in Warsaw was not observed by the police to be concerned with any improper conduct whatsoever. The present certificate is given to Mr. Klosowski under the proper signature and Government seal for the purpose of submitting the same to the Imperial University of Warsaw. Stamp duties have been collected. —Warsaw, April 29, 1886. Kasievitz, Deputy Chief of the Department. (Seal) A. Darenskov, Manager."

(9) A receipt from the Treasury of the Surgical Society "For entering the name of Severin Klosowski, two roubles."

(10) "Warsaw, November 15, 1886. — This is to certify that Severin Klosowski has been employed by me as surgeon assistant from January 20, 1886, up to the present time and during the whole of that period he performed his surgical functions with a full knowledge of the subject, and his conduct was good. To this fact I testify with my own signature, and affix my stamp.—(Signed) D. Moshkovski."

(11) "I was born in 1865, in the village of Nagornak, district of Kolo, Government of Kalish. I lived with my parents until the age of 15, attending at the same time the primary school. In 1880 my parents apprenticed me for the purpose of studying surgery to Moshko Rappaport, senior surgeon of the town of Zvolen. Having served my term of apprenticeship till 1885, I came to Warsaw, and whilst employed by Mr. V. Olshanski I also attended a practical course of surgery at the Praga Hospital. Upon the termination of my hospital practice I entered the service of Mr. D. Moshkovski, by whom I am still employed. I present herewith all my documents.—Yours faithfully, Severin Klosowski, Warsaw, November 15, 1886." (The document bears a stamp value 15 kopecks.)

(12) "Passport, given on November 24, 1886, to Severin Antonovich Klosowski, residing in the Radom Government, district of Ilshetsk, county of Khotche, village of Tyshenitsa, Nova Nil to travel to the city of Warsaw from the above date till November 1–13, 1887, upon the expiration of which the said document shall be returned to me. The civil and military authorities shall allow the bearer a free passage, and if necessary render him legal assistance. Given in Khotche, November 24, 1886. Physical description. Age, 21; born in 1865; height, medium; hair, of a dark shade; eyes, blue; nose and mouth, medium; chin and face, longish; birthmarks, none. Passport within the limits of the Kingdom of Poland. Free. —(Signed) Mazur, Magistrate of the County of Khotche. (Seal) Godlevski, County Clerk." (This was given to Klosowski on his recruiting in 1886.)

(13) "Warsaw, December 1886.— His Excellency, the Dean of the Medical Faculty of the Imperial University of Warsaw. "Petition from Severin Klosowski, surgical pupil, residing at No. 16 Muranovskaja St. "I have the honour to request your Excellency to grant me permission to undergo the examination for the purpose of receiving the degree of Junior Surgeon. I enclose herein the required documents.— Yours faithfully, Severin Klosowski."

(14) "Town of Praga, November 24 to December 6, 1886.— I hereby certify that Severin Klosowski was employed by me in the capacity of an assistant surgeon from August 20, 1885, till February 1, 1886, and during the whole of the time he fulfilled the whole of his duties with zeal, and was of good behaviour. In witness whereof I have affixed my own signature.—(Signed) C.F. Olshanski."

(15) "Ministry of Interior, Medical Administration of Warsaw. December 5, 1886.— In consequence of the application presented by Severin Klosowski, surgical pupil, the Medical Administration hereby testify to the effect that they do not see any reason to oppose his receiving the degree of Junior Surgeon. The required stamp duties have been paid.— (Signed) Dr. M. Oreszaief, Collegiate Councillor and Inspector. A. Pominski, Secretary."

(16) "Severin Klosowski has paid to the Treasury of the Warsaw Society of Assistant Surgeons, Hospital fees four roubles per month.— Warsaw, February 28, 1887. Cobalski, Senior Surgeon. Paid up till March 3, 1887."

# APPENDIX II: THE CROWN PUBLIC HOUSE

The Crown was built about 1840. Its original address was 151 Borough High Street, but when the road was renumbered between 1854 and 1875 it became 213. The area east of the Crown — between today's Newcomen Street, Tennis Street and Long Lane — was the site of four prisons: King's Bench, Marshalsea (both c. 14th and both for debtors); the c. 16th County Gaol and the c. 17th House of Correction.

When Chapman was at the Crown, the alley (Angel Place) that currently separates 213 from the John Harvard Library at 211 did not exist: the pub was part of a terrace unbroken from number 207 to 221. There was an Angel Place in Chapman's time, but it was between 205 and 207.

Its first licensee in 1841 was Henry Luke Winton; immediately preceding Chapman was William Tillman in 1901; Chapman was followed by Arthur Browne in November 1902 and then Mr Petts in 1903. In 1915 it was listed as St George's Distillery and its proprietor Emanuel Ring was, by coincidence, born in Poland just months after Kłosowski.

Later it reverted to a pub, and in the 1960s it was owned by Watney Mann. When Richard Gunner took over in 1966 four upper rooms were boarded up. Upon opening them he judged that they had been unused for about forty years. One contained a Victorian washbasin which was featured in a press photograph because it was almost certainly used by Maud Marsh and George Chapman. Mr Gunner's mother and wife had some supernatural experiences.

> Mrs Bet Gunner...claims to have heard footsteps in some of the empty rooms, and the whistle of what sounded like a kettle boiling. She will not stay in the pub at night following an incident two years ago, when she caught a glimpse of a man in one of the upstairs rooms. He walked up the stairs laughing, then vanished. Mr Gunner's wife Barbara says she has heard the sound of crying upstairs when her three children were asleep. This ended when Mr Gunner threw out a carrycot he found in the attic. Mr Mario Dempsey...who worked in the bar two years ago, has had some eerie experiences. 'One Saturday night...when I went to bed, the place was spotless, but in the morning there was a glass on the counter, as if someone had pulled up a chair and had a drink'.[615]

The Crown closed in 1976 when Watney Mann sold it to the next-door neighbours, cocoa importers Gill and Duffus, to house their staff canteen. It has since been demolished and rebuilt, but the decorative façade has been painstakingly reinstated.

*Richard Gunner at the wash basin he found in a boarded-up room at the Crown. From the South London Press.*

615 *South London Press,* 3rd September 1976

# APPENDIX III: PEOPLE

### ABBERLINE, FREDERICK
Metropolitan Police inspector during the Whitechapel murders
B1843, Dorset. Occupation: (1863) Met Police constable; (1865) sergeant; (1873) inspector; (1887) moved to Scotland Yard; (1888) first class inspector; (1890) chief inspector; (1892–1904) private detective, European branch, Pinkerton's Agency, spent three seasons at Monte Carlo casinos. Residence: (1896–1904) 313 Clapham Road, Stockwell; (1904–1929) Bournemouth. D1929.

### ADAM, HARGRAVE LEE
B1867, Camberwell. Father a clerk. Lived in south London all his life. Never married. Occupation: journalist and author. Between 1908 and 1936 wrote several books on crime, including *Trial of George Chapman* (1930). D1944.

### BADERSKA, JÓZEFINA (MRS KAMIŃSKA)
Kłosowski's sister-in-law
B1876, Mikstat, Poland. Dau of Joseph, a farmer (fl1903). Emigrated to London c. 1898. Married in Bethnal Green 1898, to cabinetmaker Stanisław Kamiński (b 14th April 1871, Gostynin, Poland). Seven sons: Edward Tadeusz b 27th April 1899, Stephen Wallace b 15th December 1901, Jan b1902, Walter b1904, Stanisław b1907, Mieczysław b1909, Henry b1911. Residence: (1901) 80 Farrance St, Limehouse; (1907) Baltimore, MA, USA; (1909) 518 South Ann St, Baltimore.

### BADERSKA (ŁUCJA) LUCY (MRS KŁOSOWSKA; MRS SZYMAŃSKA)
Kłosowski's wife
B1871 or 72, Mikstat, Poland. Dau of Joseph, a farmer (fl1903). Emigrated to London c. 1889; anglicised name to Lucy. Married Tuesday 29th October 1889, at the German Catholic church of St Boniface, Union St, Whitechapel, to Seweryn Kłosowski. Children: Władysław 1890–91, Cecilia 1892–1960. From (at latest) the end of 1897, lived with cabinetmaker Franciszek (Frank) Szymański b1876, Poland. Adopted his surname. Married Frank 20th June 1903, Polish Roman Catholic church of St Joseph and St Casimir, Cambridge Heath Rd, Bethnal Green. Children: Henry b 28th April 1899 d1983, Helena b Q4 1902, Walerya b1907, Stanisława b1909, Frank b Sept 1910. Residence: (1899) 1 Pelling St, Limehouse; (1901) 2 Pelling St (two rooms in a six-roomed house); (1903) 80 Farrance St, Limehouse; (1908) 58 Hind St, Limehouse; (1911) 23 Latham St, Limehouse, where they had two rooms in a very small six-roomed house, sharing with a Russian/Polish family of nine (street demolished; Bartlett Park occupies the site). Occupation: (1892) told ship's clerk she was a servant, grandson reported she was a tailoress. She, Frank and all the children except Cecilia moved to São Paulo, Brazil c. 1912. (Between 1870 and 1914, 100,000 Poles settled in Brazil.) *In 1928 Frank (junior) had a daughter with Irene Chalko (b1912, Lithuania) and they married the following year, when she was 16 and he 18. They had another daughter. Nothing is known of Henry, Helena, Walerya or Stanisława. There are currently a number of Szymańskis in São Paulo; presumably they are Henry's descendants.*

### Baderska, Maria (Mary) Ann (Mrs Polaczek)

Kłosowski's sister-in-law

B1868, Mikstat, Poland. Dau of Joseph, a farmer (fl1903). Married 15th May 1887, in the German Roman Catholic church of St Boniface, Union St, Whitechapel, Franciszek (Frank) Polaczek. Residence: (1887) 70 Grove St (now Golding St), off Cable St; (1889) Green St, Bethnal Green; (1891) 209 City Rd, Holborn [misspelled 'Polheck' in census]; (1895) 205 City Rd. Children: Helena b1888, Frank b1889, Anna b1891, John b1892, Janina b1894. Children registered as 'Polachek.' Mary died aged 27 in late 1895 [death registered as Mary 'Polczyk']. Frank married Maria Wenglarczyk in 1897 (see his entry).

### Baderska, Stanisława (Mrs Rauch)

Kłosowski's sister-in-law

B1873, Mikstat, Poland. Dau of Joseph, a farmer (fl1903). Emigrated to London in 1890. Occupation in 1891: tailoress. Appears in 1891 census twice. September 1892 married Varsovian cabinetmaker Wilhelm Rauch 1861–1925. Often misnamed 'Mrs Stanislaus Rauch' in court transcript and press reports. Residence: (Feb–June 1892) 26 Scarborough St; (1903/1911/1918) 292 Burdett Rd, Stepney (west side, between Agnes St and Pixley St); (1956) 30 Hainault Road, Leytonstone. Twelve children (ten alive in 1911): Jadwiga Maria b1893 (married Frank Pazda); Stanisław 1894–1918; Jan b 15th March 1896; Anna b 10th September 1897; Wilhelm Władysław, 1899–1899; Hilary Edmund (nicknamed 'Mundzio') b1901; Wanda b1904; Józef 1906–1980; Mieczysław b1909; twins Helena and Stanisława b1910; Tadeusz ('Teddy') 1912–1995. By 1923 had anglicised her name to Stella. D 6th July 1956. *Her son Stanisław, a gunner in the Royal Field Artillery, d 17th February 1918, buried Rocquigny-Equancourt Road British Cemetery, France.*

### Baderski, Stanisław

Kłosowski's brother-in-law

B1864, Mikstat, Poland. Son of Joseph, a farmer (fl1903). Emigrated to London by May 1887. Occupation: tailor. Married April 1890 to Władysława Lagiewska (b1866, Prussian Poland). Residence: (1891) 75 Nichol's Square, Haggerston; (1895) Bethnal Green; (1897) Walthamstow; (1903) 406 Hoe St, Walthamstow; (1911) 104 North Birkbeck Road, Leytonstone. The family is mistranscribed in the 1891 census as 'Baderske' and is missing from the 1901 census. Ten children: five died in childhood. Joseph 1890–1896; Julius 1892–1892; Feliksia 1894–1896; Walerya b1893 (a tailoress); Isydor b1895; Felix b1896; Mary b1897; Theresa 1899–1900; Stanisław 1902–1902; Aniela b1906. *During WWI Isydor and Felix served in the Middlesex Regiment. Felix married Maria Arasimowicz in 1925, lived in Deptford, and died in 1951. They had two sons, Bernard C. b1926 and Ted J. b1927.*

### Baderski, Władysław

Kłosowski's brother-in-law

Existence inferred from (a) news report in which Stanisław mentioned his (unnamed) brother and (b) Kłosowski's marriage certificate shows Władysław Baderski as a witness. No trace in official records, suggesting he returned to Poland or changed his name.

## BODKIN, SIR ARCHIBALD HENRY

Prosecution counsel at Chapman's trial

B1862, London. Called to the Bar 1885. Married 1891 to Maud Bush. Appointed recorder 1901. Director of Public Prosecutions 1920–30. Responsible for the prosecution of every spy tried during WWI and for the banning of publications he saw as obscene. KCB 1924. Recorder of Dover 1931–47. Chairman of Devon Quarter Sessions 1930–47. D1957.

## BODMER, RICHARD FIC, FCS

Court witness

B1856, Zurich, raised in Wales. Occupation: public analyst, Borough of Bermondsey; consulting chemist, Clinical Research Association. Office: 1 Southwark St. Residence (1901) Harold Rd, Margate. D1926, Eastbourne.

## BRAY, WILLIAM LEMAIN

Court witness

B1847, St Pancras. Married 1870 to Alice Kirby. Occupation: managing clerk to solicitor Frederick Braund, 6 Gray's Inn Square. Residence: (1891) 19 Almond Rd, Tottenham; (1901, 1903) 82 Park Lane, Tottenham. D1920.

## BUSHELL, FRANK AND EMMA

Managers at the Crown

Frank b1866, Sandwich. Emma Reynolds b1867. Married 1886. Children: Frankie Leslie b1888; Doris Mabel b 27 July 1892. Occupation: (1891) both club stewards in Ramsgate; (1901) Frank a billiard marker; (1903) managers, the Crown, Southwark. Residence: (1891) 107 High St, Ramsgate; (1902) 80 Denmark St, Lambeth. (1911) Frank in Chelsea Workhouse; no trace of Emma. Frank d1918. *1911 Frankie was a billiard marker; Doris was a waitress. Doris married Christopher Taylor in 1913. In 1918 Frankie lived at 68 Glenarm Rd, Clapton.*

## CHAPMAN, CECIL MAURICE BA

Stipendiary magistrate at Southwark police court

B1852, Wanstead Manor. Oxford graduate 1875. Served 20 years at the Bar then became a magistrate. 1899 married his widowed cousin, Adeline Chapman 1847–1931, a prominent feminist (her dau Mildred Mansel was imprisoned as a militant suffragette). Chairman, Men's League for Women's Suffrage, patron of the Women's Police Service. Residence: (1911) 24 Buckingham Gate, SW1. Books: 1911 *Marriage and Divorce;* 1925 *The Poor Man's Court of Justice: Twenty-five Years as a Metropolitan Magistrate.* D1938.

## CHAPMAN, SARAH ANN (ANNIE)

Court witness

B c. 1875. Girlfriend of George Chapman (when he was still Kłosowski) and mother of his son William b 8th August 1895, d spring 1896. Residence: (1894) 656 High Rd, Tottenham; (1895) Albert Rd, Tottenham; (1895) Edmonton Workhouse; (1903) 9 Hartington Rd, Tottenham.

### CLARKE, ALFRED
Fraudster

B1868, Edmonton. Married to Annie Mosley 1893, at St Francis de Sales RC church. Tottenham. One dau, Ada Ann Retalie Clarke b1894. Divorced 1907 on the grounds of cruelty (i.e. wifebeating) and his adultery with Mrs May Stockley, dau of Mrs Gillmor. Occupation: salesman for mineral water company; confidence trickster perpetrating frauds with cheques and loans. In 1902 he was convicted for false pretences for the fourth time, for conspiring with Hilda Oxenford (see her entry) to defraud Chapman.

### COLE, LOUISA
Court witness

B1883, London. Occupation: (1901) servant, 194 Borough High St; (1902) assistant, Edward Leftwich's bacon shop, Marshalsea Rd, Southwark; (1902, from July) cook and servant at the Crown; (late 1902) unemployed. Residence: (1902–3) 6 Boddy's Bridge, a slum alleyway off Upper Ground, Blackfriars.

### COTTER, DR PATRICK GALLAGHER MD, MS
Court witness; assisted at Maud Marsh's post-mortem

B1862, Ireland. Qualified 1884. Residence: (1891) 350 Old Kent Rd; (1893, 1901) 107 Drury Lane; (1911) 57 Caledonian Road. D1926.

### DACRE, HENRY
Court witness; trustee of Mary Spink's inheritance fund

B1858. Occupation: solicitor. Residence: (1901) Hawthornden, Otley, Yorks.

### DAVISON, WILLIAM HENRY
Court witness; sold Chapman tartar emetic in Hastings

B1842, New York. Married 1863 at Spitalfields, to Julia Fay. Residence: (1851) 22 Walton St, Chelsea; (1863) 18 Norton Folgate; (1866) St Thomas's Rd, Hackney; (1871) 98 Shakespeare Rd, Hornsey; (1891) 66 High St, Hastings (and for 18 of the years between 1873 and 1900). D1917.

### DOUBLEDAY, MRS MARTHA (NÉE BRISTOW)
Court witness; nurse to Mary Spink

B 23rd February 1852, St Luke. Dau of a waiter. Married 1874 to locksmith Charles Aldridge (d Holborn Workhouse 1885, aged 35, leaving her with four children). 1887 married warehouseman James Doubleday. Four more children. Widowed 1909. Four of her eight children died young. Residence: (1874) 3 Richmond St; (1881–1932) 9 Richmond St. D1932. *1911 occupied one room in a house shared with three other families, including those of her daughters Rose McBride and Martha Cottrell. Her son Charles and his family lived next door.*

### ELLIMAN, DR ARTHUR CHARLES MRCS, FRCP
Doctor who examined Bessie Taylor

B1866. Residence: (1901) 73 Southwark Bridge Rd. D1916, Italy.

### FRENCH, DR HERBERT STANLEY, CVO, CBE, MA, MD, FRCP

Assisted at Maud Marsh's post-mortem

B1876. Studied at Guy's Hospital, 1898–1906. Served in Royal Army Medical Corps in WWI. Physician to George V until 1930. Author, *French's Index of Differential Diagnosis*, still in print since 1912. Residence: (1906, 1909) 26 St Thomas's St; (1915 to 1951) 62 Wimpole St. D1951.

### FREYBERGER, DR LUDWIG, MD, MRCP, MRCS

Court witness; assisted at Maud Marsh's post-mortem

B1865, Vienna. Qualified 1893/4. Until 1895 was unpaid residential physician to Friedrich Engels, whose housekeeper he married in 1894. Occupation: clinical assistant, Great Ormond Street Children's Hospital; toxicologist and forensic pathologist, London County Council; barrister-at-law, Middle Temple. Residence: (1894) 122 Regent's Park Rd; (1901) 41 Regent's Park Rd. Freeman of the City of London 1901. British citizenship awarded 1897, revoked 1919 for disloyalty to His Majesty. Died Buxton, 1934.

### FULTON, SIR (JAMES) FORREST

Recorder of London

B1846, Belgium. Read law at London University. Called to the Bar 1872. Held several senior legal posts. Recorder of London 1900–1922. MP for West Ham North 1886–92. Presided over a case that led to the conviction of Adolph Beck for fraud in 1896. Eight years later an enquiry established that the conviction was a miscarriage of justice, a decision which led to the establishment of the Court of Criminal Appeal. D1926.

### GILBERT, FRANK LOVELL

Mortuary keeper

B1863, Wiltshire. Occupation: (1891, 1901) general labourer. Residence: (1891) 271 New Kent Road, Newington; (1901) 5 Boyson Road, Walworth; (1903) 9 King's Place, Borough High St. D1941.

### GLENISTER, WILLIAM JOSEPH

Court witness

B1851. Occupation: solicitor. Residence: (1881) 199 St George's Rd, Hastings; (1901, 1911) 27 Pevensey Rd, St Leonards.

### GODLEY, GEORGE

Police officer who investigated and arrested Chapman

B 31st October 1856, East Grinstead, son of a sawyer. Family name was 'Godly'. This spelling was used for anything family-related (such as headstones, census). 'Godley' was used only for police-related matters. 1881 married dressmaker Emma Mitchell. Five children; two died young. Occupation: (1871) hotel pageboy; (1877) police constable, warrant no. 61230; (1881) PC in M Division (Southwark); (1888) detective sergeant, J Division (Bethnal Green) then H Division (Whitechapel); (1899) inspector, M Division; (1905) first class inspector, K Division (Stepney). Retired 20th January 1908, became claims' inspector for an insurance company. Residence: (1881) police section house, Blackman Rd; (1891) 26 Rutland Rd, Hackney; (1901) 62 Falmouth Rd, Newington; (1911) 11 Plashet Rd, Plaistow; (1928, 1941) 32 Mayfair Ave, Ilford. D1941.

### GRANTHAM, THE HON. SIR WILLIAM

Old Bailey judge, Queen's Bench Division

B1835, Lewes. Called to Bar 1863. Cons. MP for East Surrey 1874–85, MP for Croydon 1885–1886. Appointed judge 1886. Residence: Barcombe Place, Sussex and Eaton Sq, London. D1911.

### GRAPEL, DR FRANCIS GASPAR, MD, MRCS

Court witness; Maud Marsh's GP

B1870, London, son of a barrister. MRCS 1898. Residence/surgery: 303 London Rd, West Croydon. Later moved to Hampstead. D1948.

### GREENAWAY, MRS HARRIET (NÉE BOURNE, LATER WAIT)

Court witness

B1859, Rye. Occupation: (1881) domestic servant. 1882 married commercial traveller Frank Greenaway. At least six children. Residence: (1897) 1 Cobourg Pl, Hastings; (1901) 3 Castle Pl, Castle Road, Hastings; (1911) Wandsworth.

### HADDON, JOHN AND MARY

Kłosowski's employer

John b1846. Married in Lambeth 1873 to Mary Lewis b1846 (his second marriage). Occupation: hairdresser, umbrella maker. Residence: (1881) 8 Spring Garden Pl, Stepney; (1891) 3 Market Bdgs, West Green Rd (renumbered 5 West Green Rd); (1894) 656 High Rd, Tottenham. John D1895.

### HAWARDEN, FATHER ALOYSIUS SDB

Roman Catholic priest at Wandsworth Prison

B1873, Cheltenham. Occupation: Member of the Salesians of Don Bosco. First Salesian priest to be ordained in England. Attended Battersea Salesian School (later the Salesian College). Prefect of Studies at Battersea; rector of the Salesian House at Wandsworth; founder of the parish of St Gregory at Earlsfield, south London. Chaplain at Wandsworth Prison for many years; also organised concerts for prisoners. Later, parish priest at Farnborough and then Chertsey. Residence: (1911) 64 Orbell St, Battersea. D1960, Southwark.

### HELSDOWN, MRS ANN (NÉE HOW)

Court witness

B 12th October 1868. Married 1887 to Frederick Helsdown, labourer. Nine children. Residence: (1871, 1881) Winding St; (1891) Scrivens Buildings, Crown Lane; (1896–7) 10 Hill St; (1901) Rose Cottage, Woods Passage, All Saints' St; (1911)15 Woods Passage. D1947.

### KAMIŃSKA, JÓZEFINA — SEE BADERSKA, JÓZEFINA

### KELSALL, WILLIAM HENRY

Friend of the Taylors; identified Bessie's corpse at exhumation

B1862, Agden, Cheshire. Occupation: commission agent and farm owner. Residence (1901) Woolstenholme Farm, Agden, Lymm, Cheshire. D1914.

### KEMP, WILLIAM BREWSTER

Police sergeant who investigated and arrested Chapman

B1866, Sandy, Beds; mother an organist and music teacher; father the parish clerk. Married 1886, six children. Occupation: 1887 joined Met Police, Bethnal Green; special duty at Buckingham Palace during Queen Victoria's Jubilee; CID at Hackney, then Victoria Park, then Dalston; 1907 selected to guard the Cullinan diamond (the largest polished diamond in the world) in a taxi from Bank to Liverpool St on its journey to Sandringham; sergeant by 1894; acting inspector early 1903 until c. 1906; 1911 sergeant, CID, New Scotland Yard; retired 1913, became a private detective. Residence: (1901) 3 Searles Rd, Southwark; (1911) 38 Holmewood Gdns, Brixton Hill. D1919.

### KŁOSOWSKA, CECILIA (MRS PRZYGODZIŃSKA)

Second child of Seweryn Kłosowski and Lucy Baderska

B 12th May 1892, 26 Scarborough St. Parents separated when she was two. From age five had stepfather, Frank Szymański. Married at age 16 to Albert Przygodziński (see his entry) 4th October 1908 at the Polish Roman Catholic church of Our Lady and St Casimir, Mercer Street, off Cable St, Shadwell. Residence: (1908) 58 Hind St, Limehouse; (1911) 21 Leman St, Whitechapel (on the east side, just south of the junction with Little Alie St, and accommodated seven other households, all of them impoverished, overcrowded and Jewish). Children: Cecilia May 1910-2006, Albert John 1911-1964, Eleanor c. 1913-2007, Joseph Peter c. 1914-c. 1980s, Wanda 1915-1935, Stanisław 1922-1940. Widowed 1950. D 27th April 1960, 82 Huxley Road, Leyton. *Cecilia (jnr) married Arthur Brown in 1932 and had three children: Eunice b1934, David J. b1940 and Victor b1945. Albert married Amy Hurst in 1936, had children, and changed the family surname in the 1950s. Eleanor married Robert Oliver in 1933 and had two daughters, both married with children. Joseph married in 1943, had children, and changed the family surname in the 1960s.*

### LEAK, SAMUEL

Police sergeant who helped investigate and arrest Chapman

B 29th November 1857, Lincs. Married 1883, four daus. Occupation: (c. 1877) Metropolitan Police constable; (1911) county court bailiff. Residence: (1901) Upper St, Islington; (1911) 23 Corsica St, Highbury. D1928.

### LEVISOHN, WILLIAM (WOLFF)

Court witness

B c. 1849-56, Russian Poland, son of David, a Jewish cigar-maker (d before 1887). Emigrated to London 1862. Returned home c. 1870 aged c21 to perform seven years military service as a feldsher in the Imperial Russian Army. Returned to London c. 1877. 14th May 1887 married Alice Sutton 1861-1943. Alternative names/spellings: (1891) Adolff W. Lewisohn; (1901) William Levison; (1903, 1909) William Levisohn. Occupation: (1888 and 1890s) hawker of hairdressing supplies; (1891) general dealer; (1901) cutlery salesman; (1909) interpreter of languages (on death certificate). Residences: (1881) 57 Warden Road, Kentish Town; (1887) 24 Great Garden St, Whitechapel (now Greatorex St); (1888) St Ann's Rd, Tottenham; (1891) 40 Plevna St, Tottenham; (1900) 2 Grove Villas, Stamford Hill; (1901) 32 Southey Rd, Tottenham; (early 1903) 135 Roslyn Rd; (late 1903) 32 Southey Rd, Tottenham; (1905, 1906, 1909)

13 Ida Rd, Tottenham. Died 6th January 1909 of oesophageal cancer. Death registered as William Levisohn, b1856 (but marriage record 1887 gives his age as 38). Children: David Edward Q1 1890–1916; Adolphus Henry 23rd April 1891–1967. *Both sons served in WWI, having changed their surname to Leveson. David, a lance-corporal in Queen Vic's Rifles, died in the first Battle of the Somme (named on Thiepval Memorial). Adolphus married Doris Corfe, moved to Australia, had a dau, Enid. Returned 1932 to 135 Roslyn Road, and later settled in Forest Drive, Walthamstow, close to where Chapman lodged with John Ward.*

### Loveland Loveland, Richard KC, DL, JP

Magistrate in the shares scam case

B1841, Islington. Surname changed from Oldershaw to Loveland by Royal Licence. Called to the Bar 1865. Dep. Chair, Middlesex Quarter Session 1889–96. Dep. Chair, London Quarter Session 1897–1911. QC 1897. Masonic Grand Chancellor of England. Married to Maria Nind, he lived in a 20-roomed house near Hyde Park. D1923.

### Marsh, Alfred Samuel

Brother of Maud Marsh

B May 1885, Croydon. 1908 joined reserve army; 1909 married to Ada Barnard. Child: Eider Annie Maud b1913. Residence: (1911) 28 Donald Road, Croydon. D1958. *Eider married Harry Foord in 1936.*

### Marsh, Alice May

Sister of Maud Marsh and witness in all three courts

B 23rd May 1881, Croydon. 1906 married to Joe Walton 1883–1963. Children: Hilda 1907–1993, Harold 1912–1913, Ernest 1915–1984. Residence: (1902) 63 St James's Rd, Croydon; (1911) 14 Cecil Rd, Croydon. D1961.

### Marsh, Daisy Harriett Helen

Sister of Maud Marsh and witness in all three courts

B September 1887, Croydon. Sometimes called Helen, or Nellie. Occupation: fruit shop assistant. Residence: (1902) London Rd Fruit Stores, Croydon; (1903) 14 Longfellow (*now Donald*) Rd, Croydon. 1916 married (as Daisy H.H. Marsh) to George A. Hails. Child: Ronald b1920. Daisy d1955, Hove.

### Marsh, Mrs Eliza (née Chandler)

Mother of Maud Marsh and witness at Old Bailey and Southwark police court

B 2nd December 1854, Croydon. Dau of George, a greengrocer and Sarah, a lacemaker (and, later, greengrocer). 1872 married Robert Marsh. Six children, of whom two died by 1911. Louisa b1879, Alice b1881, Maud b1883, Alfred b1885, Daisy b1887. Occupation: caretaker. Residence: (1861, 1871) 22 South End, Croydon; (1881) Park Place Cottage, Croydon; (1891, 1901) 48 Stanley Rd, Croydon; (1903) 14 Longfellow (*now Donald*) Rd, Croydon; (1911) 9 Boston Rd, Croydon. D1913.

### Marsh, Louisa Sarah (Mrs Morris)

Sister of Maud Marsh and witness in all three courts

B 2nd September 1879, Croydon. 1898 married warehouseman (later, house-painter) Edward Parker Morris 1866–1935. Residence: (1901) 32 Nigel Rd, Peckham; (1902)

Dulwich; (1903) with parents at 14 Longfellow (*now Donald*) Rd, Croydon; (1911) 38 Barset Rd, Nunhead; (1920, 1939) 26 Barforth Rd, Camberwell. Children: Clara b1899, Alfred b1902, Walter 1905–1993; Robert b1908; George b1910; Florence b1918 (possibly also Philip and Thomas). *Clara married William Bradbery and lived at 89 Crofton Rd, Camberwell, 1930s to 1960s.*

### MARSH, MAUD ELIZA

Victim of Chapman
B 17th February 1883, 1 Park Place, Dering Rd, Croydon. Residence: (1891) 48 Stanley Rd, Croydon; (1901) Duke of York pub, Croydon (servant); (1901) 24 Heath Ct, 1 Hazeldean Rd, East Croydon (servant to Elizabeth Docking); (August 1901) Outwood, Sydenham Rd, Croydon; (late 1901) the Monument; (1902) the Crown, where she was murdered on 22nd October 1902.

### MARSH, ROBERT

Father of Maud Marsh and witness at all three courts
B1853, Monk Soham, Suffolk. Son of agricultural labourer. 1872 married Eliza Chandler. Occupation: (1872) groom; (1891) carman; (1901) bricklayer's labourer; (1911) furniture dealer. Residence: (1881) Park Place Cottage, Croydon; (1891, 1901) 48 Stanley Road, Croydon; (1903) 14 Longfellow (*now Donald*) Rd, Croydon; (1911) 9 Boston Rd, Croydon. D1927.

### MARTIN, MRS ELIZABETH ANN

Court witness
Widow. Housekeeper at Albion Mansions. Residence: (1903) 126 Queen's Rd, Hastings.

### MATHEWS, SIR CHARLES WILLIE (LATER, BARONET MATHEWS)

Prosecution counsel at Chapman's trial
B1850, New York, as Charles West, he later took his stepfather's surname. Educated at Eton. 1888 married Lucy Sloper. Described as foppish, histrionic, effeminate and having a high-pitched, weak voice, he counted two monarchs among his friends. Barrister for the Treasury 1872–1886, Junior Treasury Counsel from 1886, Senior Treasury Counsel from 1888, Recorder of Salisbury 1893–1908. Knighted 1907; KCB 1911. Baronet 1917. Director of Public Prosecutions 1908–1920. D1920.

### METCALFE, FREDERICK KYNASTON

Under-sheriff of London
b1854. Occupation: solicitor at Gasquet & Metcalfe, 92 Great Tower St and under-sheriff of London, a post in which he was succeeded by his son Percy. D1914.

### MORRIS, MRS — SEE MARSH, LOUISA

### MUMFORD, MRS JANE (NÉE HALL)

Court witness
B1858. 1882 married Robert Mumford. Occupation: (1891) dressmaker; (1911) mantle-maker. Residence: (1891) 18 New St, St Luke, (one room); (1897) 19 Bartholomew Sq; (1901) 72 Bath St, St Luke; (1911) 11 Lizard St, St Luke (one room). Widowed by 1901.

No birth, death or marriage records. Appears in three censuses, each shows a different birthplace (Yarmouth, Wisbech, Hastings) and birth year (1842, 1844, 1846).

### NEIL, ARTHUR FOWLER

Police officer and author

B 31$^{st}$ December 1867, Hither Green. Son of a gardener. Married 1894 to Mary Darbyshire (1867–1914). Residence: (1891) Section House, Camberwell police station; (1901) 27 Borough High Street; (1911) 27 Cathcart Hill, Holloway. Occupation: (1888) joined Met Police, warrant no. 73638; (1901) detective sergeant; (1919) detective chief inspector; (1920) superintendent. Retired 1927. Published memoirs 1932 as *Forty Years of Manhunting* (issued as *Manhunters of Scotland Yard* in the USA), which contains a chapter about George Chapman. D1939 London.

### NEWMAN, EDWIN HENRY ARMSTRONG

Solicitor engaged by Alfred Clarke and later by Robert and Eliza Marsh

B1862. Partner, Newman & Wilson, Gracechurch St, London. Historian, polyglot, philanthropist. D1915 (killed on railway whilst working as a wartime special constable).

### 'OXENFORD, HILDA'

Fraudster sued by Chapman

Real name and age unknown. Cohabited with Walter Oxenford and assumed his surname. With Alfred Clarke (see his entry) attempted to defraud Chapman in 1902.

### PAGETT, RICHARD AND SUSAN (NÉE ROBINSON)

Court witness (Susan)

Susan b1880, St Luke. Richard b1877, Shoreditch. Married February 1900. Occupations: (1897) barmaid and potman; (1906) Richard a carman. Residence: (1897) Prince of Wales beerhouse; (1900) 84 Chapel St, Islington (Richard); 8 Edinburgh Cottages, Islington (Susan); (1902) 105 Coventry St, Bethnal Green; (1903) 100 Essex Rd, Islington; (1906) 101 Crondall St, Hoxton; (1908) 58 Rockingham St, Southwark. Children: Susan (Susannah) b 2$^{nd}$ May 1898 and Lily (Sarah) b 20$^{th}$ March 1900.

### PAINTER, ELIZABETH ALICE (NÉE BROGAN)

Court witness; friend of Bessie Taylor

B 14$^{th}$ August 1868, Old St, St Luke's. Raised in a slum called Parrot Alley, Whitecross St, Finsbury. Father (Thomas Brogan) died; 1875 mother married George Painter. Five siblings: Sarah b1871, Ada b1878, Alfred b1883, Lilian b1884 and William b1888. Residence: (1881) 11 Westmorland Pl (now Westland Pl), City Rd, Shoreditch; (1884, 1891, 1901) 20, Block M, Dufferin St, *her sisters Ada and Sarah lived 3, Block L;* (1903) 8 Argyll St, Oxford St (resident caretaker); (1911) 12 Essex House, Essex Rd, Islington (sharing a room with Sarah). Occupation: (from age 12) domestic servant; (1911) office cleaner. D1947.

### PENFOLD, ALICE

Court witness

B1871, Cuckfield. Dau of a hoop-maker. Residence: (1901) 34 Devonshire Rd, Hastings; (1903) Clive Vale, Hastings. Occupation: (1901) letting furnished rooms.

## PETRYKOWSKI, JOSEPH

Translator of Kłosowski's documents

Misspelled by court clerks as 'Petrickowski' or 'Betrikowski'. Searches (of every possible spelling) within birth, death and marriage records, electoral registers and censuses found no trace. Residence: (1903) 30 New Road, Kennington.

## POIROTTE, DR THEODORE ALPHONSUS LM, RCP, RCS

Doctor who assisted at Maud Marsh's post-mortem

B 28th May 1866, Dublin. Qualified 1893. Licensed midwife and physician. Residence: (1900) 35 Park Hill, Clapham; (1899, 1922) 343 Kennington Rd. D1928.

## POLACZEK, FRANK

Kłosowski's brother-in-law

B1866, Mikstat, Poland. Son of John, a police constable. Occupation: barber, hairdresser. Married Maria Baderska (see her entry). Married Maria Wenglarczyk 1897. No further records, indicating that he and his second family probably emigrated.

## POLACZEK, MARY — SEE BADERSKA, MARIA

## PRZYGODZIŃSKI, ALBERT

Kłosowski's son-in-law

B1875 (1911 census) or 1877 (marriage certificate), Poznań, Prussian Poland. Son of Lawrence, a farmer. Former cavalryman, bore a sabre scar on his foot. Emigrated to England 1900. 4th October 1908 married Cecilia Kłosowska (see her entry). Occupation: ladies' tailor. Residence: (1908) 57 Leman Street, Whitechapel, then, for several decades, two rooms on the top floor of 21 Leman St. According to David J. Brown, he was a tailor and designer for Peter Robinson's department store, often travelling to Paris to see the latest fashions. D1950. Six children. Both of his sons abandoned the Polish surname in favour of an English one.

## RADIN, ABRAHAM AND HETTA/ETHEL (NÉE STRAUSS)

Court witness (Ethel)

Both b1864, (Abraham on 16th November) Vilnius, (now the capital of Lithuania, then in West Russia). Married 1886, Mile End. Naturalised June 1901. Occupation: (Abraham) barber, later shop-fitter. Children: Solomon b June 1887–1954, Isaac 1889–1950, David 1892–1953, Ada 1896–1897, Harry 1898–1988. Residence and shops: (1888) 70 West India Dock Rd; (late 1888) 7 Aldgate High St (shop); (1891, 1896) 4 St Michael's Alley, EC (shop) and 57 Brunswick Bdgs, Goulston St (residence). Moved to Southend. Ethel d1935. Abraham d 26th July 1938.

## RAPPAPORT OR (RAPAPORT), MOSHKO (MOSIEK)

Kłosowski's mentor in Poland

B 24th September 1846, Warsaw, to Izrael and Perla. Occupation: senior feldsher. Apprenticed Kłosowski and also his own son Keufel. At 19 married Chana (or Chena, or Hena or Henia) Liwcia (or Lewcia) Szlaferman, aged 16, dau of Idessa and Abram. Eight children: Perla b1870, Nesza b1872, Sura (Sara?) b1874, Hadessa b1876, Kojfman 1881–1942, Maurice 1883–WW2, Keufel 1888–WW2, Gutsze 1895–WW2. Moshko died

1910. Keufel's clinic address in 1939 was Rynek 20 (perhaps also his father's). Most of Moshko's children perished in the Holocaust. *Maurice died in Auschwitz. Nesza (married name Kawa) had three children and died at Kazimierz in 1941 (her grandchildren survived and moved to Israel). Kojfman and his wife Sarah, Keufel and his wife Yehudit, and Gutsze (married name Bressler) were incarcerated in the Jewish ghetto in Zwoleń. Gutsze died in Treblinka. Keufel died in Garbatka but one of his two sons, Abraham, survived, emigrated to the USA and settled in Springfield, New Jersey, where he had a son, Kenneth, b1957.*

### RAUCH, MRS — SEE BADERSKA, STANISŁAWA

### RAYNER, FLORENCE ELIZABETH
Court witness
B 4th August 1878, 56 Westmacott St, Camberwell. Dau of James, a warehouseman, and Sarah née Freeman. Occupation: (1901) dressmaker; (1902) barmaid. Residence: (1881, 1891) 18 Havil St, Peckham; (1901) 2 Cerise Rd, Peckham; (1902) the Crown, Southwark; (1902) Foresters' Arms, 182 Peckham High St.

### RENTON, CLARA (MRS FARRER)
Mary Spink's sister
B 4th August 1861, 23 Upper Place, Leeds. 6th March 1883 married butcher John Farrer. Children: Thompson b1886, Ethel b1887, Dorothea b1888, Clara b1892. Residence: (1891) 17 & 19 Towngate, Holbeck, Leeds; (1901) 5 South Ridge Street, Holbeck. D1911.

### RENTON, JOSEPH SMITH
Mary Spink's cousin, witness at Old Bailey and Southwark police court
B 20th Dec 1861, Otley, Yorks. Son of Alfred, a maltster. Occupation: dyer, later corn dealer. Residence: (1881) Headingley, Yorks; (1883) 23 West Hillary Street, Leeds; (1891) 9 Montague Rd, Leytonstone; (1901, 1903) 460 High Rd, Leytonstone; (1911) 19 Denmark St, Leytonstone. Married 1885 to Mary Sampson. Four sons: Edgar 1888–1946, John b1889, Albany 1892–1946, Gilbert b1895. Joseph Smith Renton d1932.

### SCHUMANN, GEORGE
Court witness
B1861, Russian Poland. Married to Rose b1864, Poland. Occupation: Hairdresser and salesman of hairdressers' requisites. Residence: (1901, 1902) 37 Nile St, Hoxton. Children: Samuel b1881, Harry b1883. *George is named both 'Schumann' and 'Sterman' by H.L. Adam. Listed as 'Sheman' in the 1901 census.*

### SIMMONDS, MRS EDITH
Court witness
Residence: (1897) 1 Cobourg Pl, Hastings; (1903) 43 Manor Rd, Hastings. Occupation: servant to Mrs Greenaway (see her entry).

### SIMS, GEORGE ROBERT
Opponent of the Chapman–Ripper theory
B1847, London. Poet, novelist, playwright, social commentator, satirist, critic, reformer, amateur criminologist, sportsman and philanthropist. Residence: (1901, 1911) 12 Clarence Terrace, Regent's Park. D1922.

### SPINK, MRS MARY ISABELLA, NÉE RENTON

Victim of Chapman

B 14th August 1858, Lowtown, Pudsey, Yorks. Dau of William Renton 1835-1869, then a linen draper, later a butcher, and Annie Eliza née Smith 1836-1868. William was the son of Albaney Renton 1801-1862, a farmer and Isabella née Booth 1800-1873, both of Leathley, Yorkshire. Annie was the daughter of Joseph Smith 1810-1863 and Mary née Farrar b1820 d between 1871-1881. Married 16th December 1883, St Paul's church, Burdett Rd, Stepney, to Shadrach Spink 1853-1928. Children: Shadrach Sayer b 26th April 1884, William Alfred b 8th December 1888. Residence: (1861) 23 Upper Place, Leeds; (1871) 70 Briggate, Leeds; (1881) Raglan St, Leeds; (1883) 2 King John St, Stepney; (1884) Rose Cottage, 6 Forest Rd, Leytonstone; (1888) Sydney Villas, Mornington Rd, Leytonstone; (1891) 1 Mornington Rd, Leytonstone. (1895) Forest Rd, Leytonstone; (1896) 10 Hill St, Hastings; (1897) 1 Cobourg Pl, Hastings; (1897) Prince of Wales, 20 Bartholomew Sq, St Luke. Murdered there, 25th December 1897.

### SPINK, SHADRACH ROBERT (OR SAYER)

Estranged husband of Mary Spink

B1853, Norfolk, son of Joseph Spink 1820-1917 and Emily née Sayer 1819-1899. Occupation: (1883) railway porter; (1891) farmer's son; (1901) domestic servant; (1911) upholsterer; (1925) furniture porter. 1883 married to Mary Renton. Children: Shadrach Sayer b1884, William Alfred b1888 (whom he never met). Residence: (1853, 1861, 1871, 1881) Banningham, Norfolk; (1884) Rose Cottage, 6 Forest Rd, Leytonstone; (1891) Lamas Hall, Aylsham, Norfolk; (1901) 24 Vicarage Drive, Eastbourne; (1911) two rooms at 58a Susan's Rd, Eastbourne; (1928) 22 Albion Rd, Eastbourne. By 1901 living with his girlfriend Anna Marcia Fielding 1856-1948, formerly a schoolteacher in Lamas village. Married December 1909. Children: Anna and Matthew. D 3rd Oct 1928.

### SPINK, SHADRACH SAYER

Mary Spink's elder son

B 26th April 1884, 6 Forest Rd, Leytonstone. Birth registered by mother. Taken away by his father at the age of four. Never saw his mother again or met his brother. Married 26th April 1911, All Saints' church, Hastings, to domestic servant Elsie Jane Pettitt 1885-1934. Occupation: (1919) farrier, army veterinary corps, then clerk, bookmaker, grocer's assistant, off licence manager, publican, hotel manager. Residence: (1891) Lamas Hall, Aylsham, Norfolk; (1901) 24 Vicarage Dr, Eastbourne; (1911) 78 All Saints' St, Hastings; East Preston, Sussex; (1950s) 25 Henty Rd, Worthing. D 5th August 1954. Buried Offington Cemetery. Children: Harry Sayer (Billy) (1913-1913), Elsie Miriam Elizabeth b1915 and Peter Sayer b1924. *Elsie, a pharmacist, married Harold Gilpin, had three children (Wallace, Quentin and Bridget) and died in Lancing in 2006. Peter Sayer Spink married Pauline Todd.*

### SPINK, WILLIAM ALFRED

Mary Spink's younger son

B 8th December 1888, Sydney Villas, Mornington Rd, Leytonstone. Christened 4th January 1889. Never met his father, brother, or any other member of the Spink family.

Residence: Leytonstone; Hastings; Bartholomew Sq; Bishop's Stortford; Haberdasher St; Shoreditch Workhouse; Hornchurch Cottage Homes. Moved to Aylsham Workhouse, Norfolk, 18th June 1903 (close to the home of his grandfather, whom he never met). Occupation: (c. 1904) servant to Canon Henry Robert Hutt at the 27-room Bingham Rectory, Notts; (1908–1913) servant to Charles James Lucas, Warnham Court, Sussex (a 42-room mansion with 13 staff); (Dec 1913) servant to Eric Hambro (of Hambro's bank), Pickhurst Mead, Hayes, Kent; (1914–1918) British Army.

When Willie was at Warnham Court his brother Shadrach was living just 24 miles away, in East Preston. Neither knew the other's whereabouts; indeed, each may not even have known he had a brother. Although Willie knew (and told people) that his mother had been murdered by George Chapman, he was unaware of his parents' names, his correct age or his birthplace. He gave his father's name as 'Henry', his mother's as 'Mary Elizabeth', his birthplace as Aylsham, Norfolk and his birth date as December 1890.

On 13th Aug 1914 Willie enlisted at Bromley in 3rd (Reserve) Bn, Queen's Own (Royal West Kent Regiment). Aged 25, he had blond hair and light grey eyes, and was of slight build, standing just 5ft 3in and having a 33-inch chest. After training at Maidstone he was posted on 25th August 1915 to the 1st Bn Royal West Kents to serve with the British Expeditionary Force in France. In October 1916 he sustained a shrapnel wound to his left buttock and was sent to hospital in Chichester for a month before returning to the Front in January 1917, this time with 10th Bn. In February 1917 his regiment carried out a successful raid at Givenchy. Willie was hit again by shrapnel, this time on his right hand. Treated at Metropolitan Hospital, then 27th March 1917 sent to Chelsea VAD Hospital, Belgravia, for convalescence. Diagnosed with partial deafness in both ears. 16th April 1917 returned to Bingham rectory as a reserve in the Royal Fusiliers Labour Corps, possibly working in munitions.

On 9th October 1917 he was posted back to the Royal West Kents. The 1st Bn moved to Italy in December 1917 to strengthen Italian resistance, and Willie served briefly in the 13th French Mortar Battery. The regiment returned to the Western Front in France in April 1918 and took part in the Battle of the Lys during the German Spring offensive of 7–29th April 1918 (Operation Georgette). On 16th April Willie was reported missing presumed killed in action. Was never identified amongst the dead. He is commemorated on Panel 8 of the Ploegsteert Memorial in Belgium and on the war memorial in Warnham, West Sussex.

Pte William Spink L/10426 earned the 1914–1915 Star and the British War and Victory medals. He had named Ellen Richardson (housekeeper at Bingham Rectory) as his next of kin. The following letter was written on 11th September 1919 by Canon Hutt MA, vicar of Bingham, to the infantry record office, Hounslow:

> Dear Sir, I am requested by Miss Richardson to answer this enquiry about Pte [Private] Spink. It is a peculiar case. While he was a small child, Pte Spink's mother ran off — taking Pte Spink with her — with a man named Chapman — who was a notorious criminal & subsequently executed for poisoning 3 or 4 women — of whom Mrs Spink was one. Her child — Pte Spink — was brought up by the Workhouse Authorities & some 17 or 18 years [ago] he entered our service as houseboy. He remained with us 7

years — but ever since he left he has always made my house his home. E.g. spending his annual holiday when in service & his furlough when in the Army. The last time he was here I asked him about his relations, He told me that he did not know that he had one in the world. Hence it comes about that he has given this as his home address & Miss Richardson, my housekeeper, as his next of kin. Pte Spink made a will the last time he was with us. It is in my possession but I don't know its contents. [*There are a few more words but they are illegible.*] Yours faithfully, H. R. Hutt.

When Ellen Richardson died on 30th May 1920, she has still not received Willie's medals. Legal right to them passed to her own next-of-kin — her sister — but there is no evidence that she claimed them.

*George Chapman's great-great-granddaughter Samantha at the Ploegsteert Memorial, 2014*

### Starke, Max

Kłosowski's lodger

B1861, Russia. Occupation: hairdresser. 1897 married to Tilly Gluckstein. Children: Esther, Milly and Lilly. Residence: (1891) 2 Tewkesbury Bldgs, Whitechapel; (1901) 19 Mansell St, Aldgate; (1911, 1919) 8 New St, Gravel Lane, Houndsditch; (1929–1954) 22 Prince George Rd, Stoke Newington. Shop: 12 Stoney Lane, Houndsditch (to 1939). Naturalised 1914. D1954. *Esther married David Freedman in 1921.*

### Stevens, Mrs Martha (née Money)

Court witness; sick nurse to Bessie Taylor

B1844, Newbury. Dau of Joseph, a builder. Moved to London. Married 22nd June 1871 to Arthur Stevens, a tailor and sometime actor. Five children: Alice b1869, Harriet 1871–1884, Arthur John b1873, William b1876, Joseph 1878–1916. Separated from husband by 1891. Later adopted two children: Saul Stargratt and Adelaide Venus. Residence: Newbury; central London; 176 Union Street, Southwark; Barking. D1926, Romford.

### Stevenson, Sir Thomas MB, MD, MRCP, FRCS

Court witness

B1838, Rainton, Yorks. Occupation: analyst to Home Office; (1878–1908) lecturer in forensic medicine; president of the Institute of Chemistry and of the Society of Public Analysts. Married to Agnes Maberly. Residence: (1901) 158 Streatham High Rd; (1907) Sandhurst Lodge, 382 Streatham High Rd. Knighted 1904. D1908.

### STOKER, DR JAMES MORRIS

Court witness; physician to Bessie Taylor and Maud Marsh
B1865, Cork, Ireland. Qual 1893. Married Annie, b1875. Two children. Surgery: (1892–1939) 221 New Kent Rd. Residence: Marlesford, Croydon Rd, Beddington. D1946.

### SUNDERLAND, DR SEPTIMUS PHILIP MD, MRCS, LRCP

Obstetrician who examined Bessie Taylor
B1860, Birmingham. Qualified 1882, MD 1883. Practised in women's hospitals then privately at Wimpole Street, London. Residence: (1901, 1911) 11 Cavendish Place. Wrote medical books and also *Old London's Spas, Baths, and Wells*. D1950, Bexhill.

### SYDNEY, HENRY ISAAC

Chapman's solicitor
B1846, son of a solicitor. Married Isabelle Stirling. Seven children. Office: 300 Borough High St and 2 Renfrew Rd, Lambeth. Residence: (1899) 9 Angel Rd, Brixton; (1901) 6 Lower Kennington Lane; (1901, 1911) 97 Knatchbull Rd, Camberwell; (1920) 43 Lavender Gdns, Battersea. D1921.

### SZYMAŃSKA, MRS LUCY — SEE BADERSKA, LUCY

### SZYMAŃSKI, FRANK

Lucy Baderska's second husband
B1876, Poland. Son of Mateusz, a master carpenter. Occupation: cabinetmaker. Married Lucy Kłosowska 1903, fathered five of her seven children. Emigrated to São Paulo, Brazil c. 1912.

### TARGETT, DR JAMES HENRY FRCS

Court witness
B1862, Wiltshire. Qualified 1885. Assistant obstetric surgeon, Guy's Hospital. Later in private practice, Upper Wimpole St.

### TAYLOR, BESSIE

Victim of Chapman
B 15th June 1861, New Brook Farm, Dutton, Cheshire. Dau of Thomas Parsonage Taylor and Betsey née Whitlow (see their entry). Residence: (1871) Massey Brook Farm, Lymm; (1881) Holly Bank Farm, Broomhall. Moved to London c. 1888, worked at Streatham, Peckham, Prince of Wales beerhouse, the Grapes, Bishop's Stortford, and the Monument, Southwark, where she was murdered on 13th February 1901.

### TAYLOR, (GEORGE) PAUL

Magistrate at the police court
B1861. Called to the Bar 1885. 1895 appointed stipendiary police magistrate for Southwark and Marylebone. Residence: 7 Lancaster Gate Terrace, Paddington. D1917.

### TAYLOR, THOMAS PARSONAGE AND BETSEY

Parents of Bessie Taylor
Thomas Parsonage Taylor b1836, Dutton Hall, Dutton, to farmer John Taylor and Sarah née Parsonage. Betsey Whitlow b1829, dau of John and Betsey Whitlow of Old Farm, Stretton, nr Lymm. Married 11th Feb 1857. In 1861 Taylor was farming 96 acres

and employing six staff; in 1871 he was farming 12 acres with two staff. Residence: (1861) New Brook Farm, Dutton; (1871) Massey Brook Farm, Lymm; (1881) Holly Bank Farm, Broomhall; (1891) Hill Farm, Preston on the Hill; (1901) Hillside Farm, Dutton Rd, Preston on the Hill. Children: William Wright b1858, John b1859, Arthur b 20 April 1860, Bessie 1861–1901, Harry b1862, Mary Gertrude 1865–1893, Eliza b1866. T.P. Taylor d June 1902. Betsey d August 1902. *Arthur became a pork butcher in Warrington, married Mary and had at least three children (Margaret b1880; Joseph b1884; Thomas b1901). Harry married Emily Kelly in 1902 and took over Hill Farm, Preston Brook, where they had a son, Frank, in 1909. Eliza married Alexander Drummond in Stockwell in 1911.*

## Taylor, William Wright

Brother of Bessie Taylor

B1857, Little Budworth, Cheshire. Married in 1882 to Emma Chantler. Children (b Manchester): Thomas b1883, fruit and potato merchant (died by 1911); Harry b1886, railway clerk, later fruit seller. Residence: (1861) New Brook House, Dutton, Cheshire; (1871) Massey Brook Rd, Lymm, Cheshire; (1881) 5 Afton Sq, Salford, Cheshire, with Emma Chantler, his 'housekeeper'; (1883, 1886) Manchester; (1891) as 'William Wright', 5 Codnor St, Manchester; (1900) Peckham; (1901, 1903) 62 Lausanne Rd, Hornsey; (1905, 1911) 343 Holloway Rd, Islington. Warehouse: (1901–1912) 14 James St, Long Acre. Occupation: (1881) commission agent; (1891) potato salesman; (1911) fruit merchant (in business with Emma). *Harry married Caroline Stone in 1907.*

## Toon, Mrs Jessie

Court witness

Claimed to be married to a labourer called Frank but no record found. Occupation: charwoman. An elusive character, extensive searches found few offical records for her. A story in the *Exeter & Plymouth Gazette*, 3rd March 1903 about a Frank Macguire, 45, a woollen weaver of Etham St, Southwark, and Laura Macguire, 23, a laundress, who were charged with 'being disorderly and using obscene language in Walker-street, Borough', mentioned that Laura Macguire's real name was Jessie Toon and she was 'an important witness in the Chapman case'. There is, however, no trace of either Frank or Laura Macguire in any other records (such as birth, death, marriage, census) so perhaps these were pseudonyms. Residence: (1902) 23 Etham St, off Tabard Street, Southwark; (1903) Osborne St, off Commercial St, Whitechapel (addresses she gave to court officials). According to Booth's investigator, Etham Street was narrow, cobbled, and populated by thieves, prostitutes and 'evil-looking' people. (These slums were demolished and a football pitch covers the site.) In the 1901 census a Jessie Toon (b1871, Devon) and a Thomas Toon (b1863, Northants) lived in Tyers Street, Lambeth, with his children by his late wife and a newborn child, Thomas Walter Toon, presumably Jessie's (no trace of him in 1911 census; also no death record). A Jessie Toon also b1871 was admitted to Mint Street (Southwark) workhouse in December 1903 and again in 1905 (as Toone), and was admitted to Whitechapel Workhouse Infirmary several times between 1903 and 1911, during which time she was living in various cheap lodging houses and gave her occupation as a flowerseller. An Elizabeth Jessie Toon b1849 (or 1852) received parish relief at Shoreditch in late 1902 and died in 1913. It is impossible to say if any of these were the Jessie Toon in question.

**WALDO, DR FREDERICK JOSEPH MA (CANTAB), MD, JP, BARRISTER-AT-LAW**

Coroner who conducted Maud Marsh's inquest

B1852, Bristol. Trained at St Bartholomew's Hospital. MRCS 1879; MB (Cantab) 1880; entered medical register 1881; MD 1884. DPH, RCPS 1890. Called to Bar 1896. 1900 married to Alice Exon, and they had one daughter. 1904 published 'The Klosowski (Chapman) Poisoning Case'. Occupation: Medical Officer of Health for Southwark (no dates); Coroner for the City and Southwark 1901–1932. Freeman of the City of London. Residence: (1911, 1933) 40 Lansdowne Rd, Holland Park.

**WARD, JOHN**

Court witness; Chapman's landlord

B1843, Hillingdon, Middx. Married to Caroline, five children. Residence: (1891) Rose Villa, Lytton Rd (close to Forest Road), Leytonstone; (1895) Forest Rd, Leytonstone (*The Echo* gave the address as 'Rose Cottage'); (1901) 10 Canterbury Terrace, High Rd, Ilford; (1903) 35 Pyrmont Rd, Ilford (a turning south off the High Road). Occupation: master tailor (at 3 Church Lane in 1895).

**WAYMARK, MRS ELIZABETH JANE (NÉE BAKER)**

Court witness; nurse to Mary Spink

B 24th March 1854, 10 Clift St, Hoxton. Married 1877 to Charles Waymark. Eight children, only the first three lived more than two years: Charles 1879–1901, Mary 1880–1956, John Joseph 1882–1961, Edward 1884–1885, Ellen 1885–1886, Eliza 1887–1890, George 1888–1890, Florence 1891–1891. Widowed 1891. Residence: (1881) 25 Edward St, St Luke; (1891) 23 York Road, St Luke; (1901) Beerhouse, 106 Ironmonger Row, St Luke; (1901, 1904) 41 Windsor Terrace, St Luke. Occupation: (1871) machinist; (1901) general servant. Died St Bart's Hospital, 21st January 1910. *Her son, Charles, a railwayman, was killed at Whitecross St goods depot. In 1904 Mary married George Smith and John married Maggie Staines.*

**WENGEL, WILLIAM F**

Court witness; Chapman's employer

B1865, Germany. Son of a farmer. In London by 1885. Married 1887 to Eleanor Bligh 1869–1936, nine children. Occupation: barber and publican. Pub: (1894, 1899–1907) Lord Morpeth, 402 Old Ford Rd. Residence: (1887) 22 Great Hermitage St (now Hermitage Wall), Wapping. Salon: (1885–1911) 7 Church Lane, Leytonstone; 673 High Rd, Leytonstone; (1911) salon/residence 817 High Rd, Leytonstone. 1911 census, William was a barber and Eleanor an umbrella repairer employing her nephew as assistant. Early 1920s Church Lane salon combined hairdresser's and toy dealer. D 17th February 1921.

**WICKEN, ALFRED**

Court witness; Kłosowski's colleague

B1875, Croydon. Married 1899 to Ada Bradberry. Children: Ada b1901, Alfred b1909. Occupation: (1890s) assistant hairdresser at Haddon's; (1911) hairdresser, tobacconist and newsagent. Residence: (1898) 32 Drayton Rd, Tottenham (and shop); (1903) 2 Market Terrace, Lea Bridge Rd, Leytonstone; (1911) 18 West Green Rd, Tottenham; (1926) 71 Springfield Rd, Tottenham. D1947.

# SELECTED BIBLIOGRAPHY

Adam, H.L. (1930) *Trial of George Chapman.* William Hodge

Balzer, H. (ed) (1996) *Russia's Missing Middle Class: the Professions in Russian History.* Sharpe

Begg, P. (2004) *Jack the Ripper: The Definitive History.* Longman

Begg, P. (2006) *Jack the Ripper: The Facts.* Robson

Booth, C. (1902) *Life and Labour of the People in London.* Macmillan

Chaplin, C. (2003) *My Autobiography.* Penguin

Cooley, A.J. (1846) *A Cyclopædia of Several Thousand Practical Receipts.* Appleton

Copland, James, M.D. (1845) *A Dictionary of Practical Medicine.* Harper

Eddleston, J. (2001) *Jack the Ripper: An Encyclopedia.* ABC-Clio

Eddleston, J. (2003) *The Encyclopaedia of Executions.* Blake

Eddleston, J. (2010) *Foul Deeds in Islington.* Wharncliffe Books

Emsley, J. (2006) *The Elements of Murder: A History of Poison.* OUP

Fanthorpe, L. and P. (2003) *The World's Most Mysterious Murders.* Dundurn

Fido, M. (1993) *Murder Guide to London.* Academy Chicago

Fielding, S. (2008) *Pierrepoint: A Family of Executioners.* Amazon Kindle

Furniss, H. (ed) (c. 1908) *Famous Crimes Past and Present.* Caxton House

Goldfrank's *Manual of Toxicologic Emergencies.* McGraw Hill Professional

Gordon, R.M. (2000) *Alias Jack the Ripper: Beyond the Usual Whitechapel Suspects.* McFarland

Gordon, R.M. (2002) *The Thames Torso Murders.* McFarland

Gordon, R.M. (2003) *The American Murders of Jack the Ripper: Tantalizing Evidence of the Gruesome American Interlude of the Prime Ripper Suspect.* McFarland

Gordon, R.M. (2008) *The Poison Murders of Jack the Ripper.* McFarland

Grex, Leo (1985) *Detection (Stranger than Fiction).* Ravette

Harris, M. (1994) *The True Face of Jack the Ripper.* Michael O'Mara

Hess, K. and Orthmann, C. (2010) *Criminal Investigation.* Delmar

Honeycombe, G. (1993) *More Murders of the Black Museum.* Hutchinson

Hyde, H.M. (1953) *Carson.* Heinemann

Jakubowski, M. and Braund, N. (2008) *The Mammoth Book of Jack the Ripper.* Robinson

Leeson, B. (1934) *Lost London: The Memoirs of an East End Detective.* Stanley Paul & Co

Lynch, T. (2008) *Jack the Ripper.* Wordsworth

Marjoribanks, E. (1932) *Carson the Advocate.* Macmillan

Marriner, B. (1993) *Murder with Venom.* True Crime Library

Marriott, T. (2007) *Jack the Ripper: The 21st Century Investigation.* Blake

Moore, G. and Maunder, A. (2004) *Victorian Crime, Madness and Sensation.* Ashgate

Moss, K. (1999) *Southern Folk Medicine 1750-1820.* University of South Carolina Press

Nash, J.R. (1990) *Encyclopaedia of World Crime.* Crime Books

Neil, A.F. (1932) *Forty Years of Manhunting.* Jarrolds, issued in the USA as *Man Hunters of Scotland Yard.* Sun Dial Press

O'Donnell, K., Parlour, A. and Parlour, S. (1997) *Jack the Ripper Whitechapel murders.* Ten Bells

Odell, R. (2006) *Ripperology.* Kent State University Press

Pearson, E.L. (1936) *More Studies in Murder.* Harrison Smith & Robert Haas

Rubinstein, W.D. (2008) *Shadow Pasts: History's Mysteries.* Pearson

Rumbelow, D. (2004) *The Complete Jack the Ripper.* Penguin

Sims, G.R. (1901) *Living London.* Cassell

Stratmann, L. (2010) *Greater London Murders.* History Press

Sugden, P. (2002) *Complete History of Jack the Ripper.* Constable Robinson

Thurgood, P. (2013) *Abberline: The Man who Hunted Jack the Ripper.* History Press

Trow, M.J. (2012) *Ripper Hunter.* Pen and Sword

Wilson, C. and Pitman, P. (1962) *Encyclopedia of Murder.* Putnam

Wilson, D.A. (2011) *History of British Serial Killing.* Amazon Kindle

Wood, G.B. (1860) *A Treatise on Therapeutics and Pharmacology, or Materia Medica.* Lippincott

# LIST OF ILLUSTRATIONS

Note: Polish surnames ending in ~i have feminine versions ending in ~a, thus Józef Baderski and his daughter Lucy Baderska. George Chapman was known as Seweryn Kłosowski until 1895, but for ease of reference he is referred to throughout the index as George Chapman (usually abbreviated to GC).

Page references followed by 'n' denote footnotes (e.g. 12n); a page number in boldface after a main heading indicates an Appendix entry.